Peace Psychology Book Series

For other titles published in this series, go to
http://www.springer.com/series/7298

Ani Kalayjian · Raymond F. Paloutzian

Forgiveness and Reconciliation

Psychological Pathways to Conflict
Transformation and Peace Building

 Springer

Ani Kalayjian
139 Cedar Street
Cliffside Park NJ 07010-1003
USA
e-mail: drkalayjian@gmail.com

Raymond F. Paloutzian
Professor Emeritus of Psychology
Westmont College
955 La Paz Road
Santa Barbara, CA 93108–1099
USA
e-mail: paloutz@westmont.edu

ISBN 978-1-4419-0180-4   e-ISBN 978-1-4419-0181-1
DOI 10.1007/978-1-4419-0181-1

Springer Dordrecht Heidelberg London New York

Library of Congress Control Number: 2009929315

Printed on acid-free paper

Springer is part of Springer Science+Business Media (www.springer.com)

Foreword

We all long for peace within ourselves, families, communities, countries, and throughout the world. We wonder what we can do about the multitude of conflicts currently wreaking havoc across the globe and the continuous reports of violence in communities as well as within families. Most of the time, we contemplate solutions beyond our reach, and overlook a powerful tool that is at our disposal: forgiveness. As a genocide survivor, I know something about it. As the genocide unfolded in Rwanda in 1994, I was devastated by what I believed to be the inevitable deaths of my loved ones. The news that my parents and my seven siblings had indeed been killed was simply unbearable. Anger and bitterness became my daily companions. Likewise, I continued to wonder how the Hutus and Tutsis in Rwanda could possibly reconcile after one of the most horrendous genocides of the 20th century. It was not until I came to understand the notion of forgiveness that I was able to see the light at the end of the tunnel.

Common wisdom suggests that forgiveness comes after a perpetrator makes a genuine apology. This wisdom informs us that in the aftermath of a wrongdoing, the offender must acknowledge the wrong he or she has done, express remorse, express an apology, commit to never repeating said harm, and make reparations to the extent possible. Only then can the victim forgive and agree to never seek revenge. This exchange between the offender and victim can be a powerful force for reconciliation for interpersonal conflicts, inter-communal conflicts, and even international conflicts. Where the conflict has been protracted with offenses committed by both sides, offenders and victims may apologize and forgive each other; and from there they can make a new start where relationships are once again constructive. However, true forgiveness requires not only an apology, but perhaps more important, it requires empathy.

True forgiveness takes place when we seek to understand the offender and his or her motives. We may find that the offender was not fully in control of their actions or that they committed the offense after they themselves had been victimized. How else could a psychologically healthy person kill a neighbor, rape a child, or brutalize an elderly person? Those who engage in violence against people from other ethnic, racial, or religious groups might have been long exposed to heinous campaigns where they were taught to fear the "other." Or as was the case in Rwanda, harming the "other" was encouraged by political leaders. In other instances, doing so yields material gains such as acquiring neighbors' property. Under such circumstances, good people can do evil things. My neighbors are an example of this. They had for years been good neighbors to my parents only to then kill them in the 1994 genocide. Therefore, forgiveness requires that we become aware that despite the evil that has been committed, offenders still have some humanity and can be redeemed. However, this does not mean that we should exempt offenders from receiving justice or from making appropriate reparations – provided such justice is conducted in the most restorative way possible.

When large-scale crimes are committed, especially those of mass violence, it should serve as a reminder that something even larger is wrong with the current socio-political and economic structures. It should propel us to make reforms in order to reduce the likelihood that such evil behavior will occur again. It should remind us that these structures share some of the blame and that if the status quo continues, we can expect more of the same. Thus, we too might behave in a reprehensible way and suffer the shame and remorse that generally comes to those who display disgraceful behavior. Because of such shame, offenders often deny the evil they have done. In fact, offenders are sometimes so devastated by their acts that they seek protection by way of denial. That is why victims who can, should take the first step, and show their own readiness to reconcile. In turn, this can prompt or encourage offenders to apologize, which contributes to their healing and to the reconciliation process. However, without reconciliation, there simply cannot be lasting peace.

The ideal for conflict transformation and lasting peace is to have offenders and victims come together to dialogue, understand each other's points of view, and focus on the future rather than on the past. That is what reconciliation is all about. However, one party might refuse to come to the table and dialogue, in which case reconciliation is not possible. However, this is not a reason to give up trying to transform conflict and build lasting peace. In addition, we can embrace what I call unconditional forgiveness. We can forgive on the basis that it is the right thing to do, and that it represents a self-healing strategy.

Forgiveness does not necessarily depend on how the offender behaves or develop from reforming socio-political structures. Rather, forgiveness should be embraced because it is in accordance with that spiritual belief common to all faiths: do unto others as you would have them do unto you. In my Christian faith, we are asked not to be overcome with evil but to overcome evil with good. By doing so, we not only live up to our faith, but we also help stop the cycle of violence and prevent our mind and soul from being dominated by anger and bitterness. Forgiveness can enable people to move beyond deep-routed pain, anger, hatred, grudges, and bitterness that often result from trauma, whether human-induced or the result of natural causes. Forgiveness is a powerful tool that is at the victims' disposal that can facilitate their own healing.

Joseph Sebarenzi
Author of *God Sleeps in Rwanda: A Story of Survival and Reconciliation*

Preface

This book explores forgiveness, reconciliation, and related topics at multiple levels, from individual and group, to intergroup relations. We hope that this book fosters peace and encourages those who are tired of war, hatred, and similar dilemmas that continue to plague all peoples.

Forgiveness and reconciliation are difficult. However, they may be the keys to peace and our survival. Forgiveness can also help people move beyond the burden of pain, anger, hatred, grudges, and misunderstanding that often result from trauma, whether it is the result of human activity or natural causes. Although there are books that counsel people to forgive and reconcile, most speak to the individual and focus on prayer, meditation, or other spiritual exercises as methods of forgiving. Some are based on a specific religious tradition while others emphasize only one discipline. However, the traumas of today's world affect all individuals, families, clans, communities, cultures, societies, generations, and even nations. Therefore, books that focus on reconciliation at only one level are incomplete due to the multilayered nature of trauma. This book is comprehensive in scope and addresses forgiveness at all levels, including interpersonal, communal, and societal.

This book focuses on people while emphasizing larger units of analysis. Special attention is paid to the cognitions and behaviors of people in their unique social, historical, and cultural contexts. This approach facilitates our understanding of the structural properties that promote systemic violence and the potential reforms that can promote systemic peacebuilding. Forgiveness and reconciliation are both important aspects of this effort. This book helps to demystify the idea of forgiveness and presents concrete examples of how individuals can reframe their perspective of reality so that it is both realistic and, at the same time, peace-promoting. Part of the peace building process requires mutual trust, and the processes that nurture such trust include those that nurture forgiveness and reconciliation.

This book offers an inclusive approach. It is multidisciplinary, multiethnic, multigenerational, and international. The authors address forgiveness in the contexts of (a) current and past events in trauma-laden areas such as Rwanda, Darfur, India-Pakistan, Africa, as well as in the Western world, (b) the phenomena of unresolved and denied mass trauma such as in the case of the Ottoman Turkish Genocide of the Armenians, and trans-generational transmission of trauma and displacement, and (c) racial, ethical, religious, and developmental issues that can foster either division or harmony. Each chapter includes well-documented research combined with rich case material and offers lessons that can be applied in practical ways.

Acknowledgments

We wish to thank those who have contributed in special ways to this book. The authors comprise a uniquely assembled set of international experts. Some are academics, some work in government in war-torn countries, some work therapeutically with victims, and others specialize in working at the front lines of conflicts. Several of these authors have conducted forgiveness training and peace building in earshot of mortar rounds and live gunfire. They have put themselves on the line in order to help promote peace and we salute their efforts.

Also, we would like to express a very special thank you to Erica Louise Swenson. She worked on this project for 2 years and contributed greatly at every step of the way. She communicated diplomatically with authors, processed and evaluated drafts of chapters, and prepared material for chapters and the index. She is second to none in the competence and quality with which she executed every step. In addition, we would like to thank Ann Taves for her helpful critiques of Chapter 5, Mark Paloutzian for assistance in preparation of the index, and Elissa Jacobs for help in fine tuning several chapters.

We also express appreciation to the institutions and organizations where this work was done and to the good people that came with them. Ani thanks Fordham University Lincoln Center for providing work facilities and the steady environment where the forgiveness workshops and discussion meetings that led to this book developed. She also thanks the staff and Executive Committee of Meaningfulworld and the Association for Trauma Outreach and Prevention. Ray expresses appreciation to his home institution, Westmont College in Santa Barbara, the Faculty of Psychology at Katholieke Universiteit Leuven, Belgium, and the Center for Advanced Study in the Behavioral Sciences at Stanford University. All three settings provided excellent facilities and resources, plus a cordial social environment, to facilitate the completion of this book.

We owe a special note of gratitude to the editor of the Peace Psychology Series, Dan Christie, who was our gentle, competent, and knowledgeable guide. He provided us with invaluable wisdom and advice, and gave us a platform from which we could complete this book with pride and joy.

Ani Kalayjian
Raymond F. Paloutzian

Contents

Author Biographies

Khawla Abu-Baker, PhD, is in the Department of Behavioral Science, Emek Yezreel College. He is also a family therapist and supervisor in a private clinic in Akko, Israel.

Rhea V. Almeida, PhD, LCSW, is founder of Institute for Family Service and creator of the Cultural Context Model. She is the author of *Expansions of Feminist Theory Through Diversity, Transformations in Gender and Race: Family and Developmental Perspectives* and co-author of *Transformative Family Therapy: Just Families in a Just Society.*

Andraé L. Brown, PhD, is an Assistant Professor in the Marriage, Couple and Family Therapy Program at Lewis Clark College, Co-Director of Affinity Counseling Group and Council for Contemporary Families Fellow. Research involves development of treatment modalities that use the social ecology of families, schools, and communities to address trauma, violence, and substance abuse.

Wilma J. Busse, EdD, is a co-founder of One By One, Inc., and co-creator and facilitator of One By One Dialogue Groups. She is a psychologist and associate professor at Suffolk University, Boston, Massachusetts.

Asma Warsi Chaudry, Esq, is an attorney with the Boaz Community Corporation, an immigration legal resource center in New Jersey. Asma received an MA from New York University in Near Eastern Studies, and a JD from Rutgers University School of Law.

Dan Booth Cohen, MBA, PhD, consults individuals and organizations using an innovative group process known as Systemic Family Constellation. His doctoral degree is from Saybrook Graduate School and Research Center. He has had a diverse career as a business owner, corporate executive, author, peace activist, and counselor over the past 30 years; www.hiddensolution.com.

Anita Dharapuram, MNA, works with low-income immigrant, and refugee women at C.E.O. Women by teaching them entrepreneurship, communications, and English so they may improve their livelihoods. She recently completed her

Masters in Nonprofit Administration from the University of San Francisco, where she studied nonprofit workforce diversity as it relates to South Asian women.

Lisa Dressner, LCSW, is a founding member and co-director of Affinity Counseling Group. Her research and clinical interests include family trauma due to domestic and community violence, creating therapeutic healing communities, antiracism and white privilege, sexual abuse, contested divorces, adoption, and juvenile justice reform.

Catherine Ducommun-Nagy, MD, LMFT, is a Swiss-trained child and adult psychiatrist and family therapist. She is a Clinical Associate Professor at Drexel University in Philadelphia, PA where she teaches contextual therapy in the department of couple and family therapy. She is the president of the Institute for Contextual Growth located in Glenside PA. She has published extensively on the subject of contextual therapy and its applications and she is frequently invited to teach as a guest lecturer internationally, mostly in Europe and South America.

Martina Emme, PhD, is a founding member of One By One, Inc., and heads the Dialogue Group Committee in Germany. She has run One By One dialogue groups since 1996 and lives in Berlin, Germany.

Robert A. Emmons, PhD, is Professor of Personality Psychology at the University of California, Davis, and received his doctoral degree from the University of Illinois. He is the author of nearly 100 research articles and chapters and has written or edited four books, including *The Psychology of Ultimate Concerns* (Guilford Press) *The Psychology of Gratitude* (Oxford University Press), and *THANKS! How the New Science of Gratitude Can Make You Happier* (Houghton-Mifflin). He edits the *Journal of Positive Psychology*.

Charles E. Farhadian, PhD, Associate Professor of Religious Studies at Westmont College in Santa Barbara, California, holds his MA from Yale University and PhD from Boston University. He specializes in the relationship between religions and cultures, particularly in Southeast Asia and the Pacific region. His books include *Christianity, Islam, and Nationalism in Indonesia* (Routledge, 2005), *Christian WorshipWorldwide* (Eerdmans, 2007), and *The Testimony Project: Papua* (Deiyai Press, 2007). Currently he is co-editing with Lewis Rambo the *Oxford Handbook of Religious Conversion* (Oxford University Press).

Hagitte Gal-Ed, PhD, is an art therapist with interest in philosophy of art and epistemology. She introduced the concepts of Dialogic Intelligence© and ARTiculation© (2001) to peace education. She was on the Committee for International Education for Peace of the Parliament of the Worlds Religions (1999), and consultant for the First Conference of Israeli and Palestinian Bereaved Families for Reconciliation and Peace in East Jerusalem (2004). She created PEACE TV, a community-based television program in New York that presents dialogue-based peace education in collaboration with the Department of Peace Education and Teachers College, Columbia University.

Rosalie Gerut, MA, a daughter of Holocaust survivors, is the founding president of One by One and co-designed the Dialogue Group Model. She holds an MA from Tufts University and is a licensed educational psychologist with a specialty in trauma and recovery.

Suliman A. Giddo, MA, is Founder and President of Darfur Peace and Development Organization. He graduated of Khartoum University in Sudan, and received a Masters Degree from Staryer University in Business Administration and Post Graduate Diploma in Humanitarian Assistance from Fordham University. He has worked for the United Arab Emirates and the American Red Cross, and was adjunct professor at Indian Business College. Currently he is pursuing a PhD in Conflict Analysis and Resolution at George Mason University.

Paula Green, PhD, is founder-director of Karuna Center for Peacebuilding in Massachusetts and a Professor of Conflict Transformation at the School for International Training (SIT) in Vermont. At SIT she created and directs the Summer Peacebuilding Institute, Conflict Transformation Across Cultures (CONTACT). A psychologist, she facilitates seminars in conflict transformation and reconciliation worldwide.

Pilar Hernández, PhD, is an associate professor in the Department of Counseling and Human Services at Johns Hopkins University. Her work in the United States and Columbia focuses on traumatic stress, resilience, liberation, and community paradigms in therapy and clinical supervision.

Ani Kalayjian, RN, EdD, DSc (Hon), is adjunct professor of psychology at Fordham University Lincoln Center. She received her doctoral degree from Columbia University. She is active in filed work at disaster sites, and is President of the Association for Trauma Outreach & Prevention and the Armenian American Society for Studies on Stress and Genocide. Since 1990 she has been actively involved in the United Nations, where she focuses on human rights, refugees, women, mental health, and spirituality. She has published more than 30 articles and chapters and wrote *Disaster and Mass Trauma: Global Perspectives in Post Disaster Mental Health Management* (1995, Vista); www.meaningfulworld.com.

Ansley W. LaMar, PhD, received his doctoral degree in social psychology at the City University of New York and is now Professor of Psychology at New Jersey City University. He is also Dean of the university's College of Arts and Sciences.

Robert F. Massey, PhD, is Professor in the Department of Professional Psychology and Family Therapy, Seton Hall University, New Jersey. He received his doctoral degree from the City University of New York. He co-edited the *Comprehensive Handbook of Psychotherapy, Vol. 3: Interpersonal, Humanistic, and Existential* (2002, Wiley).

Sharon Davis Massey, PhD, is an adjunct professor at Seton Hall University. She teaches lifespan human development and provides clinical instruction in the Marriage and Family Program. She co-edited the *Comprehensive Handbook of*

Psychotherapy, Vol. 3: Interpersonal, Humanistic, and Existential (2002, Wiley). Her specialization is on how trauma arrests human development how reconciliation and forgiveness can facilitate recovery.

Augustine Nwoye, PhD, is full Professor in the Department of Psychology of The University of Dodoma, Dodoma, Tanzania. He had previously served as Chairman, Department of Psychology, Kenyatta University, Nairobi, Kenya. Professor Nwoye has developed an African paradigm for mental health and, in particular, for family and couple therapy. He also has experience in dealing with stress and multiple losses, especially surrounding HIV/AIDS and other traumatic experiences within an African context.

Paloutzian, Raymond F., PhD, received his doctoral degree from Claremont Graduate School in 1972, and is Professor Emeritus of experimental and social psychology at Westmont College, Santa Barbara, California. He has been a visiting professor teaching psychology of religion at Stanford University, and Guest Professor at Katholieke Universiteit Leuven, Belgium. His wrote *Invitation to the Psychology of Religion,* 2nd ed., (Allyn & Bacon, 1996, 3rd ed. forthcoming) and with Crystal Park co-edited the *Handbook of the Psychology of Religion and Spirituality* (Guilford, 2005). Dr. Paloutzian is Editor of *The International Journal for the Psychology of Religion.*

Antoine Rutayisire, MA, received one Masters degree in Applied Linguistics in the UK, North Wales, in 1986, and another in Modern Literature and Curriculum Development from Rwanda University. Since 1999 he has been on the National Unity and Reconciliation Commission, serving as Vice-Chairman from 2002 to 2008. His books are *Senga, Uhinduure Uhindure Gakondo Yawe (Pray to Conquer and Transform your Inheritance), Abarinzi b'Inkike (Watchmen on the Walls),* and *Umuyobozi Mwiza, Urugero rwa Mose (The Portrait of a Good Leader: the Example of Moses).* He also published *Faith Under Fire, Testimonies of Christian Bravery* based on the 1994 Rwanda genocide. *Out of the Fire: Testimonies of Healing, Forgiveness, Repentance and Reconciliation* is also forthcoming.

Barbara Tint, PhD, is the Director of International and Intercultural Conflict Resolution in the Conflict Resolution Graduate Program at Portland State University. Sue is also a consultant, facilitator and trainer in various domestic and international settings.

Viken Yacoubian, PhD, received his doctoral degree from the University of Southern California. He is founder and director of the Institute for Multicultural Research and Development and an adjunct professor of psychology at Woodbury University in Burbank, California.

Section I
Theoretical Perspectives

Chapter 1
Introduction: Issues and Themes in Forgiveness and Reconciliation

Raymond F. Paloutzian and Ani Kalayjian

Throughout the world, we continue to see violent outbreaks between individuals and groups. For many years, psychologists committed to peace viewed violence through the narrow lens of the Cold War struggle for world dominance between the United States and the Soviet Union. At that time, the prevention of nuclear war was the preeminent concern for those who called themselves peace psychologists.

Since the end of the Cold War, we have seen the growth of violence cycles in many places including Afghanistan, Bosnia, Israel, Northern Ireland, and Rwanda, where individual and collective traumas and feelings of victimization have laid the groundwork for future episodes of mass violence, sometimes even across generations, carried by collective memories of grievances and the like (Roe, 2007). These cycles of violence have challenged us to develop a more sophisticated and nuanced understanding of the causes, consequences, and prevention of violence between individuals and groups. Among the lessons we have learned is that in order to prevent future episodes of violence, it is important to intervene with forgiveness and reconciliation processes when the opportunity arises, and often this means during the aftermath of a violent episode. Clearly, in deeply divided societies, negotiated settlements are not likely to sustain peace unless groups in conflict are brought in contact and engage in a reconciliation process that acknowledges past pain and begins to envision an interdependent future (Lederach, 1997). This book offers fresh views of forgiveness and reconciliation from around the world.

Although there is a wealth of psychological and behavioral science research on war, aggression, hostility, and prejudice, topics such as forgiveness and reconciliation have been largely overlooked until the past quarter-century. This emerging body of literature suggests that the topics should be more seriously considered, if we intend to address and ultimately solve the most devastating of human problems. (See McCullough, 2008; McCullough, Pargament, & Thoresen, 2000; Worthington, 2005a, for comprehensive reviews of recent research.)

Applying our knowledge of forgiveness to peace efforts in real-world situations has only just begun. Most of the literature on forgiveness discusses it at an individual, family, or micro-level. Although this type of analysis is helpful, the lessons gleaned from such work need to be extended and applied to the macro-level. Several chapters in this book "go global" by expanding the concepts, principles,

Ani Kalayjian, Raymond F. Paloutzian, *Forgiveness and Reconciliation*, Peace Psychology Book Series, DOI 10.1007/978-1-4419-0181-1_1,
© Springer Science+Business Media, LLC 2009

experiences, and processes of forgiveness and reconciliation from the micro-level to interethnic, intranational, and/or international levels. Accordingly, several chapters in this text incorporate material and applied work devoted to forgiveness and reconciliation on a large scale (Green, Chapter 16; Kalayjian, Chapter 15; Tint, Chapter 17). In order to understand how the principles of forgiveness can contribute to peace, we must first acknowledge the factors that affect both systemic and episodic violence and peace-building.

Where Does Forgiveness Fit? Systemic Violence and Peace-Building

In order to understand the complex interplay of factors that contribute to war and to the possibility that forgiveness and reconciliation could inhibit war, we must first conceptualize the systemic processes involved (Massey & Abu-Baker, Chapter 2). A compelling schema for conceptualizing the systemic processes is presented by Christie (2006).

Christie explains that there are both episodic and structural violence and episodic and structural peace-building. The systemic approach links the intermittent instances of episodic violence, which involve direct harm to victims, with the non-intermittent harm committed indirectly to victims that results in (and may also result from) unjust social arrangements (i.e., structural violence). Thus, if one segment of a society continually receives the "short end of the stick," that is, always gets less of its proportionate share of the goods and services, then that constitutes a force of violence that feeds the probability of, and occasionally creates, a violent episode. In contrast, episodic peace-building is comprised of actions taken to manage existing or potential conflict, and this is linked with structural peace-building, that is, those factors, processes, policies, and agreements that move a society toward socially just arrangements. The potential to use this model to analyze the relative distribution of goods and resources, such as oil, water, transportation, access to medical care, and education, as well as desired intra- and interpersonal states and transactions, such as forgiveness, reconciliation, restitution, and commitment to non-transgression in the future, is great. This potential is either explicitly or implicitly incorporated into every chapter in this book.

When Christie's (2006) fourfold model is further explored, its scope and implications become clearer. For example, although peaceful and violent actions are performed by individuals, they seldom act independent of complex historic, familial, ethnic, cultural, and religious contexts. Therefore, by understanding the complex interactions between these and other elements of the process, we may be able to better manage the process and reduce the probability of conflict.

Factors that contribute to peace-building can be either negative or positive (Christie, Tint, Wagner, & Winter, 2008). Negative peace-building is comprised of interventions that manage conflicts (i.e., the perception of incompatible goals) effectively so that violent episodes do not occur. Generally, the purpose of negative peace-building is to reduce tensions between individuals or groups. In contrast, positive peace-building refers to efforts to reduce structural violence, a proactive process that promotes more egalitarian social arrangements as well as individual and collective narratives that support the sustainable satisfaction of basic needs for all people. Positive and negative peace-building can be used together when individuals and groups pursue the socially just ends by nonviolent means. As several chapters illustrate, procedures to enhance forgiveness and/or reconciliation can be applied after a conflict has occurred (negatively and reactively, e.g., Nwoye, Chapter 8) or to promote peace consciousness (positively and proactively, e.g., Gal-Ed, Chapter 7).

Issues and Themes in This Book

Ideally, all sides of a conflict would agree on how to work toward peace and would share a common understanding of the role of forgiveness and reconciliation. However, there is rarely such an agreement or understanding. Fortunately, many chapters in this book suggest ideas that could serve as points of discussion. Such points could be areas where common understanding and agreement are possible. They are expressed as issues and themes that are addressed across levels of analysis, geographic regions, historic factors, and personal and political beliefs. Some of the items are best understood as issues because there is little agreement about them. It is in the interest of peace to understand such issues and the different opinions that surround them. Other items should be thought of as themes because their central ideas weave throughout many chapters and help knit the material together.

Five Implicit and Recurring Themes

Basic survival reactions confront ethical and religious teachings. A number of authors document conflict between feelings of revenge and hostility and the desire to forgive (Giddo, Chapter 12; Nwoye, Chapter 8; Paloutzian, Chapter 5; Yacoubian, Chapter 14). A look into our ancestral past helps us understand why we are not predisposed to forgive. When humans first emerged, attacking or defending against one's predator(s) was essential for survival. Those who were able to anticipate an attack and strike first were more likely to live and reproduce than those who were not. In addition, those who were best able to defend themselves or defeat their enemies were likewise more able to survive and propagate. Such survival responses are biologically wired into our systems and are therefore phylogenetically old (Dunbar & Barrett, 2007; Kirkpatrick, 2005; McCullough, 2008).

As humans developed social arrangements in which to live, insults, theft, and gestures that precede bodily harm and other transgressions came to signal an offense (Dunbar & Barrett, 2007). Therefore, it is not surprising that our first "gut" reaction to such an offense is to counter-offend (Giddo, Chapter 12; Paloutzian, Chapter 5). However, cultural evolution led to a social system that includes processes to inhibit our tendency to counter-offend (Dunbar & Barrett, 2007; Kirkpatrick, 2005; McNamara, 2006). The paradox that persists today is that while people's initial reaction to an offense may be one of counter-aggression, cultural and religious teachings of forgiveness preach the exact opposite (Ducommun-Nagy, Chapter 3; Farhadian & Emmons, Chapter 4; McCullough, 2008). The complexities that emerge from such opposing tendencies can make it difficult to define forgiveness.

Grappling with what forgiveness means. Those who promote forgiveness often begin by explaining what it is not (Borris, 2006). They indicate that forgiving does not mean that you have to like your offender, deny your feelings, forget the crime, excuse the offense, or refuse compensation. Approached this way, a definition of forgiveness is elusive. However, chapters in this book convey some of its core aspects.

It is not sufficient to state only what forgiveness is not. Doing so leaves key distinctions unclear. If we wish to help promote positive peace (Christie et al., 2008), then we also need to state what forgiveness is. There are several critical dimensions along which forgiveness and non-forgiveness vary, and some of these dimensions are identified in this book. Also, although forgiveness and reconciliation are not synonymous, both concepts are highlighted and often commingled in this book. The authors employ several definitions of forgiveness as well as reconciliation in their chapters. Thus, we as readers are advised to be alert to instances in which these concepts are clearly distinct or separately identifiable and where they seem to overlap or be combined.

Forgiveness as a multidimensional process. Among the most basic issues with which we are faced is whether forgiveness is a category or a dimension. Occasionally, the terminology is used in a way that suggests that the author considers it something that a victim can either accept or reject. However, the authors in this book suggest a more sophisticated understanding: the psychological process of forgiveness falls along a continuum that ranges from high levels of forgiveness to high levels of non-forgiveness. Also, because forgiving is multidimensional (Worthington, 2005b), it is more often partial than total and is a process rather than an event. This process may include many small steps instead of one large step and may be implemented or received with hesitance rather than certitude (Massey, Chapter 6).

Forgiveness feelings, attitudes, and behaviors. Part of the underlying notions of forgiveness as a process is connected to whether it is viewed as being primarily attitudinal or behavioral. Attitudes are internal psychological predispositions to think, feel, and act toward the attitude object in a certain way. For example, if a person has a pro-military defense attitude, then he or she is more likely to evaluate the military of his or her country in a positive way and favor political candidates who would increase the military budget. If a person has an anti-military defense attitude, then he or she is more likely to evaluate the military in a negative way and favor political candidates who would decrease the military budget. Attitudes cannot be directly observed but must be inferred. In contrast, behavior is publicly observable and concrete. One either joins the military or does not join the military; one either performs an act of kindness toward their perpetrator or does not perform an act of kindness toward their perpetrator.

The distinction between forgiving attitudinally versus behaviorally is important for at least two reasons. First, people have to decide what their goals are when confronted with the question of what their response to the perpetrator will be. Is the victim's goal to think or feel differently toward the perpetrator than before or act in positive ways toward the perpetrator even though harmed by them or both? If both, are those responses to be arranged in a particular sequence? Second, various authors refer to forgiveness as attitudinal or as behavioral (Enright, 2001). Because of this, victims may find that the concept of forgiveness is presented with more than one meaning. Although both meanings of forgiveness are relevant for different circumstances, such considerations may seem confusing, especially for individuals who have recently been victimized.

Intrapersonal and interpersonal forgiveness. The above-discussed distinction is intimately related to the difference between intrapersonal forgiveness versus interpersonal forgiveness. Intrapersonal forgiveness refers to when an individual gives up feelings of hatred and revenge toward his or her perpetrator. Instead, the individual feels more positive emotions, even though he or she may never come to "like" the perpetrator. The contributions of Kalayjian (Chapter 15), Cohen (Chapter 9), and Gal-Ed (Chapter 7) focus on intrapersonal forgiveness. In this sense, it is possible to forgive without ever communicating with the perpetrator or without performing any forgiving act. This type of forgiveness is suggested if contact or communication with the perpetrator is impossible for any reason (e.g., Brown, Almeida, Dharapuram, Choudry, Dressner, & Hernández, Chapter 13). In any case, with intrapersonal forgiveness, the process is about one's own feelings and sense of well-being. It has little to do with the perpetrator in the sense of interaction or communication (Borris, 2006). Forgiveness at the intrapersonal level may leave the door open to self-deception. It is possible for a victim to believe that he or she has forgiven, even though he or she has not.

One way to determine whether a victim has sincerely forgiven is to explore it at the interpersonal level. For example, this could be by initiating some kind of meaningful contact, whether direct or indirect, with the perpetrator or the perpetrator surrogates, if the offender is not available. Thecontributions by Rutayisire on Rwanda (Chapter 11), Giddo on Darfur (Chapter 12), Yacoubian on Armenia (Chapter 14), Green on international relations (Chapter 16), LaMar on black forgiveness in America (Chapter 10), Tint on dialogue processes as a live contact procedure for communication among opposing sides (Chapter 17), and Paloutzian (Chapter 5) focus on forgiveness at the interpersonal level. Their preference is for forgiveness that includes communication with the perpetrator(s) in combination with some sort of action.

Five Prototypical Issues

A number of issues are addressed in one or more chapters of this book. Together with the themes identified above, they convey the complexity and far reach of the concept of forgiveness and the myriad real-world factors that must be considered in its application. We list some issues below so that you can be cognizant of them as you read this book.

Can forgiveness be conditional? One issue pertains to whether forgiveness is conditional or unconditional. Should forgiveness be conditional? Does it make sense to say to an offender, "I will forgive you, IF ...?" Instead of reflecting an internal state of forgiveness, should the victim partake in some sort of deal-making or bargaining? If genuine forgiveness means that it must be given completely and independent of whether the forgiver receives anything in return, can we realistically expect that of people (Ducommun-Nagy, Chapter 3; Massey, Chapter 6)? Giddo (Chapter 12) and Paloutzian (Chapter 5) suggest that some degree of forgiveness may be possible if certain conditions are met.

Is forgiveness realistic across generations? Some circumstances require forgiveness of events that occurred in the distant past. In such cases, the initial trauma may have been experienced by individuals who have long since passed and the trauma has been transmitted through generations to their offspring. Such is the case with descendents of survivors of the Ottoman Turkish Genocide of the Armenians (Yacoubian, Chapter 14), the Nazi Holocaust of the Jews (Tint, Chapter 17), and the India–Pakistan conflict in the aftermath of British rule (Brown, Almeida, Dharapuram, Choudry, Dressner, & Hernandez, Chapter 13). Trans-generational transmission of trauma has also been relevant to lifers in prison (Cohen, Chapter 9). The authors of those chapters address the unique issues involved in forgiving those who have caused the mass traumas of their past.

Is forgiveness culturally and procedurally specific? Not all cultures view forgiveness and related issues in the same light. The emphasis in Western countries is on the individual victim and those resources he or she can muster to forgive, initiate communication with the offender, and so forth. In contrast, in other cultures the emphasis is on group processes to promote forgiveness. For example, Nwoye (Chapter 8) presents an African approach in which the group or larger social entity plays a major role in arranging forgiveness procedures. The group, which includes the perpetrator, victim, and other relevant parties such as parents or authorities, follows a formal procedure that does not leave the question of how to proceed solely up to the victim. The procedures may even include carefully controlled public shaming of the offender. Other unique procedures may also include artistic expression (Gal-Ed, Chapter 7).

What is the role of ethnic identity? Many circumstances in which there is a need for forgiveness involve the ethnic identity of opposing sides. For example, Giddo (Chapter 12) refers to the Islamic soldiers of the government wreaking havoc on the indigenous ethnic Darfurians. Similarly, Rutayisire's Chapter 11 highlights the tribal separation of the Tutsi and Hutu that is at the heart of their genocide. Finally, self-evident ethnic–national divisions have been central to the conflicts between India and Pakistan (Brown, Almeida, Dharapuram, Choudry, Dressner, & Hernandez, Chapter 13), Armenia and Turkey (Yacoubian, Chapter 14), and Nazi Germany and the Jews (Tint, Chapter 17).

Are victims or perpetrators entitled to anything? The question of whether victims are entitled to reparations is addressed in several chapters of this volume. For example, Ducommun-Nagy (Chapter 3) discusses the many variations of the entitlement issue within the context of the ethics of forgiveness. She addresses matters such as whether a victim's entitlement should be met by the perpetrator, the state, or others and what perpetrators may or may not be entitled to. Giddo's (Chapter 12) section about how to promote peace in Darfur is replete with statements that the Darfurians should receive various reparations, replenishments, and reassurances of future safety, before forgiveness can occur.

Conclusion and Looking Ahead

We know that there is no panacea and that promoting and establishing lasting peace is not easy. However, we are confident that proactive, positive peace efforts are worth their costs and that expanding human consciousness about forgiveness and reconciliation processes is greatly needed. Forgiveness is not an idealized or fantasy state in which all will be well if we just forgive. On the contrary, there may be significant physical, psychological, or social costs associated with forgiveness, and in some cases they may be too great. For example, even though we are motivated to forgive by our ideals, actually doing so could cause more internal conflict with ourselves, external conflict with our group, or physical risk than we can bear. In such instances, an alternative nonviolent path must be found.

The authors share the UNESCO premise that "wars begin in the minds of men." However, peace can also begin in the minds of men and women. We hope these authors' writings promote positive peace.

References

Borris, E. R. (2006). *Forgiveness: a 7-step program for letting go of anger and bitterness.* New York: McGraw-Hill.

Christie, D. J. (2006). What is peace psychology the psychology of? *Journal of Social Issues, 62*(1), 1–17.

Christie, D. J., Tint, B. S., Wagner, R. V., & Winter, D. D. (2008). Peace psychology for a peaceful world. *American Psychologist, 63*(6), 540–552.

Dunbar, R. I. M., & Barrett, L. (Eds.). (2007). *Oxford handbook of evolutionary psychology.* Oxford: Oxford University Press.

Enright, R. D. (2001). *Forgiveness is a choice: A step-by-step process for resolving anger and restoring hope.* Washington, DC: American Psychological Association.

Kirkpatrick, L. A. (2005). *Attachment, evolution, and the psychology of religion.* New York: Guilford Press.

Lederach, J. P. (1997). *Building peace: Sustainable reconciliation in divided societies.* Washington, DC: United States Institute for Peace Press.

McCullough, M. E. (2008). *Beyond revenge: The evolution of the forgiveness instinct.* San Francisco: Jossey-Bass.

McCullough, M. E., Pargament, K. I., & Thoresen, C. E. (Eds.). (2000). *Forgiveness: Theory, practice and research.* New York: Guilford Press.

McNamara, P. (Ed.). (2006). *Where god and science meet* (Vols. 1–3). Westport, CT: Praeger.

Roe, M. D. (2007). Intergroup forgiveness in settings of political violence: Complexities, ambiguities, and potentialities. *Peace and Conflict: Journal of Peace Psychology, 1,* 3–9.

Worthington, E. L. (Ed.). (2005a). *Handbook of forgiveness.* New York: Routledge.

Worthington, E. L. (2005b). Initial questions about the art and science of forgiving. In E. Worthington (Ed.), *Handbook of forgiveness* (pp. 1–13). New York: Routledge.

Chapter 2
A Systemic Framework for Forgiveness, Reconciliation, and Peace: Interconnecting Psychological and Social Processes

Robert F. Massey and **Khawla Abu-Baker**

> *Then I realized something. That last thought had brought no sting with it. Closing Sohrab's door, I wondered if that was how forgiveness budded, not with the fanfare of epiphany, but with pain gathering its things, packing up, and slipping away unannounced in the middle of the night.*
>
> Khaled Hosseini, *The kite runner* (p. 359).

Forgiveness, reconciliation, and peace pose possibilities for human relations. Only humans engage in malignant aggression (Fromm, 1941/1965; 1973) interpersonally and through socio-political violence (Chirot & Seligman, 2001). These dynamics affect personal well-being; balances and levels of satisfaction in relationships; multigenerational legacies in families, cultures, nations, and geographical regions. The tenacity of altruism and aggression and their intermixture in persons and situations throughout human history connotes that understanding these processes proves complex (Pargament, McCullough, & Thoresen, 2000).

Research on forgiveness is focused mainly on individual self-experiences (Enright, 2001; McCullough, Pargament, & Thoresen, 2000). Reconciliation refers to interpersonal, dyadic, dynamics (Enright, Freedman, & Rique, 1998; Worthington, 2005). Peace connotes accord between larger groups and nations (Christie, 2006). Each process requires preconditions to result in constructive rather than damaging consequences (Armour & Umbreit, 2005; Staub, 2005). Demarcation of these processes as discrete has been questioned (Hill, Exline, & Cohen, 2005; Pargament et al., 2000). Consideration of their interconnecting requires a more integrative, systemic perspective.

A Systems Approach

With systems thinking we can conceptualize the interconnecting of psychological and social processes intertwining self, relationships, groups, and social structures in cooperation, social harm, violations of justice, forgiveness, reconciliation, and peace (Christie, 2006; Massey, 2002). A framework for understanding all of these processes, which occur in different dimensions of human development, needs to be

Ani Kalayjian, Raymond F. Paloutzian, *Forgiveness and Reconciliation*, Peace Psychology Book Series, DOI 10.1007/978-1-4419-0181-1_2,
© Springer Science+Business Media, LLC 2009

sufficiently comprehensive to encompass the establishment, violation, and restoration of justice on the personal, interpersonal, inter-group, and international levels (Hill, Exline, & Cohen, 2005; Mullet & Girard, 2000).

The systems we live in exert power over personal options and the allocation of resources beyond individual control, yet they arise, continue, and change as humans construct them (Massey, 1985/1986). Systems do not exist independently of human creativity, consent, and compliance. Social structures are not reducible to psychological dynamics, nor do they exist as sociological reifications separable from the persons who are influenced by and co-construct them (Merleau-Ponty, 1942/1963). Accurate analyses and effective interventions require appropriate attention to each dimension (Pargament et al., 2000).

Specifically human capacities make possible each of these dimensions, which are inextricably linked, reciprocally influence and circularly reinforce each other. In this chapter we delineate and inter-relate the processes which provide the scaffolding for a comprehensive systemic framework. When woven together the processes interlock in a systemically integrated tapestry clarifying the interconnecting personal and social dynamics of forgiveness, reconciliation, and peace. A family vignette will illustrate how universally human processes impact daily living in cultural contexts (Sandage & Williamson, 2005).

Illustration[1]

Personal, Interpersonal, Familial, and Cultural Processes. Yasmeen, a 31-year-old Druze woman living in Israel, came to therapy 8 months pregnant and suffering from deep depression. She had discovered that her husband, Fadi, age 33, serving in the Israeli military forces, was having an affair with a 24-year-old Druze woman. Fadi had met his girlfriend, Mona, recently when he returned to college.

Yasmeen had close and warm relationships with Fadi's family of origin. She lived on the second floor of a house while his widowed mother lived on the first floor. In Arab villages, since land and money are scarce, males build floors on top of their parents' houses. Like others in the community they live modestly and simply. As an only son Fadi was responsible for taking care of his widowed mother and for visiting all four of his married sisters according to the traditions. Yasmeen had taught herself to pursue a lifestyle similar to a single mother; she did not rely on her husband as do traditional women in her village. Since Fadi was located in a far-away location, she believed that he would respect and love her more if she were able to become independent, playing an opposite role to his mother and sisters. She wanted to impress him with her abilities. For the short run, he was freed from his own household and child-raising responsibilities, but the result for the long run was that he became isolated from the daily life of his family unit. When he relocated closer and moved back to live permanently at home, he felt like an outsider, not as a father and husband.

---

[1] This couple had been in therapy with the second author.

During the week, Yasmeen divided her time between her work as an assistant to a kindergarten teacher, her house, her children, and assisting her mother-in-law with cleaning, preparing food, taking her to the doctor, and including her when she had guests. On weekends, when Fadi arrived home, she tried to let him take care of his extended family matters and not burden him with her own problems, though she really wanted him more fully as a partner and lover. Yasmeen believed that this strategy would let Fadi appreciate her independence and her sensitivity toward protecting his limited time and energy and, as a result of her behavior, love her more.

The result boomeranged. Yasmeen was too fatigued and too lonely. Fadi never knew how skilled she was with conflict management, organizational skills, and rearing children. Fadi felt that Yasmeen did not rely on him while Mona, his mother, and his sisters were consulting with him. Fadi claimed that Yasmeen was mothering him while Mona was sharing ideas, emotions, problems, and friendship with him. Fadi continued in his denial of the extramarital affair to Yasmeen. Her brother, a student at the same college as Fadi, confirmed to Yasmeen that the affair was ongoing. Her brother insisted that he saw them together several times. Yasmeen was sure of this, but Fadi denied this each time she asked him.

Yasmeen asked her brothers for help. They advised her to file for divorce. The four brothers asked Fadi to stop cheating on their sister. He denied the relationship with Mona and claimed that the brother who said he saw them together had lied. The brothers beat up Fadi. Fadi demanded that Yasmeen make a choice between remaining in their marriage or returning to her family of origin. Yasmeen, with great sorrow, decided to cut off her relations with her family of origin. In individual sessions, Fadi agreed to abstain from contacting Mona until Yasmeen would give birth and recover from her depression.

After giving birth, Yasmeen found her cutoff from her family of origin unbearable. In reflecting on what was best for herself and her children, she was sure she loved Fadi deeply. She wanted to do whatever was necessary to reconnect him to herself and their home. She discovered her ability, willingness, and desire to regain intimacy with Fadi. In the months that Fadi stayed home longer, Yasmeen did not have pain from pregnancy, she was able to have sexual relations again, and she believed that intimacy might bring Fadi closer.

In therapy, Yasmeen recalled her childhood with her estranged parents who had not stopped quarrelling since the early days of their marriage. This caused their three married daughters to feel lonely and unprotected in their patriarchal society. Yasmeen came to the conclusion that her future would be worse had she filed for divorce. According to traditions, she would be uprooted from her cherished environment, would not be allowed to take custody of her children, and would be forced to return to her parents living in tension. If she were divorced, her opportunities for re-marriage would be almost nil whereas a divorced or widowed man might remarry a younger, more educated woman.

Yasmeen concluded that forgiveness and reconciliation with Fadi represented the best scenario for herself as a Druze woman and for her four children. Also she found that reconciliation between Fadi and her brothers would work best for her marriage. Yasmeen initiated a traditional ceremony. She took her new baby girl to the house of her older brother and put the child in his hands, thus asking him metaphorically, "Are you taking care of your daughters?" This courageous act caused the four brothers to feel guilty for not taking their sister's welfare into account while beating up her husband. They asked a traditional mediator to initiate a conciliation ceremony with their brother-in-law in his house. Her brothers came together with their wives and children and brought many gifts. This meant that they respected Fadi by coming to his home. If he did not welcome them, he would become the guilty one from then on. All parties agreed to open a new page in their relations. This process of reconciliation starting with Yasmeen and then with her siblings left Fadi with feelings of shame and guilt. He resumed individual therapy to crystallize his decision to disconnect his relationship with Mona.

Specifically Human Social-Psychological Capacities Potentiating Harm, Forgiveness, Reconciliation, Peace

Self-Processes

Development of Self and Social Attachments. Self develops in contexts through interpersonal exchanges and personal reflections. Individuals receive attributions, evaluations, and definitions of self (*me's*) from others in responses and words (Mead, 1964). The *I* of each person actively coordinates the me's into a self-image based on past and present experiences and future anticipations of self with others. Yasmeen sees herself as a wife, mother, and family member. Fadi's departing from adherence to a perception of being primarily a husband, faithful to Yasmeen, harmed her.

Perceptions of Self and Other Develop Reciprocally. Humans pursue both autonomy/distinctiveness of identity and belonging/homonomy (Angyal, 1965). Individuals yearn for *acceptance* in the forms available. A person who is safe and respected gains awareness of *good me* and perceives others as good (Sullivan, 1953). When harshness, neglect, or abuse occurs, a sense of I and me can be damaged. *Bad me* emerges in conjunction with a perception of other as bad, unreliable, or hostile. In extreme circumstances, as in sexual abuse and torture, parts of self may be submerged, denied, or split off and remain latent as *not me*, as unacceptable or rejected. In interpersonal harm self is disconfirmed, colluded against through mystifying exchanges (Laing, 1965), or discounted (Schiff et al., 1975). Through cooperation self is affirmed and feels valued (Laing, 1961). In cooperating Yasmeen and Fadi experience validation of self. Cooperation generates trust, nurtures self and identity (Erikson, 1968), and builds social structures based on legacies of fairness and justice (Boszormenyi-Nagy & Krasner, 1986; Christie, 2006). Interpersonal harm – Fadi's infidelity and Yasmeen's brothers pummeling Fadi – induces physical and psychological stress and social tensions. It undermines creative potentials and contributes to legacies of the misuse of power and of injustice. Forgiveness, reconciliation, and peace restore cooperation and trust (Makinen & Johnson, 2006). In these processes concepts and feelings about others depend on (1) whether protection against further harm is enforced, (2) whether harm continues, (3) whether others prove reliable and honorable, and (4) whether offenders, aggressors, and perpetrators are held accountable or turn repentant (Armour & Umbreit, 2005; Staub, 2005).

Self-awareness begins with prototaxic feelings and images (Sullivan, 1953). *Symbolic thinking* and *language* facilitate processing of perceptions and attributions regarding I, me, and others (Mead, 1964). Language may be used parataxically – illogically or with private meanings. Generally people clearly comprehend consensually validated, syntaxic communication, i.e., using words with commonly understood connotations and logic. Symbolic thinking and language enable persons (1) to be aware of engaging in interpersonal harm, forgiveness, reconciliation, and peace; (2) to remember these experiences; (3) to reflect on choosing to initiate, continue, or cease these activities; and (4) to evaluate the consequences of their occurrence for self and others in contexts. Forgiveness, reconciliation, and peace are impeded by prototaxic or parataxic communication and facilitated by syntaxic symbolic thinking and language.

From birth individuals are *socially motivated* and seek *contact, social recognition, and belonging* through attachments. Positive regard for self emerges from secure *attachments* (Ainsworth, 1982; Bowlby, 1988; Prescott, 1990). Injured self-concepts emerge with insecure anxious, avoidant, or disorganized/disoriented attachments (Davies, 2004; Main & Solomon, 1990). Forgiveness involves affirmation of self and restores good I and good me in supporting the needs for interpersonal security and collaboration (Sullivan, 1953). Reconciliation connotes affirmation of self and other as trustworthy, as available for secure attachment. Negative socialization can generate expectations of social mistreatment and complicate processes of validating self and claiming positive entitlement to interpersonal justice and fairness (Boszormenyi-Nagy & Krasner, 1986).

Self-processes facilitate or impede psychological forgiveness. In forgiveness positive thinking and feelings supplant negative ones (Enright, 2001; Enright & Fitzgibbons, 2000). Forgiveness results from changing motivations from negative to conciliatory (McCullough, Fincham, & Tsang, 2003). In decisional forgiveness a person alters intentions about how to behave toward another, and in emotional forgiveness moves from unforgiving emotions to orienting them positively toward the offender (Worthington, 2005). Yasmeen and Fadi engaged in these processes in transforming cognitions, emotions, and motivations from negative to positive in forgiving.

Self-Objects. Cooperation and trust facilitate construction of comforting and supportive self-objects – internal, affectively laden images of others used to repair or restore a deficient or missing aspect of self (Kohut, 1987). Self-objects formed in contexts of protection and support bolster self-esteem in times of interpersonal harm. Lack of caring parenting hampers development of supportive self-objects. Yasmeen's self-objects stemming from experiencing distress in living with bickering parents exacerbated her feeling lonely and unprotected in her marriage. Yasmeen's deep depression beyond the expected sadness of grieving over the discovery of her husband's affair was compounded by his lack of attention and support as she readied to imminently give birth to a fourth child and by socio-cultural restrictions around a wife's rights. No parent or relationship partner is perfect. Responses from parents and significant others need to be "good enough" (Winnicott, 1988, p. 114). Exoneration and reconciliation entail understanding the developmental contexts of those who caused harm (Madanes, 1990; McNeel, 1976). Forgiveness and peace imply not acting on *destructive entitlement* (feeling that one is justified in hurting someone in the present because of harm to self in the past) (Boszormenyi-Nagy & Krasner, 1986).

Culture, Self, and Social Identity. Family, culture, and society affect self. Growing up in a communal atmosphere promotes a *sociocentric cultural self* oriented to contributing to group harmony (Comas-Díaz, 1996). In cultures emphasizing individualism, efforts toward self-identity and personal success are more expected and recognized, thus fostering an *egocentric cultural self.* Evolving identities emerge within specific contexts and are permeated by consciousness of social dimensions – socioeconomic status, ethnic and racial dynamics, peace, war, terror (Comas-Díaz, Lykes, & Alarcón, 1998). Cultural interpretations and processes modulate harming and healing of self (Sandage & Williamson, 2005). Consistent with their social-cultural contexts, Yasmeen and Fadi, as Arabs and members of the Druze culture and religion living in Israel, have developed more sociocentric selves.

Individuals develop *social* as well as personal *identities* (Turner & Oakes, 1997; Tajfel & Turner, 1986). Social identities may be barricaded or bounded (Jowitt, 2001). In *barricaded* or corporate identities a person is classified only in a fixed category (e.g., ethnicity), definitively distinguished from members of other groups. With a *bounded* identity, an individual identifies with a group which partially defines self and allows for complementary, non-exclusive self-descriptions based on belonging to other groups (e.g., family along with religion). In crises and inter-group conflicts, loyalty to a barricaded identity may override the flexibility of a bounded identity and spur rejection, harm, and violence against others even when positive connections occurred previously (e.g., Bosnia, Iraq, Rwanda) (Oberschall, 2001; Prunier, 2001). This compounds obstacles to forgiveness, reconciliation, and peace (Chirot, 2001). Bounded identities allow for affirmation of self, one's own group, and the members of other groups. In Switzerland, supported by national ideologies and leaders, persons with bounded identities around ethnicity, religion, and nationality have lived cooperatively. Prior to Belgian colonization, Hutus and Tutsis lived intertwined economically, politically, and through intermarriage. Only when colonial influences imposed barricaded identities did interethnic violence erupt (Prunier, 2001; Smith, 1998). Development of bounded identities helped overcome barriers in reconciliation processes after the establishment of peace (e.g., France and Germany, Japan and United States).

Lack of social contact may polarize images and emphasize group exclusiveness (Hewstone & Cairns, 2001). Yet inter-group contact may incite aggression. When persons from other groups are viewed (1) favorably, as somewhat typical; (2) as variable; (3) as describable in multiple classifications; and (4) not as members of essentialized categories (members are distinguished by immutable and inheritable characteristics) (McCauley, 2001), the opportunities for forgiveness, reconciliation, and peace are improved. Effective interventions necessitate attention to "an ongoing dynamic of change, [for] cultural identities are not timeless, essentialized forms of consciousness, but they are in a continuous process of evolution, reformulation, quiescence, and arousal in response to the broader social and political environment in which individual and group transactions are embedded" (Tripp & Young, 2001, pp. 259–260). While personalization through meeting people from other groups may de-categorize individuals, the experiences may not generalize to groups as a whole. A combination of de-categorization (persons are not intrinsically defined by *a* category), re-categorization (perceiving persons as included within more superordinate classes including the groups with whom individuals are more or less familiar and comfortable), and cross-categorization (perceiving that persons from specific groups belong to multiple and varied classifications) blends processes underlying an evolution toward reconciliation and peace. Tanzania (incorporating African clans and lineages, the Chagga having 17 identity groups and the Maasai at least 10 plus Arabic, Indian, German, British, Islamic, and Christian influences), under the leadership of Julius Nyerere, exemplified these principles in a "politics of pluralism...[with] an impressive degree of communal comity" (p. 259).

Connecting Self and Other

Self-Transcending Consciousness, Symbolic Thinking, Language. The capacity for self-transcending consciousness (Allport, 1937/1961; Frankl, 1969; Fromm, 1955) enables humans to reflect on self, others, and relationships. Self-transcendence makes possible considering other viewpoints, empathy, conscience, love, and reaching toward spiritual realities. Symbolic thinking and language allow for memories of self-transcending consciousness and for communicating these in perpetrating harm, violence, and war and in seeking forgiveness, reconciliation, and peace. Yasmeen and Fadi would not have experienced their dilemmas nor envisioned their resolutions without self-transcending consciousness.

Social Role-Taking, Empathy. Capacity for taking the role of the other emerges as a child experiences the feelings or attitudes of others through role play (Mead, 1964). Since taking the roles and perspectives of others leads to responding in expected ways, this process comprises a cognitive foundation for social living. Community, culture, and constructive inter-group and international relations require mutually shared expectations spawning cooperation. Social role-taking grows concomitantly with the evolution of *empathy* (Selman, 1976). Forgiveness involves positively taking the role of another and exercising empathy (McCullough et al., 2003; Wade & Worthington, 2005). Taking the role of the other without empathy – in seeking understanding of the other as a means to control and manipulate the other as a devalued or denigrated object or as an enemy – results in exploitation, abuse, dehumanization, and torture. Threats to security may impede taking the role of the other. Reconciliation and peace necessitate taking the role of the other with compassion to gain an empathetic understanding of the other's experiences and to build a relationship based on mutual acknowledgment and reciprocity of good will, trust, and justice (Armour & Umbreit, 2005; Christie, 2006; Enright et al., 1998; Staub, 2005).

Yasmeen took the role of Fadi in devising the strategy of assuming many home responsibilities to free him to attend to the needs of his mother and sisters in the hope that he would rekindle his love for her. Fadi came to therapy because he felt guilty since Yasmeen was pregnant, in pain and deep depression, did not stop crying, and was becoming dysfunctional at home and in her job. Fadi's declared sensitivity to Yasmeen's psychological situation was not typical of Druze men. However, Fadi lacked full empathy and did not take the role of Yasmeen in initiating and continuing a special relationship with Mona. In the end Fadi displayed empathy toward Yasmeen and her brothers in implementing cultural beliefs by respecting customary connections.

Between Processes. Through specifically human capacities, persons interconnect over space and time. Though concepts and language abound for describing individual and interpersonal processes, we generally lack a conceptual framework and language for elucidating the interconnecting of persons in relationships and systems. Buber (1948/1957) highlighted the "realm that exists *between an 'I' and a 'Thou.'*" (Boszormenyi-Nagy & Krasner, 1986, p. 33) Natanson (1970) called "what happens *between* selves...[in] the experience of self with other selves" (p. 47) sociality. In sociality "the *between* is shared" (p. 54) and encompasses the living, the dead, and the unborn. "The basis of sociality...[lies in] the 'subjective interpretation of meaning'...The starting point for the entire conception of sociality...[flows from the premise] that the response of one person to another presupposes that each partner interprets the other's action as meaningful" (p. 56). Self-transcending consciousness, empathy, and social role-taking make this possible. Throughout life in the dialectical dynamics *between* self and other, persons live in "a structural relational context" (Boszormenyi-Nagy, 1965, p. 41) essential to being human. Because of this what happens in the *between* among humans endures if not explicitly in verbalized stories then in the dynamics of invisible loyalties over generations in the family and societal ledgers of justice and trustworthiness (Boszormenyi-Nagy & Krasner, 1986). Psychological, social, and spiritual harm and healing occur in the *between*. Forgiveness and peace extend beyond the dynamics of the persons involved to the relationships they share and the social structures they live in.

Fadi and Yasmeen in conjunction with their families had constructed a social and intimate *between* in their marriage, living arrangement, and network of family responsibilities. Fadi violated the committed between of emotional and spiritual connection with Yasmeen by engaging in an affair with Mona. A conciliation ceremony common in their culture restored a constructive between. Their estrangement and reconciliation, their recommitment of loyalty to each other, family, and culture structured the relational context and ledger of justice for themselves and their progeny over generations.

Interaction, Interperception, Interexperience. Laing, Phillipson, and Lee (1966) provided language regarding *between* processes. Persons interconnect through interactions, thinking, and feeling. Before, during, and after interactions, perceptions of self and others form. Significant perceptions/attributions regarding self and other are interdependent. When I am interacting, I think of myself in a particular way. I think of the other person in a certain manner. I also think of how the other is viewing me.

The other person is also engaging in these processes: Having a viewpoint on him- or herself, looking at me in some way, and imagining that I am conceiving of her or him from some perspective. Though sounding complicated, these perceptual or cognitive processes – *interperceptions* – occur continuously. The agreement or incongruence between the different levels of interperceptions gives rise to understanding, feeling understood, and being understood or misunderstanding, feeling misunderstood, and being misunderstood. Through *interexperiences* individuals feel more emotionally connected, responsive, and attached with persons with whom they experience relationships than with strangers no matter what the geographical distance.

Yasmeen learned of inappropriate interactions by Fadi with Mona, experienced non-supportive interactions with her parents, and fulfilling interactions with her children and mother-in-law. Interperceptions needed sorting out. Yasmeen reflected on perceptions of self as daughter of estranged parents, committed wife, injured partner, beloved daughter-in-law and sister-in-law, capable woman. She considered perceptions of others as harming husband, sometimes-helpful brothers, emotionally neglectful parents, and appreciative mother-in-law. Yasmeen surmised that Fadi in his infatuation with Mona was perceiving her in ways in which misunderstandings were arising. She was feeling misunderstood and mistreated. The interperceptions, interactions, and interexperiences of Yasmeen's brothers and Fadi changed dramatically from being respectful brothers-in-law to antagonistic and aggressive bothers around the integrity of Yasmeen to reconciling with her perspective and with her husband.

Patterns of interactions, interperceptions, and interexperiences become traditions and standards in social groups. They are frequently *internalized* and *conformed* to with greater or lesser flexibility. When pressured in situations of abuse, racism, sexism, and homophobia, a member of a stigmatized group may internalize shame-based norms of negativity as personal beliefs shaping one's own identity (Harper & Hoopes, 1990). An individual may conform in behavior, but preserve the integrity of a distinct self by not internalizing a social message. Or a disparaged person may act based on a self-affirmation (Billingsley, 1968; Sue & Sue, 2003), bolstered by a social-support system for one's being and way of living. When interpersonal and inter-group cooperation is rooted in respect for traditions and standards compatible with the interperceptions of the participants, the interperceptions are mutually supportive of the integrity, dignity, and needs of those involved, and interexperiences are comfortable. When traditions and standards in interperceptions demean self or other, harm is caused, and interexperiences are distressing. Forgiveness, reconciliation, and peace flow not simply from personal dispositional motivations but also involve relational and situational dynamics based on reciprocity or mismatching of attributions, interperceptions, and interexperiences about forgivingness and forgivability (Hoyt, Fincham, McCullough, Maio, & Davila, 2005).

Belief Systems, Meaning. The cognitive processes of attributions, beliefs, expectations, and meaning in conjunction with emotional and motivational dynamics provide maps for how to evaluate and plan in relation to self, others, and social institutions. Personal belief systems result from perceptions and memory of how to advance personal well-being and satisfying social connections. Interpersonal and

social belief systems are built through shared interperceptions in mutual understandings arrived at through consensus and enforced through socialization and legal
procedures. Core beliefs on the individual level parallel group-level world views that
constrain or trigger conflicts. Eidelson and Eidelson (2003) identified five dangerous belief domains – superiority, injustice, vulnerability, distrust, and helplessness –
which may spur conflict and harm.

Societal belief systems (*ideology*) shape social interactions and personal identities (Erikson, 1968). Leaders of countries following the Geneva Conventions, based
on syntaxic understandings, interdict inhumane treatment and torture of captured
enemies. Renouncing these agreements, when ideologies are defined as opposi-
tional, sanctions harm and violence to persons categorized as prisoners of war or
as enemy combatants. Social beliefs stipulate the rules (*norms*) for living in a group
(Fadi and Yasmeen are to honor family connections) and how individuals should act
in specific situations or relationships (*roles*) (Yasmeen and Fadi as parents caring
for their children). For Yasmeen, Fadi, and their families harming, forgiveness, and
reconciliation rituals revolve around cultural beliefs, customs, norms, and roles. An
individual may internalize norms and roles or not conform for personal or ethical
reasons (Merton, 1949/1957). Ideology based on social distinctions and a focus on
superiority/inferiority perpetuates interpersonal harm and violence (Staub, 2005).
Ideology anchored in embracing inclusiveness fosters bounded rather than barricaded identities, moving beyond solely negative attributions toward members of
other groups, the breaking of barriers to interaction, and healing histories of interpersonal harm and violence through forgiveness, reconciliation, and peace. Intractable
conflicts, as between the Israelis and Palestinians, are buttressed by a clash of narratives based on ideologies embodying perceptions of exclusive legitimacy, histories
of victimization, and irreconcilability (Rouhana & Bar-Tal, 1998). In forgiveness
and reconciliation varying belief systems must be acknowledged (Shriver, 1998).
Disregard for German beliefs about social identity and shame after World War I bred
a vortex of hostility. This was displaced in the Holocaust and erupted in World War
II leaving consequences for forgiveness and reconciliation still needing attention.
Denial of historical involvement in oppressive ideologies blocks progress. Children of perpetrators, as in Nazi Germany, shielded from knowledge of their parents'
activities, grow up amidst silence about harm done, suffer secret shame and guilt,
and feel unforgiven and unreconciled (Bar-On, 1991).

Group belief systems, symbolized by leaders' actions, stimulate reconciliation or
harm. In 1865 US President Lincoln acknowledged loss and the need to grieve. He
encouraged charity rather than malice as he promoted peace. In 1985 US President
Reagan's inclination to visit the Bitburg cemetery, in which Nazi SS soldiers were
buried, but not a concentration camp, caused a furor and represented an obstacle to
leader-level reconciliation between Germany and the United States. The prevalent
US ideology of dividing the world into good and evil, of denying defeat, of judging
self-righteously that violence can produce good (in Central America in the 1980 s),
and of avoiding grieving clashed with German and Jewish beliefs emanating from
abhorrence about the perpetuation of harm as symbolized by Nazi SS soldiers buried
in Bitburg (Shriver, 1998). The same belief system (dividing the world into good

and evil groups, not acknowledging loss, and the need to grieve) spawned US interventions in Iraq based on an ideology of suppressing the distress of remembering damage to persons, families, and both nations in Vietnam.

Meaning forms a cognitive and affective bridge interconnecting self, others, and group-level processes. Individuals experience, discover (Frankl, 1969), and construct (Gergen, 1997) meanings as core values. Meaning arises in creativity and by internalizing and conforming to social belief systems. For many, religion offers a prominent belief system for interpreting meaning (Silberman, 2005). Meanings emerge from and affect the interpretations of interpersonal harm, forgiveness (Enright et al., 1998), and peace (Christie, 2006). Meanings congruent with shared interperceptions form a basis for cooperative and satisfying interactions. Meanings identified as incompatible or antithetical lead to alienation or expressed antipathy. Social institutions (legal, educational, religious) serve as the guardians of meanings (Erikson, 1968). They promote either equitable structures fostering forgiveness, reconciliation, and peace or discriminatory and unjust structures underpinning harm and suffering, violence and war. Sharing meanings provides a foundational motivation for cooperation in a group. Imposing and silencing meanings cause harm, frequently in a context of authoritarian, oppressive power and inequitable social structures. Yasmeen and Fadi were imbued with the belief systems of their families and cultures. They discovered and constructed the meanings of their individual and social lives within the frameworks of their personalities and relationships within their contexts. They live in an international region in which meaning systems sometimes clash and lead to harm through aggression and violence (Rouhana & Bar-Tal, 1998).

Reference Groups. Reference groups (families, cultures, religions) provide norms for evaluating the relevance of meanings to a person's self, personal and social identity, and social issues. Reference groups provide communication channels regarding expected standards (Shibutani, 1955). Participants in chosen reference groups experience congruent interperceptions. When interpersonal harm occurs, membership in a reference group may prolong victimization or perpetration or provide a buffer against injury and oppression. Members of reliable and trustworthy reference groups provide encouragement. When families and familiar social institutions are damaged or destroyed, social supports for survival are impaired and new structures are needed. Spiritual connections can bind persons. They either facilitate crossing barriers and chasms in forgiveness, reconciliation, and peace or solidify barricaded identities and histories of harm to justify violations of justice, interpersonal harm, aggression, and violence.

Families, culture, and religion serve as the primary reference groups for Yasmeen and Fadi. They turn to them for membership and for norms. Yasmeen knew, as did Fadi, and did not necessarily have to put into words, though words helped particularly in reconciliation processes and in re-establishing a more satisfying family life, the expectations for each as a member of the family and culture. As Druze people they are Arabs in culture and language and belong to a branch of Muslims developed in the 11th century from Shiite Islam. While respecting religion, which is a daily influence in their lives, they are not strictly religious.

Group-Level Processes

Triangles, Threesomes. Harm, forgiveness, and reconciliation frequently involve more than two people. Triangles exist when two persons remain overly close and another is excluded or withdraws (Kerr & Bowen, 1988). Triangles generate split loyalties (Boszormenyi-Nagy & Krasner, 1986). Threesomes occur when three or more persons relate while respecting the identities and relationship possibilities of each (Guerin, Fogarty, Fay, & Kautto, 1996). Threesomes may be more culturally congruent in communally oriented cultures (Falicov, 1998). In triangling, clear thinking about the needs of each person and the authentic possibilities for comfortable and satisfying relating are lost through collusion and mystification occurring frequently in abuse (Laing, 1965). Forgiveness, reconciliation, and peace require detriangulation and relating appropriately in dyads and threesomes. While acknowledging the unacceptability of harm and abuse, each person ought to take responsibility for healing going forward (Madanes, Keim, & Smelser, 1995).

Fadi was torn between his needs for each woman. He loved Yasmeen for some reasons and Mona for others. Fadi was triangulating with the two women and experienced loyalties to each. This generated conflict interpersonally and in the community. Yasmeen's brothers triangulated with Fadi as one brother communicated with her about her husband's infidelity and as they beat him up. Forgiveness and reconciliation involved detriangulating to relate in respectful compatible twosomes and threesomes. The nations, in Yasmeen's and Fadi's region, are triangulated with split loyalties to other nations. This complicates achieving peace and the families of Yasmeen and Fadi.

Boundaries, Social Distance, In-Groups, Out-Groups. *Boundaries* demarcate accessibility between self and other (Minuchin, 1974). With *clear boundaries* age- and role-appropriate cooperative interactions transpire. *Rigid boundaries* denote exclusion. Intrusions on culturally sanctioned and personally desirable space and time indicate *diffuse boundaries*. As Yasmeen perceived a diffuse boundary between Fadi and Mona, she set up rigid boundaries with him. When Fadi insisted that Yasmeen choose between her marriage and her family, she established rigid boundaries with them. As they reconciled, Yasmeen and Fadi sought clear boundaries as spouses, with Mona excluded, and collaboration with her family. Cultural standards prescribe acceptable types of interpersonal contact – *social distances* (Hall, 1966). For Yasmeen, Fadi, and their families social distances ranged from engaged to estranged to reunited.

On the group level, norms about members' characteristics and values dictate social distance and acceptance or rejection of individuals as belonging to *in-groups* or *out-groups* (Allport, 1954). Belief systems supporting favorable perceptions of an individual or group facilitate clear boundaries, less social distance, in-group status, and greater ease in taking the role of the other (Cairns, Tam, Hewstone, & Niens, 2005; Christie, 2006). In these situations the integrity and dignity of each person with bounded identities are respected; groups are considered as separate because of mutually acceptable reasons. Belief systems about classifying another individual or group unfavorably enjoin rigid or diffuse boundaries and greater social distance, relegation to an out-group, and increased difficulty in constructively taking the role of the other. With rigid boundaries members of out-groups avoid each other. In situations of aggression and exploitation diffuse boundaries are crossed. This may lead to rigid boundaries. When persons are divided into in-groups and out-groups with barricaded identities, harm and violence may be justified based on the inhumanity of others. This evades reflecting on and taking responsibility for the responses of self and one's own group in fomenting conflict situations and the consequences for all involved. Dehumanization and dichotomization of groups underlie prejudice, exclusion, and violence (Allport, 1954). When personal and social security are threatened, defending without demonizing the other(s) becomes a challenge. Violations of human interconnectedness through interpersonal harm, torture, and killing traumatize persons on both sides, possibly for generations, as they struggle, maybe out of awareness, with unacknowledged guilt and shame begging for voice and reconciliation (Berger & Berger, 2001; Chirot & Seligman, 2001; Krondorfer, 1995). Forgiveness, reconciliation, and peace involve discovering the humanity and dignity of others and inclusion within community.

In India the Untouchables (Dalit), believed to fall below the four castes, were forbidden contact and equal status. Belief systems encoded in law govern boundaries and social distance. In Latin America the humanity of African slaves was acknowledged. They were accorded rights to legal marriage and protections against masters molesting women, thus curtailing some interpersonal harm and violence (van den Berghe, 1967). In North America slaves were regarded as property not entitled to marry and were subject to physical and sexual abuse.

Social-Structural Processes

Specifically human processes enable persons to collectively establish social structures and institutions, to develop and use tools, and to exercise group-level power, all of which facilitate, impede, or constrain interpersonal harm, violence, forgiveness, reconciliation, and peace. Social harm and violence occur beyond individual control, though individuals participate. Their impacts exceed the scope and responsibility of individuals who are not in decision-making roles and positions. Personal forgiveness and interpersonal reconciliation, while valuable, do not suffice in addressing the social-structural issues in inter-group and international conflicts, violence, and peace processes.

Social Structures. Social structures develop, endure, and are preserved over time and space because of the specifically human capacities for self-transcending consciousness, symbolic thinking, and language. Social structures arise as communal agreements about how to organize to best provide for human needs (Mead, 1964). Structures which served human needs may not do so later. Structures persist beyond their usefulness through adherence to norms, particularly when leaders derive inequitable benefits from them and when technology is used to defend them. Social structures provide parameters for interpersonal harm, violence, forgiveness, reconciliation, and peace (Christie, 2006).

Yasmeen's and Fadi's lives are embedded in social structures. Cultural and religious gender norms govern their roles, customs, and relationships. Violations of justice and their redress are circumscribed by social structures (Armour & Umbreit, 2005; Hill et al., 2005). Intrapsychic forgiveness by Yasmeen would not end Fadi's assignation with Mona, and the socio-cultural violation of marital and family integrity would persist. Were they to divorce, Yasmeen loses her rights to raise her children and to maintain contact with Fadi's mother and family who cherish her. Divorce in this context would generate further violations of parental justice in excluding Yasmeen from the care of her children and would preclude marital reconciliation.

The couple are employed in geographically indigenous social structures based on their educational levels. Each occupational social structure imposes some constraints. Fadi, as a Druze man, was required to serve in the Israeli army for 3 years after finishing high school or face imprisonment. He continued to serve for better pay. When stationed far away, he could not return home daily. This left Yasmeen under the custody of the elders, particularly her father-in-law until he passed away a year after her marriage. Serving in the Israeli army creates a chasm between Druze people and other Arabs. It also arouses dissonance for the Druze people who have tended toward isolation as a third cultural grouping in Israel. Men bring in elements of Israeli culture while women act as the keepers of Arab culture. From this cultural perspective, having a girlfriend is thought by some to be an accepted and understood Western behavior while being loyal in marriage and abstaining from infidelity is a religious, Islamic, and Druze norm. Fadi earned a BA last year, a rare accomplishment for a Druze man. Yasmeen's 2 years of training beyond high school for an education certificate is advanced for Druze women, 50% of whom do not finish high school. Yasmeen benefited from the Israeli policies of providing day care for children from 3 months after birth and free kindergarten at 3 years of age.

Fadi and Yasmeen reside in Israel as members of a cultural and religious minority within broader social structures. During the summer of 2006 they were at risk of being injured or killed by airborne armaments launched during the conflict between military forces in Israel and Lebanon.

Threats to attaining social-structural peace in the region overwhelm efforts for psychological forgiveness and interpersonal reconciliation, though these remain valid in their own dimensions. The cleavages fomenting conflict and causing harm in each situation – religion, ethnicity, class, race, region – differ in salience. The multifaceted causes and processes in ethnopolitical conflicts vary by context in the intermingling of psychological, interpersonal, economic, political, and social-structural dynamics (Mays, Bullock, Rosenzweig, & Wessells, 1998). "Structural violence and protracted state-sponsored violence and terrorism" (p. 740) implicate both societal and psychological issues. Resolution requires addressing multiple levels – "human needs such as identity, security, and recognition" in conjunction with "change...by the society at large...[involving] territory, power, and wealth" (Rouhana & Bar-Tal, 1998, p. 767) in securing peace and clearing a path for effective reconciliation and forgiveness.

Tools and Technology. The extension of social structures over space and time requires tools and technology (La Barre, 1968; Massey, 2006). Abstract and symbolic thinking, represented in language, imagination, prehensile hands, and refashioning of material and conceptual resources, makes tools possible. Tools can be utilized for biophilous and necrophilous purposes (Fromm, 1964). Biophilous uses of tools and technology affirm selves, heal injuries, support respectful and caring relationships, empower groups to provide for members' needs, and promote constructive intergenerational and inter-group legacies. Necrophilous uses of tools and technology injure selves, disrupt relationships, damage and destroy the productions and legacies of individuals, families, and groups, small and large, as well as inter-group and international connections. Uses of tools, guided by constructively taking the roles of others and empathy, nurture community, forgiveness, and reconciliation and further peace. Using tools for necrophilous purposes without empathy leads to injury and annihilation, war, ethnic cleansing, and genocide (Chirot & Seligman, 2001). Individuals and leaders of groups who constructively take the roles of others and exercise empathy do not proliferate and use nuclear weapons, do not launch intercontinental ballistic missiles, do not engage in suicide bombings, do not place profits above health and environmental safety, do not intentionally fly planes into occupied buildings, do not sanction torture, and do not authorize preemptive warfare. The necrophilous uses of tools and technology severely challenge the possibilities for forgiveness and reconciliation and highlight the dominance of social structures in undermining peace.

The tools and technology in Yasmeen's and Fadi's occupations contrast. At Yasmeen's school the objective is to nurture children's talents, personalities, and social relations through biophilous tools and technology. This helps children learn, receive positive attributions confirming their selves, gain membership in the ingroup and reference group of the better educated, and acquire beneficial resources. In the military, Fadi, his fellow soldiers, and commanders have access to and control over tools and technology which can be utilized necrophilously to heighten social conflicts and disrupt opportunities for reconciliation and peace.

Power. Uses of power bridge individual, group, and social-structural dynamics. Power can be exercised as power to, power with, and power over (Fromm, 1947, 1965). Power exists on a continuum – from power to be, affirmation, assertion, aggression, to violence (May, 1972). Negative forms of power do not emerge when constructive types prove effective. Individual power affects mostly personal development and immediate relationships. Group power moderates the range of options and the parameters of action available to individuals. Social-structural powers (legal, economic, educational institutions) significantly control distribution of and access to resources, including tools and technology, which advance or restrict individual and group levels of power. Social structures operating to enhance the powers to be, become, and affirm support a full range of human need fulfillment (Massey, 1987). Oppressive social structures constrict need satisfaction and keep people insecure and dependent on the dictates and whims of the more advantaged power holders. When persons are empowered and their groups respected, cooperation predominates. This either minimizes needs for forgiveness or enables engaging in forgiveness and reconciliation when violations of justice from human vulnerabilities and fallibility arise. When persons and groups are disempowered by restrictive, authoritarian, and oppressive social structures, violations of justice and instances of harm and violence are more likely not acknowledged and redressed, so that forgiveness, reconciliation, and peace are blocked (Armour & Umbreit, 2005; Staub, 2005).

When Yasmeen did not experience the power of affirmation from Fadi, she utilized the power of assertion to organize herself more independently and to engage in metaphorical action. She enlisted her brothers in implementing the powers to affirm and to be in relation to her newborn and her developing family. The affair elicited the powers of aggression and violence by her brothers. Fadi also activated the power of assertion with some aggression by demanding that Yasmeen cut off relations with her family before he was willing to initiate the power of affirmation for her as his wife.

The families of Yasmeen and Fadi belong to a culture and religion spread beyond the geographical boundaries of their nation of citizenship to neighboring countries. They live in the midst of warring societies seeking to exert power to control resources essential for survival and the mobilization of tools and technology – water and oil (Parfit, 2005; Specter, 2006) – and to assert the legitimacy of belief systems and boundaries based on the values and social structures of cultures and religions (Rouhana & Bar-Tal, 1998). The concerns implicated in these struggles draw in nations from around the world in international debates, disagreements, conflicting policies, and aggressive actions. Achieving peace requires social-structural changes to construct a secured and lasting context for psychological forgiveness and interpersonal reconciliation.

Societal leaders in government, the military, the media, and in large and multinational corporations – whether elected, appointed, or imposed – wield power and technology in ways which inflict interpersonal and inter-group harm or further peace, reconciliation, and forgiveness. The impacts of social-level leadership are not easily overcome by individual or small-group efforts, and the consequences exceed the parameters of forgiveness and reconciliation. Historical and contemporary examples abound of leaders initiating aggression, violence, wars, ethnic cleansing, and genocide. These disrupt personal lives, relationships, families, communities, societies, and international relations. They diminish efforts for forgiveness and reconciliation in the wake of destruction and harm. In contrast, leaders can stimulate and structure peace. If peace is to prevail when violence occurs at the societal level – so that reconciliation and forgiveness become meaningfully and securely functional – leaders need to (a) interdict violence, (b) take responsibility and apologize for aggression, (c) provide for processes and structures of reconciliation, (d) foster re-establishing bonds of social attachments, (e) advocate and enforce laws prohibiting interpersonal, inter-group, societal, and international harm, (f) engage collaboratively in fulfilling superordinate goals benefiting formerly conflicting parties, and (g) allocate power, technology, and economic resources to equitably benefit all persons and groups involved in trustworthy ways (Chirot & Seligman, 2001; Sherif, 1958). Specific issues modulate these processes in varying countries. Discussions include Argentina (Sluzki, 1990), Chile (Centeno, 2001), Iran (Kinzer, 2003), Iraq (Galbraith, 2006), Japan (Onishi, 2005), South Africa (Tutu; 1999). International persuasion based on shared standards of justice and consensus about protection of human rights becomes necessary in extreme situations. International pressures prodded progress toward diminishing harm and promoting reconciliation in Northern Ireland (Gallagher, 2001) and South Africa (Hamber, 2001). The meanings and processes of forgiveness, reconciliation, and peace vary according to the harm committed by perpetrators and bystanders or experienced by victims/survivors in each situation of harm, whether in inter-group conflicts, documented exterminations (Chirot & Seligman, 2001), or in disappearances (Sluzki, 1990).

Conclusion

Definitions and approaches to forgiveness, reconciliation, and peace vary. The *perspective presented here* is focused on the *capacities enabling humans to engage in interpersonal harm, forgiveness, reconciliation, and peace* which underlie varying viewpoints. Both *personal experiencing* and the *social contexts and structures* affect the likelihood and continuation of interpersonal harm and forgiveness, social conflicts and peace. A systems perspective embraces the specifically human interconnecting psychological and social processes required for conceptualizing, in an integrative perspective, the dynamics in interpersonal and inter-group harm, forgiveness, reconciliation, and peace. An integrative perspective encompasses explaining how self, relationships, groups, and social structures are interconnected in systems of care and violence (Cairns et al., 2005; Christie, 2006; Staub, 2005). In transforming social structures "conflict resolution must go beyond changes in perceptions, attitudes, and qualities to the creation of enduring structures that institutionalize equality, autonomy, and respect among different groups" (Fisher, 1994, p. 61 in Hewstone & Cairns, 2001, p. 335). While psychosocial projects can serve as effective interventions on the personal and interpersonal dimensions, the resolution of conflicts and the securing of peace as contexts for authentic and lasting forgiveness and reconciliation require social-structural changes and consistency (Christie, 2006).

When will they/we ever learn? Humans continue to roil in the cauldron of harm and violence, yet search for the haven of security, esteem, and peace. Seeking dominance turns to aggression. Prophets foresee that the lion will lie down with the lamb while the blind will see. Yet those with physical sight only sometimes recognize the common humanity of self and other – as both vulnerable and worthy – fearing harm and not fully trusting nor entirely believing in the wealth of the interconnecting made possible by the specifically human processes of forgiveness, reconciliation, and peace. Assessing and intervening in situations and systems of interpersonal and inter-group harm and violence in preparation for processes of forgiveness, reconciliation, and peace involve (1) evaluating the extent to which self and other are respected or not; (2) whether those involved are constructively taking the roles of the others and (3) practicing empathy or not; (4) whether their interactions, interperceptions, and interexperiences are supporting understanding or leading to misunderstanding; (5) whether their reference groups allow for mutual membership in in-groups with bounded identities or exclude the others in out-groups with barricaded identities; (6) whether their boundaries are appropriate; (7) whether their belief systems are founded on justice for all humans or on dichotomizing persons and groups as worthy or despicable; (8) whether all can join with consensual social distances or some are rejected; (9) whether tools and technology are used biophilously to benefit or necrophilously to harm; (10) whether leaders advance allocation of power, technology, and economic resources for constructive and peaceful purposes or utilize them with destructive and inequitable consequences; and (11) whether power in social structures and legacies of justice nurture the human needs of all or generate further harm and violence imperiling forgiveness, reconciliation, and peace.

References

Ainsworth, M. D. S. (1982). Attachment: Retrospect and prospect. In C. M. Parkes & J. Stevenson-Hinde (Eds.), *The place of attachment in human behavior* (pp. 3–30). New York: Basic Books.

Allport, G. W. (1954). *The nature of prejudice*. Garden City, NY: Doubleday.

Allport, G. W. (1961). *Pattern and growth in personality*. New York: Holt, Rinehart, & Winston. (Original work published 1937)

Angyal, A. (1965). *Neurosis and treatment: A holistic theory* (E. Hanfmann & R. Jones, Eds.). New York: Viking.

Armour, M. P., & Umbreit, M. S. (2005). The paradox of forgiveness in restorative justice. In E. Worthington (Ed.), *Handbook of forgiveness* (pp. 491–503). New York: Routledge.

Bar-On, D. (1991). *Legacy of silence*. Cambridge, MA: Harvard University Press.

Berger, A., & Berger, N. (2001). *Second generation voices: Reflections by children of victims, perpetrators, and bystanders of the shoah*. Syracuse, NY: Syracuse University Press.

Billingsley, A. (1968). *Black families in white America*. Englewood Cliffs, NJ: Prentice-Hall.

Boszormenyi-Nagy, I. (1965). A theory of relationships: Experience and transaction. In I. Boszormenyi-Nagy & J. Framo (Eds.), *Intensive family therapy: Theoretical and practical aspects* (pp. 33–86). Hagerstown, MD: Harper & Row.

Boszormenyi-Nagy, I., & Krasner, B. R. (1986). *Between give and take: A clinical guide to contextual therapy*. New York: Brunner/Mazel.

Bowlby, J. (1988). *A secure base: Parent-child attachment and healthy human development*. New York: Basic Books.

Buber, M. (1957). Guilt and guilt feelings. *Psychiatry, 20*, 114–129. (Original work published 1948)

Cairns, E., Tam, T., Hewstone, M., & Niens, U. (2005). Intergroup forgiveness and intergroup conflict: Northern Ireland, a case study. In E. L. Worthington (Ed.), *Handbook of forgiveness* (pp. 461–475). New York: Routledge.

Centeno, M. A. (2001). Explaining the long peace: War in Latin America. In D. Chirot & M. E. P. Seligman (Eds.), *Ethnopolitical warfare: Causes, consequences, and possible solutions* (pp. 179–202). Washington, DC: American Psychological Association.

Chirot, D. (2001). Introduction. In D. Chirot & M. E. P. Seligman (Eds.), *Ethnopolitical warfare: Causes, consequences, and possible solutions* (pp. 3–26). Washington, DC: American Psychological Association.

Chirot, D., & Seligman, M. E. P. (2001). *Ethnopolitical warfare: Causes, consequences, and possible solutions.* Washington, DC: American Psychological Association.

Christie, D. J. (2006). What is peace psychology the psychology of? *Journal of Social Issues, 67,* 1–17.

Comas-Díaz, L. (1996). Cultural considerations in diagnosis. In F. W. Kaslow (Ed.), *Handbook of relational diagnoses and dysfunctional family patterns* (pp. 152–168). New York: John Wiley & Sons.

Comas-Díaz, L., Lykes, M. B., & Alarcón, R. D. (1998). Ethnic conflict and the psychology of liberation in Guatemala, Peru, and Puerto Rico. *American Psychologist, 53,* 778–792.

Davies, D. (2004). *Child development: A practitioner's guide* (2nd ed.). New York: Guilford.

Eidelson, R. J., & Eidelson, J. I. (2003). Dangerous ideas: Five beliefs that propel groups toward conflict. *American Psychologist, 58,* 182–192.

Enright, R. D. (2001). *Forgiveness is a choice: A step-by-step process for resolving anger and restoring hope.* Washington, DC: American Psychological Association.

Enright, R. D., & Fitzgibbons, R. P. (2000). *Helping clients forgive: An empirical guide for resolving anger and restoring hope.* Washington, DC: American Psychological Association.

Enright, R. D., Freedman, S., & Rique, J. (1998). The psychology of interpersonal forgiveness. In R. D. Enright & J. North (Eds.), *Exploring forgiveness* (pp. 46–62). Madison, WI: University of Wisconsin Press.

Erikson, E. (1968). *Identity: Youth and crisis.* New York: W. W. Norton.

Falicov, C. J. (1998). The cultural meaning of family triangles. In M. McGoldrick (Ed.). *Revisioning family therapy: Race, culture, and gender in clinical practice* (pp. 37–40). New York: Guilford Press.

Frankl, V. E. (1969). *The will to meaning.* New York: New American Library.

Fromm, E. (1947). *Man for himself: An inquiry into the psychology of ethics.* Greenwich, CT: Fawcett.

Fromm, E. (1955). *The sane society.* Greenwich, CT: Fawcett.

Fromm, E. (1964). *The heart of man: Its genius for good and evil.* New York: Harper & Row.

Fromm, E. (1965). *Escape from freedom.* New York: Avon. (Original work published 1941).

Fromm, E. (1973). *The anatomy of human destructiveness.* New York: Holt, Rinehart, & Winston.

Galbraith, P. W. (2006). *The end of Iraq: How American incompetence created a war without end.* London: Simon & Schuster.

Gallagher, T. (2001). The Northern Ireland conflict: Prospects and possibilities. In D. Chirot & M. E. P. Seligman (Eds.), *Ethnopolitical warfare: Causes, consequences, and possible solutions* (pp. 205–214). Washington, DC: American Psychological Association.

Gergen, K. J. (1997). Social psychology as social constructivism: The emerging vision. In C. McGarty, & S. A. Haslam (Eds.), *The messages of social psychology: Perspectives on mind in society* (pp. 113–128). Oxford, UK: Blackwell.

Guerin, P. J., Jr., Fogarty, T. F., Fay, L. F., & Kautto, J. G. (1996). *Working with relationship triangles: The one-two-three of psychotherapy.* New York: Guilford.

Hall, E. T. (1966). *The hidden dimension.* Garden City, NY: Anchor Books.

Hamber, B. (2001). Who pays for peace? Implications of the negotiated settlement in post-apartheid South Africa. In D. Chirot & M. E. P. Seligman (Eds.), *Ethnopolitical warfare: Causes, consequences, and possible solutions* (pp. 235–258). Washington, DC: American Psychological Association.

Harper, J. M., & Hoopes, M. H. (1990). *Uncovering shame: An approach integrating individuals and their family systems.* New York: W. W. Norton.

Hewstone, M., & Cairns, E. (2001). Social psychology and intergroup conflict. In D. Chirot & M. E. P. Seligman (Eds.), *Ethnopolitical warfare: Causes, consequences, and possible solutions* (pp. 319–342). Washington, DC: American Psychological Association.

Hill, P. C., Exline, J. J., & Cohen, A. B. (2005). In the social psychology of forgiveness and justice in civil and organizational settings. E. Worthington (Ed.), *Handbook of forgiveness* (pp. 477–490). New York: Routledge.

Hosseini, K. (2003). *The kite runner*. New York: Riverhead Bookis.

Hoyt, W. T., Fincham, F. D., McCullough, M. E., Maio, G., & Davila, J. (2005). Responses to interpersonal transgressions in families: Forgivingness, forgivability, and relationship-specific effects. *Journal of Personality and Social Psychology, 89*, 375–394.

Jowitt, K. (2001). Ethnicity: Nice, nasty, and nihilistic. In D. Chirot & M. E. P. Seligman (Eds.), *Ethnopolitical warfare: Causes, consequences, and possible solutions* (pp. 27–36). Washington, DC: American Psychological Association.

Kerr, M., & Bowen, M. (1988). *Family evaluation: An approach based on Bowen theory*. New York: W. W. Norton.

Kinzer, S. (2003). *All the Shah's men: An American coup and the roots of Middle East terror*. New York: Wiley.

Kohut, H. (1987). *The Kohut seminars: On self psychology and psychotherapy with adolescents and young adults* (M. Elson, Ed.). New York: W. W. Norton.

Krondorfer, B. (1995). Remembrance and recollection: Encounters between young *Jews and Germans*. New Haven, CT: Yale University Press.

La Barre, W. (1968). *The human animal*. Chicago: University of Chicago Press.

Laing, R. D. (1961). *Self and other*. Baltimore, MD: Penguin.

Laing, R. D. (1965). Mystification, confusion, and conflict. In I. Boszormenyi-Nagy & J. L. Framo (Eds.), *Intensive family therapy: Theoretical and practical aspects* (pp. 343–363). New York: Harper & Row.

Laing, R. D., Phillipson, H., & Lee, A. (1966). *Interpersonal perception*. New York: Harper & Row.

Madanes, C. (1990). *Love, sex, and violence*. New York: W. W. Norton.

Madanes, C., Keim, J. P., & Smelser, D. (1995). *The violence of men*. San Francisco: Jossey-Bass.

Main, M., & Solomon, J. (1990). Procedures for identifying infants as disorganized/disoriented during the Ainsworth Strange Situation. In M. E. Greenberg, G. Chiccetti, & E. M. Cummings (Eds.), *Attachment in the preschool years: Theory, research, and intervention* (pp. 121–160). Chicago: University of Chicago Press.

Makinen, J. A., & Johnson, S. M. (2006). Resolving attachment injuries in couples using emotionally focused therapy: Steps toward forgiveness and reconciliation. *Journal of Consulting and Clinical Psychology, 74*, 1055–1064.

Massey, R. F. (1986). What/who is the family system. *The American Journal of Family Therapy, 14*(1), 23–39. (Original work published 1985)

Massey, R. F. (1987). Transactional analysis and social psychology of power: Reflections evoked by Jacobs' "Autocratic power." *Transactional Analysis Journal, 17*, 107–120.

Massey, R. F. (2002). Systems as interconnecting social-psychological processes: Existential foundations of families. In R. F. Massey & S. D. Massey (Vol. Eds.), F. Kaslow (Series Ed.), *Comprehensive handbook of psychotherapy, Interpersonal/humanistic/existential* (Vol. III, pp. 489–526). New York: Wiley.

Massey, R. F. (2006). Freedom with responsibility: Interconnecting self, others and social structures in contexts. *Transactional Analysis Journal, 36*, 134–151.

May, R. (1972). *Power and innocence*. New York: Dell.

Mays, V. M., Bullock, M., Rosenzweig, M. R., & Wessells, M. (1998). Ethnic conflict: Global challenges and psychosocial perspectives. *American Psychologist, 53*, 737–742.

McCauley, C. (2001). The psychology of group identification and the power of ethnic nationalism. In D. Chirot & M. E. P. Seligman (Eds.), *Ethnopolitical warfare: Causes, consequences, and possible solutions* (pp. 343–362). Washington, DC: American Psychological Association.

McCullough, M. E., Fincham, F. D., & Tsang, J.-A. (2003). Forgiveness, forbearance, and time: The temporal unfolding of transgression-related interpersonal motivations. *Journal of Personality and Social Psychology, 84*, 540–557.

McCullough, M. E., Pargament, K. I., & Thoresen, C. E. (2000). The psychology of forgiveness: History, conceptual issues, and overview. In M. E. McCullough, K. I. Pargament, & C. E. Thoresen (Eds.), *Forgiveness: Theory, research, and practice* (pp. 1–14). New York: Guilford.

McNeel, J. (1976). The parent interview. *Transactional Analysis Journal, 6*(1), 61–68.

Mead, G. H. (1964). *George Herbert Mead on social psychology* (A. Strauss, Ed.) (Rev. ed.). Chicago: University of Chicago Press.

Merleau-Ponty, M. (1963). *The structure of behavior* (A. L. Fisher, Trans.). Boston: Beacon. (Original work published 1942).

Merton, R. K. (1957). *Social theory and social structure*. New York: Free Press. (Original work published 1949).

Minuchin, S. (1974). *Families and family therapy*. Cambridge, MA: Harvard University Press.

Mullet, E., & Girard, M. (2000). Developmental and cognitive points of view on forgiveness. In M. E. McCullough, K. I. Pargament, & C. E. Thoresen (Eds.), *Forgiveness: Theory, research, and practice* (pp. 111–132). New York: Guilford.

Natanson, M. (1970). *The journeying self: A study in philosophy and social role*. Reading, MA: Addison-Wesley.

Oberschall, A. (2001). From ethnic cooperation to violence and war in Yugoslavia. In D. Chirot, & M. E. P. Seligman (Eds.), *Ethnopolitical warfare: Causes, consequences, and possible solutions* (pp. 119–150). Washington, DC: American Psychological Association.

Onishi, N. (2005, August 16). Koizumi apologizes for war; embraces China and South Korea. New York: New York Times, A4.

Parfit, M. (2005, August). *Powering the future. National Geographic, 208*(2), 2–31.

Pargament, K. I., McCullough, M. E., & Thoresen, C. E. (2000). The frontier of forgiveness: Seven directions for psychological study and practice. In M. E. McCullough, K. I. Pargament, & C. E. Thoresen (Eds.), *Forgiveness: Theory, research, and practice* (pp. 299–319). New York: Guilford.

Prescott, J. W. (1990). Affectional bonding for the prevention of violent behaviors: Neurobiological, psychological, and religious/spiritual determinants. In L. J. Hertzberg & G. F. Ostrum (Eds.), *Violent behavior, Vol. 1: Assessment & intervention* (pp. 95–124). Costa Mesa, CA: PMA Publishing Corp.

Prunier, G. (2001). Genocide in Rwanda. In D. Chirot & M. E. P. Seligman (Eds.), *Ethnopolitical warfare: Causes, consequences, and possible solutions* (pp. 109–116). Washington, DC: American Psychological Association.

Rouhana, N. N., & Bar-Tal, D. (1998). Psychological dynamics of intractable ethnonational conflict: The Israeli-Palestinian case. *American Psychologist, 53*, 761–770.

Sandage, S. J., & Williamson, I. (2005). Forgiveness in cultural context. In E. L. Worthington (Ed.), *Handbook of forgiveness* (pp. 41–55). New York: Routledge.

Schiff, J. L., Mellor, K., Schiff, E., Schiff, S. Richman, D. Fishman, J., et al. (1975). *Cathexis reader: transactional analysis treatment of psychosis*. New York: Harper & Row.

Selman, R. (1976). Social-cognitive understanding: A guide to educational and clinical practice. In T. Likona (Ed.), *Moral development and behavior* (pp. 299–316). New York: Holt, Rinehart, & Winston.

Sherif, M. (1958). Superordinant goals in the reduction of intergroup conflict. *American Journal of Sociology, 43*, 349–356.

Shibutani, T. (1955). Reference groups as perspectives. *American Journal of Sociology, 60*, 562–569.

Shriver, D. W. (1998). Is there forgiveness in politics? Germany, Vietnam, and America. In R. D. Enright & J. North (Eds.), *Exploring forgiveness* (pp. 131–149). Madison, WI: University of Wisconsin Press.

Silberman, I. (2005). Religion as a meaning system: Implications for the new millennium. *Journal of Social Issues, 61*, 641–663.

Sluzki, C. E. (1990). Disappeared: Semantic and somatic effects of political repression in a family seeking therapy. *Family Process, 29*(2), 131–143.

Smith, D. N. (1998). The psychocultural roots of genocide: Legitimacy and crisis in Rwanda. *American Psychologist, 53*, 743–753.

Specter, M. (2006, October 23). The last drop. *The New Yorker*, pp. 50–71.

Staub, E. (2005). Constructive rather than harmful forgiveness, reconciliation, and ways to promote them after genocide and mass killing. In E. L. Worthington (Ed.), *Handbook of forgiveness* (pp. 443–459). New York: Routledge.

Sue, D. W., & Sue, D. (2003). *Counseling the culturally different: theory and practice* (4th ed.). New York: Wiley.

Sullivan, H. S. (1953). *Interpersonal theory of psychiatry*. New York: W. W. Norton.

Tajfel, H., & Turner, J. (1986). The social identity theory of intergroup behavior. In S. Worchel & W. G. Austin (Eds.), *Psychology of intergroup relations* (pp. 7–24). Chicago: Nelson.

Tripp, A. M., & Young, C. (2001). The accommodation of cultural diversity in Tanzania. In D. Chirot & M. E. P. Seligman (Eds.), *Ethnopolitical warfare: Causes, consequences, and possible solutions* (pp. 259–274). Washington, DC: American Psychological Association.

Turner, J. C., & Oakes, P. J. (1997). The socially structured mind. In C. McGarty & S. Haslam (Eds.), *The messages of social psychology: Perspectives on mind in society* (pp. 355–357). Oxford, UK: Blackwell.

Tutu, D. (1999). *No future without forgiveness*. New York: Doubleday.

van den Berghe. (1967). *Race and racism: A comparative perspective*. New York: John Wiley & Sons.

Wade, N. G., & Worthington, E. L. (2005). In search of a common core: A content analysis of interventions to promote forgiveness. *Psychotherapy: Theory, Research, Practice, Training, 42*(2), 160–177.

Winnicott, D. W. (1988). *Human nature*. New York: Schocken.

Worthington, E. L. (2005). Initial questions about the art and science of forgiving. In E. Worthington (Ed.), *Handbook of forgiveness* (pp. 1–13). New York: Routledge.

Chapter 3
Forgiveness and Relational Ethics: The Perspective of the Contextual Therapist

Catherine Ducommun-Nagy

Contextual therapy can offer a very useful framework to address the issue of forgiveness, reconciliation, and peace-building that complements the framework proposed by individual psychology in general, developmental psychology, trauma psychology, or even peace psychology. Contextual therapists propose that some of the important determinants of our behavior are located outside of our psyche. They believe that one of the most important determinants of our actions lies in our expectation of fairness and reciprocity in relationships. Therefore, many of our actions can be explained by our attempt to reach some level of justice in our relationships with others. In this case, our capacity to forgive others and to make peace with them does not depend simply on our individual psychological characteristics or on our individual responses to trauma. It depends on the degree of fairness that we have encountered in our relationships and in our world in general. On that specific point, contextual therapists share the same view as peace psychologists (Christie, 2006).

This knowledge allows contextual therapists to discuss the subject of forgiveness from a unique vantage point, the point of view of *relational ethics.* In this chapter, I shall give a description of relational ethics and demonstrate that the process that leads from vindictiveness to forgiveness and peace does not simply involve changes at an emotional or cognitive level, but also changes in relationships.

Understanding Relational Ethics

From Family Therapy to Contextual Therapy

Families Fight Changes. The pioneers of family therapy discovered that our individual behavior is influenced by supra-individual determinants. They also described how our individual behavior can trigger reactions in others that could not have been predicted from the sole knowledge of their individual psychology. To describe family relationships, classical family therapists have heavily relied on the general systems theory described by Bertalanffy (1968). According to this well-known theory, systems have properties that cannot be derived from the simple observations of the parts that form them. What makes a system a system and not a pile of parts but a

Ani Kalayjian, Raymond F. Paloutzian, *Forgiveness and Reconciliation*, Peace Psychology Book Series, DOI 10.1007/978-1-4419-0181-1_3, © Springer Science+Business Media, LLC 2009

structure that systems are able to maintain over time? They also possess mechanisms that allow them to return to their original state if they are exposed to internal changes or changes in their environment. This capacity is described with the technical term of *homeostasis*. Classical family therapists have been very good at explaining how families can register changes and what mechanisms they use to return to a point of equilibrium, but they have come up short in their explanation of the nature of the forces that holds families together over time.

The Discovery of Relational Ethics. Boszormenyi-Nagy, one of the pioneers of family therapy, discovered the importance of a dimension of human relationships that had been overlooked by the pioneers of systemic family therapy: the dimension of relational ethics. This discovery led him to the founding of contextual therapy. Based on the analysis of thousands of hours of family therapy sessions, Boszormenyi-Nagy was able to demonstrate that we all keep an account of what we receive from others and what we give to them and we all expect fair returns from our investments in our relationships. He described this dimension of human relationships as the dimension of relational ethics. He was able to show that people with psychosis, whose capacity to distinguish between internal and external reality is decreased, do not lose this ability. As he said on many occasions, "The language of fairness is the last language that people with psychosis can still hear." It is even true of people with severe antisocial personalities who refuse to care about others. They too base their actions on reciprocity, albeit in a negative form. We often hear them say "Why should I care about anyone since no one was there for me when I needed it?"

Loyalty as a Source of Family Cohesion. Boszormenyi-Nagy is most famous for his discovery that it is primarily the active commitment to other family members that maintains the cohesion of the family – or, in other words, the homeostasis of the family system. This led him to the formulation that loyalty is one of the most important factors that contribute to the homeostasis of families as well as of any human group.

> Loyalty commitments are like invisible but strong fibers which hold together complex pieces of relationship "behavior" in families as well as in larger societies. To understand the function of a group of people, nothing is more crucial than to know who are bound together in loyalty and what loyalty means for them. (Boszormenyi-Nagy & Spark, 1984, pp. 40–41)

The Origins of Morality

Boszormenyi-Nagy's hypothesis that fairness, reciprocity, and trust are the needed ingredients for successful relating between family members and for the successful survival of the next generations has been confirmed by the work of many researchers in fields as diverse as evolutionary biology or economics (Ducommun-Nagy, 2002). Many of these researchers have come to the conclusion that we are programmed for fairness and reciprocity. They assume that this capacity is probably anchored in our genes. In other words, we are programmed for relational ethics and this does not depend on our mental health or on the degree of our moral development. This is a trait that we all share as members of the human species. If this is the case, it is our innate capacity for fairness and reciprocity that has led us to build our moral systems including our great religions (Ridley, 1996). Hence it is not necessary to assume that our capacity for morality has been bestowed on us by divine intervention or that our morality is only a thin veneer overlaying a core of basic amorality (De Waal, 2006).

Defining Relational Ethics

Relational ethics need to be distinguished from *value ethics*. Value ethics are defined by a set of moral values that guide us in our responses to others. In this perspective, our capacity to care about the welfare of others depends on the degree of our moral development. Furthermore, the definition of justice depends on preset values. This is not the case with relational ethics. First, our capacity to care about others seems to be related to an innate tendency to give, which is already found in young children. Therefore, we don't need to assume that our capacity to care about the welfare of others requires a high degree of moral development and a reliance on value ethics. Second, the definition of justice is never absolute. The definition of what is fair or unfair always stems from an actual dialogue between the parties involved, hence the use of the word "relational ethics." Boszormenyi-Nagy's choice of terms follows from the work of Martin Buber (1957, 1958). Maurice Friedman, who has written extensively on his work, states that

> Buber does not start from some external, absolutely valid ethical code which man is bound to apply as best as possible to each new situation. Instead he starts with the situation itself …. The responsible quality of one's decision will be determined by the degree to which one really "sees the other" and makes him present to oneself. It is here, in experiencing the relationship from the side of the other, that we find the most important key to the ethical implications of Buber's dialogue – an implication that none of the other thinkers who have written on the I-Thou relationship has understood in its full significance. Only through "seeing the other" can the I-Thou relationship become fully real, for only through it can one be sure that one is really helping the other person. (Friedman, 1960, pp. 204–205)

To better illustrate the difference between value ethics and relational ethics, one can look at the situation of parents who already have biological children and feel compelled to adopt a child out of a commitment to social justice, which is based on value ethics. From this point of view, their generous behavior is commendable. But things may look different from the point of relational ethics. Relational ethics requires that situations are examined from the vantage point of all the parties involved. In this example, before making the decision to adopt a child, parents would need to examine the consequences of the adoption not only for all the family members but also for the child: Would their biological children grow from the experience or could they be negatively affected by the new situation? Would the presence of a new child rejuvenate their aging parents or could these people suffer from a lack of attention? Parents who adopt a child later in their life often take in children with special needs. Are they sure that they have enough resources to deal with the situation both emotionally and financially, or could they end up resenting the child for being too difficult? From the point of view of relational ethics, the most generous parents and the most commendable ones are not the ones who abide to value ethics at all costs, but the ones who are capable of setting aside their moral ideals if they cannot meet them without hurting others in the process.

The Relational Definition of Justice

Since the definition of justice is neither purely objective nor purely subjective, but intersubjective, it would be wrong to assume that contextual therapists could define what is fair or unfair in a given relationship. Relational ethics lie between the realm of the value ethics of absolute principles that are defined outside of relationships and the world of nihilism where there is no ethics to talk about, because no one can define what reality is.

If we use the framework of relational ethics, ethics result from our willingness to meet with our fellow human beings and to respect their reality as a reality that is as valid as ours. Hence, our greatest culpability results not from any specific injury to the other, but from our refusal to meet the other and to recognize that his or her needs are as valid as are ours.

It would be tempting to believe that there is a strong parallel between the pre-occupations of the ethicists and the concerns of the contextual therapists. It is quite true that they both are concerned with a definition of ethics and ethical behaviors, but it would be misleading to believe that ethicists can easily understand relational ethics. In fact, it is quite the opposite. As they abide in the world of value ethics, it would be difficult for them to discuss giving and forgiving from a truly relational perspective, which is the perspective adopted in this chapter.

On the other hand, the conclusions of the founder of contextual therapy about the nature of relational ethics finds a surprising parallel in the view of two researchers who have been generally associated with a constructivist or postmodern view of family therapy, Maturana and Varela (1987): "Every human act has an ethical meaning because it is an act of constitution of the human world: This linkage of human to human is, in final analysis, the ground-work of all ethics as a reflection on the legitimacy of the presence of others" (p. 247).

The World of Destructive Entitlement

The Dark Side of Fairness

For better or worse, we care about fairness. Our brains seem to possess structures that allow us to register what we get and what we give (Barkow, Cosmides, & Tooby, 1992). We also expect reciprocity. When we give to others, we expect a fair return for our investment. Conversely, when we receive from others, we know that we are obligated to them. Our expectation of fairness in relationships can lead us to cooperate with others positively: We are compelled to give fairly when we have received fairly.

But, the world of relational ethics also has a dark side that people tend to overlook. We need to remember that our expectation of fair reciprocity can lead us to cooperate with others, but it can also lead us to become vindictive. We can easily move from a spiral of mutual giving (you give to me, I give to you) to a spiral of endless retaliation (you hurt me, I hurt you).

Our tendency to automatically retaliate for the wrongs that have been done to us constitutes one of the most serious obstacles to reconciliation in couples and one of the most serious obstacles to peace in the case of feuding groups. Throughout history, we see ethnic groups or nations that have become entrapped in endless cycles of retaliation that can prevent the establishment of a lasting peace for years or even centuries. In recent times, the two most striking examples of this situation have been the relationship between ethnic groups in the Balkans and the relationship between Israel and Palestine in the Middle East. But it would be unfair to single out these two groups, since so many other groups have also fallen into the same trap all over the world.

When we are hurt by others, we will not simply retaliate and treat them as badly as they have treated us. We will also seek compensation for our losses. If we obtain some measure of compensation for the injustices that we have incurred, it might be possible for us to move toward forgiveness. But what happens if the perpetrator refuses to acknowledge his or her responsibility toward us? What happens if the perpetrator is dead or too weak emotionally or materially to offer us any compensation?

What Is Destructive Entitlement?

Experience shows that it is often difficult for us to simply cut our losses and move on. We are, in fact, very likely to insist on our right to compensation. When we cannot count on a response from the culprit, we will present our claims to whoever is available: our partners, our children, or an innocent group if we have been hurt by a group. We will expect that these people will provide us with the redress that we are entitled to. But in doing so, we commit an injustice ourselves. These people are not responsible for our hurts and do not owe us any compensation. This is the tragedy of what contextual therapists call *destructive entitlement*, i.e., a justified claim leading to the unjustifiable exploitation of innocent bystanders. Destructive entitlement not only leads us to become unfair toward others, but it shields us from experiencing any remorse for our unfairness. Why should we experience any remorse for simply claiming our just dues? We are blind to our own unfairness because in our own eyes we are the victims, not the victimizers. This lack of remorse will lead to further damages in our relationships. Since we refuse to accept responsibility for our own wrongdoings, the victims of our destructive entitlement will accumulate destructive entitlement too.

The Multigenerational Consequences of Destructive Entitlement

Adults can generally set some limits to the exploitative behavior of others. We can put an end to the marriage with a spouse who has become too exploitative. We can put an end to a friendship with a friend who has become too demanding. If we do not accumulate too much destructive entitlement, we retain our capacity for generosity. Unfortunately, this is not true of children or groups.

Hurt Parents, Exploited Children. Countless clinical examples show that children can easily become the victims of their parents' destructive entitlement. Children are bound to their parents by many kinds of ties and they cannot put an end to the relationship if it becomes exploitative. In addition, children have a natural tendency to offer their love and loyalty even to parents who might not deserve it (Boszormenyi-Nagy, 1996). Therefore, it is very tempting for parents who have been the victims of poor parenting to turn to their children with the hope that they will receive from them the love and commitment that they did not receive from their own parents. In other words, they *parentify* their children, which is of course unfair to them. Over time, *parentified* children accumulate destructive entitlement and will later turn to their offspring for compensation. This situation can lead to the perpetuation of an exploitative pattern of relating between parents and children that can last for generations. This is because it is always fueled by the same ingredients: the parent's destructive entitlement and the child's loyal availability to respond to the parent's needs.

Group Oppression as a Source of Destructive Entitlement. According to Boszormenyi-Nagy (1996, April), what is true for families is true for larger groups as well. He believes that destructive entitlement and loyalty can fuel the negative actions of ethnic groups toward others. We know that ethnic groups who are threatened by the attacks of an oppressing group cannot easily move away to escape victimization. Even if these groups were able to migrate to a new territory, it would not result in a peaceful outcome. The move would inevitably cause the resentment of the people whose territory was suddenly intruded upon by the displaced group. This is true in the case of large-scale migrations and is also true even in the case of smaller moves of population. We know how negatively local populations can react to the arrival of even small groups of displaced persons or asylum seekers. There have been examples of such negative reactions all over Europe in the recent years. This is one of the factors that has contributed to the recent success of the extreme right in several countries.

What is true for any ethnic group that is threatened by an invading group is also true for any group that is persecuted by an oppressor or for any minority that is the object of prejudice or discrimination by a dominant group. In short, when any group becomes the victim of an attack by other groups or is oppressed by a dominant group, it can accumulate destructive entitlement.

In addition, group members who have been the victims of oppression by a dominant group may also place unfair expectations on the people to whom they are the closest, such as their spouse or their children. This could have very destructive consequences for their family life. In the end, even if the oppression did not last for a very long time, it can have devastating effects for many generations. In short, the violation of the justice of one person's basic human order can make this event a pivot around which the destiny of the future relationship between himself and his descendents revolves. (Boszormenyi-Nagy, 1985, p. 6)

Group Loyalties and Destructive Obligations. Due to group loyalty, even members of the group who have not been directly hurt feel compelled to join in the drive to retaliate.

Ethnic groups are loyalty-based like families. One of the forces that hold them together is the protection of destructive entitlement. Their members act not only on destructive entitlement but also on destructive obligations: a mixture of loyal obligation with destructive entitlement. Terrorists on one side, heroes on the other, their destructive entitlement grows in proportion with the degree of external oppression that the group has experienced. This drive can be described as a destructive obligation. Not only can this pose a serious obstacle to peace building, but it can also serve as a motivator for "terrorism." (Boszormenyi-Nagy, 1996, April, p. 14)

Destructive Entitlement as an Obstacle to Forgiveness

The most serious damage that people incur when they are wronged is that their capacity to give gets damaged. This, of course, has ominous consequences for their capacity to move toward forgiveness and reconciliation.

Here is the paradox of forgiveness: People who have received enough from life and who have been treated fairly by others can easily offer forgiveness to others because they are capable of generosity, but there are no culprits to forgive because no one has hurt them. The only people who would need to forgive others are the people who have been wronged, but they are the least likely to do so because they have accumulated destructive entitlement.

If we want to be effective in helping people move toward forgiveness, we need to understand the serious impact of destructive entitlement on the reconciliation process. People who get a fair compensation for the damages that they have incurred, or at least some acknowledgment for their hurt, are more likely to move toward forgiveness than people who meet a callous response to their quest for redress. On the other hand, this does not mean that their destructive entitlement will disappear.

We know from the court system that we can usually decide what people should get as a compensation for material damages, but that it is much more difficult to estimate what they should receive as a compensation for their pains and sufferings. In most cases, victims will remain hurt no matter how much financial compensation they receive. In addition, people who have met enough injustices in their life to turn into one-sided takers cannot experience the satisfaction that people experience when they are able to help someone else. The fact that their predicament deprives them of the possibility of giving to others constitutes in itself a source of destructive entitlement that is easily overlooked.

In the end, our destructive entitlement will not only push us to inadvertently hurt innocent third parties or to refuse forgiveness to the people who have hurt us, but it might even lead us to become blind to the merits of the persons who have hurt us, even when these people have a valid claim or even if they deserve acknowledgment for other reasons. This is exemplified by the situation of children who have been neglected by they parents.

Hurt Children, Unforgiving Adolescents. Children who are neglected by their parents experience all sorts of deprivations, first in their own homes and later in placements where they often do not receive much individual attention. They are also often parentified. By the time they reach their teens, they frequently present with the symptoms of what professionals call a Conduct Disorder. By definition, people who present with this condition are people who violate the rights of others and who do not care about the rules of society. They seem to lack a sense of justice. In reality, it is their capacity to care about fairness that gets them into trouble.

Parents who have neglected their children because of substance tend to do better in their later years. Sadly it is usually the time when their children enter adolescence and are getting worse. If parents are able to maintain sobriety for an extended period of time, they will try to get more involved in the lives of their children. As they make many efforts to try to become better parents, they hope that their children will forgive them for their past behavior, or at least give them some recognition for their current efforts. Unfortunately, most of the time, this does not happen because by that time, the children have accumulated too much destructive entitlement. In this case, they refuse to care about the needs of their parents, since their parents did not care about their needs when they were little.

While it is true that parents deserve a lot of respect for their efforts, parents often fail to see that the hurt they caused to their children cannot be erased simply by their own good behavior. They need to realize that their child is damaged in his or her capacity to give. In those circumstances, it would be unrealistic to expect that children could suddenly forgive their parents.

Contextual therapists propose that we need to see these young people as depleted givers who have given more to the adult world than they had received from it. If we can give them acknowledgment for that, they will be able to slowly decrease their reliance on their destructive entitlement and this will allow them to start caring about others again. In addition, therapists can also help parent and child to discover that they can gain from displaying some generosity toward the other. Parents can discover that they can gain from giving space to their children and children that they do not lose if they acknowledge their parents' efforts.

*Can We Give More Than We Have Received?*If we want people who have been hurt to move toward forgiveness and reconciliation, we need to help them discover that they can get an internal reward from giving that could compensate them for the fact that they have not received fairly. If they can discover that they can gain something from giving generously, and not simply from trying to get back what was taken from them, they will be not only less likely to rely on their destructive entitlement but also more likely to accept and forgive the people who had failed them. This can lead to a true reconciliation.

The World of Constructive Entitlement

Receiving Through Giving

Defining Constructive Entitlement. Contextual therapists believe that our only source of legitimate therapeutic optimism lies in the hope that people can discover that when they are generous toward others, they gain something for themselves, a *constructive entitlement* (Boszormenyi-Nagy & Krasner, 1986).

Contextual therapists describe that people who are able to give generously to others are freer to engage successfully in their own pursuit than are people who get stuck in endless claims for compensation. They are also less likely to engage in self-destructive behavior and less likely to suffer from psychosomatic symptoms. While contextual therapists have not tried to quantify the direct effects of giving on people's mental and physical heath, they have accumulated a wealth of clinical data showing that people report a subjective improvement in their functioning once they are able to make a step toward generous giving (Ducommun-Nagy, 2003).

Generous giving implies that one is ready to take the risk of giving without counting on a guarantied return from that action. For contextual therapists, the act of giving is neither fully altruistic nor fully selfish. It is not an act of pure altruism, because we can get something from it. But it is not a selfish act either. As long as we are sincere in our effort to benefit others without expecting a similar effort on their part, we are not hypocrites. On the other hand, if we give to others only because it is good for us to give, we would be worse than hypocrites. We would, in fact, be engaging in an exploitative type of behavior, because we would simply be using these people as a means to an end. This certainly would not earn us any constructive entitlement.

Giving or Taking? When we take the risk of giving to others, we need to be prepared to meet an unfair response. Hence, we need to be capable of generosity. We could cut off our relationship with someone who refuses to reciprocate, but we cannot make people give back what they received from us if they refuse to do so. It is naïve to believe that therapists can restore the fairness of damaged relationships or the broken trust between people.

Therapists can support people to present their claims, but they cannot guarantee that this will result in a positive response on the part of the wrongdoers. In addition, there are times when we know in advance that the individuals whom we are trying to help will not be able to reciprocate because they are in no position to do so. This is the case, for instance, with severely handicapped or terminally ill people.

In the end, we need to decide for ourselves what is worse for us: to encounter an unfair return for our giving or to refuse to take the risk of giving. If we believe that we can only give to others if we can expect an exact return for our investment, we leave the world of close relationships to enter the world of commercial exchanges. If we do that, we may experience less hurt and disappointments, but we will also experience a lack of human connectedness.

Conversely, if we accept to meet people where they are, to find out about their needs and to respond to them to the best of our abilities, without worrying about what we can get from the relationship, we can gain something that we could not obtain otherwise: an increased human value.

Generous People Are Realists. What contextual therapists have discovered empirically in their clinical work is consistent with the findings of several researchers in the field of evolutionary biology, economy, and mathematics (Ducommun-Nagy, 2002, 2006). This is exemplified by the work of M. Nowak who is both a biologist and a mathematician who directs The Program for Evolutionary Dynamics at Harvard University. He and his team have shown that the most promising strategy to increase our profit is indeed a strategy of fair reciprocity, but this is not enough. We also need to be occasionally capable of generosity and forgiveness (Nowak, Page, & Sigmund, 2000). This generosity is needed to get us out of a spiral of mutual recriminations and revenge if we have gotten stuck in a spiral of negative reciprocity. We cannot guarantee that our gesture will result in a positive response, but if we do not take the risk, there is no chance at all that the situation will change. In the end, when we display a generous attitude toward others, we are neither fools nor saints, but simply realists. The notion that we are better off if we treat each other fairly has recently become the subject of popular books, like for instance *The Power of Nice* (Kaplan Thaler & Koval, 2006).

The Healing Moment in Contextual Therapy

The discovery that we can gain from giving has led to the definition of a new therapeutic principle: the principle of *receiving through giving* (Boszormenyi-Nagy & Krasner, 1986). It has also led to a new definition of the healing moment in therapy. The healing moment is not simply the moment when people can obtain a fair acknowledgment and a fair restitution from the wrongdoers, and thus a moment of increased fairness in the relationship. In this new perspective, it becomes the moment when the receiver gains in an obvious fashion because he or she is the direct benefactor of the giving and the giver receives back from the act of giving, in an indirect fashion. Giving does not simply lead to an increase of human worth in the giver but it also allows the giver to gain an existential confirmation that could not be obtained outside of a relationship.

The Paradox of Autonomy. Boszormenyi-Nagy (1985, 1987c) believes we are dependent on the presence of others to achieve autonomy. He defines this dependence as an *onticdependence.* In this perspective, autonomy becomes a paradoxical notion since we generally assume that autonomy is connected with independence, not with interdependence or dependence. He borrowed his ideas from the existentialist philosophers who all believe that our very existence as autonomous selves depends on the presence of an Other (Theunissen, 1984). This is not just a philosophical view but also the view of some scientists who have studied our social and biological characteristics in comparison with the same characteristics in other species.

A good illustration of the thoroughly social nature of our species is that second to the death penalty, solitary confinement is the most extreme punishment we can think of. It works this way because we are not born as loners. Our bodies and our minds are not designed for life in the absence of others (De Waal, 2006).

The Five Dimensions of Relational Reality. More recently, Boszormenyi-Nagy (2000, April) added that one of the determinants of our actions lies in our existential need for a connectedness with others, not just in our need for fairness. In his new model, he proposes that relational reality can be described according to five dimensions: the dimensions of (1) factual reality and biological determinants, (2) psychology, (3) systems and transactions, (4) relational ethics, and (5) the new ontic dimension. Hence, his new model entails the original four dimensions described in all the previous literature on contextual therapy and a new fifth dimension that is only discussed in a few texts (Ducommun-Nagy, 2002, 2006).

> Only through responsibly addressing the Thee (you) do I become an I. According to this dialogical principle, mutual regard for each other is in the best existential interest of both relating partners. It is true not only via each party's extractively self-serving benefits but, more fundamentally, through the partners' mutual definition of each other's autonomous, differentiated personhood. In this ethically self-delineating and self-validating sense, giving becomes inseparable from receiving. (Boszormenyi-Nagy, 1987d, pp. 302–303)

In this perspective, we are not simply being generous when we offer caring, loyalty, or forgiveness to others, but we are also attempting to maintain a tie with people on whose presence we depend existentially. Existentially, it is not the absence of justice in our lives that makes us the most vulnerable, but the absence of relationship. For that reason, we fare better if we can be loyal to a non-deserving parent than if we cut this parent off.

Forgiveness as a Source of Autonomy. From this vantage point, forgiveness becomes a resource not simply because we can get an indirect return from our generosity toward the ones we forgive, but also because forgiveness allows us to maintain a relationship with people despite their wrongdoings. Since we are inevitably hurt by many people, we would be at risk for a great isolation if we were unable to forgive at least many of them. Since we need their presence in our lives to confirm our existence as autonomous selves, we would loose if we were unable to forgive them because it would decrease our chance to reach autonomy.

The Path Toward Forgiveness

As therapists, we might be able to see that people can benefit from forgiveness, but how can we bring people to make this discovery for themselves? What are the obstacles that they need to overcome before they can move toward forgiveness and reconciliation? We have seen that any injustice can set in motion our destructive entitlement, but our claim will vary as a function of the degree of culpability that we attribute to the wrongdoer and the degree of justice or injustice of our world. If we remember that the definition of justice is never an absolute, the definition of what constitutes an injustice and of what needs to be repaired can only be derived from a genuine dialogue between all the participants in the relationship.

Multidirected Partiality

Contextual therapists use a two-pronged approach to help people decrease their reliance on destructive entitlement. The model that they propose can also be used by mediators or by anyone who tries to assist adversarial groups in reaching some level of reconciliation. In the case of family therapy, the therapist starts by encouraging the family members who believe that they have been hurt or wronged to present their claims. Victims are supported to present their claims clearly and to formulate what would be required to reach reconciliation. Subsequently, they are also asked to listen to the justifications of the other parties and to show some willingness to try to understand their predicament. Boszormenyi-Nagy (1987b) coined the term *multidirected partiality* to describe this strategy.

As each family member is offered a chance to present his or her side, and each of them starts to gain a better understanding of the positions of the others, a number of things happen: The victims are more inclined to forgive the perpetrators if they have received a fair acknowledgment of their claims from the therapist or if they can see that the wrongdoer was a victim too. Similarly, wrongdoers might be more motivated to apologize and to offer amends if they have been offered some modicum of fairness by the therapist and if they reach a better understanding of the consequences of their actions for the one whom they have hurt.

Meeting Allows More Forgiving. Multidirected partiality requires not only that each participant in the relationship should have a fair chance to present his or her side. In addition, it also requires that each person is offered a fair chance to earn constructive entitlement by getting the chance to give to others. For this reason, the therapist needs to be attentive to the fact that a premature forgiving by the victim could deprive the perpetrator a chance of earning constructive entitlement by offering apologies or reparations.

For all these reasons, people who are able to meet in person are more likely to reach some resolution in their conflicts than people who are meeting only through appointed emissaries. For instance, people who are getting through a divorce are more likely to put aside their resentment and move toward a peaceful settlement if they are willing to meet each other in person, with the help of a mediator, rather than if they rely solely on their lawyers.

Forgiveness and the Balance of Giving and Receiving

Our ability to forgive others does not depend solely on the degree of our destructive entitlement. It also depends on the balance of giving and receiving that exists between us and the culprits. We will be more likely to extend forgiveness to someone whom we can also see as a giver than to someone whom we see as a pure taker. This can be illustrated by the situation of two women who were the victims of a similar crime. In each situation, a woman was violently attacked and raped by a man as she was walking home at night. Each could have died in the attack. Both were seriously traumatized, but not injured significantly. There was no evidence of pregnancy or sexually transmitted disease. From that point on, the two situations were vastly different.

The Unforgivable Criminal. The first woman was a young professional woman who was walking back home from work after dark. After the attack, she was helped to contact the police. Following that, she received a full array of services offered to rape victims. She also received a lot of support from her family, colleagues, and friends. Eventually, her assailant was arrested because he was filmed by a surveillance camera and was a known recidivist. The only thing that the victim wanted is that this man could be put in jail for as long as the law permitted and to put the entire event behind her. She received nothing from the criminal other than violation and pain and did not have the slightest impulse to forgive the man.

The Forgiven Assailant. The second woman, Tania, was a young woman who had succeeded in creating a stable life for herself despite a history of extreme defiance toward authority figures during her teens, which is the time when she got raped. Her childhood was marked by a lot of emotional deprivations and she had turned rebellious. She was a good student who never missed school. On the other hand, she was never home. Most nights, she stayed out very late to party with friends. She used to smoke marijuana and to drink. She was diagnosed with a severe Conduct Disorder. She attended outpatient therapy and was even hospitalized briefly. She did not feel that therapy was helpful, but she remembers that her therapist was extremely concerned for her safety. She had told her bluntly that if she continued to stay out at night, she would end up dead. Tania reports that she felt invulnerable and could not believe that anything bad could happen to her. She was soon proven wrong.

On a summer night, she was walking home in the middle of the night when she realized that she was being followed by a man. In no time, he proceeded to assault her and to rape her. At that very moment, she remembered the words of her therapist and assumed that her last hour had come, but her aggressor did not kill her. This put an end to her feeling of invulnerability. She also had to admit that her therapist knew things that she did not know and that she needed to start listening to the advice of adults.

Despite the years that have gone by since the time of the rape, Tania has still occasional flashbacks of the scene. She re-experienced the fear of being killed. At other times, she feels very ashamed of the sexual nature of the encounter, even if she was not responsible for it. For all these reasons, she is still very angry with her aggressor, who was never caught. Nonetheless, she is emphatic that she has forgiven him. How come? She believes that in a weird way, he saved her life. "He did not kill me and used a condom. Because of him, I learned my lesson and I could change my life before it was too late. Someone else could have killed me or given me HIV and then it would have been too late."

She also believes that the rape has been the event that scared her enough to change her life. This man was inadvertently more successful in helping her to stop her destructive behavior than her own mother or her therapist. Tania felt that he did deserve credit for that and therefore she was willing to forgive him for the bad things he did to her.

Forgiving Depends on Receiving. How is it possible that a person who has been diagnosed with a Conduct Disorder and who presents residual symptoms from the trauma can forgive her assailant, while a person who has a good life and plenty of support to overcome the trauma refuses to do so? From these two examples, we can confirm that the answer lies in the balance of giving and receiving between the perpetrator and the victim: One person, the young professional woman, sees the assailant as a pure taker. There is nothing that she can credit him for, hence she has no reason to extend any generosity to him. The second woman clearly describes that the assailant was not only a taker but also a giver. This allowed her to move toward forgiveness despite the great amount of destructive entitlement that she had accumulated in the course of her young life.

Belief Systems and Forgiveness

Forgiveness and Exoneration

Boszormenyi-Nagy (1996, April) makes a distinction between forgiveness and exoneration. Forgiveness implies that we give up a claim toward another person whom we still see as the culprit. In other words, we let go of our claim toward the perpetrator and we also forgo any expectation that this person should be punished on our behalf. But we do not have to let go of the notion that this person is a true wrongdoer. Exoneration leads to a very different situation. Through the process of exoneration, we clear the person from the accusation itself, so there is no more need for actual forgiveness.

For instance, we can be very hurt by the limitations of a severely handicapped child who cannot return our caring or by the unrealistic demands of a very sick person. We do not need to forgive them, because there is nothing to forgive. We simply need to come to terms with the reality of their limitations and, through that, we exonerate them from any guilt. On the other hand, is there any excuse for the fact that a parent has taken more from a vulnerable child than he or she was willing to give?

Who Is Accountable for the Shortcomings of Our Parents? When it comes to the parent–child relationship, contextual therapists tend to place more emphasis on the process of exoneration than on the process of forgiving, for a number of reasons.

If we are willing to learn more about the life of our parents, we might discover that they have been victims too. We will also discover that they are no different from us. They too seek some fairness in their lives. We might realize that the damages they caused to us did not result from their malice, but from a legitimate effort at getting some reparation for the injustices of their own lives, even if this effort had negative consequences for us. In any event, we cannot blame our parents for the situations that have led them to become exploitative. For instance, they cannot be blamed for the shortcomings of their own parents. This is true of these people too. How far do we need to go back before we can find the true culprits? If we can see that, we may be able to exonerate our parents for their wrongdoings.

Even if we cannot reach that stage, our effort will have positive results. It will be easier to forgive our parents if we can have at least some understanding of their side. Also, as we care to find out more about our parents, we also earn some measure of constructive entitlement. This will free us to forgive them, even if we cannot expect a direct acknowledgment of our effort because our parents are too impaired in their capacity to give to be able to thank us, or because they are already dead. In short, even when we cannot fully exonerate our parents for their behavior, it will be easier for us to forgive them if we try to understand their predicament.

Is there really anyone to blame for the injustice that we incurred in having parents who where unable to meet our needs? Who will compensate us for it anyway? We cannot sue the stork who dropped us at their doorstep instead of bringing us to the home of parents who had a more fortunate childhood and who would have been more able to provide for us. So can this injustice ever be repaired? In many ways it cannot, since no one is directly responsible for our predicament.

Distributive and Retributive Injustices

Distributive Injustices. There are many situations in which a person or a group gets hurt and encounters a fate that is much harder than the fate of others, but the damage does not result from an injury to a relationship that has been caused by a specific person or a specific group. There is an identifiable victim, but no identifiable culprit, as in the case of victims of a natural disaster. Contextual therapists define these kinds of injustices as *distributive injustices.*

Retributive Injustices. By contrast, there are injustices that occur when one party causes damage to the other party or injures the fairness of the relationship by exploiting the other, as in the case of the parent who turns to the child for compensation of past injustices. Since retributive injustices occur to people who are in relationships with others, the healing of these injustices also needs to occur in the context of the relationships these people have. We have already examined the process of reconciliation between parent and child and seen that the process is similar for groups. If a group is responsible for an injustice toward another group, it should be able to offer some redress or at least, minimally, some acknowledgment of responsibility and some effort at avoiding to cause further damages.

In many circumstances of our lives, we are the victims of a combination of these two kinds of injustices. In the example of the parentified child, the fact that the child is exploited by a needy parent constitutes a retributive injustice. On the other end, the fact that the child is born to that parent and not to a parent who is more capable of generosity constitutes a distributive injustice.

Who Is Responsible for the Injustices Done to Groups? When we discuss injustices that occur to a group, it is even more difficult to determine what results from a retributive injustice and what results from a distributive injustice. To take the example of the victims of the December 2004 tsunami, we can say that the fact that the earth moved in the part of the world where they lived, rather than somewhere else, constitutes a distributive injustice. No person or group can be blamed for that. On the other hand, the fact that they did not benefit from the same protection as other inhabitants of the earth, who live in areas equipped with advanced warning systems, constitutes a retributive injustice. This injustice would not have occurred if governments or international organizations had cared about them as much as they cared about other populations.

Things get even more complicated when we look at the fate of African populations that have been decimated by famine in the recent years. Children who suffer from malnutrition are the victims of a distributive injustice, since nobody can be blamed for the fact that they were born in an area of the world where nature is very harsh. But are we truly innocent? In fact, if we live in the industrial world, we may share responsibility in the fate of these African children simply because we consider that driving a car without any restrictions and maintaining the temperature of our homes at a comfortable level at all times is a basic right. In reality, as we insist on these standards, we contribute directly to the global warming that has led to dramatic climatic changes that have started to threaten the survival of people whom we will never meet. It is not only true of African populations but for many other populations as well.

How Do We Account for Distributive Injustices?

When we are the victim of a true distributive injustice, we are not likely to accept the idea that what happens to us is simply the product of randomness. How many people can honestly accept that whatever happens to them has no meaning in terms of justice and fairness? How many people are ready to believe that what happens to them is simply the product of the random combination of zillions of factors? If we assume that we are biologically equipped for assessing all the situations that we encounter in terms of giving and receiving and in terms of fairness, we will indeed try to account for the differences that occur between our life and the life of others in terms of justices and injustices. We will be compelled to bring back a retributive element to the world of distributive injustice.

Our tendency to account for the events of our lives in terms of justice or injustice is universal. We need to find some explanation for the origin of distributive injustices. What will vary are our responses. Each of us will come to different conclusions about the origins of these injustices and the nature of the redress. This will depend on our cultural and religious backgrounds. This will in turn affect our response to a harsh fate and it will also affect our capacity to forgive others for their wrongdoings.

Contextual therapists know from clinical experience that distributive injustices can trigger as much destructive entitlement as retributive ones: Parents who have become orphans at a young age will be tempted to parentify their children. People who have a serious medical illness may turn into demanding spouses. On the other hand, people who believe in a retributive system that they can locate outside of the realm of ordinary reality will be less likely to seek compensation for the injustices of their lives in the realm of close relationships.

For instance, we may believe that what happens to us today is a retribution for past deeds, either in our current life or even in past lives if we believe in reincarnation: We have a good life because we behaved well and a bad one because we behaved badly. Since we are fully responsible for our present circumstances, we cannot honestly turn toward others for redress. We will get redress only by changing our own behavior. If we believe in God and in an afterlife, we will accept our fate because we will see it as God's will and because we believe in God's justice.

Our religious beliefs will affect our capacity to forgive the people who have actually hurt us. We will be more likely to forgive them if we see that we have created the circumstance that put them on our paths or if we believe that the injustices of this life will be repaired in our afterlife. Topics such as this are addressed by Farhadian and Emmons (Chapter 4).

The Supra-Individual Determinants of Forgiveness

Forgiveness as a Group Process

Up to now, we have examined the issue of forgiveness as a relational process between two people, the victim and the perpetrator. We also need to address the fact that forgiveness occurs in a larger relational context. When we forgive someone, we are not alone. We are also part of a larger system: a family or a group.

Family Homeostasis as an Obstacle to Reconciliation. We have already seen that family systems and groups in general have a tendency to resist change and to maintain a status quo. How can this affect the process of forgiving? If a person tries to forgive someone outside of the family, it is common to hear other family members saying: "Why do you need to forgive this person?" or "Don't make peace with these people, they will just take advantage of you." The person who has taken the initiative of offering forgiveness to a culprit may bend to the pressure of the group and retreat. This is not too surprising. What is more surprising is that if someone else in the family or in the group makes a similar move later, the person who had made the initial step toward forgiveness will not second that move. Instead, he or she will most likely chime in with the people who are against peace. Is this the result of an inconsistency? In fact, it might not be the case if we think in terms of family homeostasis.

Collusion to Avoid Changes. Boszormenyi-Nagy (1987a) proposed the term *collusive postponement of mourning* to describe the effort that family members make to spare each other from the pains and losses that could result from a true change in the family. The reconciliation between a group member and an outsider could lead to the departure of one family member from the group or it could bring a stranger into it. In general, family members collude to avoid changes that could threaten the structure of the group. This means that as long as there are enough people to fight the idea of forgiveness, anyone can move to the position of the forgiver without threatening the group's homeostasis. It is therefore irrelevant to try to find out who is on the side of forgiving. If we want to predict if a group member will be able to move toward forgiveness against the expectation of his group, it would not serve us to know many details about his or her individual psychological characteristics. What we would need to know is the degree of his or her commitment to respond to the expectations of the group.

Forgiveness as a Source of Loyalty Conflicts. Almost by definition, the expression of our loyalty to a group requires that we refrain from displaying solidarity with another group. This expectation constitutes in itself a very serious obstacle in the peace-building process. How can we display any interest in reconciling with an adversary without becoming immediately disloyal to our group? In this context, it is understandable that people who are willing to make peace with an opponent group, against the prevalent attitude of vindictiveness in their own group, can encounter a serious resistance of their group or even put their life in danger. We know too well what happened to two major promoters of peace, Gandhi in India and Rabin in Israel.

Multidirected Partiality as a Tool to Decrease Loyalty Conflicts. What can we do if our family or our group resists our efforts to make peace with someone? What if our family or a larger group accuses us of disloyalties if we try to move toward reconciliation? It is not the purpose of this chapter to discuss the management of loyalties, but some general guidelines can apply. If loyalties play a role in a person's inability to forgive others, the first step that a therapist or a mediator can take is an application of multidirected partiality. The therapist or the mediator needs to help all the participants in the relationship to explore the consequences of forgiveness for all the parties involved, not just for the victim and the culprit. They need to explore in what way people could be hurt by the process of reconciliation and ask the people who want to move toward reconciliation to hear the concerns of the ones who resist it. As they get a fair chance to present their side, these people may become more open to examine the situation from the vantage point of the ones who want to move toward peace or even from the point of view of the perpetrators. This approach might lead the group as a whole to become more tolerant to the idea of reconciliation. This, of course, will relieve the people who want to move toward forgiveness from the accusation of being disloyal to the group.

It is therefore imperative that mediators who are involved in peace-building at the level of large groups try to help as many people as possible to see the advantages of reconciliation. Otherwise, the people who try to move toward reconciliation with an opponent group will be accused of disloyalty and put themselves in danger.

Finding the Freedom to Forgive

What can we do if the group as a whole is unable to move in the direction of recon-ciliation? People who want to move toward forgiveness are not limited to simply abiding to the group's expectation as their only option for how to express their loyalty to their group. Since what threatens the group is, for the most part, the fear of losing its members, people who want to move in the direction of reconciling with an outsider need to find a way to reassure the group of their commitment in a way that does not sacrifice their own aim of reconciliation.

Invisible Loyalties as an Obstacle to Forgiveness. Let us take the example of a woman who has recently separated from her husband because he had an extramarital affair. She may want to forgive him because she believes that her marriage is worth salvaging. Her parents will resent her efforts at reconciliation if they feel that she has become more available to them since she has separated from her husband. This would put the woman in a bind, because she will start to realize that she cannot pursue her own goals without being disloyal to her parents.

Her predicament may push her to express her loyalty to her parents in an indirect and invisible way. For instance, she can suddenly become more vindictive toward her husband, despite the fact that she is still intent on reconciliation. She may not even understand the origin of this change of attitude. On the surface, she will remain disloyal to her parents since she is still intent on salvaging her marriage. But, in an indirect way she may be in fact loyal to them, because her new behavior could lead to a failure of the reconciliation process. We can say that she has become invisibly loyal to her parents. In order to succeed in her own pursuit, this woman would need to find a way to reassure her parents about her loyalty in a visible and non-destructive manner.

Loyalty as a Source of Personal Freedom. If we can reassure the people who count on our loyalty that we are committed to the relationship with them, it will be easier not to meet all their expectations. For instance, the woman of our example could take the initiative of reassuring her parents that she will continue to visit them regularly even if she returns to the marriage. As she tries to meet their needs to the best of her ability, she will feel less guilty if they continue to express their dissatisfaction. We need to remember that loyalty does not have to be synonymous with dependence and submission. As long as we are genuinely committed to care about our families, we do not have to respond to all of their expectations (Ducommun-Nagy, 2006).

To a great extent, the process described for families is similar for groups. However, groups are even more dependent on a direct expression of our loyalty in the form of a rejection of the stranger than our families are. In the above example, the woman may displease her parents if she returns to her marriage, but if the couple has a child, the reconciliation also benefits the woman's parents: They depend on this baby to secure their biological posterity. In that way, ultimately, but indirectly, the woman will have remained loyal to her parents even if she has betrayed their expectations.

On the other hand, since groups that are not based on blood ties depend solely on our personal commitment for their continuity, they will be much more threatened by our commitment to strangers and we will have much less avenues to reassure them of our loyalty. One of the avenues that is open to us is to promote the cause of our group or to succeed in its name. For instance, we will certainly be able to reassure our group of our loyalty if we become a sports hero wearing its colors. We simply have to think about the enormous amount of group loyalty that is mobilized by any sports meeting, from the Olympics to the meeting between the most insignificant local groups.

Thus, when sports heroes are appointed as Ambassadors of Peace for the UN, it might be a smart move not simply because they attract an enormous public attention but for another reason: Since they cannot be accused of disloyalty to the nation or the ethnic group that they represent so well, they might indeed be freer to speak for peace between groups than many other people are.

Multidirected Partiality as a Tool for Peace

While contextual therapists focus generally on close relationships and apply multi-directed partiality to couple and family relationships, multidirected partiality has implications for many other situations in which people or groups need help to move toward reconciliation and peace, very specifically feuding ethnic groups. Boszormenyi-Nagy (1996 April, 2002) has written specifically about the situation of ethnic groups whose claims are ignored. We know that they might rely on destructive actions to provoke the attention of the world. This can become a motivation for group terrorism.

Multidirected Partiality and the Prevention of Group Terrorism. Boszormenyi-Nagy has made the hypothesis that if we could extend partiality to these groups and offer them a forum to present their claims in an organized fashion, they would be less likely to act destructively (Boszormenyi-Nagy, 1996 April, 2002). He had proposed a long time ago that since the UN cannot provide a forum for the claims of non-self-governing groups, another forum should be created. These groups could then present their positions to that forum, document their claims by whatever evidence they could gather, and hope for a fair hearing of their sides.

> How many places in the world witness terroristic warfare that goes back to hundreds of years of confrontation? The fact is that for ethnic groups, there is no authoritative international or U.N. agency to turn to. A farsighted U.N. reform would need to develop one. It takes a long time to introduce significant changes on a world-wide level, yet should we not systematically explore that process, which would be needed for exoneration between any two (or more) ethnic parties? There is no therapist of national-ethnic groups, but it would be worthwhile to explore how the multidirected partiality model could be made into a practical one in preparation for actually dealing with international law that is not based on the use of bombs, warships and rockets. What does it take to make the international legal-political structure become more "up to date"? (Boszormenyi-Nagy, 1996 April, pp. 14–15)

Unrepresented People Need to Be Heard. In some ways, Boszormenyi-Nagy's wish has been heard. There is an organization, The Unrepresented People and Nations Organization, which has a similar goal. Its seat is in Den Haag, The Netherlands. In exchange for a promise to renounce terrorism, the organization offers these groups support to document their claims and present them in front of established international organizations. With time, several ethnic minorities or suppressed nations that the group has represented have indeed been able to present their claims in front of international organizations and some have even gotten true national independence in the process (Ducommun-Nagy, 2006).

Conclusions

What Do We Gain When We Forgive Others?

Many therapists have agreed that forgiveness is often a necessary step toward healing (Wade & Worthington, 2005; Worthington & Wade, 1999). This is also the view of the contextual therapists and it is now easier to understand why. If giving constitutes a healing moment in therapy, then of course forgiving is not only necessary for healing, but it is healing in itself. This is because it earns us constructive entitlement and increases our human worth. Furthermore, forgiveness sets us on the path to autonomy because it allows us to remain connected with others and allows us to ascertain our existence as autonomous selves. All these elements explain why forgiveness is such an important step in our healing from trauma and injustices.

If all of this is correct, then forgiving might not be such a "head-in-the-cloud" attitude or a self-defeating proposition. It can become a wise action that can benefit the forgiver at least as much as the one who is pardoned.

Relational Ethics as a Determinant of Peace

The work of Boszormenyi-Nagy on the importance of relational ethics as a determinant of our behavior has added a new level of knowledge in our effort to understand all the factors that are involved in the process of peace-building. As contextual therapists, we share with individual therapists the belief that our actions are determined by our biological make-up, by the givens of our environment, and by our individual psychology. With the systemic family therapist, we believe that our freedom of action is modulated by the constraints of the larger systems to which we belong. We see also that our very existence as autonomous human beings depends on our capacity to relate to others, to give to them, and to offer them forgiveness. But, we believe that it is in the dimension of relational ethics that we need to look for the explanations of our behavior when it comes to understand how we can regain the capacity to forgive people who have hurt us and to move toward peace.

References

Barkow, J., Cosmides, L., & Tooby, J. (1992). Cognitive adaptation for social exchanges. In J. Barkow, L. Cosmides, & J. Tooby (Eds.). *The adaptive mind: Evolutionary psychology and the generation of culture.*Oxford: Oxford University Press.

Bertalanffy, L. von (1968). *General system theory*. New York: Brazillier.

Boszormenyi-Nagy, I. (1985). A theory of relationships: Experience and transactions. In I. Boszormenyi-Nagy & J. Framo, J. (Eds.), *Intensive family therapy*. New-York: Brunner/Mazel (first published in 1965).

Boszormenyi-Nagy, I. (1987a). The concept of change in conjoint family therapy. In *Foundations of contextual therapy: Collected papers of Ivan Boszormenyi-Nagy* (pp. 35–53). New York: Brunner/Mazel. (Original published in 1965).

Boszormenyi-Nagy, I. (1987b). From family therapy to a psychology of relationships: Fictions in the individual and fictions in the family. In *Foundations of contextual therapy: Collected papers of Ivan Boszormenyi-Nagy* (pp. 54–78). NY: Brunner/Mazel, (Original published 1966).

Boszormenyi-Nagy, I. (1987c). Relational modes and meanings. In *Foundations of contextual therapy: Collected papers of Ivan Boszormenyi-Nagy* (pp. 79–97). New York: Brunner/Mazel. (Original published in 1967).

Boszormenyi-Nagy, I. (1987d). Transgenerational solidarity: The expanding context of therapy and prevention. In *Foundations of contextual therapy: Collected papers of Ivan Boszormenyi-Nagy* (pp. 292–318). New-York: Brunner/Mazel. (Original published in 1986).

Boszormenyi-Nagy, I. (1996, April). *Forgiveness and exoneration.* Presentation at the National Conference on Forgiveness in Clinical Practice, University of Maryland, Baltimore, MD. (Unpublished manuscript.)

Boszormenyi-Nagy, I. (2000, April). *General plenary address.* Presented at the 14th annual Conference of the Hungarian Family Therapy Association, Szeged, Hungary.

Boszormenyi-Nagy, I. (2002). Foreword. In R. F. Massey & S. Davis Massey (Eds.), *Comprehensive handbook of psychotherapy: Vol. 3, interpersonal/humanistic/existential* (pp. xi, xii). New York: Wiley.

Boszormenyi-Nagy, I., & Spark, G. (1984). *Invisibles loyalties.* New-York: Brunner/Mazel. (First published in 1973).

Boszormenyi-Nagy, I., & Krasner, B. R. (1986). *Between give and take: A clinical guide to contextual therapy.* New York: Brunner/Mazel.

Buber, M. (1957). Guilt and guilt feelings. *Psychiatry, 20,* 114–129. (Original published 1948).

Buber. M. (1958). *I and Thou.* New York: Scribner.

Christie, D. (Ed.). (2006). Post-cold war peace psychology: More differentiated, contextualized, and systemic. *Journal of Social Issues, 62*(1). [Whole issue.]

De Waal, F. (2006). *Primate and philosophers, how morality evolved.* Princeton, NJ: Princeton University Press.

Ducommun-Nagy, C. (2002). Contextual therapy. In R. F. Massey & S. Davis Massey (Eds.), *Comprehensive handbook of psychotherapy: Vol. 3, interpersonal/humanistic/existential* (pp. 463–488). New York: Wiley.

Ducommun-Nagy, C. (2003). Can giving heal? Contextual therapy and biological psychiatry. In P. B. Prosky & D. V. Keith (Eds.), *Family therapy as an alternative to medication* (pp. 111–137). New-York: Brunner-Routledge.

Ducommun-Nagy, C. (2006). Ces loyautés qui nous libèrent. Paris: Lattès.

Friedman, M. S. (1960). *Martin Buber, the life of dialogue.* Chicago: The University Press.

Kaplan Thaler, L., & Koval, R. (2006). *The power of nice: How to conquer the business world with kindness.* New York: Reed Elsevier.

Maturana, H. R., & Varela, F. (1987) *The tree of knowledge.* Boston: Shambala.

Nowak, M., Page, K., & Sigmund, K. (2000). Fairness versus reason in the ultimate game. *Science, 289,* 1773–1775.

Ridley, M. (1996). *The origins of virtue, human instincts and the evolution of cooperation.* New York: Penguin Books.

Theunissen, M. (1984). *The other.* Boston: MIT Press.

Wade, N. G., & Worthington, E. L., Jr. (2005). In search of a common core: A content analysis of interventions to promote forgiveness. *Psychotherapy: Theory, research, practice and training, 42*(2), 160–177.

Worthington, E. L., Jr., & Wade, N. G. (1999). The psychology of unforgiveness and forgiveness and the implications for clinical practice. *Journal of Social and Clinical Psychology, 18,* 385–418.

Chapter 4
The Psychology of Forgiveness in the World Religions

Charles Farhadian and Robert A. Emmons

Understanding the psychology of forgiveness within the religions is critically important these days as religions seem to be among the most robust forces that can either help or hinder all kinds of human relationships. The topic of forgiveness occupies a central place in all of the major world religions, with the assumption that there is something wrong with the human condition. That is to say, something or many things need to be repaired, and the religions offer a variety of insight, wisdom, and aid to do so.

Relationships Between Religion and Forgiveness

In order to tease out some of the salient themes of the psychology of forgiveness within the religions, this chapter offers reflections on five basic questions about the relationship between the religions and the processes of forgiveness. Naturally, even the question of which religions to include in the discussion can leave readers wishing for more. Here we offer reflections on some aspects, not all, of the major religious traditions of the world, Hinduism, Buddhism, Judaism, Christianity, and Islam, with the hope that readers will want to pursue the same and related themes on their own. To limit our purview we do not consider the immense array of religions known collectively as New Religious Movements and traditional religions, with recognition that the major religious traditions listed above account for the vast majority of religionists today, which are well over 4.4 billion people! This chapter illuminates broad themes of the psychology of forgiveness within the religious traditions through consideration of the following five orientating questions: (1) How do religions foster characteristics that facilitate forgiveness processes? (2) How do religions oppose characteristics that discourage processes of forgiveness? (3) How might religions impede processes of forgiveness? (4) What role do public religious rituals play in the facilitation of forgiveness? (5) What is the relationship between the religions and personal and corporate transformation that may give rise to the processes of forgiveness?

Having listed these questions, we should state the obvious: religions in themselves do not "facilitate forgiveness," they in themselves do not "discourage

Ani Kalayjian, Raymond F. Paloutzian, *Forgiveness and Reconciliation*, Peace Psychology Book Series, DOI 10.1007/978-1-4419-0181-1_4,
© Springer Science+Business Media, LLC 2009

forgiveness," nor "impede processes of forgiveness." Religions don't act – human agents do. This is the human element of religion and in part the focus of this chapter. We cannot lose sight of the human agents who engage the traditions, allowing those traditions to profoundly shape their individual and corporate identities, as well as their understanding of the "other" – that general category of difference that can provide the source of creativity or impetus for destruction. Religions are experienced and practiced by human beings. Perhaps that is where we should begin, with the acknowledgment that human beings provide variable interpretations of their own religious traditions, a fact that introduces a multitude of complexities into the discussion of the psychology of forgiveness in the world religions. Recognizing that religions are deeply embedded in social, cultural, and psychological domain helps us avoid seeing the religions as simply a list of doctrines and practices, however important these are to understanding the religious traditions, and encourages the appreciation of the role that human personalities and psychologies play in the interpretation of a religion.

Who forgives? Human beings? God? Ancestors? Who is forgiven? What is necessary for forgiveness to be a social reality? What role can religions play in the processes of forgiveness? One of the unique features of religions is that they generally do provide a means of forgiveness and a way to live in greater harmony with fellow human beings, the natural world, and the Divine. Religions can offer sources of new knowledge and transformational notions that can enhance forgiveness between human beings and communities. The new knowledge (e.g., wisdom) offered by the religions can challenge prevailing notions or be cajoled to benefit the carriers of that knowledge, sometimes to the uplifting of the human community or to the detriment of others. It is crucial to recognize that the concept of forgiveness implies a corollary concept – sin. Whatever term religion uses to describe it, all religions affirm that something has gone awry with human beings and the Divine or pattern of the universe. Something is wrong and needs to be mended, whether that is the human inability to see the truth or a fractured relationship between the human and the Divine. Forgiveness of the human offence against the Divine, essential harmony of the created order, or fellow human beings is one of the goals of the world religions.

How Do Religions Foster Characteristics That Facilitate Forgiveness?

How do religions excuse an offence or disharmony that disrupts the human relationship to God or with the essential pattern of the universe? More specifically, how do religions encourage followers to develop qualities of empathy, compassion, mercy, and humility and other virtues that may encourage forgiveness? It is important to note that religions challenge human beings to live in ways that consider others as fellow human beings and the affects of individual and corporate behavior on others. Religious traditions present ideals, often presented in the form of stories, narratives, parables, visual and dramatic arts, and formalized into doctrines, that communicate the characteristics of a faithful follower of the religious tradition. All religious traditions recognize that something is amiss with the human condition (e.g., sin, disharmony, selfishness), and each tradition offers its remedy. Generally, the monotheistic traditions suggest that the Divine, God (Allah), initiates forgiveness – that salvation in fact requires the forgiveness of all kinds of transgressions (God is holy and those that follow God must be holy or made holy), whereas the Asian traditions (i.e., Hinduism, Buddhism, Taoism, Confucianism) generally present ways in which followers can either purify themselves, gain knowledge of the deepest structure of the universe, or align themselves to the pattern of the universe in order to be saved or improve their present and future life.

The monotheistic traditions (i.e., Judaism, Christianity, and Islam) affirm the need for reconciliation with God, who has initiated a means through which one can live harmoniously with God and others. Forgiveness and reconciliation, while related, are two different moments, with forgiveness being the necessary first step toward reconciliation. In Judaism, the prophets stressed the insufficiency of sacrifice without a transformation of the heart (Jeremiah 4:4) and that the context of Divine forgiveness involves a contrite heart from which confession arises. According to Judaism, God's nature is to forgive, and the use of the language of covenant relationship (e.g., God is to people like father is to son) challenges people to forgive others because they are forgiven by God. The Talmud states, "He who sins and regrets his act is at once forgiven" (B. Hag. 5a). Likewise, Christianity teaches that God's forgiveness exemplifies how human beings should treat one another. Christ died "for our sins" (I Cor. 15:3) so that human beings can be forgiven, and several New Testament parables illustrate this central Christian affirmation. One of the most universally recognized Christian prayers, the Lord's Prayer, uses the expression, "Forgive us our debts, as we also have forgiven our debtors" or "Forgive us the wrongs that we have done, as we forgive the wrongs others have done us" (Matt. 6:12), tying together God's forgiveness with the call for humans to forgive one another. Likewise, in Islam, God (or Allah) is one who forgives (Qu'rān 39:53, 2:286), yet believers are also told to forgive, "They avoid gross sins and vice, and when angered they forgive" (Qu'rān 42:37), for forgiveness is rewarded by Allah, "And the recompense of evil is punishment like it, but whoever forgives and amends, he shall have his reward from Allah; surely He does not love the unjust" (Qu'rān 42:40). Consequently, in the monotheistic traditions, it is because God forgives that human beings can forgive others. Forgiveness is fundamentally rooted in the nature of God who initiates forgiveness.

Within the religious traditions that originated in Asia (e.g., Hinduism, Buddhism, Taoism, and Confucianism), the constellation of sin and forgiveness functions quite differently, for Hinduism and Buddhism argue for the primacy of *dharma*(i.e., truth, teaching, duty) that needs to be maintained, while Taoism and Confucian affirm that health and happiness are directly related to one's ability to follow the force of the Tao. The central concepts of dharma and Tao, while not referring to a personal or knowable God as affirmed in the monotheistic traditions, does provide a standard apart from which one will fail to gain individual and social harmony or salvation (e.g., liberation). Forgiveness, then, relates not to a personal force or Divinity that excuses one's "sin," or failure to follow the laws of dharma and Tao, but rather to a re-establishment and re-alignment to those principle manifest forces.

Generally, prayer and submission are the main instruments that get us "right" with the Divine, the law of *dharma*, and *yin-yang* cosmology (i.e., Taoism and Confucianism), for prayer as ritual serves a communicative function between human and Divine or between human and cosmic pattern. Here prayer and submission are closely tied, since prayer is by nature a form of surrender in the religions – it inherently places the believer in a position of acquiescence vis-à-vis the Divine or cosmic force. No real prayer places the individual above the gods. As the phenomenologist Mircea Eliade (1907–1986) suggested, re-alignment with the gods renders fundamental, existential reorientation possible (Eliade, 1957). And the ritual of prayer is one of the major avenues of that kind of re-alignment. According to the religious traditions of the world, forgiveness is truncated unless it gives rise to an improvement in the human relationship to other human beings and to the environment. The final destination of Divine or cosmic forgiveness, that is, its empirical reality, is its manifestation in human and communal relationships. All of the world religions offer guides and techniques to prayer and submission, striving for forgiveness. In the monotheistic traditions, scriptural injunctions and religiously ideal persons, such as Jesus or Muhammad, model the use of prayer and submission as a communicative and action-oriented device aimed toward receiving forgiveness from God.

Jesus' prayer on the cross, "Father, forgive them, for they do not know what they are doing" (Luke 23:24), is a prayer on behalf of others. Jesus demonstrates forgiveness in the Garden of Gethsemane when he heals the severed ear of the Roman guard who was a member of the group that arrested Jesus while he was praying. Within the Jewish tradition, and particularly during the Yom Kippur Liturgy, petitions for forgiveness are frequent: "Forgive us the breach of positive commands and negative commands, whether or not they involve an act, whether or not they are known to us." In the history of Islam, it was revealed to Muhammad, "Hence, turn towards your Sustainer [alone] and surrender yourselves unto Him ere the suffering [of death and resurrection] comes upon you, for then you will not be succoured" (Qu'rān 39:54). Muslims are emboldened to pray specifically for forgiveness, aiming to be "...those who are patient in adversity, and true to their word, and truly devout, and who spend [in God's way], and pray for forgiveness from their innermost hearts" (Qu'rān 3:17).

The religious traditions that originated in Asia emphasize specific practices that enable human beings to bring the practitioner into submission to the cosmic forces that govern all life. Prayer and meditation are significant contributors to mending sins of imperfection, disillusionment, and disharmony, leaving the believer out of sync with cosmic forces (*adharma*) and rendering her dis-eased. Hinduism and Buddhism tend to stress prayers and meditative practices that bring about an enlightened state, where personal offences against the impersonal forces and laws of the universe (e.g., Brahman, Noble Truths) are mitigated, enabling the individual to achieve greater awareness and compassion for one another. Within Hinduism this may entail practices as diverse as hiring a professional band of Brahmin priests who can employ Vedic hymns, to rituals that appease nature deities, to engaging in deep meditation, where one seeks unity with the Divine essence (Brahman), to deep self-reflection with the aim of realizing the nature of the Divine within. Within Buddhism, practices can range from silent meditation facing a wall to the study of sacred Buddhist texts at a Buddhist university or chanting the name of a bodhisattva of compassion who can help the believer cross the sea of suffering.

How Do Religions Oppose Characteristics That Discourage Forgiveness?

It is common for the religions to be misunderstood, particularly by the non-religious or anti-religious, as simply harbingers of all forms of narrow-mindedness, with moral constraints and divine injunctions being the manifestation of religiosity itself or, worse, of some pathology. On the one hand, religions have seemed to play major roles in legitimating all sorts of violence in history. On the other hand, all religious do prescribe ideal behaviors and discourage others, with an eye to advocating those practices and behaviors that uplift the human person. Religions also resist several characteristics that impede processes of forgiveness, such as narcissism, revenge, and pride. How so?

First, divine injunctions, or cosmic principles, which limit the self-centered ego, provide moral constraints on the believer and help to develop moral consciousness corresponding to the religious ideals. Moral consciousness is thus connected to one's relationship to God and to one another and strikingly is frequently connected to belief in a final Judgment Day. The monotheistic traditions recognize a God who is judge and who will judge our lives at the consummation of time. As such, divine injunctions, as recorded in the great sacred texts of the monotheistic traditions, affirm that human beings are to forgive each other – and they will be judged in part on that basis. According to the Christian tradition, "For if you refuse to forgive others, our Father will not forgive your sins" (Matthew 6:15; Cf. Luke 6:37). The "don'ts" of religion include specific behaviors noted in the sacred texts and histories that are antithetical to the tradition and its vision of a better human society. The Ten Commandments delineate such attitudinal restraints and is usually recorded using several negations, "Do not worship any other gods," "Do not make any idols," "Do not murder," and so on. Divine injunctions communicate that we as individuals are not entirely autonomous (literally, "laws unto ourselves"), but rather are responsible for our own behaviors in the sight of God. Revenge itself is never advocated, since judgment is the prerogative of God. Similarly, the religious traditions that originated in Asia anathemize characteristics of self-centeredness, revenge, and pride, in part because of the social and cosmic disharmony these characteristics yield. Confucius' Silver Rule reads, "Do not do unto others what you do not want done to you" (Analects XII.2, XV.23; Cf. Matthew 7:12), and advocates what is "appropriate" in each human encounter. According to Islamic theology, the chief failing of human beings is rebellion and pride (Qu'rān 96:1–3, Qu'rān 20:122–3), with the opposite virtue being submission (literally, *Islam*). As the often-phrased Hebrew Proverb goes, "pride comes before the fall" (Proverbs 16:18).

Second, the power of the religious community to communicate social disapproval acts as another robust constraint to characteristics that would obstruct forgiveness in individual believers. Social disapproval is an immensely influential force. Religious individuals attempting to live by the admonitions of the sacred texts and the traditions stemming from those early records are validated in their religious journeys in large part by the community that affirms they are "right" within the tradition. Do they exhibit the characteristics advocated by the religious tradition? Which attitudes and virtues are most valued and how are they maintained? The vast corpus of religious and civil laws, as concretized forms of social disapproval, bear testimony to the importance of sustaining stable societies by deterring behavior incongruous with human flourishing, with forgiveness being one of the foundational virtues to social harmony. The idea that a religion's primary function is to rein in socially non-normative behavior and promote socially normative behavior has a long history in the social-scientific study of religion (Durkheim, 1965, 1912; Malinowski, 1935). Research has found that individual religiousness is associated with greater adherence to conventional norms (Saucier & Skrzypinska, 2006). Furthermore, in many studies of delinquent and high-risk behaviors, religious beliefs and behaviors are often conceptualized as measures of "conventionality," along with other, more typical measures of conventionality such as measures of the perceived wrongness of norm violations such as stealing, lying, harming others, and damaging others' property (see McCullough & Willoughby, 2009, for a review).

Third, it is far too easy to gloss over the differences between religions, as though they are essentially the same thing, dressed up in different linguistic and cultural garb, just different paths to some unitive destination. In fact, while the religions do share many significant similarities, they are also quite different in important ways. Individual and social identities are impacted deeply by religious belief, practice, and community commitment. That is to say, religions function as boundary-making devices as well, for good or ill. Who is "in" and "out" of a religion depends upon the parameters of orthodoxy set by the founders and interpreters of the tradition, usually with robust debates about those specific boundaries throughout the history of each religion. Processes of forgiveness too exhibit a degree of variation since the parameters of forgiveness are outlined by each tradition differently. Forgiveness may be extended in some religious traditions only under a narrowly defined set of conditions, such as particular ritual actions or formulaic sayings, while in other traditions, forgiveness may be extended by anyone at anytime regardless of particular ceremonial events. Needless to say, and to add a degree of complexity to our topic, various interpreters of a given tradition may have different perspectives on the conditions under which forgiveness is requested or offered, as well as the methods of forgiveness.

How Might Religions Impede Processes of Forgiveness?

First, we highlight that individual and group identity coheres in part because of the function of personal and corporate boundaries that maintain a sense of individuality. Boundaries are a part of healthy identity construction. However, there are many kinds of boundaries and some are so robustly restrictive that they give rise to inward-looking, prejudicial orientations of an "us/them" mentality. Religious fundamentalism refers to holding defensive attitudes toward one's religious beliefs and is associated with strong boundaries between in-group and out-group. A recent study found that fundamentalism is positively related to pro-forgiveness attitudes but not to forgiveness behaviors (Brown, Collin, & Campbell, 2007). This study is important because it implies that the link between forgiveness and religiousness might be more complicated than has been previously assumed. Using a religious measure that assesses fundamentalism may be less likely to predict actual forgiveness than it is to predict attitudes about forgiveness, and attitudes are not the same thing as behaviors. Intrinsic–extrinsic religiousness also appears to affect forgiveness; people who hold their religious beliefs for extrinsic reasons are more retaliatory than are intrinsics following interpersonal provocation (Greer, Mitchell, Varan, & Watson, 2005).

Second, it may not be the religions themselves or any set of religious doctrines that impede processes of forgiveness, especially when the world's religions offer specific rituals and protocols for forgiveness, but rather the obstruction of forgiveness could be the result of the misappropriation of the religious tradition itself. For decades scholars of religions predicted the demise of religions in the contemporary world. However, the past few decades have shown that the opposite has occurred, with dramatic resurgence of religions on all continents. Along with the overall explosion of religions across the globe has been the dramatic rise in religious fundamentalisms that have in many instances exploited the "us/them" mentality by attempting to eradicate perceived enemies of the given tradition. Since the 9/11 events of 2001, the world's attention has been focused primarily on Islamic fundamentalism or so-called political Islam. But isn't it possible for a follower of any religion to interpret their particular tradition in fundamentalist terms, whereby being intolerant of any perspective different than their own? For example, Hindutva ideology in India, a form of Hindu fundamentalism that has been the foundational ideology that gave rise to several violent clashes with Muslims and attacks on Christian congregations, and the burning alive of an Australian Christian missionary and his sons has shown itself to be quite intolerant of things considered "not Hindu" (not local). What Westerners call fundamentalism refers originally to a late 19th century movement within Protestant Christianity, during a conflict between modernists and fundamentalists. Today fundamentalism refers more generally to religious intolerance, but the term can be applied equally to religiously legitimated forms of racial, ethnic, or tribal intolerance. Needless to say, religious people usually follow their tradition because they believe it to be true and it provides meaning for them. One reason why religious fundamentalism impedes the process of forgiveness is not because believers affirm the truth of their tradition but because it is a sociological opposition, sometimes expressed in physical violence, that seeks to eliminate "the other" and allows no public space for the emergence of a civil society.

Finally, on the ground, where we all live, rather in the abstract realm of theological concepts, the histories and conditions of subjugation can dramatically impede processes of forgiveness. Life can be messy, marked by human inconsistencies. Even as the religions valorize forgiveness, on a human level the act of pardoning somebody can be nearly impossible to achieve. Wounds run deep. Generational wounds run deeper still, since the memories of committed offenses may have been memorialized and deeply burned into the social consciousness of large groupings of people who, from an early age, are taught to hate or despise the other (see Volf, 2007). Religious differences can create false bases for conflict, and group conflict and violence in the name of religion can be supported and fomented by religious leaders (Staub, 2005). Consequently, religions may not encourage and may actively discourage forgiveness when presumed perpetrators are members of other faith groups.

What Role Do Public Religious Rituals Play in Facilitating Forgiveness?

Humans are ritual beings. Much of what we do and how we act is done ritualistically. That is to say, there are numerous prescribed actions, behaviors, and symbolic gestures, which shape our human discourse and encounters every day. In Western cultures, when we meet someone we usually shake hands rather than pat their heads. Well-mannered individuals say, "Thank you," when served in a restaurant. When we bump someone we ask for forgiveness, even if informally: He says, "Sorry about that" and she replies, "That's okay." With a minimal amount of ritual exchange, the social fabric is mended. Rituals have a communicative function that can help sustain communities. On one level, ritual actions can powerfully communicate respect and honor to other persons, thus they are performed on a human level for other human beings for the preservation of the relationship, even for a moment. So there are direct social consequences of engaging ritual behavior, such as maintaining social harmony and unburdening ourselves from feelings of guilt for offending others. On another level, rituals can be communicative events between and among human beings and the Divine. It is one thing to bump someone while walking down the street, but quite another to break the laws of God or oppose the natural order of creation. Religious rituals have a communicative function between human beings and the Divine. Public religious rituals can be brief or long, simple or elaborate.

What is important about public religious rituals? What makes such rituals efficacious? Should one feel a certain way during the ritual performance? Does one need to feel genuine guilt or a deep sense of remorse for the offence that was committed? The world religions stress different requirements for public rituals. In some forms of Hinduism, such as those with Vedic influences, contrition is less important than the right performance of the ritual itself. But most world religions, including much of the Hindu tradition, note the seriousness of ritual actions and the remorse that ought to accompany the ritual performance. The inner life must want to correspond to the communicative ritual. Acts of penance and restitution are frequent elements of spiritual confession across traditions (Pargament, 2007). Purification rituals are designed to restore the relationship between the perpetrator and the victim, or more commonly, between the perpetrator and the Divine (Pargament, 2007).

Furthermore, public religious rituals solidify social identity and the ideals of the community. Through public religious rituals, communities stand before God and one another, acknowledging their personal and corporate limitations, impurities, and sinfulness. From the perspective of evolutionary theory, public and private religious behaviors (i.e., ritual activities such as fasting, prayer, worship, tithing, confession) can be regarded as "costly" in that they incur significant effort without prospect of immediate returns. In their roles as signaling devices these religious rituals and behaviors can become reliable indicators of commitment (of the person enacting them) to the religious community (see Rappaport, 1999, for a similar analysis). By engaging in these religious practices the religious adherent is saying, in effect, "Look, I would not be devoting so much time to these irrational and useless activities unless I was truly committed to the group." Identifying who is in and not in compliance with the rules facilitates group cohesion and cooperation (Sosis, 2005).

Finally, public religious rituals of forgiveness represent the public commitment to forgiveness. Can there be any more serious accountability for forgiveness than communicating with one another before the presence of God or of cosmic order? Many religions even note the presence of an audience of saints, spirits, or deities at important times of meeting between human beings and God. These rituals may include a public commitment or vow to expressing an intention to seek atonement and forgiveness, or to forgive one's transgressor. A vow to God carries greater moral weight and authority than a vow to a mere human. The Hebrew Bible states, "If you make a vow to the LORD your God, do not be slow to pay it, for the LORD your God will certainly demand it of you and you will be guilty of sin. . .whatever your lips utter you must be sure to do." In the mind of the pledge-maker, severing a divine vow would bring severe punishment, while performing the behavior would bring ultimate rewards.

Does Personal or Corporate Religious Transformation Facilitate Forgiveness?

Religions matter most when they make a difference in the lives of individuals and communities. It is one thing for academics to discuss the nature and theory of religion, and the accompanying abstractions of the topics within the purview of religious studies, but it is quite another for people and societies transformed by religion to make sense of their religious lives in the midst of a world fraught with human inconsistencies, social problems, and the histories of trauma, which need forgiveness. A religion holds little value unless the truths or insights of that religion animate people's lives, guide their decision-making, and help them live better with other human beings, the environment, and the Divine. Marking each religion are both "this-worldly" and "other-worldly" orientations, which sociologist of religion Max Weber explored in several of his writings.[1] Generally, ascetic traditions and monastic movements, such as Buddhist *bhikkhu*(monks), Buddhist *bhikkhuni*(nuns), Christian monks and nuns, Hindu *sadhus*(ascetics) and *sannyasa*(renouncers), and Muslim Sufi orders tend toward being "other-worldly" in their orientation, as spiritual life is directly to the world beyond immediate, empirical reality. Likewise, these same traditions exhibit characteristics that focus on a "this-worldly" spiritual orientation as well. Weber's famous work on the Protestant ethic and the spirit of capitalism, the Buddhist valorization of charitable outreach, the Hindu emphasis on engaging the world as a sacrifice to the gods (*Bhagavad Gita*), and the Muslim notion of social justice implicit in all Five Pillars of Islam illustrate the "this-worldly" quality of the same traditions that can also be "other-worldly" in their orientation. The spectrum of "this-worldly" and "other-worldly" orientation is important because it reminds us that not all believers of a given tradition hold the same value for social and personal engagement in this world. Consequently, the process of forgiveness begins with the affirmation that the religious ideals impact this world directly, without being simply an exercise in making things right with the gods alone. Religions that combine both "this-worldly" and "other-worldly" orientations seem best positioned to be active players in establishing long-term forgiveness among peoples. It is worthwhile to note that religious leaders play leadership roles in nearly all Truth and Reconciliation Commissions.[2] Their presence signifies the importance of religion, and what sociologists have called "spiritual capital," in the discourse about forgiveness across cultures and societies.

Forgiveness matters because salvation and knowledge of the Divine or cosmic law is in part dependent upon the believer's ability and willingness to pardon others. Forgiveness is an ideal, but nevertheless is presented within the reach of religionists, whether with the help of God (e.g., Christianity, Islam, or Judaism) or by sheer self-reliance (e.g., Theravada Buddhism). Forgiveness is a Divine act that enables individuals to be close to the Divine by reflecting on the nature of God, and being personally or corporately transformed by the Divine, then by forgiving others. Several passages within the sacred texts of the world religions exemplify the close

---

[1] See Max Weber's work, *The Theory of Social and Economic Organization*(New York: The Free Press, 1947); *The Protestant Ethic and the Spirit of Capitalism*(New York: Scriber's Press, 1958); *Economy and Society: An Outline of Interpretive Sociology*(Berkeley: University of California Press, 1978); *The Sociology of Religion*(Boston: Beacon Press, 1993); *Religion of India: The Sociology of Hinduism and Buddhism*(New York: The Free Press, 1958); and *The Religion of China: Confucianism and Taoism*(1951).

[2] For instance, a partial list of Truth and Reconciliation Commissions, with their religious leadership, includes Argentina (Roman Catholic Bishop Jaime de Nevares, Rabbi Marshall Meyer, and Methodist Bishop Carlos T. Gattinoni), East Timor (Clergymen Jovito Araujo and Agustinho de Vasconcelos), Ecuador (a representative of the Ecuadoran Bishops' Conference), Nigeria (Rev. Matthew Kuka), Panama (Catholic Alberto Santiago, Protestant Bishop Julio Murray), Peru (Dean of Catholic University, Salomon Lerner Fresnes, Father Gaton Garatea), South Africa (Anglican Archbishop Desmond Tutu), and Uruguay (Archbishop Nicolas Cotungo, Jesuit priest Claudio Williman).

connection between the initiative of the Divine in the act of forgiveness and the intimacy with the Divine that results when people are forgiven. And there are always social and spiritual implications of forgiveness. For instance, the Hindu sacred texts note, "If we have sinned against the man who loves us, have ever wronged a brother, friend, or comrade, the neighbor ever with us, or a stranger, remove from us this stain, O King Varuna" (*Rig Veda* 5.85.7); "Though a man be soiled with the sins of a lifetime, let him but love me, rightly resolved, in utter devotion. I see no sinner, that man is holy. Holiness soon shall refashion his nature to peace eternal. O son of Kunti, of this be certain: the man who loves me shall not perish" (*Bhagavad Gita* 9:30–31). In Mahayana Buddhism, the fundamental importance of the practice of chanting the name of the Buddha promises to elicit forgiveness:

> Let him utter the name, Buddha Amitayus. Let him do so serenely with his voice uninterrupted; let him be continually thinking of Buddha until he has completed ten times the thought, repeated, 'Adoration to Buddha Amitayus' (*Namu Amida Butsu*). On the strength of his merit of uttering the Buddha's name he will, during every repetition, expiate sins which involved him in births and deaths during eighty million kalpas. (Contemplation Sutra, Pure Land Buddhism, 3.30)

In Judaism, God initiates forgiveness for God's sake: "I, I am He who blots out your transgressions for my own sake, and I will not remember your sins" (Isaiah 43:25). Forgiveness in the Judeo-Christian tradition leads to personal transformation: "Hide they face from my sins, and blot out all my iniquities. Create in me a clean heart, O God, and put a new and right spirit within me" (Psalms 51:9–10). In Christianity, the crucifixion of Jesus Christ enables God's forgiveness to be made efficacious: "In him (Jesus Christ) we have redemption through his blood, the forgiveness of our trespasses, according to the riches of his grace which he lavished upon us" (Ephesians 1:7–8). Within Islam, Allah forgives: "Say, 'If you love Allah, follow me, and Allah will love you, and forgive you all your sins; Allah is All-forgiving, All-compassionate'" (Qur'an 3.31); "Say, 'O my Servants who have transgressed against their souls! Despair not of the mercy of Allah: for Allah forgives all sins: for He is Of-forgiving, Most Merciful'" (Qur'an 39:53). Taking refuge in the Divine, or trusting in cosmic law (e.g., dharma, Tao), changes people at the deepest levels. What's important here is the human imitation of the Divine. In the words of phenomenologist Mircea Eliade, "By imitating divine behavior, man puts and keeps himself close to the gods – that is, in the real and the significant," giving us a new existential situation out of which we can engage the world (Eliade, 1957, p. 202).

What Have We Learned from the Scientific Study of Forgiveness?

Research is answering fundamental questions about what forgiveness is and isn't, how it develops, what are its physiological correlates and physical effects, whether it is always beneficial, and how people – if they are so motivated – might be helped to forgive. There are benefits to forgiveness and costs to unforgiveness. The negative social, emotional, and physical consequences of unforgiveness (especially if chronic) on overall health, including increased disease risk, have been demonstrated (Friedberg, Suchday, & Shelov, 2007). To the extent that forgiveness acts as one path out of unforgiveness, it may reduce these negative states and associated behaviors and mitigate their detrimental consequences. By the same token, the ability to forgive has been shown to lead to reductions in anxiety and depression, better health outcomes, increased coping with stress, and increased closeness to God and others (Krause & Ellison, 2003).

Factors That Influence Willingness to Forgive

Forgiveness has usually been treated by both researchers and applied psychologists as synonymous with forgivingness – as a characteristic of the individual (the offended party in a transaction) that is relatively consistent across relationships and across offenses within a given relationship. Religion is one factor thought to be important in forgiveness. Pargament (1997) documented several ways in which forgiveness is divine: (a) forgiveness has been encouraged for thousands of years by major world religions, (b) religion offers models and methods of forgiveness (e.g., the parable of the Prodigal Son), (c) forgiveness can be sanctified – that is, imbued with sacred qualities (in many religions, the deity possesses a forgiving character), and (d) religion offers worldviews and guidelines that help people reframe their attitudes toward their offenders and specify conditions under which forgiveness should be granted. A religious discipline that might facilitate forgiveness, for example, is journaling (Koch, 2004). A recent study found that writing about the benefits of interpersonal transgressions was effective at promoting forgiveness compared to two other tasks (McCullough, Root, & Cohen, 2006). Religiously based ceremonies, testimonies, and memorials can facilitate the healing process of forgiveness for those who have been the victims of group violence (Staub, 2005).

Religions often differ in their commandments about when to forgive. For example, the Talmud argues that in order to be forgiven, transgressors must first make an explicit admission of wrongdoing, repent not to repeat the offense, and offer restitution to the offended. On the other hand, Christianity prescribes that forgiveness should be offered unconditionally (McCullough, Pargament, & Thoresen, 2000). Theological warrants on forgiveness can be subjected to empirical research. For example, interesting research has shown that people who feel forgiven by God are more likely to forgive others unconditionally, whereas requiring transgressors to perform acts of contrition is related to more distress and poorer mental health (Krause & Ellison, 2003).

The empirical association between religion (or religiousness) and forgiveness is not straightforward. Many studies have indeed shown that religious persons value forgiveness, say their faith helps them forgive, and that religious involvement is positively correlated with the disposition to forgive (forgivingness). But there is also the religion–forgiveness discrepancy: there is almost no correlation between religiousness and forgiveness responses to specific transgressions (see McCullough, Bono, & Root, 2005, for a review of the literature on religion and forgiveness). When an association is found, it is very weak, though in the expected direction. Yet a recent study showed that religious people were actually more retaliatory (behaviorally) against a norm-violator, even though they reported themselves to have been more forgiving (Greer et al., 2005).

Personality is another factor that predicts willingness to forgive. McCullough and Hoyt (2002) examined forgiveness ratings across a variety of transgressions in close relationships (with friends, parents, and romantic partners) and concluded that some people are dispositionally more willing to forgive than others. Specifically, between 22% and 44% of variance in respondents' willingness to forgive a specific transgression was attributable to stable individual differences in forgivingness. Personality factors that best predicted forgivingness in that study were agreeableness (positively) and neuroticism (negatively). With regard to the place of forgiveness in personality, Ashton and Lee (2001) recently posited that forgiveness/non-retaliation is one of three major traits that underlies prosocial tendencies and can account for individual differences in the major dimensions of agreeableness and emotional stability. A lifestyle characterized by forgiveness is often thought to be also characterized by love, empathy, humility, and gratitude (Worthington, 1998), though empirical research on forgiveness and these positive virtues is not yet definitive.

Forgiveness Interventions

Forgiveness appears to be a learnable skill. To date, more than two dozen forgiveness intervention studies have been reported, mostly using brief, small-group formats. These structured interventions involved counseling and exercises that were used to help people move from anger and resentment toward forgiveness. They have addressed a wide range of offenses and client characteristics. Most intervention studies rely on some form of process model of forgiveness, Enright's (2001) being the gold standard. Enright's model represents the forgiveness process as having four phases: Uncovering, Deciding, Working, and Deepening. For example, the Deciding phase involves three subprocesses: (a) insight that old resolution strategies are not working and have a high cost, (b) willingness to consider forgiveness as an option, and (c) commitment to forgive the offender. Results have generally been promising, especially in demonstrating that grievances or hurts can be reduced significantly and that willingness to forgive an offender can be increased through forgiveness training. Forgiveness interventions have been shown to be successful in alleviating depression, anxiety, and grief in post-abortion men (Coyle & Enright, 1997); depression, anxiety, and self-blame in incest survivors (Freedman & Enright, 1996); and anger and resentment in cases of marital infidelity (Gordon, Baucom, & Snyder, 2005). Some interventions have been at the group level, tackling issues such as human rights abuses, intergroup conflict and war, and ethnic and religious violence (Moeshberger, Dixon, Niens, & Cairns, 2005).

Some studies have compared religiously based interventions (incorporating, for example, personal petitionary prayer and scripture meditation) with secular interventions. Consulting one's religious scriptures, as Rachlin (2000) proposed, can be effective for initiating self-change because scriptures can give behavioral guidance that is more likely to be followed because the advice is believed to emanate from a sacred source. Interestingly, though, two published studies that included spiritual exercises did not produce additional benefits beyond the secular intervention. For example, in one study of college women who had experienced infidelity, emotional/verbal abuse, physical abuse/threats, rape, or unwanted breakup, women in both the secular forgiveness intervention and the spiritually integrated forgiveness intervention experienced decreases in anger, anxiety, depression and increases in forgiveness immediately and at follow-up, relative to the no intervention control group (Rye & Pargament, 2002). In another study with a community sample of divorced adults (Rye et al., 2005), a rigorous experimental design was used pitting a secular intervention against a religiously based one. No differences were found on outcomes when religious and secular conditions were compared, nor did intrinsic religiousness moderate intervention effects. Thus, with respect to mental health, secular and spiritually based forgiveness programs appear equally effective.

An important question to ask, in the context of religion and forgiveness, is whether forgiveness interventions are equally effective across different groups of people? In particular, there appear to be differential effects of these interventions for men and women. It's been known for some time that sex may be related to treatment outcomes in general group counseling, with women generally responding more favorably to short-term group therapy than do men (Ogrodniczuk, Piper, & Joyce, 2004). With respect to forgiveness, men appear to be less willing than women to (a) consider forgiveness as a way to respond to a hurt and (b) forgive a specific hurtful event. Other research has suggested that men tend to report more anger and desires for revenge against an offender (Wade & Goldman, 2006). Thus, forgiveness interventions, particularly at a group level, must be sensitive to the gender composition of that group. Wade and Goldman (2006) found that in a review of intervention studies, participants' sex and the number of men in each intervention group were related to forgiveness-related outcomes. There was a relationship between sex and response to group treatment. The more men who were in a group, the more likely women were to diminish desires for revenge and the less likely men were to cultivate empathy for their offenders. Thus, women appeared to benefit from the increased presence of men in the groups. This finding could have important implications for religiously based forgiveness interventions, given the fact that women are much more likely to be religious than men so that participation in religious groups is heavily skewed by sex (Stark, 2002).

Conclusion

Despite the Divine initiative in the process of forgiveness and the ideals presented by each religious tradition, the actual response to divine forgiveness and the extension of forgiveness to others is the prerogative of the human actor who has the privilege to enact forgiveness within the human community. The religious ideals mean little if they do not give rise to personal and social change, and forgiveness is a universal requirement for healthy civil societies and mutual enrichment, particularly across ethnic and religious divides. According to the world religions, the cost of not forgiving others ranges from social exclusion to worse, genocide or outright demonization of "the other." The world religions can be the source of goodness and goodwill toward one another or be employed to legitimate horrendous violence to the human community. We end our chapter where we started, with the recognition that religions themselves don't act – it is the human person or community that acts in the world to forgive others. The religions of the world can provide the source and processes of forgiveness, but only as far as human beings and communities of faith avail themselves of religious truths and insights provided by those religions.

References

Ashton, M. C., & Lee, K. (2001). A theoretic basis for the major dimensions of personality. *European Journal of Personality, 15*, 327–353.

Brown, R. P., Collin, B. D., & Campbell, N. J. (2007). Fundamentalism and forgiveness. *Personality and Individual Differences, 43*, 1437–1447.

Coyle, C. T., & Enright, R. D. (1997). Forgiveness intervention with postabortion men. *Journal of Consulting and Clinical Psychology, 65*, 1042–1046.

Durkheim, É. (1965). *The elementary forms of religious life*(J. W. Swain, Trans.). New York: Free Press.

Eliade, M. (1957). *The sacred and the profane: The nature of religion*. Orlando, Florida: Harvest/HBJ Publishers.

Enright, R. D. (2001). *Forgiveness is a choice*. Washington, DC: American Psychological Association.

Freedman, S. R., & Enright, R. D. (1996). Forgiveness as an intervention goal with incest survivors. *Journal of Consulting and Clinical Psychology, 64*, 983–992.

Friedberg, J. P., Suchday, S., & Shelov, D. V. (2007). The impact of forgiveness on cardiovascular reactivity and recovery. *International Journal of Psychophysiology, 65*, 87–94.

Gordon, K. C., Baucom, D. H., & Snyder, D. K. (2005). Treating couples recovering from infidelity: An integrative approach. *Journal of Clinical Psychology, 61*, 1393–1140

Greer, T., Mitchell, M., Varan, V., & Watson, S. (2005). We are a religious people; we are a vengeful people. *Journal for the Scientific Study of Religion, 44*, 45–57.

Koch, C. J. (2004). *Journal keeping: Exploring a great spiritual practice*. Notre Dame: Sorin Books.

Krause, N., & Ellison, C. G. (2003). Forgiveness by God, forgiveness of others, and psychological well-being in late life. *Journal for the Scientific Study of Religion, 42*, 77–93.

Malinowski, B. (1935). *The foundations of faith and morals: An anthropological analysis of primitive beliefs and conduct with special reference to the fundamental problem of religion and ethics*. London: Oxford University Press.

McCullough, M. E., Bono, G., & Root, L. M. (2005). Religion and forgiveness. In R. F. Paloutzian & C. L. Park (Eds.), *Handbook of the psychology of religion and spirituality* (pp. 394–411). New York: The Guilford Press.

McCullough, M. E., & Hoyt, W. T. (2002). Transgression -related motivational dispositions: Personality substrates of forgiveness and their links to the Big Five. *Personality and Social Psychology Bulletin, 28*, 1556–1573.

McCullough, M. E., Pargament, K. I., & Thoresen, C. E. (Eds.). (2000). *Forgiveness: Theory, practice and research*. New York: Guilford Press.

McCullough, M. E., Root, L. M., & Cohen, A. D. (2006). Writing about the benefits of an interpersonal transgression facilitates forgiveness. *Journal of Consulting and Clinical Psychology, 74*, 887–897.

McCullough, M. E., & Willoughby, B. L. B. (2009). Religion, self-regulation, and self-control: associations, explanations, and implications. *Psychological Bulletin* (135), 69–93.

Moeshberger, S. L., Dixon, D. Niens, L., & Cairns, E. (2005). Forgiveness in Northern Ireland: A model for peace in the midst of the "troubles". *Peace and Conflict: Journal of Peace Psychology, 11*, 199–214.

Ogrodniczuk, J. S., Piper, W. E., & Joyce, A. S. (2004). Differences in men's and women's responses to short-term group psychotherapy. *Psychotherapy Research, 14*, 231–243.

Pargament, K. I. (1997). *The psychology of religion and coping*. New York: The Guilford Press.

Pargament, K. I. (2007). *Spiritually integrated psychotherapy*. New York: The Guilford Press.

Rachlin, H. (2000). *The science of self-control*. Cambridge, MA: Harvard University Press.

Rappaport, R. (1999). *Ritual and religion in the making of humanity*. Cambridge: Cambridge University Press.

Rye, M. S., & Pargament, K. I. (2002). Forgiveness and romantic relationships in college: Can it heal the wounded heart. *Journal of Clinical Psychology, 58*, 419–441.

Rye, M. S., Pargament, K. I., Pan, W., Yingling, D. W., Shogren, K. A., & Ito, M. (2005). Can group interventions facilitate forgiveness of an ex-spouse? A randomized clinical trial. *Journal of Consulting and Clinical Psychology, 73*, 880–892.

Stark, R. (2002). Physiology and faith: Addressing the 'universal' gender difference in religiousness? *Journal for the Scientific Study of Religion, 41*, 495–507.

Sosis, R. (2005). Does religion promote trust? The role of signaling, reputation, and punishment. *Interdisciplinary Journal of Research on Religion, 1*, 1–30.

Saucier, G., & Skrzypinska, K. (2006). Spiritual but not religious? Evidence for two independent dispositions. *Journal of Personality, 74*(5), 1257–1292.

Staub, E. (2005). Constructive rather than harmful forgiveness, reconciliation, and ways to promote them after genocide and mass killing. In E. L. Worthington, Jr. (Ed.), *Handbook of forgiveness* (pp. 443–459). New York: Routledge.

Volf, M. (2007). *The end of memory: Remembering rightly in a violent world*. Grand Rapids, MI: Eerdmans.

Worthington, E. L., Jr. (1998). The pyramid model of forgiveness: Some interdisciplinary speculations about unforgiveness and the promotion of forgiveness. In E. L. Worthington, Jr. (Ed.), *Dimensions of forgiveness: Psychological research & theological perspectives* (pp. 107–137). Radnor, PA: Templeton Foundation Press.

Wade, N. G., & Goldman, D. B. (2006). Sex, group composition, and the efficacy of group interventions to promote forgiveness. *Group Dynamics: Theory, Research, and Practice, 10*, 297–308.

Chapter 5
The Bullet and Its Meaning: Forgiveness, Nonforgiveness, and Their Confrontation

Raymond F. Paloutzian

One of the biggest challenges that a person can face is to forgive those who killed those they love. This is so whether the killer is a single individual acting alone, or a member of an opposing social class, nation, or bygone empire. In such a situation the pain is so great, the hurt goes so deep that if someone tells you that you should forgive, it twists the knife that is already deep inside your chest and causes it to go deeper, causing more grief and agony than before.

When I saw my sister murdered and my father wounded, I felt this kind of pain. When it was intimated and I believed that I was supposed to forgive the man who committed the murder, it simply made the pain worse. It took 17 years for me to figure out where I stood – to settle the conflict that lived inside my chest. It took the rest of my adult life to articulate the social psychological processes at the core of how humans confront the issues raised by such events and how we can construct new and different meaning(s) in life when we look these issues squarely in the face.

I have learned about the historical, cultural, ethnic, familial, and personal factors that affect our mental states and social worlds as I confronted the opposing desires inside myself to forgive and not to forgive. Through learning about the complex interactions of these factors, I began to understand why we feel a desire to forgive and at the same time are repelled by the thought of doing so. Being a victim can motivate a person toward opposite reactions. Growing up as an Armenian in the United States, I learned about the Ottoman Turkish genocide of the Armenians, and although our family was repulsed by what the Ottomans had done, we were equally repulsed at the thought of a counter-attack or revenge. Thus, I acquired intimate knowledge of how we come to feel, behave toward, and make decisions about the enemy, the perpetrator, the oppressor, and about how we can feel great conflict in relation to them. The principles and processes that are at work undergird this chapter. The integration of them cuts to the core of what it means to be a human – to love, lose, hate, and perhaps to forgive an individual, group, or nation. I learned that an attempt to forgive is always tentative and the outcome is always uncertain.

Ani Kalayjian, Raymond F. Paloutzian, *Forgiveness and Reconciliation*, Peace
Psychology Book Series, DOI 10.1007/978-1-4419-0181-1_5,
© Springer Science+Business Media, LLC 2009

The Dilemma

The concept of forgiveness reflects a high ideal of how people ought to feel or act toward an offender. It is a difficult concept to put into practice because it goes against our built-in propensity to either counter-attack an offender or seek retribution through group or societal means (Exline & Baumeister, 2000; McCullough, 2008). Why does forgiveness, which is explicitly promoted by many great religions (Farhadian & Emmons, Chapter 4, this volume; Rye, 2005; Rye et al., 2000) and is depicted as healthy by psychological research (Luskin, 2002; Worthington, 2005a), seem to run counter to our innate tendencies? What psychological processes operate to foster or inhibit forgiveness, and how do we choose from the many possible responses to human tragedy, i.e., when life hands us a dirty deal?

We can begin to elaborate upon these questions by using my own experience as a stripped-down, clear, basic case study. I wish to use the case of my sister's murder and the shooting of my father in order to begin to address the far more complicated dilemmas inherent in large-scale traumas. I do not mean to equate this one murder with the murder of many or to genocide. However, I do think that examining this case can reveal core processes related to forgiveness in brutal simplicity.

Murder and Forgiveness

In the case that follows, I conceal names of individuals and state agencies, locations, dates, and other nonsubstantive details for purposes of confidentiality and safety.

The Dirty Deal

When I was a young man, my sister was shot in the head by her husband; he also shot my father in the chest. I saw these events. My sister died immediately. My father lived to old age and carried the bullet slug in his arm until he died. The murder occurred after my sister and her husband had been married for only a few years. His violence toward her started small and escalated over time. It began with a slap, a shove, then he knocked her downstairs, hit her, beat her, tied her up with a rope and raped her, put a knife to her throat (for which he was brought to court; the judge let him go), and several months later he killed her with a .38 pistol.

One evening he knocked on the front door of our house, where my sister had come to live after coming to feel that it would be too dangerous to stay with him. When she was in sight, he pulled the gun out of his pocket and shot. The first bullets missed everybody. Then one bullet hit my father in the chest while my sister ran screaming. He chased her and then pinned her behind a door while my mother struggled to get the gun out of his hand. He shot my sister in the left temple. Her body fell over my mother and they both fell to the floor. As my sister's body lay across my mother's lap, my sister's body jerked badly while blood was gushing from her brains, mouth, and hole in her head, and spreading all over my mother's lap. I was 20; my sister was 22.

My sister's husband was tried in the downtown courthouse for one count of murder in the first degree and one count of attempted murder. The jury found him guilty of both charges. He was sentenced to life in prison. He was released after 12 years. Prior to his release, I had correspondence with the State Prison Authority asking that he never be released, indicating that my family was terrified of him. I highlighted that he had already demonstrated that he would perform violent acts against other people including us, and that although I understood the legal issue of offender's rights, there were cases such as this in which the offender's rights and the victim's rights were in conflict. I argued that, because of his demonstrated record of violent behavior especially toward us, the authorities should decide on behalf of the victim. I received a letter that said that the authorities had it on record to inform us 60 days in advance if he should ever be released. Later, he was released without informing us. My father was later told that it was for the offender's protection. The offender is now a senior citizen and has battered and harmed at least four wives and has threatened the lives of others.

How Ought One to Respond?

In the months and years following the event, I had great difficulty knowing how I was supposed to respond. What was I supposed to "do with" what had happened? My "moral" inclinations made me feel like I ought to want to forgive, but the devastation and horror of what I had seen and the deep loss I felt dictated the opposite – I hated the perpetrator and would have liked revenge. In my fantasies and dreams, I imagined opposite scenarios. In one case, he would die; sometimes I was his executioner. In the other case, he would show remorse and sorrow and I would be a helpful friend. I felt like I was supposed to express goodness, love, and forgiveness, while I actually felt hate, disgust, and revulsion toward him.

The sense that I ought to forgive was rooted deeply in my family. As a second-generation Armenian, I was acutely aware of the Ottoman Turkish genocide of the Armenians (Kupelian, Kalayjian, & Kassabian, 1998; Yacoubian, Chapter 14, this volume), but I also knew that not all Turks were bad. On the contrary, some Turks saved Armenian lives by hiding them in their homes and basements when the Ottoman soldiers came to kill them. My grandparents saw both sides. Thus, I was taught that prejudice, holding a grudge against a person merely because of the group he or she happened to be born into, is wrong. Hence if we err, we should do so on the side of human compassion, kindness, and forgiveness, not on the side of hatred. Forgiving "the Turks," as well as specific Turks, was a virtue.

In addition, forgiveness was a value in my own religious and philosophical outlook at that time. My understanding of it was shaped by a strong belief in Western individualism, the notion that each person can strive for and accomplish whatever he or she is willing to work hard for. Extending this idea to the process of forgiveness meant that I ought to be able to forgive the offender so long as I was willing to do so – since each person is in control of his or her own reactions. Each person, I believed, is responsible for what he or she does; thus I was responsible for whether or not, or to what degree, I forgave. The buck stopped with me. The sense that I could and should be in control of my feelings resulted in intense conflict between the desire to forgive and the desire not to.

Finally, after 17 years I knew where I stood. First, my struggle over whether to forgive and love my enemy or hate him ended. I decided that I did not want to love my enemy. Second, I decided to keep the desires I had that my sister would still be alive and that the prison authorities would have kept the murderer in prison, instead of letting those desires go as a way of gaining comfort. I decided that my sister's murder was not for sale. The outcome was that I gave up trying to control my feelings, simply accepted them, and the dilemma was resolved. As a psychologist, I never thought that this was an ideal resolution. It would have been an interesting puzzle to integrate the different motivations that came from the two sides of myself, the victim and the psychologist, but that was not possible. The position I came to was the only stance my victim self could accept with integrity. As a consequence, I lived with the tension between them.

The psychologist side of me kept up with the latest research on forgiveness, which began to appear in significant amounts approximately a decade ago (Enright & North, 1998; McCullough, Pargament, & Thoresen, 2000a). The literature typically placed the emphasis on forgiveness at the intra-individual level. One common idea was that the victim could generate forgiving attitudes and feelings toward the perpetrator within themselves without communicating with or acknowledgment from the perpetrator. Although we know that victims are helped by such cognitive and affective changes (Borris, 2006), I thought that this idea was inadequate or incomplete because it seemed that something more than only a change inside of one's own mind was needed to fully work through the traumas and pain. Some kind of interpersonal communication or behavioral transaction seemed necessary for complete forgiveness to occur.

As a result of editing this book and learning much from its authors, I came to realize that the individualist Western approach is not adequate when a person is faced with the realities of victimhood. At such times, people need others to guide and support them when trying to obtain justice. This suggests that alone, one can go only so far down the road of forgiveness. To go further, there needs to be a real interpersonal transaction between the victim and the perpetrator. And the effects can be further enhanced with social supports from one's group, government, or applicable entity of authority (cf., Nwoye, Chapter 8, this volume; Rutayisire, Chapter 11, this volume).

Forgiveness Shades of Gray

In the real world we must live with murky variations of concepts and categories that can initially seem clear and simple, such as "forgiveness." In life, forgiveness is a process that people have to work through over time, and victims can exist in any number of places during that process. This process is comprised of many dimensions (Worthington, 1998). Each dimension falls on a continuum on which a person can be relatively high or low, with infinite variations in between. As examples, where a person is in the forgiveness process depends on where they fall along a number of continua such as the following:

1. the degree to which the emphasis is on feelings *versus* behaviors;
2. if the emphasis is on feelings, the degree to which the person is encouraged to generate feelings of forgiveness *versus* identify and accept his or her feelings whatever they might be;
3. the degree to which the process is comprehensive in the scope of offenses that it covers;
4. the degree to which the process is closer in time to beginning *versus* ending;
5. the degree to which the process has come to resolution or closure;
6. the degree to which its outcome is positive *versus* negative;
7. the degree to which it is or was public *versus* private.

The number of combinations of "where someone might be" on the forgiveness continua can be generated by combining all the variations of the above-mentioned factors. Because of the myriad combinations that are possible, our understanding of the forgiveness dilemma for one person can be very incomplete; and if this is a shortcoming in our understanding in the case of one person, it is a far greater shortcoming in the case of a nation. What is needed for forgiveness may not be clear or not be possible. Therefore, an unambiguous process and conclusion is more likely the exception than the rule. In ambiguous cases, the dilemmas involved in forgiveness can seem especially confusing and magnified.

Below are some issues that should be considered as we make our way through the circumstances that confront us in the task of forgiving. In particular, I extend a point inherent in number 2 above because I found that distinction especially hard to negotiate. The difficulty has to do with the difference between accepting my feelings because they were accurate and honest *versus* arriving at a positive feeling of forgiveness because it was something I was supposed to do.

Feelings, Forgiveness Feelings, and Actions

Emphasis on Feelings. As suggested by the list above, scholars and practitioners of forgiveness grapple with whether forgiveness is best defined as attitudinal, emotional, cognitive, or behavioral (Enright, 2001; McCullough, Bono, & Root, 2005; McCullough, Pargament, & Thoresen, 2000b; Worthington, 2005b). Undoubtedly, in its fullest form, forgiveness involves a complicated mix of these dimensions. How one views this issue affects one's belief about whether communication with the offender is necessary and the degree to which an emphasis is best placed on how the victim feels or what the victim does. If the emphasis in treatment is on emotions, then it is crucial to distinguish between encouraging forgiveness feelings in particular and promoting acceptance of all feelings whatever they may be. A victim can get confused if this distinction is not clear.

Clinical and counseling psychology literature on forgiveness often puts an emphasis on the feelings that the victim must accept and work through (Enright, 2001; McCullough et al., 2000a; Worthington, 2005a). This is very important if the person is going to go on and live comfortably. Wherever the person may be along the forgiveness continua, it is important that he or she is encouraged to accept his or her feelings "as they are." Accepting feelings is one step that may bring some relief. In many cases, however, full resolution may require more than just accepting feelings. More is often not possible if the offender is unavailable or the risk of confrontation is too great. Because of these issues, many victims may never have a full sense of resolution.

Toward a Behavioral Bottom Line. Now let me take the challenge of forgiveness one step further by restating it in more concrete, behavioral terms, while still acknowledging the important role of feelings. If you "really" forgive the offender then how do you feel and what do you do? Do you feel compassion for the perpetrator(s)? Do you invite them over for tea? Do you inculcate positive attitudes and/or motives to help them or to promote their well-being? Can you still want them dead and at the same time arrive at a state of forgiveness of them? Views of forgiveness that separate feelings of forgiveness from forgiving behavior (e.g., Borris, 2006) would seem to imply or at least allow for this.

My journey has led me to highlight the bottom line question, "What behaviors do I perform if I forgive the offender that are different from the behaviors that I perform if I do not forgive the offender?" Behavior is the acid test of forgiveness in exactly the same way that it is the acid test of love. It pushes the issue of someone purporting to forgive someone else to its limits because it asks what the forgiver will actually do, rather than merely dealing with changes in the person's attitudes, thoughts, or feelings.

Considering this behavioral emphasis, perhaps people attempt to forgive not only for the sake of their own peace of mind but also for the sake of establishing or at least attempting to partially restore a relationship with the offender, larger group, community, or state. Thus, you may forgive *for* yourself – you can go some distance toward feeling more comfortable by accepting your feelings or thinking differently about the offender. But you may also forgive *not only* for yourself. You may also forgive for others and for the sake of your relationship with them and possible future relationships. Therefore, this means that attempting forgiveness in a totally self-contained way may be psychologically incomplete. Forgiveness in the fullest sense would seem to require the active participation of all sides.

Western Individualism. In individualistic societies such as the United States we place most of the responsibility for forgiveness on the shoulders of the victim. We do this on the assumption and with the hope that he or she can (and should) find the emotional resources to forgive. Western individualism has led to the view that internal attitudinal and emotional changes can occur even though external reality may not change. Plainly stated, in this view, the reality of the situation depends on how you look at it – how you cognitively appraise it. The emphasis on the attitudes of the victim in many cases simply places an extra burden on the shoulders of victims that makes it harder for them to find closure in the wake of being innocently harmed.

Although the appraisal process is essential to forgiveness, there is a drawback to this view. It implies that if you do not forgive, it is your fault – as if reality is only in your mind, perceptions, and appraisals. But our problems are not only in our minds; they do exist in external reality. Further, the drawbacks that can result from an over-individualistic emphasis can be exacerbated by certain religions that teach that the only thing a person needs in order to forgive is faith in God. In such cases, those who are unable to forgive (whether affectively, attitudinally, motivationally, or behaviorally) may have to ultimately forgive themselves for failing to forgive the offender.

Cross-Cultural Perspective. An emphasis on individual forgiveness in the West contrasts with the way forgiveness processes are viewed and implemented in other cultures. Some African cultures involve group processes whereby the offender is expected to give a public confession, show evidence of genuine remorse, and commit him or herself to making amends. These displays are accompanied by the victim showing contriteness and by publicly accepting the apology and terms (e.g., Nwoye, Chapter 8, this volume). It is a group and interpersonal, not an intra-individual, process that helps forgiveness emerge in a more complete form. Perhaps such a procedure meets needs to confront the perpetrator that victims may automatically bring to the group setting. For example, a victim may need to feel protected, may need to hear the offender confess, and may need some kind of restitution. We examine each of these below.

A Bilateral Transaction Ideal. Forgiveness in its most complete form is an interpersonal bilateral transaction that includes a personal decision and a public commitment to behave in a different way than one might have initially been inclined to do right after the transgression. Just as with the offense itself, with forgiveness, it is what one ultimately does that counts. I believe this principle applies whether we are talking about forgiving one person for a single offense or about forgiving a nation for offenses whose trauma has been transmitted across generations (e.g., Brown et al., Chapter 13, this volume; Cohen, Chapter 9, this volume; LaMar, Chapter 10, this volume; Yacoubian, Chapter 14, this volume).

Examples of Victims' Needs

Protection from Perpetrator. If this is accomplished (e.g., by death of the offender, offender in prison for life with no possibility of parole, offender lives on the other side of the Earth, an army stands in between "them" and "us"), then a victim may be more able to consider some level of forgiveness. So long as I continue to be or feel at risk, I am likely to be self-protective and keep an implicit or explicit counter-attack highest on my response hierarchy. For example, both the Palestinians and the Israelis feel forever unsafe from each other and each continues to attack and counter-attack the other. Neither side seems any closer to agreeing to cease hostilities, let alone to forgiving the other, than they were during the second half of the last century. In such cases, perhaps forgiving is likely to be interpreted as a sign of weakness or vulnerability, thus inadvertently (and incorrectly) appearing to the opponent as if one is on the verge of losing face and giving in – something that would probably result in a very unsafe feeling.

Need for Confession. Some amount of forgiveness can be achieved if the offender never confesses to the crime. However, a higher degree of forgiveness seems more likely if the perpetrator confesses, demonstrates genuine remorse, and takes action to make amends. In some cases confession may not be possible, such as those in which the perpetrators are dead. In those cases, some sort of acknowledgment of the crime or discussion by the agent-descendents of the perpetrators may help facilitate the forgiveness process. Dialogue processes that bring opposing parties together for structured discussions (Tint, Chapter 17, this volume) also seem to be helpful in moving both sides toward forgiveness and reconciliation. Such a process could not occur, however, without some agreed-upon baseline for confession, acknowledgment, and honest communication. The more this occurs, the more forgiveness is possible.

Without this kind of openness and honesty, the victim is left with no communication, no consideration, no closure. That is what my family got from the offender and the state. Complete closure is not possible without direct, honest communication and remorse from the offender(s) themselves. Without it, the victim is left forever, to some extent, hanging – even though some degree of comfort may be gained by inculcating genuine feelings of forgiveness.

Amends and Equity. The notion of equity means that the scales have to be balanced, that the playing field be leveled, that there be payment for an offense. Equity means fairness. This means that because an offense cannot be unperformed, some kind of active performance by the offender is needed to address the grievance created by the offense. This is why methods of dealing with victimhood at only an intra-individual level can, in my view, help only partially. Such methods omit the interpersonal transaction needed to go further through the forgiveness process. The greatest degree of equity can be attained when such transactions occur and when the offender makes amends in concrete ways.

In a case such as that of my family, one can forgive partially perhaps, but not fully, because neither the offender nor the society in which the crime occurred provided the necessary means for doing so. Victims can forgive to a greater degree along a greater number of continua if, e.g., the state does its part to set the needed processes in motion. This requires apprehending the offender, bringing the offender and the victim together, and arranging for systematic, long-term dialogue with the goal of righting the wrong in ways that are identifiable and accountable.

In order to facilitate equity and amends-making, governments should modify laws and procedures that imply that a crime committed is only or primarily against the state. This is not so! A crime violates the laws of the state, yes, but it is also committed against specific victims. It is they who have been harmed. The victims deserve to have their government follow procedures that encourage offenders to admit wrongs, not only to the state but also to the victims.

Conclusions

The above discussion leads to at least four conclusions. First, a victim is more likely to forgive to a greater degree if the offender admits to having committed the crime, confesses, shows remorse, asks for forgiveness, and makes amends. Second, a victim is more able and apt to forgive if he or she feels safe from future harm. This is more likely if there are public safety policies and procedures in place to ensure that the victims are safe. Third, because a crime is both a violation of a public law and an act against individuals, forgiveness is easier if the victims see their government initiate a process of restitution and reconciliation. How many of the above are at work in my families' case? And in the other cases written in this book?

Forgiveness and Reconstruction of Meaning

Finally, the highest examples of forgiveness show it not as simply a positive emotional or mental state for one's own psychic or health benefit or as a motivation toward behavioral change. It includes emotions, mental states, and motivations, but it takes shape in its fullest form as an interpersonal process that unfolds over time and may continue indefinitely. This can best develop if it is understood as a transaction between people who are at odds with each other but who decide to work together as collaborators for a better, more peaceful future. Thus, as a process it is open-ended and its outcome is uncertain.

It makes little sense to think in terms of simple categories like "Forgiveness Yes" or "Forgiveness No." Our knowledge and the probability that we will live in peace will go a lot further if we instead understand that this is a dimension with saintly, rare, and complete instances of forgiveness at one extreme and hostile, grudge-nurturing, death-promoting instances of nonforgiveness at the other. For most of us, our response to being harmed is probably somewhere in the middle.

The process of reconstructing a life and worldview that includes forgiveness is difficult. It requires one to not merely create a new personal identity but to construct a new meaning of self that does not include the old self, but includes the *loss* of the old self. The absence of the old self is always present, and any accurate meaning following the loss requires recognition and acceptance of this. An understanding of these processes and resolution of the issues can lead to an ultimate challenge, i.e., to demonstrate forgiveness by behavior just as one demonstrates love by behavior. An attempt to forgive ought not to be undertaken with a positive illusion but with knowledge that it is done with the hope of peace.

References

Borris, E. R. (2006). *Forgiveness: a 7-step program for letting go of anger and bitterness.* New York: McGraw-Hill.

Enright, R. D. (2001). *Forgiveness is a choice: a step-by-step process for resolving anger and restoring hope.* Washington, DC: American Psychological Association.

Enright, R. D., & North, J. (Eds.). (1998). *Exploring forgiveness*. Madison, WI: University of Wisconsin Press.

Exline, J. J., & Baumeister, R. F. (2000). Expressing forgiveness and repentance: benefits and barriers. In M. E. McCullough, K. I. Pargament, & C. E. Thoresen (Eds.), *Forgiveness: theory, research and practice* (pp. 133–155). New York: The Guilford Press.

Kupelian, D., Kalayjian, A. S., & Kassabian, A. (1998). The Turkish genocide of the Armenians: Continuing effects on survivors and their families eight decades after massive Trauma. In Y. Danieli (Ed.), *International handbook of multigenerational legacies of Trauma* (pp. 191–210). New York: Plenum Press.

Luskin, F. (2002). *Forgive for good: A proven prescription for health and happiness*. New York: Harper Collins.

McCullough, M. E. (2008). *Beyond revenge: The evolution of the forgiveness instinct*. San Francisco: Jossey-Bass.

McCullough, M. E., Pargament, K. I., & Thoresen, C. E. (Eds.). (2000a). *Forgiveness: Theory, practice and research*. New York: Guilford Press.

McCullough, M. E., Pargament, K. I., & Thoresen, C. E. (2000b). The psychology of forgiveness: History, conceptual issues, and overview. In M. E. McCullough, K. I. Pargament, & C. E. Thoresen (Eds.), *Forgiveness: Theory, research, and practice* (pp. 1–14). New York: Guilford.

McCullough, M. E., Bono, G., & Root, L. M. (2005). Religion and forgiveness. In R. F. Paloutzian & C. L. Park (Eds.), *Handbook of the psychology of religion and spirituality* (pp. 394–411). New York: Guilford Press.

Rye, M. S. (2005). The religious path toward forgiveness. *Mental Health, Religion, and Culture, 8*(3), 205–215.

Rye, M. S., Pargament, K. I., Ali, M. A., Beck, G. L., Dorff, E. N., Hallisey, C., et al. (2000). Religious perspectives on forgiveness. In M. E. McCullough, K. I. Pargament, & C. E. Thoresen (Eds.), *Forgiveness: theory, research, and practice* (pp. 17–40). New York: Guilford.

Worthington, E. L., Jr. (Ed.). (1998). *Dimensions of forgiveness*. Radnor, PA: Templeton.

Worthington, E. L., Jr. (Ed.). (2005a). *Handbook of forgiveness*. New York: Routledge.

Worthington, E. L. (2005b). Initial questions about the art and science of forgiving. In E. Worthington (Ed.), *Handbook of forgiveness* (pp. 1–13). New York: Routledge.

Section II
Individual and Interpersonal Levels

Chapter 6
Forgiveness and Reconciliation: Essential to Sustaining Human Development

Sharon Davis Massey

This chapter highlights the inextricably interwoven benefits to personal, interpersonal, communal, and societal development of reconciliation and forgiveness, two interrelated processes which help to restore trust, reinstate integrity, and foster security within the individual, dyad, family, community, and larger interpersonal and social systems. Together they help to make continuing interaction with others a safe-enough affair so that a couple or family can support the development of individual members and so that a community or larger group can function adequately to nurture the persons, families, and ethnic and other identity groups that compose it.

Social Ruptures and Trauma Threaten Human Development

Traumatic ruptures in relationships between individuals and within and between groups occur at all levels in human systems and quickly spread from the level at which they originate, impacting others. This "ripple effect" often endures over time and across generations, as illustrated in the vignettes below.

Fallout from Nuclear Trauma Continues

One nation ended a war that cost many lives in several nations by dropping atomic bombs on two large cities in an "enemy" country, killing great numbers of noncombatant civilians, i.e., women, children, the elderly (Hersey, 1986; Walker, 2005). The signature image of the mushroom-shaped cloud that rose above Hiroshima, repeatedly replayed in newsreels by the "winning" nation, the United States, as a symbol of its superior strength and its capacity to ensure the safety of its own citizens and those of its allies, became over decades the feature of nightmares for both children and adults, ordinary citizens, and policy makers, in the victorious nation and allied countries and in others considered friendly, neutral, and hostile to their concerns (Sagan, 1995). Perpetual unease between nations that do and do not yet have nuclear arms speaks volumes to the need for finding less traumatic ways of resolving very serious rifts at the international level.

Ani Kalayjian, Raymond F. Paloutzian, *Forgiveness and Reconciliation*, Peace Psychology Book Series, DOI 10.1007/978-1-4419-0181-1_6, © Springer Science+Business Media, LLC 2009

Colonization Continues to Affect Colonizer and Colonized

In a different display of power, several nations embarked earlier on a course of imperialism, colonizing people from other cultures across large swaths of several continents. Colonization, too, proved to be a two-way street in which "foreign" cultures, languages, people, and the problems spawned by enforced inequality in human relationships spilled across national and cultural boundaries and spread, both in lands that were subjugated and in those of the colonizer (Fanon, 2005, 1961; Memmi, 1991/1965). Institutional racism, poverty, unequal political power, inadequate educational and employment opportunities, and distrust of each other's cultural ways were built into the failed policies of colonization and remain today as continuing threats to personal, interpersonal, and communal development. They are exacerbated in areas where slavery and apartheid were used to further reinforce dominance by one group over another. Recently second-generation youth (descendents of persons colonized in the Maghreb and sub-Saharan regions of Africa), now living in France with their families as naturalized but unwelcome citizens, have protested inequities they, their families, and communities still endure.

A Demobilized Child Soldier Cannot Go Home Again

A child in Sierra Leone, kidnapped at age 6 from his home, was forcibly "recruited" into military service and made to engage in terrifyingly violent acts against his own people by persons wishing to effect change at the national level (Singer, 2005). As a 13-year-old "veteran" with 7 years of military experience his unit was demobilized. He wanted to return home and to go to school, but feared realistically that his family and community might be unwilling to forgive him or to reconcile with the events that made him a soldier at age 6.

Community, family, and personal development are interrupted in scenarios such as those described above, as groups are subjugated, lives are lost, personal relationships broken, cities shattered, families and villages scattered. In these vignettes we see that the present world offers multiple reasons for learning about reconciliation and forgiveness, the maintenance and restoration of positive relationships, reunification, and the construction of peace.

Social Support Helps Keep Development on Track

The integrity and positive functioning of all support systems are needed for optimal human development (Winnicott, 1995). Families can best move forward in their own development and in meeting the developmental needs of their members in a peaceful community that can provide for the basic human security needs: food, housing, education, job opportunities, and mental and physical health care (Nef, 2006; Thomas, 2000). Conflict co-opts energy, focus, and supplies needed for sustaining growth and disrupts and often destroys the human networks that support personal and collective survival and growth.

In the twenty-first century, children are increasingly exposed to and impacted by war. A child may be buffered from irreparable harm through secure attachment to an early caretaker prior to a disruptive or traumatic event or by an ongoing relationship with supportive adults during and after exposure to trauma (Macksoud, Aber, & Cohn, 1996). In their work with nursery-school children during and in the aftermath of bombings in London in World War II, Freud and Burlingham (1943) noted that children whose parents helped them modulate the strong emotions aroused by trauma fared better in terms of mental health than children whose parents or other adult caretakers did not. Unfortunately civilians, parents, and children alike, who used to account for 5% of war casualties, now constitute 90% (Machel, 2001).

A Parent Helps Her Child to Reconcile

A 12-year-old Muslim boy in Bosnia was injured when a shell fired by "the enemy" entered his home (Raymond & Raymond, 2000). His mother took him immediately to the medical center, where he underwent surgery. She stayed with him through the night and after the surgery told him that his arm had to be amputated (just above the elbow) and that he should not be upset about it. With her support he reconciled to his new circumstances, did not personalize his misfortune, and said he did not wish for this to happen to other children. The meanings he assigned to this experience did not include shame, self-blame, or hatred for others:

> If you consider what could have happened, I am lucky to be alive. I have some use of my arm. I can work with it and get around. ... I am not to blame for it. But what can you do? It happened. Shells don't have eyes. What can I say? It happened. (p. 21)

Observers felt it was unlikely this child would grow up seeking to inflict such an injury on others.

Research confirms (Siegel, 1999) that when caretakers are attuned and responsive to their children's emotional states and help them interpret challenging situations in ways that amplify positive states and reduce negative ones, the child learns to modulate his or her mental state, develops trust, feels secure, experiences a positive sense of self and others, and learns how to build and maintain positive relationships.

Dialog Helps to Build Community and Construct Peace

Cross-cultural research (Moghaddam, 1998) indicates that in *all* cultures ongoing dialog in which participants speak truthfully about their diverse experiences and listen with trust to one another's divergent views is essential to the positive function of groups and to the maintenance of community.

In Colombia the father and a female, teenage cousin of a 14-year-old youth were shot to death by one of many armed groups, guerilla and paramilitary organizations and the army, fighting in a seemingly endless war (Cameron, 2001). The father, a dentist, and the cousin, who was acting as his receptionist, had no relationship to the hostilities. The youth's only "transgression" against the attackers was his involvement in the Children's Movement for Peace. Following their violent deaths, this young man, after significant internal struggle, decided to honor their memory by continuing to work for peace. No doubt the adolescent's capacity to reconcile with the reality of the death of his father and cousin, to work through his anger and initial wish to retaliate, and to continue his work for peace are related to his having so often engaged in dialog – with other similarly traumatized children and adults through the Children's Movement for Peace in Colombia – about the desperate need for and positive gains that can only come from constructing a peaceful community that includes and benefits all parties.

We see in the vignettes above that there are multitudinous ways in which the richly interwoven, resilient, and durable social supports essential to sustaining human development that are normally available, when all goes well in everyday family and community life, can be torn asunder. Traumatic ruptures can happen in relationships at any systemic level and promptly spread to and negatively impact other levels. Without intervention their repercussions can continue, over time and across generations, to diminish personal development and to foster societal regression (Bowen, 1976). Fortunately, therapeutic intervention and dialog that gives voice and affords genuine interest in their perspectives to all parties affected by a problem can lead the way toward reconciliation, forgiveness, and the healing of trauma-affected persons and communities (Akbar & Forst, 2005; Davoine & Gaudillière, 2004; Hellinger, 2003).

Reconciliation and Forgiveness Give Rise to and Arise from Security

In humans the process of reconciliation appears developmentally linked to the early, natural phenomenon of the parent or caretaker's helping a small child to calm, *to conciliate*, during or following a period of threat, i.e., to again feel peaceful, comfortable in one's skin, and in relation to self and significant others, thus lending to the disconsolate child, as it were, the adult's own sense of competence or ability to navigate in a world that presents challenges which are overwhelming to the child, until the child over time grows to acquire that capacity. An early parent–child relationship in which the child has basic trust (Erikson, 1997) that the caretaker will dependably attend to his or her security needs provides the child multiple experiences of regaining a sense of composure, calm, and self-regulation after a perceived threat to the self. The child internalizes a model of comfortable connection with another who can be counted on for nurturance and protection. This, I think, is the ontological basis for the felt need experienced by adults for reconciliation in the aftermath of emotional and interpersonal disruption.

The felt threat may be to oneself or to the self–other relationship and can be caused by oneself or by someone or something else. In either case the felt need to exert some effort to "right" the order that has been upset, to reestablish a sense of personal comfort, and to connect with others on whom one can rely over time, with whom one can share one's subjectivity (Stern, 1985) and explore what meanings to assign to personal or shared experiences (Siegel, 1999) have their origins in the universal developmental need of children for secure attachment to a protective and benevolent caretaker (Bowlby, 1988).

Ivan and Catherine Nagy (Ducommun-Nagy, 2002) remind us that not only children but all humans are characterized by an "ontic" dimension; that is to say, we do not and cannot exist apart from others. Human viability is dependent upon attachment. Optimal development is facilitated by the ability to establish and maintain mutually supportive links with other persons and groups (Massey & Combs, 2002). Ruptures in significant relationships at all systemic levels threaten personal and group security, thus ongoing development. Faulty relationships both create and are generated by insecurity.

Reconciliation is a natural process engaged in by children and adults seeking to regain a sense of unencumbered relationship to self and others and wishing to come to terms with an event or interpersonal rift that has been experienced as threatening to the self or to a valued relationship. Conciliation has much to do with the capacity for self-soothing. When the capacity of an ordinarily self-assured child to re-group after an unsettling circumstance has been exceeded, the thoughtful caretaker intervenes, providing the secure psychological base (Bowlby, 1988), interpretive dialog (Siegel, 1999), and conciliatory intent needed to enable the child to reconcile in the aftermath of the temporarily paralyzing event and to move forward. *Forgiveness* includes giving up rancor and the desire to punish or to exact a penalty in relation to an event or from a person who has caused someone discomfort or harm. Reconciliation and forgiveness are recursively influential. The search for and beginnings of reconciliation open the door to forgiveness. The offer and receipt of forgiveness consolidate, deepen, and help to finalize reconciliation.

Forgiveness and Reconciliation Are Common, Essential Everyday Processes

As St. Exupéry (1970/1943) noted, what is essential may be invisible to the eye. Often what is most ordinary is most difficult to see, therefore to understand and to fully appreciate. Because they are essential to the maintenance of ongoing relationships, the two processes of reconciliation and forgiveness are ubiquitous. In the context of a secure relationship they may go scarcely noticed by the participants, being so integral a part of their ongoing interactions. Yet they are precisely the part that helps to maintain a shared sense of security in having a trustworthy, reciprocally valued relationship. Reconciliation and forgiveness are grounded in the mutual investment of the participants in the relationship and emerge from their attentiveness to mending the small ruptures that inevitably occur as two or more persons navigate their way forward in their personal and shared lives. In parent–child relationships they are foundational to children's learning appropriate interpersonal behavior as well as to their figuring out how to cope with unsettling interpersonal or external events.

Reconciliation and forgiveness are essential to supportive relationships. Reconciliation and forgiveness are at the heart of what Kegan (1982) calls *natural therapy*, i.e., the everyday personal and interpersonal problem-solving that occurs when people seek advice from and make use of the support of friends, family members, coworkers, or other trusted acquaintances. They provide the everyday means of coping with life's smaller disruptions and of getting beyond troublesome disappointments in our relationships with ourselves and with others. *Unnatural therapy* is Kegan's term for clients' working through personal, interpersonal, or family issues with a psychotherapist. The goal of unnatural therapy is not different from that of natural therapy. The intent is to return persons who are not functioning adequately vis-à-vis their natural support systems, and vice versa, back to these natural supports as soon as they can be successfully re-linked in a way that is functional for and supportive of both.

When relationships are strained or broken due to smaller or larger relational injustices, ethical balance can be restored and reconciliation and forgiveness constructed through informal dialog with friends or family, or in a more formal therapy setting with the assistance of a trained professional (Boszormenyi-Nagy & Krasner, 1986; Hellinger, 2003). With provision of security, they can also be negotiated wherever conflicted groups of persons agree to meet with the intent of collaboratively coming to terms with the repercussions of trauma caused by their own or others' harmful behavior (Akbar & Forst, 2005; Allen, 2005; Tutu, 1999).

Psychotherapy is normatively sought when interpersonal and family discussion is unavailable, has proven insufficient for resolving the problem at hand, or is felt to be unsafe. Continuing debilitative effects of trauma on persons and consequently on their relationships with others may best be addressed through psychotherapy (Apfel & Bennett, 1996; Solomon & Siegel, 2003). When larger systems, such as ethnic groups or nations, are in conflict and fail to approach reconciliation, intervention from regional, national, or international bodies, creative diplomacy, and the assistance of nongovernmental organizations can be helpful (MacLean, 2006; Montvale, 2006; Nef, 2006). Typically, negotiations for reconciliation and re-establishment of peaceful relationships are entered into by partners of equal power and status (two children who fought at school, a husband and wife who wish to overcome a marital argument, two countries settling a border dispute). When this proves inadequate, a facilitator with higher status or power may be invoked: a parent or teacher on behalf of school children, a marital counselor or divorce mediator on behalf of a sparring couple, and a regional or international group on behalf of quarreling nations.

The Self, Support Systems, and Security Are Shaped by Context

Self does not exist as a separate entity or in a vacuum, but arises in interaction with a specific and ever-evolving ecological context of interlocking support systems without which life cannot be sustained (Bronfenbrenner, 1986; Winnicott, 1995).

Humans are dependent, first for survival and then for ongoing security, on the provision of physical protection, food, shelter, and the trustworthy and caring attention of others who are instrumental in supplying these (Maslow, 1943; Thomas, 2000). It is obvious that infants and small children are dependent on the beneficence of their caretakers and contexts for survival. The relative ease and consistency, or lack of the same, with which caretakers and contexts are able to note and respond to infants' and children's needs determines whether they survive, their quality of life, and the parameters of their development (Davies, 2004). It is commonly accepted that children are dependent for life and well-being on the persons and systems that support them and that they learn the ways of their parents or other caretakers, i.e., of their support systems. What is often overlooked, in terms of giving priority to and assigning responsibility for the upkeep and repair of human systems, is that in this regard we are all children.

Self, Other, Community, and Context Are Interdependent

All human support systems are inextricably interlinked in a delicate ecology (Martínez, 1997; Wilber, 1985) such that when one support system is harmed the others suffer as well, as we have seen in the vignettes that introduced this chapter. Each individual is not only a complex biochemical, psychosocial, and spiritual being (Kalayjian, 2002; Martínez, 1997) and a functional unity; personal well-being and developmental progression are dependent on one's staying comfortably positioned in the context of a nested series of well-functioning, interdependent, and ever-evolving support systems (Winnicott, 1995).

In a linear mode of thought the concepts of *self* and *other* and of *individual* and (any given) *group* are somewhat carelessly cast as opposites, therefore conceptualized as not overlapping, or as not participating in one another, which of course is not true. Each of us participates in many groups: the family, the community, and others. One does not become somehow "not oneself" when also functioning effectively as a group member. Pressing what needs to be an ecological and systemic way of understanding human reality into a linear mode leads to inappropriate "either–or" conceptualizations, when "both–and" constructions better represent reality. Human existence is dependent on interaction of and with others and cannot be sustained without group effort. Awareness of *self* emerges in the context of relationships with *others* and cannot happen otherwise. A secure sense of self arises in positive early relationships (Mead, 1964; Stern, 1985).

Because one's personal development and that of others is interdependent, each of us enhances our own potential through contributing to the positive function of all systems, from smallest to largest, in which we hold membership. Others' well-being and positive function redound to one's own benefit, and vice versa. Self and other are two poles of a dyadic unity (Buber, 1970). Separately we do not survive (Ducommun-Nagy, 2002). Self and society are, similarly, inseparable (Pfuetze, 1954). Without community, individuals, and ultimately the human species, cannot endure.

Insecurity Creates Obstacles to Reconciliation and Forgiveness

Basic trust in self and others (Erikson, 1997) and authentic dialog among all parties involved (Akbar & Forst, 2005; Boszormenyi-Nagy & Krasner, 1986) are essential to building, maintaining, and restoring functionality and ethical balance in relationships. They also play key roles in the desire and capacity to reconcile with or to forgive oneself and others. Trauma destroys trust in persons who previously felt secure (Van der Kolk, 2003). Insecurity in traumatized adults is often passed to their offspring (Hesse, Main, Abrams, & Rifkin, 2003; Harkness, 1993). Persons whose family legacy includes distrust and dysfunctional relationships will have difficulty trusting others' overtures toward reconciliation and forgiveness.

It is especially challenging to reconcile with intentionally or regularly perpetrated injustice, as that can be experienced as meaning that the person targeted is not accepted or valued, perhaps not even "seen," by those who caused the harm. The experience of being devalued can lead one to retaliatory devaluation of the person or group that harmed oneself and contribute to negative, tit-for-tat perceptions and interactions. If boundaries around identity are rigidly set, security threatened, and groups engaged in tit-for-tat response patterns, each seeking to dominate the other, the risk of serious human rights violations is heightened. Concern for the security of one's own group may become inflamed and animosity toward the out-group equally passionate (Kunda, 2001).

It is thought that soldiers who commit atrocities are led to do so by ceding morality to the group (Nadelson, 2005). The most violent criminals justify their violence by comparing their actions to an internal or "phantom" community of violent others to which they feel they belong (Athens, 2003). Such social supports can be virulent. Personal *and* interpersonal security need to be the norm if support systems are to be protective both of self and of others.

Love and acceptance engender security. Prejudice, hatred, and physical harm arouse fear and externalizing responses (anger, retaliation), particularly in males, or internalizing responses (depression, mental illness), more often in women (Perry, 1997). While hurdles such as those described above can be overcome, they constitute some of the factors that make reconciliation and forgiveness more difficult to construct for some persons and in relation to some antisocial acts. Personal experiences and social contexts shape one's approach to interpersonal transactions, including whether one is inclined to move toward, away from, or against antisocial behavior and whether or not one chooses to engage in reconciliation or forgiveness.

Without positive intervention, negative patterns tend to endure and can amplify (Bowen, 1976). A leader wishing to exploit and direct the energy of an ethnic group may encourage them to increasingly identify with a shared past trauma (Volkan, 2004). Greater fusion with one another based on identity with the trauma can increase emotionality at the expense of rationality, reduce rational approaches to problem resolution, and trigger emotional cutoff between in-group and out-group and between conflicted members of the same group. "Societal regression" such as this heightens the potential for conflict (Bowen, 1976). Heightened emotionality and physiological arousal decrease the capacity to calm and tolerance for verbal discussion and collaborative problem-solving, which are needed both for maintaining community and for reconciliation in the aftermath of hostility. The person who cannot calm has less capacity for constructively confronting perceived threat to the self and cherished others, thus diminished incentive to reason with others before succumbing to terror or resorting to violence (Perry, 1997). Hyperarousal, self-aggrandizement, anger, poor impulse control, and violence are among the symptoms that result from trauma. Ross (2003) aptly describes a "trauma vortex" into which traumatized societies can be led and helpfully describes the role media personnel, who are vulnerable to being drawn into the vortex as they cover traumatic events, can play in helping to heal fear, terror, and violence.

Security Is Essential to Reconciliation

A troubled child who is securely attached can be calmed by a word or gesture indicating that a parent understands and empathizes with the youngster's discomfort. A small child who was angry with a parent moments earlier may then seek comfort in the parent's embrace and ask to perch for awhile on the parent's lap, to calm and to reconcile. An adolescent may heatedly voice an opinion in opposition to that of a parent on one subject then ask for and accept advice on another. A wife may simply need for her anger or disappointment to be heard and accepted, not countered. There are many ways to calm, to reconcile, and to reaffirm a relationship that is secure.

Growing up in disorganized and violent surroundings, or later exposure to trauma and chaos, is harsh on the mental and physical health of both children and adults. If one's basic needs are unmet, the environment is chaotic and those responsible for providing security are unavailable, present but unable or unwilling to offer protection and comfort, or threatening, it is difficult to calm and reconciliation is hard to construct.

Security is needed, in the form of viable, supportive social structures, for communities, families, and individuals and is particularly crucial to the survival of those who are vulnerable. Combat veterans, for example, whether children or adults, often suffer from post-traumatic stress disorder. Although they have exited the war, it has not and does not readily leave them. Funds and facilities for meeting the needs of victims of traumatic stress, whether from natural or human-caused trauma, even for children pressed into military service to do the work of adults, are typically woefully inadequate (Nadelson, 2005; Singer, 2005). Security implies attentive, constant, and continuing support. One's capacity to calm, reconcile, and heal from trauma is dependent on it.

The Appropriateness of Reconciliation and Forgiveness Is Debated

The intent of reconciliation and forgiveness is to reclaim, in a relationship, in the family, or in the larger community, a person or group whose behavior is seen as having transgressed social norms or ethical principles. While their accomplishment is not directly linked to the restoration of relational justice, which at times is impossible, the issue of justice is the common backdrop against which reconciliation and forgiveness are contemplated and undertaken (Exline, Worthington, Hill, & McCullough, 2002). Their end is not to cause shame or blame, although these will inevitably be evoked in honest discussions of harm done and in the course of negotiations to reconstruct a safe social order or a secure relationship. Their purpose is not to abandon or isolate a person or group, but to re-link persons whose social support systems have been ruptured, to reunite in functional relationships persons who have been emotionally cut off from one another.

Cultural, religious, and personal differences account for disagreements in the discussion of when forgiveness and reconciliation may be deemed appropriate. Some persons want to assure that aggrieved parties reconcile with or forgive one another only after being made fully aware of the extent of the culpability of both (Krog, 2000). Others sanction forgiveness only after an expression of repentance on the part of the person or persons held culpable (Schimmel, 2002). Some would prefer that efforts be made at reparation before forgiveness be granted or may highlight the role of the arts in helping people to digest and come to terms with cultural trauma (Soyinka, 1999). Others hold that, while neither repentance nor reparation may be attained, a truthful, public statement made by perpetrators and victims of what occurred can open viable space for the possibility of reconciliation and forgiveness at the personal, interpersonal, and societal levels (Tutu, 1999). Still others find that, in the end, humility, remaining aware of one's own sinful nature, and restoration of relationship, while not forgetting or overlooking an atrocity that has occurred, are essential to maintaining one's personhood, to moving forward in one's own and the community's developmental trajectory, and ultimately key to one's redemption (Volf, 1996).

Some work to make an atrocity structured to be invisible and personal a visible and communal concern so that community members can support one another in holding perpetrators accountable (Robben, 2000). Some find granting forgiveness almost impossible and a betrayal of those who lost their lives to human atrocity (Wiesenthal, 1969/1997). For some, revenge remains the preferred response to a given injustice (Cose, 2004). Of the foregoing strategies, most are viable avenues toward healing and moving ahead. Lack of forgiveness paired with lack of reconciliation may support stagnation. Revenge can fuel tit-for-tat responses, as in street gang rivalries or interethnic hostility.

Youth Are Blamed for Genocide

In Rwanda several hundred Hutu boys, aged 8–16, were accused of active participation in genocide and housed with adults in a crowded prison after hostilities ended (Raymond & Raymond, 2000). When the objection was made that children and adults should not be housed together, the boys were relocated to a "rehabilitation camp" in a remote, rural area where they received little instruction and were expected to work a part of each day on a neighboring farm. Six years after the 3-month war of 1994 ended, reconciliation and forgiveness had not yet been afforded to these youth. In June 2007, the US military was seeking to prosecute a young man who at age 15 threw a grenade that killed a US soldier (Glaberson, 2007). He was captured in 2002 and held in captivity on foreign soil, without trial, for 5 years, at which point his case was thrown out as not fitting the criteria for military tribunals then being held. More than one nation has held children accountable for crimes related to wars that grown-ups initiate and they are drawn into. In relation to adult perpetrators of trauma against individuals or the community, there can be even greater animosity and more incentive toward retaliatory behavior or to strip perpetrators or combatants of the right to due process and block any avenue toward reconciliation with and re-inclusion in community.

In regard to sustaining the development of the human species, what we must begin to understand with much greater sophistication is that to the extent that imprisoned or warehoused children (or adults) tend to be attached to families and identified with communities (most are), these support systems are similarly impacted by the treatment meted out to their members. In reality we do not maim, martyr, or marginalize persons one by one. Each of us is attached to a string of related and concerned others.

Forgiveness and Reconciliation Heal Persons, Communities, and the Social Fabric

The vignettes in this chapter pertain to children by design, as instinctively there is more sympathy regarding how children's perceptions, motivations, and behaviors may be shaped by their developmental experience and by compelling contextual factors. This facilitates conceptualizing, from an ecological-systemic and developmental perspective, how we might best protect and facilitate their well-being, how we should construe their culpability when they engage in antisocial behavior (for example, when induced into soldering), whether or how to punish them, and how best to intervene to rehabilitate and re-socialize them toward positive interpersonal and civic behavior as adults.

One former child soldier (Beah, 2007) has written a book recounting his experience as a child combatant. When his community and family were torn asunder by internal warfare in his country, he fled with other young boys who sought security in other villages that rebuffed them, fearing for their own safety if they took the boys in. Shortly they were inducted into the military, harshly trained, each supplied with an AK-47 and drugs to help them cope with the savagery they then witnessed and perpetrated. Fortunately for him, his "enemies," and those of us who can learn from his experience, he was rescued by UNICEF workers and relocated to a rehabilitation camp where he received the counsel of a nurse who heard his story, earned his trust, and participated in his rehabilitation. He was later sent to the United States to explain at the United Nations the lot of child soldiers. He is one of relatively few young men caught in a life of such brutal violence and then exonerated. Had he not been rehabilitated and forgiven the violence he perpetrated, he would not be living freely among us. Had he not reconciled with his experience and written about it, we would not know his story and would understand less about what initiates and what may bring an end to child soldering.

Internal violence in nations disrupts regions, communities, and families, thwarting development, and threatening their capacity to sustain the individual and collective lives of humans, young and old, and the cultures and contexts that have nourished them. Sadly, humans have perpetrated many gross injustices against one another and continue to do so.

The world community has much to acknowledge, to discuss, and to overcome. As we begin to understand the issues that lead to and result from human atrocities, perhaps we can begin to build a communal will to work toward their prevention, while also beginning to develop pragmatic and just means for their resolution. Studies of the social behavior of primates in captivity show that aggressive and peaceful social patterns that are common to different species, for example, rhesus monkeys (aggressive) and stumptail monkeys (tolerant, easygoing), are learned rather than innate (De Waal, 2005). Aggressive patterns were moderated when adolescent members of the two groups were placed together. Bonobos have learned to overcome negative emotions (aggression, fear) after a bout of belligerent behavior toward members of a different community in order to move shortly afterward toward positive interaction (grooming, play, sex). This offers hope that humans may yet learn to extend the benefits of reconciliation, forgiveness, and peacemaking to the societal level as well.

References

Akbar, A., & Forst, B. (Eds.). (2005). *After terror: Promoting dialog among civilizations.* Cambridge, UK: Polity.

Allen, J. R. (2005). After the bombing: Public scenarios and the construction of meaning. In J. R. Allen & B. A. Allen (Eds.), *Therapeutic journey: Practice and life* (pp. 1110–1117). Oakland, CA: TA Press. (Original work published 1999).

Apfel, R. J., & Bennett, S. (1996). *Minefields in their hearts: The mental health of children in war.* New Haven, CT: Yale University Press.

Athens, L. H. (2003). Violentization in larger social context. In L. Athens & J. T. Ulmer (Eds.), *Sociology of crime, law and deviance, vol. 4: Violent acts and violentization: Assessing, applying and developing Lonnie Athens' theories* (pp. 1–41). New York: JAI/Elsevier Science.

Beah, I. (2007). *A long way gone: Memoirs of a child soldier.* New York: Farrar, Strauss & Giroux.

Boszormenyi-Nagy, I., & Krasner, B. R. (1986). *Between give and take: A clinical guide to contextual therapy.* New York: Bruner-Mazel.

Bowen, M. (1976). Theory in the practice of psychotherapy. In P. Guerin (Ed.), *Family therapy* (pp. 42–90). New York: Gardener.

Bowlby, J. (1988). *A secure base: Parent-child attachment and healthy human development.* New York: Basic Books.

Bronfenbrenner, U. (1986). Ecology of the family as a context for human development: Research perspectives. *Developmental Psychology, 22,* 723–742.

Buber, M. (1970). *I and thou.* New York: Scribner. (Original work published 1927).

Cameron, S. (Ed.). (2001). *Out of war: True stories from the front lines of the Children's Movement for Peace in Colombia.* New York: Scholastic Press.

Cose, E. (2004). *Bone to pick: Of forgiveness, reconciliation, reparation, and revenge.* New York: Atria.

Davies, D. D. (2004). *Child development: A practitioner's guide* (2nd ed.). New York: Guilford.

Davoine, F., & Gaudillière, J.-M. (2004). *History beyond trauma: Whereof one cannot speak, thereof one cannot stay silent.* New York: Other Press.

De Waal, F. (2005). *Our inner ape.* New York: Penguin.

Ducommun-Nagy, C. (2002). *Contextual therapy.* In F. Kaslow (Series Ed.); R. F. Massey & S. D. Massey (Vol. Eds.) *Comprehensive handbook of psychotherapy: interpersonal/humanistic/existential* (Vol. 3, pp. 463–488). New York: Wiley.

Exline, J. J., Worthington, E. L., Jr., Hill, P. C., & McCullough, M. E. (2003). Forgiveness and justice: A research agenda for social and personality psychology. *Personality and Social Psychology Review* 7, 337–348.

Erikson, E. H. (1997). *The life cycle completed.* New York: Norton.

Fanon, F. (2005). *The wretched of the earth.* New York: Grove. (Original work published 1961).

Freud, A., & Burlingham, D. T. (1943). *War and children.* Westport, CT: Greenwood.

Glaberson, W. (2007, June 3). A legal debate in Guantánamo on boy fighters, pp. A1 and A35. *The New York Times.*

Harkness, L. L. (1993). Transgenerational transmission of war-related trauma. In J. P. Wilson & B. Raphael (Eds.), *International handbook of traumatic stress syndromes* (pp. 635–643). New York: Plenum Press.

Hellinger, B. (2003). *Peace Begins in the Soul: Family constellations in the service of reconciliation.* Heidelberg, Germany: Carl-Auer-Systeme Verlag.

Hersey, J. (1986). *Hiroshima.* New York: Vintage.

Hesse, E., Main, M., Abrams, K. Y., & Rifkin, A. (2003). Unresolved states regarding loss or abuse can have "second-generation" effects: Disorganization, role inversion, and frightening ideation in the offspring of traumatized, non-maltreating parents. In M. F. Solomon & D. J. Siegel (Eds.), *Healing trauma: Attachment, mind, body and brain* (pp. 168–195). New York: Norton.

Kalayjian, A. (2002). Biopsychosocial and spiritual treatment of trauma. In F. Kaslow (Series Ed.); R. F. Massey & S. D. Massey (Vol. Eds.) *Comprehensive handbook of psychotherapy: interpersonal/humanistic/existential* (Vol. 3, pp. 615–637). New York: Wiley.

Kegan, R. (1982). *The emerging self: Problem and process in human development.* Cambridge, MS: Harvard University Press.

Krog, A. (2000). *Country of my skull: Guilt, sorrow and the limits of forgiveness in the new South Africa.* New York: Three Rivers Press.

Kunda, Z. (2001). *Social cognition: Making sense of people.* Cambridge, MA: MIT Press.

Machel, G. (2001). *The impact of war on children.* London: Hurst & Company.

Macksoud, M. M., Aber, L., & Cohn, I. (1996). Assessing the impact of war on children. In R. J. Apfel & S. Bennett (Eds.), *Minefields in their hearts: The mental health of children in war* (pp. 218–230). New Haven, CT: Yale.

MacLean, G. A. (2006, Winter-Spring). Human security and the globalization of international security. *The Whitehead Journal of Diplomacy and International Relations*, VII(1), 89–99.

Martínez Miguélez, M. (1997). *The emerging paradigm: Toward a new theory of scientific rationality,* (S. D. Massey, Trans.). México, DF: Trillas.

Maslow, A. H. (1943). A theory of human motivation. *Psychological Review,* 50, 370–396.

Massey, S. D., & Combs, L. (2002). An interpersonal-systemic and developmental approach to supervision. In F. Kaslow (Series Ed.); R. F. Massey & S. D. Massey (Vol. Eds.) *Comprehensive handbook of psychotherapy: Interpersonal/humanistic/existential* (Vol. 3, pp. 669–698). New York: Wiley.

Mead, G. M. (1964). *George Herbert Mead on social psychology* (A. Strauss, Ed.). Chicago: University of Chicago Press. (Original work published 1934).

Memmi, A. (1991). *The colonizer and the colonized.* Boston, MA: Beacon. (Original work Published 1965).

Moghaddam, F. M. (1998). *Social psychology: Exploring universals across cultures.* New York: W. H. Freeman.

Montvale, J. F. (2006, Summer-Fall). Track two diplomacy: The work of healing history. *The Whitehead Journal of Diplomacy and International Relations,* 7(2), 15–25.

Nadelson, T. (2005). *Trained to kill: Soldiers at war.* Baltimore, OH: The Johns Hopkins University Press.

Nef, J. (2006, Winter-Spring). Human security, mutual vulnerability, and sustainable development: A critical view. *The Whitehead Journal of Diplomacy and International Relations,* 7(2), 55–73.

Perry, B. D. (1997). Incubated in terror: Neurodevelopmental factors in the "cycle of violence." In J. B. Osofsky (Ed.), *Children in a violent* society (pp. 124–149). New York: Guilford.

Pfuetze, P. E. (1954). *Self, society, existence: Human nature and dialogue in the thought of George Herbert Mead and Martin Buber.* New York: Harper.

Raymond, A., & Raymond, S. (2000). *Children in war.* New York: TV Books.

Robben, A. C. G. M. (2000). The assault on basic trust: Disappearance, protest, and reburial in Argentina. In A. C. G. M. Robben & M. M. Suárez-Orozco (Eds.), *Cultures under siege: Collective violence and trauma.* Cambridge, UK: Cambridge University Press.

Ross, G. (2003). *Beyond the trauma vortex: The media's role in healing fear, terror, and violence.* Berkeley, CA: North Atlantic Books.

Sagan, C. (1995). *A path where no man thought: Nuclear winter and its implications.* New York: Vintage Books.

Saint-Exupéry, A. (1970). *The little prince.* (Richard Howard, Trans.). New York: Harcourt. (Original work published 1943).

Schimmel, S. (2002). *Wounds not healed by time: The power of repentance and forgiveness.* New York: Oxford University Press.

Siegel, D. J. (1999). *The developing mind: How relationships and the brain interact to shape who we are.* New York: Guilford.

Singer, P. W. (2005). *Children at war.* New York: Pantheon.

Solomon, M. F., & Siegel, D. J., (Eds.). (2003). *Healing trauma: Attachment, mind, body and brain.* New York: W. W. Norton.

Soyinka, W. (1999). *The burden of memory, the muse of forgiveness.* Oxford: Oxford University Press.

Stern, D. (1985). *The interpersonal world of the infant: A view from psychoanalysis and developmental psychology.* New York: Basic Books.

Thomas, C. (2000). *Global governance, development, and human security.* London: Pluto.

Tutu, D. (1999). *No future without forgiveness.* New York: Doubleday.

van der Kolk, B. A. (2003). Posttraumatic stress disorder and the nature of trauma. In M. F. Solomon & D. J. Siegel (Eds.), *Healing trauma: Attachment, mind, body and brain* (pp. 168–195). New York: W. W. Norton.

Volf, M. (1996). *Exclusion & embrace: A theological exploration of identity, otherness and reconciliation.* Nashville, TN: Abingdon Press.

Volkan, V. (2004). *Blind trust: Large groups and their leaders in times of crisis and terror.* Charlottesville, VA: Pitchstone Publishing.

Walker, S. (2005). *Shockwave: Countdown to Hiroshima.* New York: HarperCollins.

Wiesenthal, S. (1969/1997). *The sunflower: On the possibility and limits of forgiveness.* New York: Schocken Books.

Wilber, K. (1985). *No boundary: Eastern and Western approaches to personal growth.* Boston, MA: Shambhala.

Winnicott, D. W. (1995). *The family and individual development.* Boston, MA: Routledge. (Original work published 1965).

Chapter 7
Art and Meaning: *ART*iculation© as a Modality in Processing Forgiveness and Peace Consciousness

Hagitte Gal-Ed

Although theoretical and empirical works in peace psychology and forgiveness proliferate, a serious examination of art in the context of processing peace meaning and
forgiveness has not been as evident. Critical information, such as art's co-evolution
with human consciousness, its psychological function as a meaning system that
is unique in centering on processes of realization and change essential to accomplishing peace, and its potential role in forming a consciousness of peace and in
processing forgiveness and healing, has largely been ignored. But the potential
contribution of art to peace is great.

Challenges

The Problem

In spite of the use of art in various psychotherapeutic modalities, including art therapy, not many practitioners approach its potential function beyond the conventional
perceptions about its ability to stimulate the mind, stir emotions, and provide a
reflection of both. By and large, the use of art in these practices remained confined to a theoretical territory delineated between "expression" and "interpretation"
governed by psychoanalytic diagnosis and post-modern analyses.

A few decades ago, this approach was challenged by such thinkers as Martin
Buber (1947, 1965) and Abraham Maslow (1966a, 1966b, 1986a, 1986b), who
approached art on par with knowledge within a context of humanistic psychology
and psychology of being, and more currently by Maurice Friedman in his discussion of the healing dialogue in psychotherapy (1973, 1985, 1991). They related to
art as a systematic realm of meaning making generated and perpetuated by the
inherently human capacity to engage in dialogic relations and relationships. They
saw dialogue as the existential mode of being human and considered the experience of meeting another person in genuine dialogue as a realm of new awareness –
emancipation, healing, self-actualization, and mutual change toward well-being and
peace-in-becoming. This approach and its specific implications for psychology and
humanistic psychotherapy (Buber-Agassi, 1999) are illustrated by the exemplary
Healing Through Meeting modality of Hans Trub (1952). Buber's treatment of art
as a dialogue-based meaning making system pointed at the connection between

Ani Kalayjian, Raymond F. Paloutzian, *Forgiveness and Reconciliation*, Peace
Psychology Book Series, DOI 10.1007/978-1-4419-0181-1_7,
© Springer Science+Business Media, LLC 2009

the making of art and consciousness development before sociobiology (Wilson, 1981, 1998) and metacognition (Metcalfe & Shimamura, 1996), and many current researchers in neuroscience were able to provide their empirical support (Solso, 2003; Spivey, 2005). Buber's insights about art as a dialogic realm of the human as a physical and spiritual whole were developed as a philosophy of mankind (or anthropology, as he preferred to call it).

Buber's exploration of the meaning of art within the dialogic mode of being illuminated the persistence of art throughout human civilization due to its concrete and cognitive contribution to improved individual and societal adaptability, survival skills, well-being, and spiritual growth before sociobiology provided its explanation of epigenetic processes on the brain–mind–culture continuum (Bedaux & Cook, 1999; Wilson, 1981, 1998). Consequently, by providing an explanation of the co-evolution of art and consciousness, art and the sciences move increasingly closer, causing critical perceptional changes in art psychology (Arenheim, 1971, 1986; Solso, 2003) and art history (Spivey, 2005), and even in the psychology of science (Maslow, 1966a, 1966b) and philosophy of science (Bhaskar, 1986, 1991). At the same time these developments also provide scientifically solid ground for a new understanding of the psychological and epistemological role of art as an independent modality in psychotherapy, its connection with the idea of freedom and its dialogic realism promoting a consciousness of peace.

Responding to the Problem

Inspired by the concepts of dialogic being, healing through meeting, and humanist psychotherapy, I have made art's unique role in human consciousness development the focus of my research interest and a conceptual framework for developing a new modality in practicing art therapy and education for peace (Gal-Ed, 2000). For 20 years I have experimented with this approach with a variety of audiences in diverse local and international frameworks, including individual trauma (1972, 1975), education for peace through art (1974–1986), social/ethnic/religious conflicts (1980–1986), group processing loss and grieving (1986), a large-scale outdoor peace culture event in New York City (NYC) (1989), an international research program of education for peace through the arts (1989–1992), an international interfaith convocation for peace at the United Nations (1999), and creating and producing *Peace TV*, a cable program in NYC (2001–present).

After conducting a long and complex process of comparative analysis between Buber's dialogic anthropology, peace research, human studies, and field data, I defined this unique capacity for dialogue as Dialogic Intelligence – DIN© – and arrived at a grounded theory of art as dialogue-based process of realization and transformation that I termed *ART*iculation© (Gal-Ed, 2001), a system of meaning processing and consciousness change.

My concern in this chapter, however, is not to discuss art as a meaning system in general merely because it is important. I have illustrated this importance before through the etymological model of the Hebrew word *Amen* as a paradigm for peace education. *Amen* is a Hebrew word radically representing interaction between art and faith as psychological meaning systems within a communal existence guided by a vision of bringing a civilization of peace to realization (Gal-Ed, 1999). Recent studies argue that both our human limitations and our capacities are qualitatively susceptible to change and in the process of evolution produced a brain, as Robert Solso states (2003), "that had an internal sense of beauty, harmony, and pleasure as well as of repulsiveness, discord, and dissonance," (p. 15). These very attributes played a critical role in the development of consciously experienced art, verbal and other communication systems, social orders, and moral standards and judgments; this is documented in a trail of artworks demonstrating these effects in great variety throughout the history of human civilization. Understanding the co-evolution of the brain and art – the sensory-cognitive system and the details of human evolution in relationship to consciousness as Solso suggests – is a critical step to understanding art as a meaning system and perhaps the origin of all meaning systems.

At the same time, critical to understanding this power of art is that in the world as we know it, only we humans have the imaginative capacity to make symbols and to represent not only the world around us but also what goes on within our heads – thoughts, emotions, feelings, and dreams. Even more importantly, the dialogic approach emphasizes our ability to make connections among all these faculties and, in so doing, generates new meanings, supports metacognition, and changes our perceptions as we go along our evolutionary path. The history of how we developed and exercised that power includes how we learned "to tell stories, to create social hierarchies, to connect with the environment, to express the supernatural, to make images of ourselves – and to mitigate the hard fact of our mortality," states Nigel Spivey (2005) in his book *How Art Made the World: A Journey to the Origins of Human Creativity* (p. 14). As a human experience, art is the only manifestation of the human capacity to give concrete representations to meanings as they just begin to emerge into consciousness (Kaplan, 2000; Malchiodi, 2006). From a dialogic perspective, at the core of art as a meaning making experience is a tension between dissatisfaction and longing for a perfected relation. This tension is productive and powerful in its potential to bring about new knowledge emancipation and conceptual transformation.

The Dialogic Dimension of *ART*iculation

"In the course of becoming human there appear, incomprehensible in their origin, two constituent factors of the human person closely bound to each other: dissatisfaction with being limited to needs and longing for *perfected relation*" (Buber, 1965, p. 163, italics emphasis of author). This particular meeting, or even tension, between the dissatisfaction with a limited state of being and the longing for perfected relation represents a bond of concrete realism between the being of art and the being of peace. "All this dissatisfaction and longing," continues Buber, "exclusiveness and inclusiveness, we find again in the realm of art" (p. 164). Concrete experiences of both art and peace take place in the realm of this particular tension, a realm of knowing by being in-relation. An existential mode of being human, this realm is characterized by dialogue, mutual change, emancipation of new meanings, and growing consciousness. Dialogue is an inherently human capacity. However, "There is no ordering of dialogue. It is not that you *are* to answer but that you *are able*" (Buber, 1947, p. 35, italics in original). Dialogue, therefore, entails the ability for choice making and through it we experience freedom and autonomy. Therefore, it is the very realism of dialogic relation that endows art a meaning system so deeply shared with the realism of peace.

This further explains the psychotherapeutic potential of art in processing both trauma and forgiveness. "It is not craft – the ability to shape wonderfully balanced tools," stresses Spivey, "not embellishment – the sense of beauty in colour and form" alone that endows art with therapeutic potential.

> The human production of art may be full of craft and decorative intent, but above all, and definitively, the art of humans consists in our singular capacity to use our imagination. Like the habit of walking on two legs, this capacity for visual symbolizing arrived... when we combined the dexterity of our hands with the power of our brains and learnt the knack of representation. (Spivey, 2005, p. 14)

Acquiring and mastering the "knack of representation" is a key lesson in human evolution and a common principle operating in art and in the processing of peace consciousness. While the meaning system model can be a useful way to illuminate what those psychological and epistemological processes are, in this chapter, however, my focus is limited to the role ARTiculation processes are already proving to have in the service of processing forgiveness and peace meanings through learning the "knack of representation."

Like peace, mastering representation while processing meaning is always experienced as being – becoming. ARTiculation is a concrete form of processing the experience of being – becoming, bringing it to realization, and giving it representation. These are key manifestations of its dialogic realism. A rationale for the dialogic realism of ARTiculation as a therapeutic modality can be presented in relation to Dialogic Intelligence by the following points:

- There is no dialogue outside a relation. Dialogue means being in-relation.
- Relation is a realm of meaning in the making and revealed connectedness.
- As such, all relations and relationships are dynamic processes of gradual change; a phenomenon integral to the realism of the universe of life of which we are a part.
- Dialogue is not just a form of verbal exchange. Rather, it is a mode of being, and a specific approach to understanding being and life phenomena through in-relation experiences.
- The capacity to engage in dialogic relations is inherently human; it can be illustrated by the function of imagination and manifested concretely through processes of meaning making, which practically bring this capacity to improved realization. As such, it constitutes a particular form of intelligence I call Dialogic Intelligence.
- As a human experience, dialogic relation is life affirming.

- As a human experience, dialogue is a process of mutual change.
- Dialogic Intelligence helps to bring the realism of change to various forms of concrete realization, thus bringing new consciousness to emancipation.
- In the context of Dialogic Intelligence, change means to accept the fact of change and its various phenomena as the realism of the universe of life and to discover practices that will make it possible for humans to participate in this reality in a life-affirming way.
- In the context of Dialogic Intelligence, the meaning of peace can be brought to realization by participating in the life of dialogic relations and mutual change consciously, thus affirming the Other as Thou – a partner in encounter, promoting well-being for all.
- For people guided by notions of power and control, the concrete realism of dialogue and mutual change is a scary proposition, as it represents the opposite of war and killing.
- To enhance Dialogic Intelligence is a human survival necessity on all levels of human relations and interactions. The current consequences of expanding globalization are a clear indication of poorly developed Dialogic Intelligence.
- A genuine dialogue demonstrates a concrete possibility for bringing about a perfected human reality, a desire expressed by the notion of peace.
- ARTiculation, a concrete realm of meaning processing since the beginning of human civilization, is an essential category and dimension of Dialogic Intelligence and a vital realm for its development.

Examples from Art History

The history of art provides a wealth of examples for this phenomenon. When asked about the meaning of his art, Matisse replied, "I do not paint things but the *relationship* between them" (italics emphasis of author).

Artists have always been on the cutting edge of human perception and consciousness development by providing representations to otherwise un-accessible cognitive processes (e.g., Paleolithic cave art). They have documented war and man-made trauma (e.g., ancient kingdoms, Altdorfer, Picasso, Kalo), addressed political violence and power abuse (e.g., Goya, Daumier, Manet), struggled for freedom and civil rights (e.g., Gericault, Delacroix), and generated collective perceptual and cultural change (e.g., Impressionism, Surrealism, Abstract, Marcel Duchamp). More complicated to define are representations of peace. Would a tranquil landscape (e.g., Millet), domestic scene (e.g., Vermeer), or still life (e.g., Cezanne) do? Would allegories (e.g., Botticelli, Rembrandt, Gauguin), geometric abstractions (e.g., Mondrian, Rothko), or minimalist renderings (e.g., Agnes Martin) do? The visual transformation of the dove after its departure from Noah's Ark in the Hebrew myth can be traced in the wings that transformed human figures into angelic beings and reappeared as a bird in Picasso's *Child with a Dove* and the *Dove of Peace*. Contemporary artists, aware of the art/consciousness connection as well as its psychotherapeutic powers for themselves and for society, address the urgency for peace consciousness by using innovative multimedia approaches to produce artworks in nature (Goldworthy, Drury, Christo) or by focusing on selected social and political issues, processing them and displaying them in public arenas outside of the traditional galleries and museums (Christo, Wodicko, Kelly, Ali). In the context of awakening peace consciousness and processing forgiveness, the works of Wodicko and Karavan are of special significance and deserve a deeper analysis beyond the scope of this chapter. Their complex working processes demonstrate the dialogic function of art and its power in processing meanings of human violence, war, forgiveness, and peace on the collective cultural level.

These examples highlighted for me the psychological and epistemological merits of Buber's treatment of art within the context of dialogue as a realm of new consciousness emancipation. When art is practiced as a dialogic experience, it brings together the processes of choice making, realization, and change as a concrete framework for meaning processing, psychotherapy, healing, cognition, and peace consciousness in the making. This is a radical move from art as merely a metaphor for life to being a concrete realm of change and growth itself.

ARTiculation Encountering Human Violence

In the face of currently increasing human violence and conflicts triggered by expanding tendencies for modernization and globalization, my rationale for ARTiculation suggests that its dialogic attributes, i.e., bringing about realization and change, can explain its timely significance in studying violence within a context of psychology of being (Maslow, 1968a, 1968b) and in processing issues of identity and consciousness on the individual, social, and cultural levels together. The relevance of ARTiculation to processing trauma, healing, dialogue, forgiveness, and reconciliation can be thus measured by the gaining of that inner strength referred to by Gandhi.

Research conducted with 24 psychiatric patients, in which 10 art therapy sessions were held in conjunction with the administration of psychotropic medicines, and the use of the Rosenberg Self-Esteem Scale and Progress Evaluation Scales for a 9 month follow-up period showed that gains in self-esteem and socialization skills achieved at the conclusion of the art therapy sessions were maintained at follow-up (Borchers, 1985). A longer term case study I conducted (1989–2001) included a 6 year follow-up period of in-depth interviews with an American senior high school student who used video as his ARTiculation tool in a dialogue-based international program of education for peace through the arts with American, Israeli, and Palestinian participants. This study decisively showed that gains in dialogic awareness and peace meaning made through the ARTiculation experiences continued to increase for this individual throughout the 6 year follow-up period.

Encouraging as such results may be, the study of ARTiculation and its potential as a psychotherapeutic modality is in its infancy, perhaps in part because practicing ARTiculation as a process combining art and science in theoretical and applied research requires specific training. Much more remains to be discovered about the nature of *ART*iculation processes and their potential effect to promote peace consciousness or to serve as a psychotherapeutic modality.

*ART*iculation in the Context of Processing Forgiveness with Adolescents

Published psychological works on forgiveness often argue for its benefits, especially in psychotherapy (McCullough, Thoresen, & Pargament, 2000; Witvliet, Phipps, Feldman, & Beckman, 2004; Worthington, 2005). Usually, anecdotal testimonies of patients are brought to illustrate successful ends of such processes. These works mostly focus on adult populations and tend to represent the therapist's voice and his/her ideological, religious, or theoretical bent. These works, unfortunately, do not address the rapidly growing need for similar attention on the part of the younger generation.

Emphasis on Adolescents

Adolescents are largely overlooked in texts on forgiveness. Current works on the effect of abuse of children and adolescents (Cohen, Mannarino, & Deblinger, 2006; Gil, 1996, 2006; Miller, 1990, 1997, 2005) flesh out both the effect and the extent of traumatic experiences at an early age and provide supportive evidence for a growing number of questioning voices concerning the therapeutic values and meanings of conventional verbal processing of forgiveness, especially with adolescents (Lamb & Murphy, 2002). A unique approach to addressing the complex therapeutic needs of adolescents is found in Shirley Riley's (1999) *Contemporary Art Therapy with Adolescents*. Art as a therapeutic modality that provides "mind-brain-body synthesis with art expression" (Riley, 2004, p. 185) has long been a central objective of art therapy (Thompson, 2003). However, as many chapters in the present volume illustrate, the processing of forgiveness continues to take place mostly with adults and through verbal articulations, rarely supported by art, except for its limited use as a diagnostic tool. At the same time, the present volume is making a contribution to the urgent task of forgiveness processing in the context of raising peace consciousness by offering a wide range of approaches, thus demonstrating the productivity of trying solutions through diverse modalities and interdisciplinary theoretical and applied research. It provides a welcoming environment for new research and approaches.

My current work with adolescents focuses on the processes of transformational learning, change, and consciousness development through mastering visual and multimedia representations. The *ART*iculation modality as I designed it approaches the young person as a dynamic whole, an autonomous being of complex creative dialogic relations beyond the verbal, intellectual, or conceptual abilities alone. My present study is guided by the question: What does an intentional practice of *ART*iculation as an intervention modality with individuals and small groups within the context of a regular high school art class reveal about their ability to process experiences of violence, trauma, healing, forgiveness, and peace? My first task was to identify important meeting points between my modality and defined forgiveness goals.

According to the American Psychological Association (APA) *Forgiveness – Research Briefs* (2006), many psychologists identify forgiveness as

> a process (or the results of a process) that involves a change in emotion and attitude regarding an offender. . . . an intentional and voluntary process, driven by a deliberate decision to forgive. . . results in a decreased motivation to retaliate or maintain estrangement from an offender and requires letting go of negative emotions toward the offender. In any event, forgiveness occurs with the victim's full recognition that he or she deserved better treatment, one reason why Mahatma Gandhi contended that "the weak can never forgive. Forgiveness is an attribute of the strong." (APA, 2006, p. 4)

I find this multifaceted definition a readily available meeting point between forgiveness and *ARTiculation*, especially since, as Gandhi claimed, the "weak can never forgive," and one must first become "strong." In this context, my investigation of the merit of *ARTiculation* processes for forgiveness processing is focused on its capacity to do just that – to help participants discover and constructively own their inner strength.

To process forgiveness in the context of Dialogic Intelligence requires mechanisms that address a person in his/her dialogic relations and relationships, including imagination, the processes of choice making, and the experiences of changing and growing autonomous. Through its complex processes of realization and autonomy emancipation, *ARTiculation* does just that. The following example illustrates.

Artist & Leader Program

Since September 11, 2001, I have been investigating the potential benefits of *ARTiculation* in the framework of a regular American high school system with inner-city adolescents who are troubled by various forms of violence, conflicts, and abuse. These experiences shape their views of the human world and hinder their ability to move on and to function constructively. For this particular framework I integrated central issues from education for peace, dialogue, forgiveness, and reconciliation into the regular art education curriculum and created a program I called *Artist & Leader*. The program is a work in progress and was selected for the outreach initiative of PBS Art-21.

In this program I introduced selected contemporary artists and their innovative artistic methodologies as applied in their *ARTiculation* processing of issues similar to those of my students. Although their artworks provide a symbol and metaphor for a search for meaning, more important is the understanding of how their *ARTiculation* efforts become themselves the process of meaning processing. Looking at such contemporary art making from the perspective of Dialogic Intelligence clearly demonstrates their *ARTiculation* experiences as a change-promoting process of realization. Such contemporary artists become important agents in the collective search for meanings of peace and in processing forgiveness. By giving a voice to the voiceless and by giving images and forms to imageless ideas or unspeakable human atrocities, these artists play a leadership role in the communal social awareness for increasingly growing audiences in need for forgiveness. In their works, art making is synonymous with the process of new consciousness in the making. Such contemporary artists provide alternative role models for a troubled young generation.

Artist & Leader also became an opportunity to expand the art making experience of my students by acknowledging their traumatic experiences, addressing their urgent developmental issues, discussing their perceptions of reality, and the lack of peace images. The specific meanings of these problems are processed by approaching art as a realm of meaning making and by using the communication and compositional elements and principles of art consciously to this end. In this context, the dialogue of art making and the dialogue of forgiveness processing connect and reverberate in each other until they reach a level of saturation from which new issues emerge, followed by a desire to start a new creative project. This became an eye-opening experience for all.

Presented here is the first phase of the project. My purpose is to illustrate the psychotherapeutic implications of *ARTiculation* as a modality in processing violence, trauma, forgiveness, and peace consciousness within an educational framework. The primary objective of this phase was to establish a safe environment and basic trust among all of us as the foundation for mutual respect and a genuine dialogue on sensitive personal matters, learning difficulties, and social issues. This environment is essential in order to allow students to turn these themes into subjects of art projects and meaning processing. I started with an introduction to the program, its learning objectives, its dialogic environment and principles, its approach to art making as a process of meaning realization, and an explanation of our participatory responsibilities. This initial discussion was followed by this sequence:

1. Students watched the Susan Rothenberg episode in the PBS, ART:21 documentary series and discussed how artists use elements and principles of art and design to make statements and process meanings of personal experiences.
2. Students started sketching a storyboard of a memory of their own and decided to produce a video documenting their work (the class was equipped with digital cameras, video recorders, and an iMac computer with an iMovie program facilitating editing and DVD burning).
3. Students watched the Ida Applebroog episode and discussed the artistic process of choice making when processing meanings of personal and social traumatic situations.
4. Students completed storyboards (using pencil, watercolor, and words) and discussed the social collective aspect of art making.
5. Students discussed current personal and social issues that affect their communities, their country and humanity in a global context, and started sketching designs and models for Community Art Projects of their own. They were given an opportunity to choose to work individually or in small teams of 2–3 participants and were encouraged to explore possibilities using mixed media.

6. Students watched the Michael Kelly episode and discussed effective mixed-media and crossed-media applications in non-conventional forms, particularly in dealing with issues of adolescence and growing up in their communities as they know them.
7. Students started executing their Community Art Projects. The process took a few weeks and involved extensive one-on-one dialogues, reflections, changes, class art critique and feedback, and writing Artist Statements.
8. Students watched the Krzysztof Wodicko episode and were given a questionnaire with the following items on it:

   • How does he use art to address the issues of abuse of power, violence, and trauma?
   • How does he get the audience involved in the work of art? And why?
   • How does he address the issues of memory and forgiveness?
   • What is your opinion: Should there be forgiveness for such human atrocities and traumas?
   • If forgiveness is considered, explain what would be an act of forgiveness? Who should be forgiven, and how exactly?
   • If forgiveness is not considered, what actions can be taken to overcome the trauma and go on with life?
   • Can art help people live with their traumatic memories? Can art help people overcome trauma and grow?
   • How do you want to use art in such cases?

9. Students continued working on their projects.
10. Students watched the episode of Laylah Ali and discussed crossed-media collaboration as well as the relationships between words, concepts, and images in processing meanings of social injustice.
11. Students watched the episode of Josiah McElheny and discussed the complexity of creating images of multi-dimensionality and peace.
12. Students completed their Artist Statements and prepared a presentation of their artworks and videos for their peers at school.

By the end of this phase, students were using a variety of materials including video, painting, drawing, clay (combined with other materials), masks, Mylar (mirroring plastic), and large cutout boards. Working in multi-dimensional media resonated with the participants' ability to consciously *ARTi*culate multi-dimensional aspects they discovered in their search for meanings. Videotaping was integral to the actual learning experience of the group. The practice of videotaping among all other creative learning materials represented a particular stage in the *ARTi*culation process; one in which we think about our thinking, and *ARTi*culating it in the ordinary communication manners of spoken words and body gestures. For the students, this experience becomes a concrete practice of (a) metacognition within the context of their learning process and (b) integrating their newly found meanings into their regular mode of communication. In this context, the dialogic power of the video becomes a concrete tool for an integrative understanding of themselves while going through their respective search for meaning. This, too, required a high level of artistic choices and thereby of meaning making on the part of the students. The final videotape includes participants' interviews and artworks and is available for therapeutic or educational audiences through my seminars and workshops.

While this project is still in progress, some benefits are already evident:

- The environment of healing through dialogue allows processing change through choice making, change, and new choices. This provides the students with a range of choices not only regarding materials and concepts but also regarding the length of time necessary for their individual processing, as well as for their participating in the group's video documentary.
- Students feel safe to address personal and collective experiences of trauma and violence, explore their meaning through various learning technologies, and make this information the subject of their artworks.
- The actual experience of the dialogic principles in the learning process and in practicing *ARTiculation* generated for the group an atmosphere of trust, openness, support, and constructive feedback.
- In this environment students felt free to express authentic thoughts and feelings about a variety of sensitive issues, including forgiveness.
- Students discovered new artistic opportunities for themselves, improved their artistic choice-making and representational abilities.
- Students expressed improved sense of self-esteem and confidence.
- Three out of 20 participants did not finish their artworks as of yet, and 5 chose not to be interviewed on camera but were excited to appear while continuing to work and willingly showed their artworks on video and on display.

Cases and Artwork

The following examples were selected to illustrate students' artistic choices and their meaning processing experience. The reader is invited to make connections between their artworks and the Artist Statements to see how their individual processing needs are reflected.

M.E.

M.E., a 10th grade boy with very limited previous experience in art, used clay, sticks, and words to *ARTiculate* what's on his mind when thinking about how he experiences violence. Interesting to note is the certain resemblance between images from prehistoric art or the African Juju healing rituals and these images by an American boy from a middle class white family. Working mainly with found objects, raw brown air-dry clay, and markers allow him to establish a sense of the "immediacy" and "concreteness" of violence in his real-life experiences. So is the shaping of the human heads in a raw un-polished manner. In this case, his lack of artistic skills and refinement correlates with his actual life experiences. In contrast, his skills with digital technology were superior to any other participant in this class, and he played a key role in the videotaping. The gap between his evidently lower dexterous ability and, in contrast, his superior ability to handle digital technology illustrates a troubling phenomenon of this young generation.

Human intelligibility evolves through dexterity. Dexterity is a human epigenetic developmental basis. Illustrated by our prehistoric ancestors as well as present time human infants, cognition, language skills, and abstraction develop through preliminary concrete dexterous experiences. The *ART*iculation modality addresses the requirement of the process of meaning making for ongoing dexterous elaboration. M.E. manifests a developmental need to stay in the dexterous stage longer than others, perhaps because it has not been satisfied earlier or damaged during an early stage of his school education. Only after seeing the words he wrote on the sticks could I become aware of the quality of his difficulty in making sense of his predicament. By the way he gave it *ART*iculation he was able to better engage in dialogues about it. Going through what seems like a "primitive" phase of expression actually opened up the way for an effective communication both with me and with his school counselor. Our dialogues resulted in more sophisticated artistic choices and at the same time growing understanding of the new meanings in relationship to reality. By utilizing more advanced artistic challenges and choices he found a way to better deal with his own issues of forgiveness. For the time being, M.E.'s work is still in progress, and he has not yet provided an Artist Statement.

Picture 1   M.E. (clay heads)

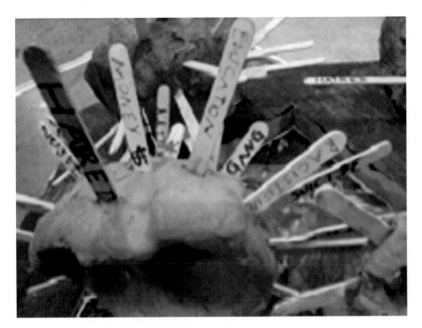

Picture 2   M.E. (clay heads, close up)

L.C.

The next example of processing violence from a personal experience of abuse takes a different approach. L.C., an 11th grade girl, uses paints very effectively. She discovered this gift of hers while working with me last year. In the present work, she is using this skill to bring feelings, emotions, and thoughts to a coherent integration within one compositional whole. This presents a very serious challenge in terms of the artistic choices she must make. What makes it so complicated for her is the fact that a composition consists of dialogic relationships between the different elements, just as it is in society and human relations. Her process, therefore, clearly illustrates the dialogic reality of peace. For her, it also demonstrated a whole new understanding of the realism of "forgiveness." The reader is invited to read her Reflection, where she explains her choice-making process in order to realize just how challenging this task is. In her Artist Statement she goes on to address the audience directly.

L.C. demonstrates an advanced stage in her ability to engage in a deep process of *ART*iculation, manifested by her compositional formation as well as her choices regarding color scheme, texture, brush strokes, and use of words. Altogether, her work demonstrates an effective way to engage in dialogic relations on many levels. In her search to give a form to her complex truth and make her authentic identity present, she reworked this composition four times around, using only brush and paint, layering them immediately on the board. From the outset, she asked to place the board upright so she could create this painting standing, at an eye level, allowing her to face/encounter her issues eye-to-eye. This seemingly technical choice, too, is in fact a concrete form of a dialogic relation in action.

L.C. wrote her reflection in response to one of our dialogues during the course of her work. She refused to be interviewed on camera but wrote her Artist Statement immediately upon completion of her painting.

L.C.'s Reflection

I had two decisions to make. I could either speak about my painting in an interview or write it out for you. I chose to be silent about this. What will it take to make people realize the extent of their damage? We have lost lives, we have lost the good in people, we have lost all humanity that was ever in us. We may not share the same blood but we are all human beings, and we are all equal.

I want you, my audience, to first look at the painting. Look at it as if you are looking into a mirror, but don't think of yourself as a bad person or part of the problem. We hear a lot that the "society" is the cause of the pain in the world. But who exactly is society? WE are society. WE live in this world we've created every day. What have we made it? Young girls, women, and men suffer. Whether it be they suffer from anorexia, drug addiction, rape, living with or being an alcoholic. The pain goes beyond the limit. Whatever the cause may be it does not affect just one person. It affects the people around them also.

What you have read above this is something that echoes my project. Some of the things that were said were not appropriate so I took them out. But I hope you'll read it and take it into deep consideration.

What is the reason you don't speak about issues? If you know someone you love is suffering why is it that you do nothing and say "Oh he/she will be alright. This is just a phase it's no big deal."? A loss of a family member is devastating, and we are now in war. I understand that people have a different way of dealing with their feelings and the pain but we need to speak up. (L.C., 11/2/06)

L.C., addresses her audience in a direct dialogue. In both her artwork and her statement she engages in conversation with her potential audience. She created a meeting space where she can be the host of an important dialogue about meanings. She is even brave enough to approach her audience with challenging questions – something she probably could not have done at the time of her traumatic experience. Having gained clarity, courage, and self-esteem through her *ART*iculation learning process, she now possesses the ability to approach the world with a new sense of strength, which can only come with making effective choices. Making effective choices in her artwork is key to obtaining an inner structure of making effective choices for herself in other life situations.

Artist Statement

I chose to show more than one problem in my work. I didn't feel that just by showing one issue was good enough and was going to get across to people. I made a full-scale painting of a human head. The person looks as if he/she is crying and is very sad about something that's happening or happened. I wanted the figure to look like it was screaming, so I gave it a wide open mouth. Inside the mouth I scratched in the words liar,

Picture 3 L.C., 11th grade girl, processing trauma and violence; acrylic on cardboard, 36″ × 40″, 2006

cheater, fake, ugly, fat. Those words are common these days. I hear people being called that often because of the way they look or the way the act. I used acrylic paint so I can layer the paint and it would be easier to scratch the words around the back of the person. The words are scratched in with white paint and a black background. I used words such as discrimination, rape, hate, crime, abuse, poverty, anorexia, racism, war, love, envy, depression, murder, suicide, and drugs. Being a high school student I see things in the world that are problems everyday. A lot of people don't think much of any issue in the world. We as children see them more than an adult would and they have high effects on us. Because of all these problems it may be hard for us to communicate with other people. *Principal Investigator Karen Rudolph, a professor of psychology at Illinois says, "Our findings have important implications for understanding how both youth and their social worlds influence the course of children's relationships."* (Italics by L.C.)

The audience is a very important part of my project. They are the ones who will put their point of view on it. I chose to make a full scale painting so that when someone walks up close to it they'll see the human figure as themselves. And they'll see the emotion and what happens to people when you judge them, or what happens when there's an issue and you don't address it. There will be no sound involved in my project. I'm not sure yet where I want to display it. It has to be a place people walk by so they'll stop and walk towards it. I want my audience to have an experience as if they've stepped into another world. They've opened a door out of the dream world we tend to live in and walked into reality. I think that most of the artist's work I viewed have inspired me with this painting. Some had used large materials to work with like buildings or walls. By using something large to show your work you get a lot out of it. Your work draws more attention to the audience. (L.C., 11/6/06)

J.G.

In the following example, J.G., an 11th grade girl, is processing meanings of violence and trauma in a 3-D format and peace in a 2-D format. J.G.'s artwork combined with her Artist Statement speaks for itself.

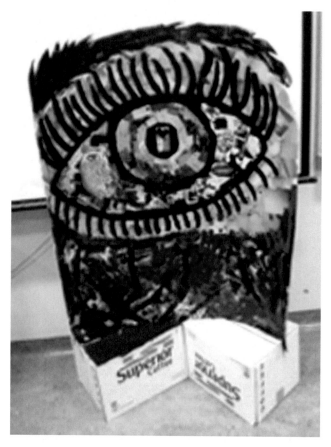

Picture 4   J.G., "Why?" acrylic and collage on cardboard, 36″ × 46″, 2006, work in progress

Artist Statement

Everyone goes through pain everyday. Not the pain that you feel on the outside but the pain that you feel emotionally in the inside. My project is titled "Why?" and it's based on pain through my eyes as a 16 year old girl trying to make her way through life. The image of the half face with the words in them is a quote about pain by Jim Morrison, who is a famous musician from the band "The Doors". The quote talks about pain and how everyone views it. The quote has a very strong meaning and point to my project and that is why I included it. I put all the images inside an eye because it is said the eyes are the windows to the soul, and I think that has a deeper meaning and it shows the pain and the emotion through my eye. I also included various images such as a dark hallway, a traffic light, swings, and other images to show not only just pain in general; but to show loneliness, loss, depression, love, fear, acceptance, guilt, and anger all in one work of art. I want the viewer to see what I see and to feel what I feel. The project is about my past and the struggles I myself have been through. But it also shows what other teens can go through every single day. (J.G., 11/8/06)

Picture 5 J.G., "Supporting Hands," acrylic on paper, 18″ × 20″, 2006, work in progress

Many students said that we lack images of peace that resonate with reality. "Supporting Hands" was created in response to my question "When you think of peace, what do you see in your mind?"

Teamwork: H.G., T.F., and V.G.

When it came to designing Community Art Projects representing social issues, over half of the participants preferred to work in teams of two or three. Following are examples of their artworks and statements.

H.G, T.F., and V.G., three 10th grade girls, processing collective trauma in 3-D form:

Picture 6   H.G, T.F., and V.G., "Judgment," clay, cardboard, Mylar, metal wire, acrylic, 24″ × 30″ × 12″, 2006

The work of this group clearly demonstrated that in the *ART*iculation modality, the artwork itself *is* the ground-base experience for the higher cognitive process of meaning making. This group has successfully created an Orwelian-like image of a society controlled by some big brother's eye. In the course of making this image, these young artists have been discussing a large variety of wrongdoing and traumatic experiences related to this social issue. It was fascinating to watch how every artistic decision took the discussion of "Judgment" in a new direction. This, in turn, heightened their art critique and aesthetic choices, practically making connections between the constructive artistic judgment and a destructive social experience of judgment. From the outset, it was clear who provided the leadership. This leader insisted that every member of the group will do their best, share responsibility, and contribute to the Artist Statement. This work represents a result of a successful collaborative endeavor. It also demonstrated to the participants the effect of a genuine dialogue and its quiet power to generate mutual change. In their experience of harmonious collaboration they realized what a dialogue-based peace entails.

Artists' Statement

Judgments are made about other people everyday. Everyone determines who they want to talk with and trust by judging them at first sight... Every action you do, hand you shake, and smile you give is observed by another. Even as you are being judged you are judging others as well. People judge people without even knowing who they are... This is a problem because people are being accused of being who they are not...people are just misunderstood...

We have used clay to make the people and painted them using a variety of dark colors on them. The people are always in a down position with their heads facing the ground because we wanted to show that when people are judged they feel sad and misunderstood for who they are. The rough ground represents the cruelty of judging. The eye symbolizes the people who do the judging towards others. It is on a hill because when people judge and they think badly of the person they are judging the judger feels they are better than the person they are judging. The shining pupil has the words people usually think of when they judge others.

We do believe that Community Art Projects can make a difference in people's lives because it changes the way they see the world. People walk through life not knowing all the problems that occur in the world. The problems that happen in our everyday life are ignored because we are so used to seeing them that they seem to be a normal occurrence. When artists create pieces of art that present a problem, that may not be big but is important, society is forced to see what is happening. Through the view of another eye, people can see the problems and can make a change in their life to stop it. For example, the art piece "Judgment" we have created shows how people are quick to judge others, like judging a book by its cover. When people see this, one by one they will try to stop judging and the problem will be faced and resolved! (H.G., T.F., and V.G., 11/6/06)

C.G. and N.J.

C.G. and N.J., 10th grade girls, created "Hunger: A Global Trauma" in 3-D format and "Peace is Your Other Half" in 2-D format:

These students asked if they could chose to work on a global trauma, instead of a personal one. They did a research on the Internet on the subject of child starvation.

Picture 7   C.G. and N.J., "Hunger: A Global Trauma," clay, photograph, sticks, acrylic, 10″ × 9″ × 8″, 2006

In order to address the experience of utter poverty they selected clay painted with earth-like color, sticks, a photocopy, and glue. In their depiction, they turned reality around placing the picture of the hungry child inside the bowl, thus provoking the audience with the question "how can we have peace when children are dying of hunger?"

Artists' Statement

Our project is based on the topic of world hunger and starvation. I chose this topic because sometimes in the morning, really early, a sponsor our children commercial comes on and it always makes me feel horrible for a child to have to live in those circumstances. For the display of my project I would like to place it in a wide open black dark space with light shining only on the piece all the time. The emptiness of the room represents the emptiness of the children's stomachs. I chose the color scheme for our artwork to be dark like the thoughts and dreams of the children. The project is a bowl and a picture frame. The bowl is made of clay like earth, like where the children get their food. It is not perfect in any shape but that is a way to show the not even close to perfect lifestyle these poor children grow up in. Placed in the bowl is a picture frame with a picture of a boy eating. This is a symbol of a lucky boy who got food. I want the audience to feel generous to them and help them more. I want them to feel bad and appreciate what they have and be grateful they aren't in that position... You have to interpret this project in your own way and really think about what you can do. (N.J. and C.G., 11/14/06)

Picture 8 **"Peace is Your Other Half," Acrylic, 22″ × 28″, 2006**

Later, I challenged them "what for you would represent peace?" Similar to others earlier, they too see peace in human intimacy. It seems that for these students, peace can be experienced when love and intimacy are found.

Artists' Statement

Peace has many meanings. Our definition of peace is companionship because that is when you are the happiest. Our project isn't necessarily about just any kind of peace, it is about peace at heart. Our project is a large painting of a man and a woman. The people are inter-woven by legs and arms representing the closeness they have. The painting is made of the complementary colors, yellow and violet, and their tones. The contrast makes the picture pop out at you. Most people think peace is "no violence", but there are many kinds of peace. Peace can be happiness, love, laughter, or sadness. From our point of view peace is companionship. (C.G. and N.J., 12/15/06)

Summary

This research is a long-term work in progress. The *ARTi*culation modality is distinguished by the dialogic realism of the artistic creative process as *both* a context and text. Peace, forgiveness, and artistic creation share the same realism. Because of the dialogic nature of *ARTi*culation and its effect as an intentional intervention modality, it was important at this early stage to present the visual images along with the artists' statements. Only in relation to each other can the artworks, side-by-side with the verbal statements, present to the reader the specific dialogic – as opposed to dialectic – efficacy of the *ARTi*culation experience. The above examples represent the beginning of a therapeutic effect generated by the dialogic character of this modality and demonstrate how its processes of creative realization allow the participant to elaborate the meaning of traumatic experience and to process forgiveness within a larger context of peace consciousness in the making.

References

American Psychological Association. (2006). *Forgiveness: A sampling of research results*. Compiled by the American Psychological Association on the Occasion of the 59th Annual DPI/NGO Conference, United Nations Headquarters. New York.

Arenheim, R. (1971). *Entropy and art; an essay on disorder and order*. Berkeley and Los Angeles: University of California Press.

Arenheim, R. (1986). *New essays on the psychology of art*. Berkeley and Los Angeles: University of California Press.

Bedaux, J. B., & Cook, B. (Eds.). (1999). *Sociobiology and the arts*. Amsterdam/Atlanta, GA: Editions Rodopi.

Bhaskar, R. (1986). *Scientific realism and human emancipation*. London: Verso.

Bhaskar, R. (1991). *Philosophy and the idea of freedom*. Oxford: Blackwell.

Borchers, K. (1985). Do gains made in art therapy persist? A study with aftercare patients. *American Journal of Art Therapy, 23*(3), 89–91.

Buber-Agassi, J. (Ed.). (1999). *Martin Buber on psychology and psychotherapy: Essays, letters, and dialogues*. Syracuse, NY: Syracuse University Press.

Buber, M. (1947). *Between man and man*. London: Routledge & Kegan Paul Ltd.

Buber, M. (1965). *The knowledge of man*. London: George Allen & Unwin Ltd.

Cohen, J. A., Mannarino, A. P., & Deblinger, E. (2006). *Treating trauma and traumatic grief in children and adolescents*. New York: The Guilford Press.

Friedman, M. (1991). *Encounter on the narrow ridge: a life of Martin Buber*. New York: Paragon House.

Friedman, M. (1973). *Martin Buber, the life of dialogue*. New York: Harper & Row.

Friedman, M. (1985). *The healing dialogue in psychotherapy*. New York/London: Jason Aronson, Inc.

Gal-Ed, H. (1999). *AMEN as paradigm for peace education*. Paper presented at The Parliament of the World's Religions, Cape Town, South Africa.

Gal-Ed, H. (2000, spring). Art as a paradigm for peace. *Jewish Education News*, Special Focus on The Arts in Jewish education, CAJE Publication.

Gal-Ed, H. (2001). *The making of art and the knowledge of peace: A grounded theory study of video ARTiculation as a learning tool in a dialogic program of peace education*. PhD Dissertation, New York University.

Gil, E. (1996). *Treating abused adolescents*. New York: The Guilford Press.

Gil, E. (2006). *Helping abused and traumatized children: integrating directive and nondirective approaches.* New York: The Guilford Press.

Kaplan, F. F. (2000). *Art, science and art therapy: repainting the picture.* London: Jessica Kingsley.

Lamb, S., & Murphy, J. (Eds.). (2002). *Before forgiveness: cautionary views of forgiveness in psychotherapy.* Oxford: Oxford University Press.

Malchiodi, C. (2006). *Art therapy sourcebook* (2nd ed.). New York: McGraw-Hill.

Maslow, A. (1966a). Isomorphic interrelationships between knower and known. In G. Kepes (Ed.), *Sign, image, symbol.* Braziller. Reprinted in Matson, F. W., & A. Montagu (Eds.), *The human dialogue: Perspectives on Communication.* New York: Free Press.

Maslow, A. (1966b). *The psychology of science: a reconnaissance.* New York: Harper & Row.

Maslow, A. (1968a). *Toward a psychology of being* (2nd ed.). New York: Van Nostrand.

Maslow, A. (1968b). Toward the study of violence. In L. Ng (Ed.), *Alternatives to Violence.* New York: Time-Life Books.

McCullough, M. E., Thoresen, C. E., & Pargament, K. I. (Eds.). (2000). *Forgiveness.* New York: Guilford Press.

Metcalfe, J., & Shimamura, P. A. (1996). *Metacognition: Knowing about knowing.* Cambridge, MA: The MIT Press. New Ed.

Miller, A. (1990). *Banished knowledge: Facing childhood injuries.* New York: Doubleday.

Miller, A. (1997). *The drama of the gifted child: The search for true self.* New York: Basic Books.

Miller, A. (2005). *The body never lies: The lingering effects of cruel parenting.* New York: W. W. Norton & Co.

Riley, S. (1999). *Contemporary art therapy with adolescents.* London/Philadelphia: Jessica Kingsley Publishers.

Riley, S. (2004). The creative mind. *Art Therapy: Journal of the American Art Therapy Association, 21*(4), 184–190.

Solso, L. R. (2003). *The psychology of art and the evolution of the conscious brain.* Cambridge, MA/London, England: The MIT Press.

Spivey, N. (2005). *How art made the world: a journey to the origins of human creativity.* New York. Basic Books.

Thompson, A. R. (2003). *Counseling techniques, improving relationships with others, ourselves, our families, and our environment* (2nd ed.). New York: Brunner-Routledge.

Wilson, E. O. (1981). *Genes, mind, and culture.* Cambridge, MA: Harvard University Press.

Wilson, E. O. (1998). *Consilience: The unity of knowledge.* New York: Knopf.

Witvliet, C. V. O., Phipps, K. A., Feldman, M. E., & Beckman, J. C. (2004). Posttraumatic mental and physical health correlates of forgiveness and religious coping in military veterans. *Journal of Traumatic Stress, 17*(3), 269–273.

Worthington, E. L., Jr. (Ed.). (2005). *Handbook of forgiveness.* New York: Brunner-Routledge.

Chapter 8
Promoting Forgiveness Through Restorative Conferencing

Augustine Nwoye

The theme of forgiveness has long been neglected in the counseling and psychotherapy literature. Yet it is an important concept in the context of reducing interpersonal conflict and hostility, particularly here in Africa, where interpersonal and inter-ethnic hostilities (such as in Rwanda, Uganda, Sierra Leone, Nigeria, Liberia, Democratic Republic of Congo, and Burundi) and multi-racial conflicts (as in South Africa, Zimbabwe, Angola, Mozambique, etc.) have been rife. Fortunately, this undeserved neglect of the concept has changed in recent decades. These are the decades when research and writing on forgiveness constructs began to gain momentum among professional counselors, psychologists, and theologians (McCullough, Bono, & Root, 2005; McCullough, Pargament, & Thoresen, 2000; Worthington, 2005) and among family therapists (Jenkins, 2006). This change has given rise to a number of theories of forgiveness now extant in the literature. In studying those theories an important conclusion that comes up again and again is that what creates the need for forgiveness is the problem of betrayal; a notion that creates the impression that the problem of forgiveness is typically encountered in the context of intimate relationships. However, adopting such a notion leaves unaddressed the related idea that the need for forgiveness also arises in the context of interpersonal assaults and gross social humiliations.

The current literature has suggested that forgiveness as a response to betrayal can only come about after the injured party has been able to pass through the normal three stages of recovering from psychological trauma, namely (a) impact, (b) a search for meaning, and (c) recovery; it is, therefore, a private state of the mind. However, this point of view tends to see the enablement of forgiveness a personal matter, with emphasis on intrapersonal sources of forgiveness to the neglect of its interpersonal roots. To close the gap, I wish to demonstrate in this chapter how the practice of restorative conferencing can be used as a method of promoting forgiveness that draws attention to aspects of mature forgiveness that are more transactional in nature. They involve not only the person doing the forgiving and the person that is forgiven but also a witnessing community, present as organizers of, and observers and facilitators to, the transactions.

Ani Kalayjian, Raymond F. Paloutzian, *Forgiveness and Reconciliation*, Peace Psychology Book Series, DOI 10.1007/978-1-4419-0181-1_8,
© Springer Science+Business Media, LLC 2009

Clarification of Concepts

Defining Forgiveness

Enright and Coyle (1998) and Enright, Santos, and Al-Mabuk (1989) define forgiveness as "a willingness to abandon one's right to resentment, negative judgment, and indifferent behaviour toward one who unjustly hurt us, while fostering the underserved qualities of compassion, generosity, and even love toward him or her" (pp. 46–47). Those researchers who support the above notion of the positive qualities of forgiveness view it as a spiritual practice. In contrast, Exline and Baumeister (2000) used the notion of debt and its cancellation to identify what happens when one accepts to forgive another. In their view, "When one person harms or transgresses against another, this action effectively creates an interpersonal debt. Forgiveness involves the canceling of this debt by the person who has been hurt or wronged" (p. 134). Hebl and Enright (1993) and Wade (1989) elaborate that this cancellation could take multiple channels, including those that are cognitive, affective, behavioral, and/or spiritual (Exline & Baumeister, 2000).

The above observations suggest that when people forgive, their responses toward people who have offended or injured them become more positive and less negative. Thus one can agree with McCullough et al. (2000) that forgiveness can summarily be defined as an intraindividual, prosocial change toward a perceived transgressor that is situated within a specific interpersonal context. This particular definition implies that when someone forgives a person who has committed a transgression against him or her, it is the forgiver (specifically, in his or her thoughts, feelings, motivations, or behaviors) who changes. In this sense, forgiveness is seen to be a psychological construct.

What is argued in this chapter, however, is that forgiveness has a dual character: it is interpersonal as well as intrapersonal. Taking this perspective means that forgiveness occurs in response to an interpersonal violation (usually a betrayal or an assault) and the individual who forgives necessarily forgives in relation to someone else. Therefore, even while being a psychological phenomenon, forgiveness is interpersonal in the same sense that many other psychological constructs are interpersonal in nature (e.g., trust, prejudice, empathy), each having other people as its point of reference. In particular, forgiveness is facilitated or hindered by the attitude of the offender to what he or she has done to the injured party. Therefore, it is also interpersonally sourced, as will be clarified shortly below.

What Forgiveness Is Not

Achieving a firm grip on the notion of forgiveness must include an attempt at understanding what forgiveness is not. Most theorists and researchers, such as Enright and Coyle (1998), emphasize that forgiveness should be differentiated from "pardoning" (a legal term), "condoning" (a justification of the offense), "excusing" (implying that the offender had a good reason for committing the offense), "forgetting" (implying that the memory of the offense has simply decayed or slipped out of conscious awareness), and "denying" (suggesting an unwillingness to perceive the harmful injuries that one has incurred).

Equally important in trying to understand what forgiveness is, and is not, is the need for a related understanding of the counterpart of forgiveness, namely repentance, which is applicable to the person who committed the transgression. Most authorities agree that repentance should be taken to refer to a manifestable attitude of remorse in the face of an offence, which encourages the offender to offer an apology for his or her misconduct. Understood in this way, the conclusion can be made that although repentance is not the same thing as forgiveness, it facilitates forgiveness (Jenkins, 2006). This is because the offender's spirit of remorse followed by an apology is more likely to provoke the spirit of compassion on the part of the victim in favor of the transgressor, with this process culminating in the injured person's decision to forgive the transgressor. However, the religious perspective on forgiveness (Worthington, 2005; McCullough et al., 2005) appears to show that in some Christian traditions the offender's repentance is not necessary for forgiveness to occur. Williams (2000), for instance, points out that "According to the model of Christ on the cross (Luke 23:34), forgiveness, or at least the petition for God the Father to forgive, does not depend first of all on repentance by the offender" (p. 33). The notion of repentance that informs the present chapter is not the type that is assumed in the above tradition.

The Forgiveness Process

Having dealt with the "what" of forgiveness and how it relates to repentance, we now explore the "how" of forgiveness. Gordon and Baucom (1998, p. 426) emphasize that the "how" of forgiveness consists of three important processes: (a) achieving a realistic, non-distorted, and balanced view of what went wrong; (b) gaining a release from being consumed by negative affect or the spirit of revenge toward the offending party; and (c) securing a lessened desire to punish the offending party. In addition, Jenkins (2006) suggests that another important point to remember in examining the process of forgiveness is that mature forgiveness entails a complex interaction including the person who is forgiving, the person who is being forgiven, and a dyadic interaction between these two people. This means that mature forgiveness is achieved in dialogue. To date, however, the attention of writers and researchers has focused more on the experience and reaction of the person doing the forgiving than on the one being forgiven. This present discussion of the practice of restorative conferencing as a method of promoting forgiveness will try to extend this focus to include aspects of promoting mature forgiveness that are facilitated by a constructive and voluntary dialogue between the protagonists, executed in the presence of a witnessing community.

Factors That Promote, Not Hinder, Expression of Forgiveness

Related to the idea that achieving mature forgiveness is an experiential process is the current understanding that a number of factors can promote rather than hinder the expression of forgiveness. Exline and Baumeister (2000) elaborating on this agree that "Victims are much more likely to forgive perpetrators who respond in repentant ways" (p. 136). Their studies show that target respondents expressed greater readiness to forgive those perpetrators who acknowledged that they committed the offense, offered sincere apologies, asked for forgiveness, expressed feelings of guilt or sadness, and did something positive to "make up" for the offense. In contrast, they found that "defensive responses by the perpetrator, such as insincere apologies, downplaying or covering up the offense, and blaming the victim, were associated with lower levels of forgiveness" (Exline & Baumeister, 2000, p. 136). These findings were in line with those by others that suggest that people are more likely to forgive perpetrators who apologize (e.g., Darby & Schlenker, 1982; McCullough et al., 2005; McCullough, Worthington, & Rachal, 1997; Ohbuchi, Kameda, & Agarie, 1989; Worthington, 2005) or confess wrongdoing (e.g., Jenkins, 2006; Weiner, Graham, Peter, & Zmuidinas, 1991). However, barriers to expressing forgiveness have also been noted (Exline & Baumeister, 2000). They can arise through fear that transgression will be repeated, fear of appearing weak, belief that justice will not be served, and loss of benefits of victim status. Similarly, defensive reactions such as self-justifications or refusal on the part of the offender to accept responsibility generally lead to harsher judgments of perpetrators and a greater desire to punish them (Gonzales, Haugen, & Manning, 1994) and therefore an inability to achieve forgiveness (Jenkins, 2006).

Barriers to Expression of Repentance

Just as there are barriers to achieving forgiveness, there are also a number of factors that can cause barriers to expression of repentance. According to Exline and Baumeister (2000), "One major barrier to expressing repentance is that perpetrators are likely to perceive the charge as inaccurate, excessive, or unfair" (p. 140). In their view, the usual tendency is for the perpetrators to perceive their transgressions as less harmful and serious than victims do, creating what Baumeister (1997) has termed the magnitude gap, a phenomenon that appears to reflect self-serving distortions on the part of both victims and perpetrators. This implies that the victims' account of the injury they have suffered at the hands of transgressors is often partial (Bruner, 1990).

Researchers have also shown that fear of punishment such as severe pragmatic costs or restrictions associated with accepting responsibility for an offence can also cause a barrier to expressing repentance. Exline and Baumeister (2000) agree with this notion and suggest that perpetrators may be able to protect themselves from sanctions if they can conceal that they committed a certain act. In the African context, another important factor that can present obstacle to expression of repentance is the problem of shame (Jenkins, 2006). And here the understanding is that even in the absence of fear of external punishment for confession, people are often reluctant to express repentance because they find doing so too shameful.

Can the Barriers Be Broken?

The major purpose of this chapter is to highlight how the practice of restorative conferencing can be used to promote forgiveness in a victim of a specific interpersonal misconduct. To achieve this, a case example will be given that reports a nasty episode that took place in an African community in which a classroom teacher was assaulted by her own student, creating the scene of a "victim" and an "offender." The restorative conferencing procedure was instituted in order to promote the spirit of remorse, repentance, and apology on the part of the offender and that of compassion and forgiveness on the part of the victim.

The lesson intended is that in the African context, forgiveness is an interpersonal process with a social dimension. To illustrate this, the discussion will include an examination of what restorative conferencing means and entails as a communal ritual for promoting forgiveness, the procedure used in practicing it, the philosophy and significance of its practice, and the actual rituals that are implemented in the use of such a technique in promoting forgiveness in the modern African context.

Restorative Conferencing

Restorative conferencing is the new alternative model that was introduced to replace the old and revenge-dominated approach for dealing with offenders, particularly young offenders (Consedine, 1995; Trebilcock, 2001; Wachtel, 1999). It takes the form of an organized dialogue between the protagonists (the victim and the offender), both members of a given community. The aim of the dialogue is to repair the harm done to the victim by the offender by allowing all concerned (victim, offender, and their parents and supporters), plus a representative of the institution or community within which the offence occurred and the protagonists belong, to meet in a well-managed, protected, and psychologically safe environment and review what happened, the reasons for its occurrence, and the preferred outcomes. This presentation shows that unlike the old retributive system that focuses only on charging the offender, the outcome of which leads to retaliatory justice of imprisonment, restorative conferencing emphasizes the need for dialogic exchanges between the perpetrator and the victim; the ultimate result is promotion of peace and forgiveness (Consedine, 1995; Kamya & Trimble, 2003; Trebilcock, 2001; Wachtel, 1999). Thus, Rivett (2003) was alluding to the dialogue of restorative conferencing when he observed that "In the latter dialogue, both perpetrator and victim witness and hear the pain of the other and are transformed by the experience" (p. 445).

Structure, Process, and Principal Features

In West and East Africa, as is also the case in Australia, New Zealand, and South Africa, restorative conferencing typically takes place in a room where everyone can sit in a circle or, as in my own practice, in a semi-circle. Authorities (Consedine, 1995; Trebilcock, 2001; Wachtel, 1999) suggest that it is important that everyone invited to the conference comes there freely, not forced, and that the environment is protected in a way that makes each member feel safe, not harassed. To achieve this effect the sitting plan is organized in such a way that the victim or victims sit with their family/supporters and the offender(s) sit with theirs. Other invited members sit somewhere in the middle. The facilitator usually places him-or-herself equidistant from victim and offender (Consedine, 1995; Trebilcock, 2001; Wachtel, 1999).

My experience of its use cautions that for the conference to bear the expected fruit, the facilitator will have personally contacted all expected to be present prior to the conference, ideally face to face. The aim is to prepare them for the meeting and to respond to any possible confusions and queries about it. The conference is intended to be an ultimately positive experience from which the victim and the offender can walk away, as Rivett (2003) mentioned, better able to move on and put the incident behind them. Consequently, the objective of the meeting is not hidden from the members until the day of the meeting. The facilitator, the convener, instead shares the rationale for the conference with them, including the expected dividends to accrue to both the victim and the perpetrator of the offence, for availing themselves.

Psychologically speaking and from the offender's perspective, the process is usually an agonizing experience. For it typically involves accepting responsibility to a shameful offence in the presence of one's parents and/or admirers. In addition, hearing and witnessing the victims as well as their own parents attest to the adverse effects their misconduct has had on them deepens their discomfort. This is particularly so to those for whom such a meeting might be the first time they are enabled to give thought to the consequences of their assault on others, including their own families. Nevertheless, it is expected that by the end of the conference the offenders are able to move forward, perhaps having expressed remorse and even an apology (although this is not forced). Depending on the offence, and particularly in the African context, mere expression of apology is not accepted as enough to influence forgiveness. In successful conferencing, practical reparation is also agreed upon and an agreement is often signed by all present. In some cases, particularly where young offenders are involved, their parents can volunteer some practical support to help the offenders behave differently in the future.

For the victims, on the other hand, the meeting is an opportunity, perhaps for the first time, toward understanding why the incident actually happened. This is often a pressing psychological need for victims because not knowing can lead to anxiety, ambiguity distress, loss of confidence, feelings of failure, and self-searching, leading to chronic stress and an inability to cope with everyday life. However, for successful conferencing, victims also need to know that an offender fully appreciates the harm they have caused. Consequently, if the conference succeeds in helping the offender(s) feel remorse for what they have done and to offer an apology, and if the offer of some kind of reparation is a positive outcome, the victim can be better helped to move on and put the incident behind them. However, these are not inevitable outcomes of the conference. But they are sufficiently common that in my own practice they are part of the main expected outcomes.

An important feature of restorative conferencing is the involvement of everyone present in planning the way forward. The victims and their supporters are asked what they would like to see come out of the conference, and so are the offender's supporters and the offender him- or herself. This contrasts with more punitive ways of dealing with inappropriate behavior where the opinion of the victim is not sought. In restorative conferencing, consensus is generally reached and an agreement signed by everyone. A copy of this agreement is distributed to everyone at the end of the conference. This has proved to be a significant element in repairing the harm done. It helps the offender to stick to his or her resolution to make up for the injury done to the victim (Consedine, 1995; Trebilcock, 2001; Wachtel, 1999). In the modern African context, restorative conferencing has been suggested for use in schools, colleges, and local districts to deal with cases of bullying, truancy, interpersonal conflict, disruptive behavior, and behavior warranting summary exclusion such as vandalism or assaults against authority. It is also recommended even in adult–adult infractions experienced in Rwanda, Sierra Leone, Liberia, Ethiopia, Burundi, South Africa, Zimbabwe, Sudan, Somalia, Israel, Palestine, and Iraq.

Historical Information

The first restorative conference was held in New Zealand as part of the Children, Youth, and Families Act of 1989 (Consedine, 1995; Wachtel, 1999). This law grew from discontent among the Maori regarding the way courts dealt with their young people in criminal and social welfare matters. Eventually the government decided that a wide range of youth issues would be dealt with through the process of a "family group conference" (FGC). This decision means that instead of attending court, the extended family of a young person would work together with officials to develop plans to address the offence in question. Presently, the practice of restorative conferencing as a method of restoring harmony among opposing parties is no longer confined to the people of New Zealand. It is now practiced in such other countries as South Africa, United States, and Kenya (Consedine, 1995; Trebilcock, 2001; Wachtel, 1999).

Reintegrative Shaming

This refers to the psychological cost, which the victim must bear if he or she is to avoid the option of a jail term or institutional expulsion following his or her infraction, when the latter is to be addressed and resolved within the context of restorative conferencing. This means that the term reintegrative shaming refers to the shame the offender feels in seeing his or her offence or criminal behavior publicly disapproved of and roundly condemned by those he or she admirers and respects (Braithwaite, 1989; Harris, 2006). Such shame is referred to as reintegrative in the sense that although it is emotionally costly to bear, its negativity is mitigated by the offender being accepted back into the community. This occurs after he or she has tendered a sincere apology for the offense and offered some other reparative acts that are intended to reflect sincere remorse and a genuine search for forgiveness – leading ultimately to his or her winning an act of forgiveness from the offended person(s).

Reintegrative shaming is in contradistinction to what is done in the traditional retributive approach. The latter aims to punish and humiliate offenders by often sending them to prison without offering them a way to make amends or to right the wrong and shed the "offender" label. In such a punitive system, offenders typically become stigmatized, alienated, excluded, and pushed toward negative subcultures (Harris, 2006). In contrast, the offender who suffers reintegrative shaming during restorative conferencing is seeing his or her offence disapproved of while still being treated as a valued human being. In this way, the process of restorative conferencing enables offenders to take responsibility, apologize, and identify ways to repair the harm and contribute to their reacceptance in the community. In that way, after suffering the shame of owning responsibility for their misconduct in the presence of their parents and significant others, and thereafter tendering an apology and a promise of reparation, the offender is reabsorbed into the community and sheds the offender label (Braithwaite, 1989; Consedine, 1995; Harris, 2006; O'Connell, Wachtel, & Wachtel, 1999; Trebilcock, 2001; Wachtel, 1997, 1999).

Phases of Restorative Conferencing

Consensus is that there are three main phases in the successful organization and management of restorative conferencing (Consedine, 1995; Trebilcock, 2001; Wachtel, 1999). These are (i) preparation, (ii) facilitation, and (iii) closure/follow-up. Successful restorative conferencing demands adequate preparation. The following is a list of activities that must be taken into account to achieve effective preparation for the conference:

(a) Have a clear understanding of the incident.
(b) Determine if a conference is needed.
(c) Meet with the offender about the case and establish their admission of responsibility.
(d) Send an invitation to all necessary participants.

Others include the need to speak or meet with all participants and securing their attendance; ensure that participants understand the conference process and its purpose; ensure that participants know how to contact the facilitator, to reserve a suitable room for the meeting; ensure that participants know the date, time, and place and how to get there; ensure that all participants have transportation; develop a suitable seating plan; be familiar with the conference facilitator's script, containing established guide on how to proceed and who should do what during the conference; and give some thought about how the conference might unfold.

Other important planning considerations include the need to determine if one needs assistance, e.g., a co-facilitator, a translator/interpreter, or an observer to give you feedback; determine which language is common to all involved and needs to be used; plan for what may happen if the conference does not reach an agreement or the offender fails to satisfy the agreement; and secure all the necessary items for a successful conference (Brendtro, Brokenleg, & Van Bockern, 1990; Consedine, 1995; Kamya & Trimble, 2003; Trebilcock, 2001). The necessary items for implementing the conference include a copy of the conference facilitator's script; agreement forms and other required forms; the conference seating plan; participant seating labels; a "Do not disturb" sign to be pasted at the door of the room where the meeting is being held; a box of tissues; and refreshments.

Facilitating the Conference

Restorative conferences are influenced by indigenous values. These values are reflected in sacred and spiritual practices valorized in African worldview. Among such practices is the ritual of invocation and other performative experiences that help to raise the mind of the members to the spiritual meaning of the meeting. For this reason, in my practice and in those simulated in my training sessions, such conferences are opened and/or ended with spiritual messages, prayers, songs, and other sacred practices like reading the relevant scripture passages to attune the people to the spirituality of the meeting. It is essential that this aspect of the conferencing process be planned appropriately and with utmost sensitivity to the culture, religion, and other aspects of diversity of the participants present (Consedine, 1995; Trebilcock, 2001; Wachtel, 1999).

For the conference to be successful, the facilitator should be completely neutral and as transparent as possible. S/he should avoid being drawn into the discussion or taking sides, but should redirect questions and their communication to the group as a whole. One of the ways to promote this is through use of, and sticking to, the script.

Closing Rituals

In my own practice and in most other restorative conferences, refreshments are served after the conference. In Africa, eating and drinking together promotes belonging and a sense of community (Ejizu, 1994; Ekwunife, 1997). In restorative conferencing, it also provides an informal way in which conference participants can spend time together after the intensity of the conference itself. In my own practice I exploit these values to the maximum. It is during the refreshments that the facilitator prepares the agreement and asks participants to sign it. After the meal and as they prepare to depart, participants often express signs of healed relationships through affectionate responses such as hugs to one another.

Illustrative Case Example

The case presented below will be used to clarify what is done or not done in the use of restorative conferencing to promote forgiveness. In the presentation the details of the people and the school made reference to have been withheld for purposes of confidentiality.

In a Kenyan Classroom

On one ill-starred Wednesday morning in the month of March 2001, a nasty and grim experience took place in one classroom in a large public secondary school in Kenya. The case involved a fracas between a dedicated and well-experienced female mathematics teacher and one of her rude male students who was obsessed with the need to make a name for himself as a terror to great teachers in the school. To achieve this aim, he had continued to be a thorn in the flesh of the teacher in question. He engaged in distractive and other kinds of funny behaviors while the class was going on, all aimed at making the teacher feel miserable each time she came to class. But being a well-trained teacher with considerable experience in teaching mathematics, she tried to weather through the storm of the student's evil machinations by ignoring it and other related techniques. However, on the fateful day, the student felt bent on achieving his negative aim of rattling the teacher in the eyes of his classmates.

He did not succeed in doing this while the class was on. He had to wait until the end of the class to do his worst. And so, as the teacher ended the class and was about to pick up her bag and her teaching materials to depart, the student leaped out of his seat, rushed to the space near the exit door as the teacher approached the same door. He met the teacher at the point of her arriving at the door to negotiate an exit. Standing shoulder to shoulder with the teacher in a competitive mood of trying to rush out first, before the teacher could do so, the teacher felt helmed in. For this reason, she looked up with a surprise and stern look, as if to ask, "What is the matter boy?" But wearing a defiant pose, and looking straight to the teacher in the face, the boy responded with the second finger of his right arm placed on the right side of his nose, in a posture of one about to blow out one's nose with mucus onto an enemy's face. Such a demeanor in the African context reflects a grave sign of insult and arrogance to an authority. And some class members witnessing what the boy was doing were stunned with bewilderment. Some of them even tried to use guarded laughter to contain their anxiety and shame due to the entire infraction.

But the student did not stop at that. As the teacher tried to hurry out of the door to escape further humiliation, the student added more injury to the teacher's humiliation. This is because, as the teacher turned away from him to leave the room, the student got hold of her skirt from the behind; swiftly throwing up, exposing the teacher's underwear. The teacher noticed what happened and first pulled down the skirt. Then she turned in anger and shock to the boy, screaming out the question, what is that? At this stage, the boy with some air of arrogance just walked away from the scene, to the utter bewilderment of his mates for the boy's gross misconduct. The teacher, overcome by shame and shock, broke down in tears and literally rushed out of the scene and went straight to the head teacher's office to report the incident.

She could not tell her story immediately when she arrived at the head's office. She was overcome by anger, shame, and shock. She sobbed profusely, leaving the head teacher utterly confused about what was the matter. However, at long last she was able to control her emotions to tell her story. She ended the report, presenting the head teacher with one choice for the school to choose from: "It is either me or that boy," she said, "since I cannot imagine myself stepping into that class again, with him there!"

The head teacher responded swiftly to the teacher's complaint. He called a meeting of the school disciplinary committee in which he reported the incident. The committee invited the prefect of the class to tell more details of what happened, from the students' perspective. On confirming that the incident took place as reported by the teacher, the committee at first thought of giving immediate expulsion to the student – as required by regulation. But then the school counselor intervened saying that they could reserve that action as a last resort until the practice of restorative conferencing had been attempted and it failed to work. She explained what this process entails and offered to facilitate its application in the case. The committee agreed to her intervention. To prepare the ground for that process, the student was suspended while the teacher was given a week off from duty to enable her to take sometime to herself to recover from the shock and stress of the incident. And for the class as a group, this week served as "interval therapy" (the wearing away of the shock of the experience with time).

Discussion

Applying restorative conferencing to the above case involved the counselor first contacting the student and his parents about the incident. The aim was to secure their motivation to attend the meeting and to be assured that the student is prepared to take responsibility for the case and would come to the conference to clarify what happened, why he did what he did, and that he would be ready to offer a genuine apology and engage in other restitution tasks the teacher might demand before she can forgive him. S/he also contacted the teacher and got her to accept the need for the meeting and her willingness to attend.

After contacting all involved, the counselor, acting as the facilitator, decided on the day for the meeting and communicated this to the student and his parents, the teacher and her supporters, and to the representative of the school administration. All agreed on the appropriateness of the date and time for the meeting and assured the counselor of their participation. After they said they would be able to find their way to the meeting, the counselor sent out official invitation to all parties involved.

Fig. 8.1 This is a semi-circular sitting plan for restorative conferencing.

After this was done s/he secured the room as well as other items for the conference, including the chairs. The chairs were arranged in a semi-circular form as depicted in Fig. 8.1.

A total of nine persons were present at the meeting to handle the above-reported case. This included three from the offender's side, three from the victim's side, and three from the community or institutional setting where the incident took place – in the present case, the head teacher, the disciplinary master, and the counselor.

Before concluding the preparation, the facilitating counselor went through the standard checklist of activities (noted above) and items required for a successful practice of restorative conferencing. During the meeting, the counselor played the role of master of ceremonies for the conference, welcomed members, and made reference to the objective of the meeting. She also invited the head teacher or her representative to act as chairman of the meeting. The meeting began with the ritual of invocation, which, in the present case, involved an opening song and prayer intended to tune the members to the spiritual meaning of the meeting and to show that God was an unseen guest in the meeting who would listen to the stories and the proceedings of the day. This measure was in synchrony to the spirituality and worldview of the participants.

After this invocation stage, the chairman took over the proceedings and formally introduced the case to the members present. He began by reminding members that the disciplinary master could confirm the traditional school disciplinary process, which involved expelling the student for what he had done. But instead, he had decided to try the option of this conference in order to create an opportunity for possible restoration of harmony between the offender and the victim. In particular, this conference might allow them to find out what really happened, learn its effects on the victim, and hear what the victim may require before she could be ready to forgive the offender.

With this introduction done, he gave the teacher the chance and the space to address the meeting. Her speech was intended to tell the members what happened and the pain she suffered consequent upon that. The student was given the floor next to respond to the charge. In the case under discussion, the teacher was able to tell the story as it happened without any exaggeration. And the result was that the student had no ground for a defensive response. He admitted responsibility and manifested remorse by kneeling down, soliciting for forgiveness for his offence. He said he had been very much shamed of it and could not understand the spirit that pushed him to offend the teacher in the way he did. The chairman, in following up this manifest sign of remorse presented by the student, returned to the teacher with a request to hear from her what she would like done by the student before his appeal for forgiveness could be granted. In response, the teacher demanded that mere apology is not the only thing necessary. She indicated that the student humiliated her in the presence of his classmates and that to annul that horrendous image, the student has to put the apology in writing and read it openly to her in their class, kneeling down. She further demanded that this ritual of apology be done in the classroom and be witnessed by the disciplinary master and the school counselor.

The chairman then directed the attention to the student and asked him if he is ready to do as demanded by the teacher. He agreed to do so. This made both the parents and everybody feel relieved. At this point the chairman indicated that he had to sign this decision in a formal agreement. This indicated that should he change his mind, the expulsion option would then take effect. The student also agreed to sign the agreement, supported by his parents.

With things at this stage, the chairman asked the teacher to show a sign of forgiving the student by accepting a proposal to have a handshake of peace with him. To facilitate this process the school counselor told the student to walk over to the teacher and to offer her the apology, this time verbally before the handshake. This he did trying to kneel down in doing so. In response, the teacher pulled him up and accepted the handshake; and they both gracefully hugged each other. All the members present received this gesture with ululation and a sense of accomplishment. The parents of the boy also hugged the teacher and gave a hug to all around in appreciation for a time well spent.

Following the above gesture, refreshments were served and the agreement was signed. The next morning the student made good his promise. He presented himself and read his open apology letter to the teacher in the full view of his classmates with the counselor and the disciplinary master present. With that done, reintegrative shaming took place on the part of the student, annulling the student's misconduct and the expected expulsion that should have occurred in this case. And with that, the teacher felt that appropriate restitution has been done in the face of the case, and thus feeling satisfied with the entire process for annulling the boys' misconduct, resumed coming to the class, with the student reaccepted into his class group.

Implications for Peace Among Warring Nations and Communities

What is clear in this chapter is that this approach to promoting forgiveness following an infraction or conflict between two people or groups can be practiced with necessary amendments to suit each case. It can have a good effect in brokering peace among conflicting peoples of the different nations of our postmodern world; this could include people in countries such as Iraq, Sierra Leone, Democratic Republic of Congo, Liberia, Sudan, and Somalia. However, the above discussion cautions that a number of conditions must be fulfilled before such a method can succeed in promoting forgiveness among conflicting peoples or nations. One condition is that the victim must tell the story without exaggerating the charge. The other is that the offender (whether an individual or a corporate body) must accept responsibility, show remorse for the offense, and offer a sincere apology and a committed readiness to perform any rituals of restitution needed to appease the victim for the hurt done to him or her (or it, if the victim is a community) (Darby & Schlenker, 1982; Komorita, Hilty, & Parks, 1991; McCullough et al., 1997; Ohbuchi et al., 1989; Weiner et al., 1991).

A principal difference of worldview between the West and the rest of the world is the presumption by most Western leaders that offended people or nations should be able to forgive and move forward in the face of their offence, with little or nothing being done by the offender to appease the offended beyond mere saying of sorry for the offence done to them. Contrary to this dismissive way of looking at the economy of forgiveness, the present chapter demonstrates that in the African context, offering of apology, although necessary, is not sufficient to annul a grave injury on another caused by one's own or a nation's misconduct. This conclusion is instructive, particularly in the context of international relations where the offending nation or its leadership may believe that appeasement of the pain of the victim could be secured by mere pronouncement of apology. The present discussion shows the inaccuracy of this orientation. What has been noted is that, at least in the African context, something much more than just saying one is sorry must be done to win a victim's heart following an injury done to him or her. This is particularly so in instances where the victim's face, good name, or physical property has been damaged. In such cases, in addition to an apology, the offender will be expected to pay some compensation to the victim for the damage. Where the damage suffered is psychological such as that in the above anecdote, the ritual of a written apology to be read in the presence of those who witnessed the offence might become a necessity.

References

Baumeister, R. F. (1997). *Evil: Inside human violence and cruelty*. New York: W. H. Freeman.

Braithwaite, J. (1989). *Crime, shame and reintegration*. Cambridge, UK: Cambridge University Press.

Brendtro, L. K., Brokenleg, M., & Van Bockern, S. (1990). *Reclaiming youth at risk*. Bloomington, Indiana: National Educational Service.

Bruner, J. (1990). *Acts of meaning*. Cambridge: Harvard University Press.

Consedine, J. (1995). *Restorative justice: Healing the effects of crime*. Lyttleton, New Zealand: Ploughshares Publications.

Darby, B. W., & Schlenker, B. R. (1982). Children's reaction to apologies. *Journal of Personality and Social Psychology, 43*, 742–753.

Ejizu, C. I. (1994). African traditional religious rituals and symbols. *Prodialogo, 87*, 243–258.

Ekwunife, A. N. (1997). The quinquagram of igbo traditional religious cultural values: An essay in interpretation. *Nsukka Journal of the Humanities, 8*, 69–97.

Enright, R. D., & Coyle, C. T. (1998). Researching the process model of forgiveness within psychological interventions. In E. L. Worthington, Jr. (Ed.), *Dimensions of forgiveness: Psychological research and theological perspectives* (pp. 139–161). Philadelphia: Templeton Foundation Press.

Enright, R. D., Santos, M. J. D., & Al-Mabuk, R. (1989). The Adolescent as forgiver. *Journal of Adolescence, 12*, 99–110.

Exline, J. J., & Baumeister, R. F. (2000). Expressing forgiveness and repentance: benefits and barriers. In M. E. McCullough, et al. (Eds.), *Forgiveness: Theory, research and practice* (pp. 133–155). New York: The Guilford Press.

Gonzales, M. H., Haugen, J. A., & Manning, D. J. (1994). Victims as "narrative critics": Factors influencing rejoinders and evaluative responses to offenders' accounts. *Personality and Social Psychology Bulletin, 20*, 691–704.

Gordon, K. C., & Baucom, D. H. (1998). Understanding betrayals in marriage: A synthesized moel of forgiveness. *Family Process, 37*(4), 425–450.

Harris, N. (2006). Reintegrative shaming, shame, and criminal justice. *Journal of Social Issues, 62*(2), 327–2006.

Hebl, H., & Enright, R. D. (1993). Forgiveness as a psychotherapeutic goal with elderly females. *Psychotherapy, 30*, 658–667.

Jenkins, A. (2006). Shame, realisation and restitution: The ethics of restorative practice. *Australian and New Zealand Journal of Family Therapy, 27*(3), 153–162.

Komorita, S. S., Hilty, J. A., & Parks, C. D. (1991). Reciprocity and cooperation in social dilemmas. *Journal of Conflict Resolution, 35*, 494–518.

Kamya, H., & Trimble, D. (2003). Response to injury: toward ethical construction of the other. *Journal of Systemic Therapies, 21*, 19–29.

O'Connell, T., Wachtel, B., & Wachtel, T. (1999). *Conferencing handbook: The new real justice training manual.* Pennsylvania: The Piper's Press.

Ohbuchi, K., Kameda, M., & Agarie, N. (1989). Apology as aggression control: Its role in mediating appraisal of and response to harm. *Journal of Personality and Social Psychology, 56*, 219–227.

McCullough, M. E., Bono, G., & Root, L. M. (2005). Religion and forgiveness. In R. F. Paloutzian & C. L. Park (Eds.), *Handbook of the psychology of religion and spirituality* (pp. 394–411). New York: Guilford Press.

McCullough, M. E., Pargament, K. I., & Thoresen, C. E. (2000). *Forgiveness: Theory, research and practice.* New York: The Guilford Presss.

McCullough, M. E., Worthington, E. L., Jr., & Rachal, K. C. (1997). Interpersonal forgiving in close relationships. *Journal of Personality and Social Psychology, 73*, 321–336.

Rivett, M. (2003). The family therapy journals in 2002: A thematic review. *Journal of Family Therapy, 25*, 443–454.

Trebilcock, R. V. (2001, Winter/Spring). *Restorative practices: Indigenous roots of restorative conflict resolution practices – Overview of current trends and review of processes.* Canada: Ontario.

Wachtel, T. (1997). *Real justice: How we can revolutionize our response to wrongdoing.* Pennsylvania: The Piper's Press.

Wachtel, T. (1999, February 16–18). *Restorative justice in everyday life: Beyond the formal ritual.* Paper presented at the Reshaping Australian Institutions Conference: Restorative Justice and Civil Society. The Australian National University, Canberra.

Wade, S. H. (1989). *The development of a scale to measure forgiveness.* Unpublished doctoral dissertation, Fuller Theological Seminary, Pasadena, CA.

Williams, J. L. (2000). Christianity; section in Rye et al., Religious perspectives on forgiveness. In M. E. McCullough et al. (Eds.) *Forgiveness: Theory, research, and practice* (pp. 17–40). New York: Guilford.

Weiner, B., Graham, S., Peter, O., & Zmuidinas, M. (1991). Public confession and forgiveness. *Journal of Personality, 59,* 281–312.

Worthington, E. L. (Ed.). (2005). *Handbook of forgiveness.* New York: Routledge.

Chapter 9
Guilt, Responsibility, and Forgiveness: Lessons from Lifers in Prison

Dan Booth Cohen

For three decades, I have organized, facilitated, and participated in peace building events and actions around the world. Some of these experiences have been exquisite and inspiring, while others have revealed important lessons about the shortcomings in our peacemakers' toolkits.

I once helped organize a 100-mile, 8-day peace walk for an international group of 50 students from 11 countries, including participants from both sides of violent conflicts. After 8 days, the group was radiating love, understanding, and respect. The heart of each walker had opened; they were able to look beyond surface differences and see the common humanity within each of us.

On our final night, we sat in a circle and spoke heartfelt words about how our world view had changed. The sharing brought many laughs and tender moments. Near the end of the round, a boy named Erich, whose face was badly disfigured from cancer surgery, shared his story. In a fragile voice he spoke of feeling ignored and excluded amidst the laughter and hugs, long talks, and strong emotions that surrounded him. His hurt served to caution us that we have much more to learn. He whispered that his latest biopsy report was grave. It was a sobering moment. Intoxicated by feelings of self-satisfaction, we were oblivious to the dying boy in our midst.

Another time, I facilitated a 3-day dialogue group in Nuremberg with German and Jewish-American teens. Near the end, after completing several powerful experiential processes, we engaged in a group dialogue about the Israeli-Palestinian conflict. The teens favored political and social solutions based on the principles of compassion, equality, and mutual respect. They yearned for all the people of the land to live side-by-side in relative harmony.

One of the young German women, who had been a key organizer of the event, took her turn to speak. She shared her view that the expansionist and militarist actions of the Israeli Defense Forces in the occupied lands of Palestine undermined the prospects for peace and reconciliation. From there, her monologue drifted into criticisms of Jews and their intrinsic character that had more than a whiff of Nazi-inspired anti-Semitism. A chill fell as the young Jewish-Americans grew increasingly uncomfortable, then literally frightened. The rant of the German girl, whom we had freely befriended for several days, had a nearly traumatizing effect as it stirred to memory the fates of European Jewry. Finally, the German facilitator

Ani Kalayjian, Raymond F. Paloutzian, *Forgiveness and Reconciliation*, Peace Psychology Book Series, DOI 10.1007/978-1-4419-0181-1_9,
© Springer Science+Business Media, LLC 2009

interrupted and attempted to smooth over the damage with conciliatory words. The trust we had built over three intensive days of dialogue evaporated in a few moments.

These stories serve to contextualize my efforts to understand peace building in the context of meaning systems and psychology. Our approaches rely largely on education, dialogue, and cognitive awareness. These are powerful and effective tools, but those of us who work with victims and perpetrators of trauma and their descendents often encounter their limitations. To augment these approaches, we need ways to uncover and resolve the unconscious impulses and cognitive blind spots that perpetuate the harmful behaviors we strive to overcome.

These tools have eluded peace psychologists partly because constructs such as forgiveness, reconciliation, and open-heartedness are abstractions that are difficult to define and measure. Evidence-based and empirically supported psychology tends to push research and practice away from subjectively oriented processes, while faith-based and spiritually oriented approaches risk being little more than naive fantasies.

The Family Constellation Process

This chapter looks at forgiveness from the perspective of "lifers" in Massachusetts state prison who participated in a phenomenological systemic group process known as a Family Constellation. The Family Constellation process (Cohen, 2005, 2006a, 2006b, 2009a, 2009b; Lynch & Tucker, 2005) developed in Germany during the 1990s (Franke, 2003; Hellinger, 2001, 2002, 2003; Hellinger, Weber, & Beaumont, 1998; Mahr, 1999; Ulsamer, 2005). Its philosophic and therapeutic stance derives from an integration of existential-phenomenology (Heidegger, 1927/1962; Husserl, 1913/1972; Merleau-Ponty, 2002), family systems therapy (Boszormenyi-Nagy & Spark, 1973; Moreno, 1945; Satir, 1987), and indigenous spiritual mysticism (Boring, 2004; Feldman, 2001; Lao-Tzu, 1993; van Kampenhout, 2001).

The basic procedures for creating a Constellation are simple, evolving from methods developed in psychodrama. A group of individuals, generally un-related, sit in a circle of chairs, led by a trained facilitator. One member (client) presents a pressing personal issue. The facilitator asks about the family of origin, seeking facts about traumas or events from the past that may have trans-generational consequences.

The facilitator asks the client to select members from the group to represent people who are important to the issue and to place them in a spatial relationship to one another. The client is instructed to place the representatives without comment according to whatever inner impulse might guide them in that moment. Once the representatives are positioned, the client sits and observes without speaking.

After several minutes of silence and stillness, the representatives often begin to experience emotions or physical sensations that are perceived as arising from an attunement to those they represent. A living portrait emerges of the connection between the presenting issue and the trans-generational family system. The aim is first to reveal invisible loyalties (Boszormenyi-Nagy & Spark, 1973) and second, through the facilitator's intervention and the movements of the representatives, to portray an image of resolution. Often, additional representatives are brought in to represent deceased family members who were excluded or suffered a painful fate.

The Constellation concludes when each representative has found a place that grants them relief or release. Lastly, the client replaces his or her own representative to experience the feelings of love and reconciliation in the re-ordered system. Afterward, there is minimal discussion or processing. The client is instructed to let the healing image sink in and to allow the presenting issue to slowly find its way toward resolution. A Constellation group frequently augments a course of psychotherapy. It is not considered therapy itself, nor a substitute for any form of treatment.

Two Case Examples of Forgiveness from a "Lifers" Prison Group

These two cases come from this author's experiences in a monthly Constellation circle with a group of "lifers" in the Massachusetts state prison system (Cohen, 2006a, 2009a, 2009b).

The first client, whom I call James, was convicted as an accessory to first-degree murder and sentenced to life in prison without parole in 1963 when he was 19 years old. Now in his sixties, he is in his fifth decade of incarceration. A few years into his imprisonment, he was befriended by a Catholic chaplain. The priest became James' surrogate father, spiritual teacher, and best friend. James had recently learned that Father M. had terminal lung cancer.

James set up representatives for his father, brother, stepfather, and Father M. He stood across from the family members and spoke a soliloquy to each one. He never met his father, nor did not even know his name, as his mother took the secret to her grave. He confronted the father, "Here's your son you abandoned. Look at me. I was convicted of murder as a boy and sent to prison for the rest of my life. Look what you did to me." His eyes were wet with tears.

His brother had also abandoned him, never making contact after he was imprisoned. "Where are you? What happened to you? How could you disappear off the face of the earth and leave me here alone?" His stepfather was an alcoholic, child-beater, and rapist. James described in grisly detail the abuse and beatings he suffered at the hands of this man.

Then he turned to the priest, whom he had placed at his side. Through all the years of isolation and incarceration, Father M. had always visited and always been kind, even sending a small monthly allowance. James expressed his love and heartfelt thanks to the only person who had stood by him as a constant source of friendship, support, and guidance.

Turning back to the trio of "sinners," James said, "I forgive you all from the bottom of my heart." His expression of forgiveness felt large and sharp, like he was running a sword through them as well.

To this point, with so much speaking, the process was closer to a role-play than a Constellation. The question was whether James' forgiveness could go further. I asked him to be silent and placed a representative for the Mother of All (a woman volunteer) to the left, and a man for God in Heaven to the right. In this configuration, these two figures stood at opposite poles with the other representatives between them.

As the room grew silent and still, we felt the presence of something sacred. The perspective shifted, with these five individuals now framed by the profound vastness of all creation. The image that emerged was the Mother as an archetype of the Alpha, the source from where everything comes. Opposite her was the Father, in this scene symbolic of the Omega, where everything goes in the end. On this scale, everyone comes into life, lives for some time, and dies. The "saints" are neither bigger nor better than the others. As the novelist Shirley Hazzard (1980) wrote, "Of those who had endured the worst, not all acted nobly or consistently. But all, involuntarily, became part of some deeper assertion of life" (p. 171).

After taking this in for some time, James said to each representative, "I agree." Gone was the sharpness of before. This was forgiveness, based not on judgments of virtue and sin, but on deep compassion and humility.

Several months afterwards, James reflected on his experience:

> The Constellation allowed me to not hurt as much anymore; not to hate myself for all the harm I caused other people and to not hate any of the people that abused me. Now, I have forgiveness, love, patience, and compassion in my heart. ("James," personal communication, May, 2006)

In the second example a group member, called here Ron, explained that after 30 years of incarceration he would have his first Parole Board hearing. He described his crime, a shockingly violent and grisly murder. His childhood had been characterized by beatings, neglect, and degradation at the hands of an alcoholic father.

In his twenties, he parked his car illegally and went for a night of drinking. The car was towed. In a rage, he attacked an employee at the tow lot with a tire iron, beating him to death and beyond. After his arrest the next day, the police brought him to see the patch of pavement where blood and flesh were spread. He was sentenced to 30 years-to-life.

His question was, "How can I ask the State for mercy when I cannot forgive myself for what I did?"

I asked for a volunteer to represent the victim. A man (also a "lifer") immediately raised his hand and stepped into the circle. Without a word, he lay on his back on the tiled floor, slightly spread-eagled with his eyes closed. Ron stood before him. The victim lay perfectly still. The offender stood over him for several minutes, shaking, tears wetting his cheeks, growing weaker with each breath. This portrayed the present situation. There was no opening for forgiveness. Any attempt to foster it would be forced and false.

I asked the victim what he was feeling. He said, "Nothing. Absolutely nothing." There was no door to forgiveness because the victim was gone forever, thus could not grant it, and Ron had no right to fabricate it.

Intervening, I asked the victim to stand and face Ron with his eyes open. After a few minutes, the victim grew angry over the injustice of his life being terminated senselessly and needlessly. Ron was bereft and hopeless.

I asked Ron to succinctly state the honest truth: "I killed you and I lived. Had I not killed you, we both would have lived." He added, "I am sorry." This softened the victim somewhat. It felt slightly better to be seen and acknowledged.

Next, I brought two male volunteers to stand shoulder-to-shoulder with the victim. They represented anyone in the offender's life, now and in the future, who angered, offended, threatened, or harmed him. I suggested these words for Ron to say, "This is my solemn vow. [To the two new representatives] Whenever I confront *you*, the man I killed will be present in my heart and mind. [To the victim] *You* will always be there to inform and guide my response."

On hearing these words, the victim reported that his attitude shifted. Being seen, seeing the offender's remorse, and hearing his promise to be remembered gave the victim a feeling of peace and a willingness to open his heart.

One-by-one, each "lifer" was asked to step forward and stand with their friend. They silently bowed to the victim (of Ron's crime and implicitly their crime as well). They told Ron, "I will support you in keeping your vow."

The victim was now at peace with his own demise and with his killer. He said, "Maybe being remembered like this will save someone else's life." In this situation, complete forgiveness could not be achieved. It was a lifelong path that required earning a small measure with every step.

The man who represented the victim in this Constellation shared about his experiences several months later:

> I allowed myself to be used as an empty vessel to be filled with the energy, to allow my body to be open and my head clear. ... Not right away, but afterwards, I felt freedom. The load is lighter. The issue carries me, I no longer carry it. After being in prison for 33 years, finding freedom is beautiful. (Anon, personal communication, May, 2006)

Mahr (2005) wrote, "The bond between perpetrators and victims is literally deeper than any other family bond" (p. 5). We saw this confirmed here. It is not a bond of love or affection in the conventional sense, but a bond of the inexorable shared fate between the murderer and victim. Owing to the irreversibility of taking of a life, neither can ever be without the other. Even though the victim ceases to exist, his influence remains strong. What emerged in this Constellation is consistent with Mahr's (2005) experience:

> As soon as the dead are remembered and their fates acknowledged, they are able to withdraw and become guardians of the living, bestowing their blessing and benevolence on them. In this way, even after decades, the living and the dead can help to heal each other. (p. 4)

The Phenomenological Stance

Any attempt to extrapolate or generalize meaning from Constellations immediately raises ontological and epistemological questions. There is a growing body of case study evidence that supports the accuracy of representative perception and the benefits to clients (Franke, 2003; Lynch & Tucker, 2005; Schneider, 2007). However, this research falls well short of the gold standard of randomized controlled studies. A wealth of favorable testimonials from practitioners and clients is no indicator of validity, as the same could be claimed by carnival fortune tellers.

However, the Constellation process does come from a well-respected lineage: phenomenological-existential psychology. One can trace its origins through such philosophers and psychologists as Spinoza, Emerson, Thoreau, Kierkegaard, Brentano, Stumpf, Husserl, James, Jung, Heidegger, Assagioli, Merleau-Ponty, Buber, and Maslow (Cohen, 2009a).

Phenomenology emerged in nineteenth century psychology as an alternative to the positivist, reductionist schools that saw all mental activity as purely physical responses to stimulus of the brain. Phenomenology was concerned with restoring meaning to existence in light of the discoveries of science. The American transcendentalists, led by Emerson and Thoreau, sought to restore the validity of imagination and creativity as vehicles for advancing knowledge. "The function of reason, they claimed, was not the discovery of truth, but that of arranging, methodizing, and harmonizing verbal propositions in regard to it" (Taylor, 1999, p. 64).

In its philosophical sense, phenomenology is concerned with the recognition of deeper structures and the revelation of their meaning. Dreams, desires, fears, obsessions, and impulses give shape to behavior patterns that defy the mapping techniques of the most skillful behaviorists. Phenomenological evidence is closer to the subjective insights found in literature than to the statistical outcomes of variate-controlled experiments. As the novelist Shirley Hazzard poetically observed, "The calculations were hopelessly out. Calculations about Venus often are" (Hazzard, 1980, p. 16).

Hellinger (2001) explains his phenomenological stance as follows:

> There are two inner movements that lead to insight. One reaches out, wanting to understand and to control the unknown. This is scientific inquiry….The second movement happens when we pause in our efforts to grasp the unknown, allowing our attention to rest, not on the particulars, which we can define, but on the greater whole. (p. 2)

It may seem implausible that representatives in a Constellation can perceive feelings and sensations that are germane to the client. Why should we accept that their feelings and sensations are congruent with those of actual living and deceased family members? Are they not more likely to be personal projections that have little bearing on the issue at hand?

The reliability of representative perception was proposed by Satir's (1987) family sculpture technique, the immediate antecedent to Hellinger's Family Constellations. In response to one or more clients being absent from family group appointments, Satir had assistants stand in their place. She observed, "If I put people in physical stances, they were likely to experience the feelings that went with that stance" (Satir, 1987, p. 68).

Similarly, the French existential philosopher Merleau-Ponty (2002) understood the human body, as opposed to only the brain, to be the basic instrument of discernment, "I experience this sensing/perception as a modality of a general existence which penetrates me without me being the instigator" (p. 249). For him, what Constellation facilitators call "representative perception" is the fundamental prerequisite to knowledge.

For forgiveness, which is inherently abstract and subjective, meaningful psychological interpretations can be based on phenomenological rather than experimental evidence. In this regard, Corveleyn and Luyten (2005) advocate ontological pluralism, using qualitative approaches to grasp understanding and meaning and quantitative approaches to analyze data and extract general laws. These approaches can complement each other for mutual enrichment. The phenomenological stance allows us to understand how forgiveness applies in situations that occur at the extremes of human behavior.

The Systemic Perspective

Peace psychology is grounded in a systems perspective. The persistence of episodic and structural violence is viewed as "manifestations of interactions among a host of destructive inputs that are embedded in social, cultural, and historical factors" (Christie, 2006, p. 6). Peace building contributes conciliatory inputs, such as conflict resolution processes and nonviolent social justice movements, as a way to counterbalance or mitigate violent momentum within the existing systems. Generally, the systemic orientation of peace psychology draws from political science and sociology.

Trans-generational forgiveness also takes a systems perspective with the starting point being the system of particular individuals. German psychiatrist Albrecht Mahr, who has worked extensively in the aftermath of war and ethnic conflict in Germany, Rwanda, and Bosnia, frames the question of collective versus individual systems this way:

> My experiences with group trauma strongly suggest that there are no large group issues which are not deeply interconnected with real people and their individual fates. Of course, there are collective phenomena built upon many individuals, but the personal and the collective are best treated as integrated entities. (Mahr, 2005, personal communication)

The study of trans-generational forgiveness begins and ends with a real human, an individual who belongs to, and is moved by, many small and large systems. When the individual and collective spheres are worked with simultaneously – both across communities and generations – participants are touched by the universality of human suffering and love. These directly experienced insights into the individual/collective concretely increase self-knowledge of the inner world of being.

With thousands dying each day from violence and exploitation, peace psychology needs to influence large political and economic systems to have a measurable effect. The essential disadvantage in these attempts is that cities, such as Dresden or Hiroshima, can be destroyed in a day, while it takes years, if not generations, to heal the damage brick-by-brick and heart-by-heart.

In the aftermath of the September 11, 2001, attacks, the American public over-whelmingly favored a violent military response. In the minds of most Americans, achieving homeland security through compassion and forgiveness is as foolhardy as building elaborate sand castles at low tide. However, as the wars in Afghanistan and Iraq have painfully demonstrated, the cost of destructiveness is immeasurably high. Eventually conflicts exhaust themselves, creating an opening for healing.

Trans-generational forgiveness presumes that individuals are bound to their groups in deep, mostly unconscious ways. The strongest systemic force that holds the person to the group is the bond of personal love between children and parents. Conscious and unconscious systemic forces maintain continuity, balance, and order in the group, but often have fateful consequences for individual members. An obvious example is a soldier who sacrifices his life to defend the motherland. To comprehend trans-generational forgiveness, it is necessary to examine in close detail the function of conscience, guilt, and innocence in human relationships.

Conscience

Children are taught to follow their conscience. According to the popular image, a devil sits on one shoulder and an angel on the other. The devil's is the voice of evil and the angel speaks on behalf of good, even of God. A good conscience guides us toward actions and words that are beneficial. A bad conscience is the price we pay when we behave in ways that are harmful or sinful. In this way, feeling guilt is an internal regulator that steers the individual toward the path of righteousness. A person who commits terrible crimes or harmful acts is said to have no conscience or a distorted or suppressed conscience (Arendt, 1958).

Eugene de Kock is a white South African who directed the most brutal and mur-derous unit of South Africa's military in the 1980s and 1990s. His job was to fight the opponents of apartheid using tactics that included mass murder, torture, assassi-nation, kidnapping, and rape. Men under his command conducted relentless attacks against black South Africans. Many of those killed were activists in the African National Congress (ANC), South West Africa People's Organization (SWAPO), and other anti-apartheid groups, but many were civilians, including women and children, with the bad fortune to fall under the tracks of his efficient killing machinery.

Pumla Gobodo-Madikizela 2003 is a black South African psychologist, a mem-ber of the county's Truth and Reconciliation Commission that was established by the new government after the dissolution of the apartheid state. She conducted a series of interviews with de Kock following his testimony before the Commission and subsequent imprisonment. In her book about these experiences, *A Human Being Died That Night*, she confronts the question of de Kock's conscience.

> Where was his conscience when he returned again and again to murder those the Apartheid government identified as its enemies? How does conscience get suppressed to the point where people can allow themselves to commit systematic acts of murder against others? (p. 50)

Arendt, in her book *Eichmann in Jerusalem* (1963), asks similar questions about one of the most murderous members of Hitler's inner circle in Nazi Germany. Adolf Eichmann commanded the Nazi military apparatus that systematically murdered as many as 10 million Jews, Poles, Germans, Gypsies, homosexuals, and others considered undesirable by the state (Berenbaum, 1990, pp. v–vi). Arendt asks whether his capacity to direct such an operation meant that he was without conscience, a psychopathic sadist free from the ordinary constraints that inhibit such acts.

Arendt and Gobodo-Madikizela concluded that these men did possess consciences. Arendt used the term "banality of evil" to describe Eichmann's apparent detachment from the suffering he caused. De Kock professed that the killings he perpetrated anguished him, but these feelings never dissuaded him from his bloody job.

In both Germany and South Africa the soldiers, police, guards, administrators, and functionaries who comprised the apparatus of state-sponsored genocide went about their daily duties with a clear conscience. Hellinger asserts, "A clear or guilty conscience has little to do with good and evil; the worst atrocities and injustices are committed with a clear conscience" (Hellinger, Weber, & Beaumont, 1998, p. 3).

The evidence accumulated from the phenomenological, systemic lens is that the inner voice of conscience guides people to be loyal, to be bonded with their families and groups that are essential for survival. Tucker (2005) writes, "A good conscience means we are acting in line with our group. . . . It depends on choosing one over another, discriminating between those who belong and those who do not" (p. 14). If there is an enemy from outside, threatening the group, conscience becomes more persistent to mobilize the energy to fight.

The Nazis viewed Jews as *Ausländeren*, outsiders who were infiltrating and diluting the Germanic race. The genetic "purity" of the German people, their very survival, was felt to be threatened by intermarriage and integration of darker-skinned, non-Christian, Semitic people. The Nazis justified exterminating the threat, using the analogy that Judaism was a cancer within the body of Germany (Lifton, 1986).

Peter Malkin (Malkin & Stein, 1990), who captured Eichmann on the streets of Buenos Aries, wrote about testing whether he had a conscience. Malkin told Eichmann about his beloved nephew who was captured and murdered at Auschwitz. Malkin expected this heartbreaking story would cause Eichmann's conscience, if he had one, to generate feelings of guilt and remorse. Instead, Eichmann, looking genuinely perplexed, responded, "But he was Jewish, wasn't he?" (p. 214).

It is not that Eichmann had no internal inhibitors toward evil behavior, but that his tightly wound circle of belonging excluded Jews. The exterminator does not bond with the termites nor does the surgeon feel compassionate toward the tumor.

De Kock felt justified fighting for South Africa. He reflected thus:

All indications were that South Africa would go the way of the rest of Africa if the ANC took over. . . . The hue and cry was 'Fight, resist, sacrifice, or you will be wiped out by the black man.' Rule by the black man was a sure means of destruction of the country. (Gobodo-Madikizela, 2003, p. 73)

De Kock was Christian, but his conscience remained clear when the fight was to defend his people against their enemies. It was only when the boundaries of his circle of belonging became blurred that his conscience troubled him.

De Kock tells of a field operation in Namibia in 1981. His unit prayed each morning. That day's prayers came from the Book of Psalms: "He is the God who avenges me, who subdues nations under me, who saves me from my enemies" (Psalm 18). Later that day, the unit came across four enemy fighters. After a brief exchange, three of the guerillas were killed and the fourth captured. In searching their possessions, de Kock was surprised to find a Bible, its pages worn from frequent reading. De Kock said, "A SWAPO man is supposed to be a communist, who is supposed to be the enemy, the personification of the Antichrist."

De Kock can kill the Antichrist without guilt. The discovery of the well-worn Bible shatters that perception. The two are now fellow Christians, members of the same group, so the killing invokes a guilty conscience. De Kock's conviction in his righteousness wavers, "They may have read the same Scripture lesson that said the enemy will be given into *your* hands. Whose side is God on now" (Gobodo-Madikizela, 2003, pp. 70–71)?

Guilt and Innocence

If conscience regulates belonging, not ethical behavior, feelings of innocence and guilt do not correspond with righteousness or evil. In the lexicography of trans-generational forgiveness, "guilt and innocence are almost the opposite of what comes to mind when the words are spoken in other contexts" (Tucker, 2005, p. 18). Re-defined, innocence flows from connection and guilt from separation.

Throughout life, individuals always are part of a family, born into a particular religion, or ethnic group, economic class, nationality, or neighborhood. People can forsake their heritage or move their domicile, but they can never change the original circumstances of their birth. From a systemic perspective, the bond between family members endures regardless of external circumstances.

Human relationships always involve an exchange of giving and taking, gaining and losing, offering and receiving. In ordinary familial and social relationships the exchange between giving and taking is in relative equilibrium. Feelings of guilt and innocence are internal regulators to keep these exchanges in balance. "Guilt and innocence are clearly bound to loyalty" (Tucker, 2005, p. 17).

When we give, we expect to receive in return; when we take, we feel the need to give. Unreciprocated giving creates an expectation, a feeling of connectedness to the other person. This connection is thus felt by conscience as innocence. Conversely, unreciprocated taking creates an obligation. The obligation is felt as a debt that separates or divides the person from whoever gave something up. Systemic conscience feels such separation as guilt.

Hellinger observed, "Guilt feels like transgression and as fear of consequences or punishment when we deviate from a social order. We feel innocence, with respect to social order, as conscientiousness and loyalty" (Hellinger et al., 1998,

p. 6). This constant exchange of giving and taking is a positive force that invisibly maintains balance, bonding, and order in the system. Unfortunately, the interplay between individuals in family systems often falls out of equilibrium and can stay out of equilibrium for generations. When this occurs, individuals and groups lose a healthy balance of exchange and instead become entangled in persistent patterns of perpetration and/or victimization.

Forgiveness

In ethics and politics, forgiving is an act designed to overcome the inevitable errors and injuries that are ubiquitous in human relationships. When we forgive, we recognize and respond to offenses against us by interrupting, instead of repeating, cycles of resentment. To Arendt's (1958) understanding, "Trespassing is an everyday occurrence...which needs forgiving, dismissing, in order to make it possible for life to go on. ... In this respect, forgiveness is the exact opposite of vengeance" (p. 240).

Ordinary forgiveness frees both the victim and the offender from the confinement of vengeance and blame, which left unimpeded, could recycle indefinitely. Committing a criminal act upends the balance in relationship between the victim and the offender. The offender, by virtue of having unrightfully taken something, incurs a debt, both to the victim and to society. To restore balance, civil societies have legal systems that administer punishment. Whether through physical pain, incarceration, financial penalty, or exile, punishment is designed to even the score. After the offenders have "paid their debt" they are entitled to be free from further obligation and restored a position of good standing in the community.

Receiving forgiveness represents a special way for a guilty person to have their state of innocent belonging restored. By receiving forgiveness those who caused harm are excused from having to be further punished. By offering forgiveness, victims no longer hold claims over them.

Arendt in formulating the necessity of forgiveness also draws limits around it. She points to acts designated as "radical evil," which are so destructive and irreversible that they can be neither punished nor forgiven (p. 241). The challenge of this book is to extend the healing power of forgiveness into situations that cross the borders of trespass into the territory of radical evil.

Gobodo-Madikizela (2003) acknowledges that applying Arendt's philosophy of forgiveness to acts of radical evil has unexpected consequences:

> Although forgiveness is often regarded as an expression of weakness, the decision to forgive can paradoxically elevate a victim to a position of strength. ... The victim becomes the gatekeeper to what the outcast desires – readmission into the human community. ... In this sense, then, forgiveness is a kind of revenge. (p. 117)

There is a risk when the forgiver adopts such a superior position, as the "good one" absolving the "bad one," that the gesture is a form of vengeance thinly disguised as an act of virtue. In cases of radical evil, this type of forgiveness does not offer a lasting resolution. Instead, what better serves trans-generational healing is an attitude toward forgiveness built on compassion.

An Indigenous Approach to Forgiveness

We can find formulas for trans-generational forgiveness in the ritualized practices of many indigenous cultures. For example, the village of Shefar'Am in Israel lies on the ancient trade routes linking Beirut, Damascus, and Jerusalem. The villagers practice the traditional Palestinian peacemaking process known as *Sulha* which has its roots in early Semitic writings, Christian scriptures, and Islamic Arab literature. "*Sulha* is first and foremost based on forgiveness" (Jabbour & Cook, 1993, p. 31). This form of forgiveness is a community-based process that involves not only the offender and victim but also their immediate and extended families, a council of trusted elders, and members of the community-at-large. It integrates words and deeds.

Sulha begins when a traumatic event, such as murder, occurs in the community. It is understood that, without a reconciliation process, the killing can initiate a blood feud between the families of the victim and murderer that can spill into the next generation. The *Sulha* is led by a group of respected elders each of whom is viewed as wise, fair, honest, and trustworthy. The elders control the process, which sometimes takes months to achieve a full resolution. Forgiveness within the context of the *Sulha* requires that the offender publicly acknowledges their guilt, expresses remorse, and offers meaningful (even if sometimes symbolic) restitution. The grandparents, parents, and children in the affected families come together for an elaborate public ceremony. In front of the community, the victim's family accepts the offer of reconciliation and swears not to seek revenge. The ceremony ends with speeches, prayers, handshakes, and a shared meal.

Trauma and Forgiveness

When traumatic crimes and injustices committed in one generation are not resolved, successive generations are drawn into the fray. Within the United States, the impact of mass traumas such as African slavery and the genocide of the Native Peoples still reverberate in collective consciousness. Immigrant groups, who escaped from extreme circumstances such as the Nazi Holocaust, Armenian genocide, or Vietnam War, pass the legacy of these events to their descendants. Without fully comprehending their impulses, children and grandchildren often feel compelled to complete what they did not start, atone for what they did not do, or inflict punishment on the living for crimes committed by those who are now dead.

Trans-generational forgiveness cannot be achieved with a simple apology and its acceptance. When the acts that caused harm are irreversible, the pathway to forgiveness places special demands on both sides. For the perpetrators, or their descendants, forgiveness requires acknowledging guilt, expressing sincere remorse, and offering a reasonable restitution. For the victims and their descendants, forgiveness is an act of deep compassion and humility that restores the sweetness of life to the living.

Forgiveness leaves the guilt with the perpetrator and frees the victims from the desire for vengeance. It comes when perpetrators, victims, and their descendants include each other as full members of the human community. The fate of all individuals involved are accepted and respected, even those who committed acts described by Arendt (1958) as "radical evil." Such forgiveness is never complete in life.

Even though they have perished, the victims and perpetrators of crimes and mass trauma maintain their presence in the lives of others. One of the men in my prison group told me this story. He has been incarcerated 33 years as an accessory to first-degree murder. During the crime, he left his co-defendant with the victim. The victim screamed "Help me!" as he was being stabbed to death. This man did nothing to stop the killing. He was caught, convicted, and sentenced to "life without parole." Five years into his sentence, there was an attempted mass prison break from his cellblock. He retreated as fighting broke out between prisoners and guards. He heard a guard, who had been set upon by a group of prisoners, screaming, "Help me!" At that moment, he felt the spirit of his murder victim come to life within him. The spirit compelled him, propelled him out of the room to save the guard's life, which he did.

Afterward, he did not reflect philosophically about this event. But through our experiences with Constellations in prison, it clicked for him that this was a very concrete example of the victim–perpetrator bond and an illustration of how forgiveness works in cases of acts of radical evil. Forgiveness is not complete. His guilt is not absolved, or even reduced. But through the victim–perpetrator bond, a life on the verge of being lost was saved. With this, he earned a measure of forgiveness and his dignity.

A child who loses a parent continues the relationship, carrying pain and love in their hearts. Invisible loyalties can become a burdensome weight, whispering the message, "Because you suffered and died so tragically, I cannot find joy. I will avenge the injustice of your death." This engenders a sense of innocence because it brings the survivor into closer contact with the deceased.

In forgiving, the child can ask instead, "Would my father want me to sacrifice my own life after his? Or would he want me to take my life and make something good from it?" The answer, accumulated from phenomenological evidence of Constellations, is consistent: Neither vengeance nor sacrifice changes the fate of the living or the dead for the better. At its core, trans-generational forgiveness is compassion based on acceptance of the past, acknowledgment of the existential equality of all people, and reverence for the vast beauty of life.

References

Arendt, H. (1958). *The human condition*. Chicago: The University of Chicago Press.
Arendt, H. (1963). *Eichmann in Jerusalem: A report on the banality of evil*. New York: Viking.
Berenbaum, M. (1990). *A mosaic of victims: Non-Jews persecuted and murdered by the Nazis*. New York: New York University Press.
Boring, F. M. (2004). *Feather medicine: Walking in Shoshone dreamtime: A family system constellation*. Taramac, FL: Lumina Press.
Boszormenyi-Nagy, I., & Spark, G. M. (1973). *Invisible loyalties: Reciprocity in intergenerational family therapy*. Hagerstown, MD: Harper & Row.
Christie, D. J. (2006). What is peace psychology the psychology of? *Journal of Social Issues, 62*(1), 1–17.
Cohen, D. B. (2005). *Begin with the work: Family constellations and larger systems*. In J. E. Lynch & S. Tucker (Eds.), *Messengers of healing: The family constellations of Bert Hellinger through the eyes of a new generation of practitioners*. Phoenix, AZ: Zeig, Tucker & Theisen.
Cohen, D. B. (2006a). I carry your heart: I carry it in my heart. *The Knowing Field: International Constellations Journal, 8*, 43–48.
Cohen, D. B. (2006b). "Family constellations": An innovative systemic phenomenological group process from Germany. *The Family Journal: Counseling and Therapy for Couples and Families, 14*(3), 226–233.
Cohen, D. B. (2009a). Systemic Family Constellations and their use with prisoners serving longterm sentences for murder or rape. *Dissertation Abstracts International 70 (02)*. (Publication No. AAT 3344884).
Cohen, D. B. (2009b). *I carry your heart in my heart: Family Constellations in prison*. Heidelberg, Germany: Carl-Auer-Systeme Verlag.
Corveleyn, J., & Luyten, P. (2005). Psychodynamic psychologies and religion: Past, present, and future. In R. F. Paloutzian & C. L. Park (Eds.), *Handbook of the psychology of religion and spirituality*. New York: Guilford Press.
Feldman, D. H. (2001). *Qabalah: The mystical heritage of the children of Abraham*. Santa Cruz, CA: Work of the Chariot.
Franke, U. (2003). *The river never looks back: Historical and practical foundations of Bert Hellinger's family constellations* (K. Luebe, Trans.). Heidelberg, Germany: Carl-Auer-Systeme Verlag.
Gobodo-Madikizela, P. (2003). *A human being died that night: A South African woman confronts the legacy of apartheid*. Boston: Houghton Mifflin.
Hazzard, S. (1980). *The transit of Venus*. New York: Viking.
Heidegger, M. (1927/1962). *Being and Time* (J. Macquarrie & E. Robinson, Trans.). New York: Harper & Row.
Hellinger, B. (2001). *Love's own truths: Bonding and balancing in close relationships* (M. Oberli-Turner & H. Beaumont, Trans.). Phoenix, AZ: Zeig, Tucker & Theisen.
Hellinger, B. (2002). *Insights: Lectures and stories* (J. ten Herkel, Trans.). Heidelberg, Germany: Carl-Auer-Systeme Verlag.
Hellinger, B. (2003). *Peace begins in the soul: Family constellations in the service of reconciliation* (C. Beaumont, Trans.). Heidelberg, Germany: Carl-Auer-Systeme Verlag.
Hellinger, B., Weber, G., & Beaumont, H. (1998). *Love's hidden symmetry: What makes love work in relationships*. Phoenix, AZ: Zeig, Tucker & Theisen.
Husserl, E. (1913/1972). *Ideas: General introduction to pure phenomenology* (W. R. Boyce Gibson, Trans.). NY: Collier.
Jabbour, E. J., & Cook, T. J., Jr. (1993). *Sulha: Palestinian traditional peacemaking process*. Montreat, NC: House of Hope Publications.
Lao-Tzu. (1993). *Tao Te Ching* (S. Addiss & S. S. Lombardo, Trans.). Indianapolis, IN: Hackett.
Lifton, R. J. (1986). *The Nazi doctors: Medical killing and the psychology of genocide*. New York: Basic Books.

Lynch, J. E., & Tucker, S. (Eds.). (2005). *Messengers of healing: The family constellations of Bert Hellinger through the eyes of a new generation of practitioners.* Phoenix, AZ: Zeig, Tucker & Theisen.

Mahr, A. (1999). Das wissende feld: Familienaufstellung als geistig energetisches heilen [The knowing field: Family constellations as mental and energetic healing]. In H. Wiesendanger (Ed.), *Geistiges heilen fr eine neue zeit [Intellectual healing for a new era].* Heidelberg, Germany: Kŝel Verlag.

Mahr, A. (2005). How the living and the dead can heal each other. *The Knowing Field: International Constellations Journal, 6,* 4–8.

Malkin, P., & Stein, H. (1990). *Eichmann in my hands.* New York: Warner.

Merleau-Ponty, M. (2002). *Phenomenology of perception.* Oxford: Routledge.

Moreno, J. L. (1945). *Psychodrama.* New York: Beacon House.

Satir, V. (1987). Going beyond the obvious: The psychotherapeutic journey. In J. Zeig (Ed.), *Evolution of psychotherapy* (pp. 58–68). New York: Brunner/Mazel.

Schneider, J. R. (2007). *Family constellations: Basic principles and procedures* (C. Beaumont, Trans.). Heidelberg, Germany: Carl-Auer-Systeme Verlag.

Taylor, E. (1999). *Shadow culture: Psychology and spirituality in America.* Washington: Counterpoint.

Tucker, S. (2005). The weight of words. In J. E. Lynch & S. Tucker (Eds.), *Messengers of healing: The family constellations of Bert Hellinger through the eyes of a new generation of practitioners.* Phoenix, AZ: Zeig, Tucker & Theisen.

Ulsamer, B. (2005). *The healing power of the past: The systemic therapy of Bert Hellinger.* Nevada City, CA: Underwood.

Van Kampenhout, D. (2001). *Images of the soul: The workings in shamanic rituals and family constellations.* Heidelberg, Germany: Carl-Auer-Systeme Verlag.

Section III
Intergroup, Societal, and International Levels

Chapter 10
A Black Social Psychologist's Perspective on Racial Forgiveness

Ansley W. LaMar

Despite the changes and, perhaps, in some cases, because of them, race relations in the United States continue to be a major concern for social scientists. Eighty years of research has provided insight into the causes and pervasiveness of racial bias, strategies for eliminating racial bias, and the effects of racial bias (Fiske, 2004). And given the deleterious effect that racism has had on Black Americans (see, e.g., Clark & Clark, 1957; DeGruy-Leary, 2005; Grier & Cobbs, 1968; Kardiner & Ovesey, 1951; Robinson, 2000; Steele, 1997) eliminating racism and improving race relations remain important goals.

Some argue that race relations would improve if Black Americans were offered reparations or a real attempt was made at racial reconciliation (see, e.g., Robinson, 2000 and Tutu, 1999). On the other hand, there is research that suggests that Black Americans may be able to improve their circumstance and race relations in the United States by practicing forgiveness. Forgiveness, as an approach to creating social harmony, has been advocated by Martin Luther King, Jr. (1957) and more recently, in another social context, by Rwandan social activist Immaculee Ilibagiza (2006). The research on forgiveness as an alternative to retribution and other methods for resolving perceived injustices and inequities has received little attention (Exline, Worthington, Hill, & McCullough, 2003). This chapter then will explore the feasibility of forgiveness as a strategy for improving race relations by referring to relevant social psychological research. Special attention will be paid to the literature on intergroup relations, prosocial behavior, moral disposition, and racial identity.

The Dynamic Complexities of Forgiveness

Forgiveness is a complex psychological construct which may include the notions of denial, forgetting, pardoning, condoning, and reconciliation (Exline et al., 2003). Fincham and Kashdan (2004), however, offer a definition that appears to capture the core features that distinguish forgiveness from related constructs. According to Fincham and Kashdan, "forgiveness is ... a freely chosen motivational transformation in which the desire to seek revenge and to avoid contact with the transgressor is lessened." This definition does not imply that extending forgiveness requires

Ani Kalayjian, Raymond F. Paloutzian, *Forgiveness and Reconciliation*, Peace Psychology Book Series, DOI 10.1007/978-1-4419-0181-1_10, © Springer Science+Business Media, LLC 2009

ignoring the offender's actions (McCullough, Worthington, & Rachal, 1997) or restoring a relationship with the offender (Worthington, Sandage, & Berry, 2000), but it does acknowledge that it may be necessary to interact with the transgressor. This is an important consideration. Even though many Black and White Americans live in racially homogenous communities they work together and frequent the same public arenas.

In addition, the Fincham and Kashdan definition acknowledges that the victims, in this case African Americans, who have forgiven an injustice may remember the transgression, but will find ways to reduce the pain, anger, and desire for restitution and revenge associated with the offense. The victims will also feel free to interact with the transgressor(s) and will allow for the possibility of a renewed relationship, but will not feel obliged to restore that relationship. As has been acknowledged elsewhere (see, e.g., Wade & Worthington, 2005) reestablishing a relationship with the offender could be detrimental to the forgiver.

This last point is especially important because perceived discrimination remains a dominant force in the lives of many Black Americans. For example, only 39% of Blacks, as compared to 68% of Whites, described race relations as good within the military and 25% of Blacks described discrimination in performance evaluation as their most bothersome incident in the military (Scarville, Button, Edwards, Lancaster, & Elig, 1999). In addition, 55% of Blacks reported that they believe that discrimination hinders their career advancement within the government (U.S. Merit Systems Protection Board, 1997). These authors have written that "Based upon the subtle but real differences in treatment and a history of discrimination in society in general as well as in the Government, it is not surprising to find that minorities generally believe that they continue to be the victims of discrimination. What is surprising is the extent of the differences in perceptions between minorities and nonminorities. Very few nonminorities believe that flagrant discrimination against employees from any minority group exists in the Federal Government" (p. 41).

More recently, a survey conducted by the Gallup Organization discovered that 47% of Blacks as opposed to 10% of Whites felt that Blacks were treated less fairly than Whites "On the job or at work," 46% of Blacks as opposed to 15% of Whites felt that Blacks were treated less fairly than Whites "In stores downtown or in malls," and 64% of Blacks as opposed to 30% of Whites felt that Blacks are treated less fairly than Whites "By police." The Gallup Organization concluded that "Black Americans ... hold much less positive views than do Whites on a variety of questions about how fairly Blacks are treated in their local community..." (ABCNews.com, 2000).

These findings are not surprising. White endorsement of blatant forms of racism has declined dramatically over the past 60 years (Bobo, 2001). But as of 1995, approximately 20% of Whites still believed that Blacks and Whites should be legally barred from marrying each other, 50% of Whites said they would object if their children went to a school where the majority of students were Black, and 70% of Whites said that they would move if Blacks came to their community in large numbers (Fiske, 2004). Blatantly prejudice attitudes may have declined, but they have not been eliminated.

These findings do not exonerate the more liberal White American. A substantial body of research (see, e.g., Katz & Hass, 1988) has determined that "...although the majority of Whites try to be open-minded and relaxed about racial issues, they still harbor prejudiced attitudes" (Franzoi, 2000) and practice more subtle forms of discrimination (Fiske, 2004). It appears that at least some portion of the discrimination that Blacks perceive is produced by the behavior of Whites.

The Ambivalent Nature of Forgiveness

Despite these reports of perceived mistreatment and the evidence that the expression of racial bias has become increasingly subtle in the United States (Dovidio et al., 1997) there is obviously a desire for improved race relations. Shelton and Richeson (2005), for example, have found that Black and White students want greater contact with each other. This optimistic finding can be explained in a number of ways. The Black students in their study could (a) believe that they have experienced less discrimination than other Black Americans (Taylor, Wright, & Porter, 1994), (b) be at an advanced stage of moral development (Enright, Santos, & Al-Mabuk, 1989), (c) have an especially well-developed racial/cultural identity (Cross & Vandiver, 2001), or (d) have a strong external incentive for establishing friendly relations with Whites.

Other Black Americans, however, are not inclined to establish friendly relations with Whites. Not forgiving, blaming, and feeling entitled to revenge may be, for some Black Americans, an eminently rational position. First, given the nature of the historical and contemporary injustices that African Americans have experienced, many may feel that forgiveness is morally inappropriate (Affinito, 1999). Second, some Blacks may feel that the anger maintained by not forgiving maintains the moral pressure needed to make certain the United States becomes a more racially just society and maintains the progress toward equality that has been made (Holmgren, 1993).

Some reasons for not forgiving may, however, be self-serving. Anger toward Whites for past injustices is normative in many Black communities. An individual who supports this norm may receive substantial social support and avoid ostracism (Exline et al., 2003). Not forgiving may also allow some Black Americans to protect their self-esteem by holding White Americans responsible for their less than favorable life circumstance (Snyder & Higgins, 1988).

Forgiving, however, does appear to confer some personal and social benefits on the forgiver. In the Black community, physical ailments, such as hypertension and heart disease, and psychological ailments, such as depression, have been attributed to genes, poor nutrition, insufficient medical care, and anger due to chronic racism and discrimination. In support of the anger due to chronic racism hypothesis, at least one author (DeGruy-Leary, 2005) has argued that the physical and psychological aliments Black Americans experience could reflect post-traumatic slavery syndrome (PTSS).

> PTSS is a condition that exists as a consequence of multigenerational oppression of Africans and their descendants resulting from centuries of chattel slavery. A form of slavery which was predicated on the belief that African Americans were inherently/genetically inferior to Whites. This was then followed by institutionalized racism which continues to perpetuate injury. (DeGruy-Leary, 2005)

Because hostility and anger are known to be related to heart disease and other medical and psychological ailments (Miller, Smith, Turner, Guijarro, & Hallet, 1996; Williams & Williams, 1993), any intervention that serves to reduce these emotions should also impact favorably on the individual's psychological and physical well-being. Encouraging forgiveness, therefore, may be one way to improve the physical and psychological well-being of Black Americans. Research has demonstrated that (a) there tends to be an inverse relationship between an inclination to forgive and levels of anger and hostility and (b) interventions designed to increase forgiveness also resulted in less anger, hostility, depression, and better reported physical health (Witvliet et al., 2001; Kaplan, 1992) and greater authentic happiness (Seligman, 2002).

Unfortunately, the research supporting the benefits of forgiveness is still in its infancy and must be viewed with caution. Future researchers may find the presumed relationship between forgiveness and the forgiver's psychological and physical well-being to be a statistical anomaly. Also, there may be circumstances where forgiveness could result in exacerbated post-offense physical or mental distress for the forgiver (Cose, 2004; McCullough & Witvliet, 2002). Similar to a person suffering from post-traumatic stress disorder, the forgiver, if s/he still has unresolved feelings related to his/her trauma, may re-experience the ordeal in the form of flashback episodes, memories, nightmares, or frightening thoughts, especially when exposed to events, objects, or people reminiscent of the trauma. And finally, Black Americans can achieve the presumed medical and psychological benefits of forgiveness by writing or talking about the transgression (Niederhoffer & Pennebaker, 2002). Racial forgiveness as a viable race relations strategy for the *individual* Black American, therefore, remains arguable.

Collective forgiveness, however, may require a different perspective. A number of researchers and social commentators do believe that forgiveness can help restore interpersonal harmony (see, e.g., Enright & Fitzgibbons, 2000; Schimmel, 2002) and can be used to create a climate that supports more positive *intergroup* relations (Ripley & Worthington, 2002). The psychological disposition of the forgiver and the social context in which forgiveness takes place are, however, critical in determining whether intergroup relations would improve.

Moral and Dispositional Attributes That Facilitate Forgiveness

People may forgive for personal, interpersonal, or group interest or they may forgive because they believe it is the principled thing to do. One meta-analysis of varied studies (Underwood & Moore, 1982) found that the level of moral reasoning predicted prosocial behavior. In a similar vein, Enright et al. (1989), using a framework established by Kohlberg (1963), discovered that an individual's level of moral reasoning was positively correlated with their stage of reasoning about forgiveness. Apparently a person can be in one of six stages: (a) revengeful forgiveness, (b) restitutional forgiveness, (c) expectational forgiveness, (d) lawful expectational forgiveness, (e) forgiveness as social harmony, and (f) forgiveness as love. Theoretically, then, only those African Americans who believe forgiveness can be used to create social harmony or who see forgiveness as a form of love can be expected to forgive.

Reed and Aquino (2003) provide empirical support for this hypothesis. They found that when an individual's moral identity assumes high self-importance, i.e., his self-conception is privately and publicly organized around moral considerations, then he is more likely to forgive an out-group member for a transgression against his group. A strong moral identity appears to be associated with an individual's willingness to include members of an antagonistic group in his circle of "moral regard." Individuals at a high level of moral development are able to see, despite their suffering, that they and their victimizers belong to the same community. Research using the Multidimensional Inventory of Black Identity, an instrument that has been found to predict the frequency of Black interaction with Whites, suggests that a Black person's willingness to forgive may also be influenced by his racial/cultural identity (Sellers, Rowley, Chavous, Shelton, & Smith, 1997).

Cross (1991) and others (e.g., Helms & Parham, 1992) have argued for a stage conception of Black Identity Development. In the expanded version of his "Nigrescence" model, Cross (Cross & Vandiver, 2001) has identified four stages of development and eight distinct identities.

Stage one, the Pre-encounter stage, has three identities: (a) the Assimilation Identity, which is characterized by a pro-American reference group orientation that emphasizes the commonalities between being an African American and the rest of American society (Sellers et al., 1997) and a tendency to deny the importance of race; (b) the Miseducation Identity, which is characterized by viewing the Black community in terms of a negative stereotypes; and (c) the Self-Hatred Identity, which is characterized by the Black American viewing himself negatively because he is Black.

Stage two, the Encounter stage, is characterized by a dissonance-producing event or series of events that cause the Black individual to reevaluate his reference group orientation. This "rude awakening" results in the individual moving into Stage three, the Immersion–Emersion stage, which has two separate identities: (a) the Intense Black Involvement Identity and (b) the Anti-White Identity. The Intense Black Involvement Identity is characterized by an over-romanticized view of the Black experience and the Anti-White Identity is characterized by a tendency toward demonizing White people and rejecting what is perceived as being White culture.

Stage four, the Internalization stage, which is characterized by a "proactive Black pride, self-love, and a deep connection to, and acceptance, by the Black community" and a shift of "uncontrolled rage toward White people to controlled anger at oppressive systems and racist institutions" (Cross, 1991) also has three identities, all of which share a tendency toward system-blame and activism and having a pro-Black, rather than anti-White, reference group orientation. The individuals who occupy these stages are characterized as follows: (a) The Black Nationalist Identity individual concentrates on improving the circumstance of Black people; (b) The Biculturist Identity individual has a pro-Black orientation and a focus on one other cultural orientation, for example, gender or nationality; and (c) the Multiculturist Identity individual has a positive Black Identity and focuses actively on two or more cultural identities. Unlike the Black Nationalist Identity individual, the Biculturist and Multiculturist individuals share a desire to build coalitions beyond the Black community.

In sum, then, we should expect Blacks in the Pre-Encounter stage to not be concerned with racial forgiveness. They will either deny that racism exists or that s/he has experienced any racial injustice or hold the White community responsible for any perceived injustices. We can also expect that Blacks in the Immersion/Emersion stage, with their especially strong in-group orientation and out-group hostility, will be the least likely to forgive White Americans (Aquino & Reed, 2002). In addition, we can expect that if they were to forgive Whites, they would forgive only after revenge had been enacted or some sort of restitution had been made. This claim is partially supported by Vandiver, Cross, Worrell, & Fhagen-Smith (2002) who found an inverse relationship between a measure of the Immersion–Emersion Anti-White stage and a scale designed to assess the belief in commonalities of all humans regardless of race (Sellers et al., 1998). Furthermore, research by Exline (Exline, Baumeister, Bushman, Campbell, & Finkel, 2004) has demonstrated that individuals who have a greater sense of injustice express greater skepticism about the appropriateness of forgiveness.

A Black person who is in the Immersion/Emersion stage invests considerable time learning about African/African American culture, assumes an especially strong Afrocentric perspective, and perceives the White community as being monolithic, racist, and hostile toward Black interest. Spending time in this stage is important; it serves as a "crucible" that allows the individual to develop an integrated and secure social identity which then provides the foundation needed for a positive group identity. It is, however, a cognitively simple stage that does not take into consideration the complicated nature of race relations in the United States.

Individuals in the Internalization stage of racial/cultural identity development, however, have a more differentiated understanding of race and race relations. They demonstrate a greater willingness to acknowledge that no racial group is perfect, that all groups have favorable and unfavorable characteristics, and that all groups have members that engage in altruistic and less-than-altruistic behavior (Cross, 1991). They also seem to understand that the behaviors of both Blacks and Whites have commendable and not so commendable motives (Katz, Wackenhut, & Hass, 1986). This differentiated understanding of race relations of the "internalized" Black is probably caused by and results in a reluctance to completely attribute racially offensive behavior to the disposition of the offender. Blacks at this stage of development can, presumably, recognize the structural and situational determinants of racism.

The readiness to make external attributions regarding the cause of racist behavior may, however, cause significant challenges. While seeing the situational determinants of the perpetrator's behavior may facilitate the forgiveness process (Wade & Worthington, 2005), it may also be a source of significant distress. Attributing the racist behavior of an individual to his personality, and denying that it has a situational determinant, may make it more difficult to forgive, but once forgiveness is conferred the forgiver can "move on." Making a dispositional attribution allows one to "localize" the cause of the transgression and the transgressor. If, on the other hand, the racist behavior is seen as being caused by a racist system, forgiving becomes problematic. The cause of the transgression still exists and another transgression from another transgressor remains likely. To completely forgive Black Americans who make external attributions, i.e., hold the "system" responsible for historical and contemporary injustices they have experienced, must work to change that system to ensure that the transgressions do not continue.

We can, then, hypothesize that Blacks who are in the Internalization stage, with their (a) focus on system rather than individual blame, (b) willingness to acknowledge the complexity of human motivation, and (c) tendency to avoid attributing an individual's behavior solely to his personality, set the stage for forgiveness (see, e.g., Wade & Worthington, 2005). Research, also by Vandiver et al. (2002), lends partial support to this assertion. Being in the Internalization Multiculturist stage is associated with greater acceptance of other cultural groups.

In addition to having a more complex view of Whites, the Internalization Multiculturist identity individuals may also be more willing to forgive because they have a relatively broad definition of their in-group. Wohl and Branscombe (2005) noticed that victimized group members who were induced to have a maximally inclusive social group, i.e., humankind, were more likely to forgive contemporary members of a historical perpetrator group and the historical perpetrator group.

The core feature that allows the Black American who has a high level of moral development and the Black American who is at an advanced stage of racial/cultural identity to forgive appears to be a maximally inclusive social identity, that is, a psychological predisposition to occupy a social category that includes White Americans.

To Whom Should Forgiveness Be Conferred?

Transgressions committed in the past against members of a group can still, generations later, evoke strong emotional reactions in current members of the abused group (Liem, 2007; DeGruy-Leary, 2005) and have behavioral consequences. Robinson (2000), and before him Grier and Cobbs (1968), for example, has argued convincingly that the legacy of slavery and discrimination is responsible for the dismal social and economic state of a significant portion of contemporary Black America. If this is so, then present day Black Americans can hold responsible and choose to forgive any individual who was actively involved in maintaining slavery, the slave trade, and the post-reconstruction exploitation of Blacks. This includes those businessmen and political leaders, both historical and contemporary, who actively obstructed Black participation in the political and economic life of the United States or passively allowed it to take place.

In addition, if forgiveness is being seen as a way as to eliminate the deleterious psychological and physical effects of racism, forgiveness may need to be conferred on others who are not White. For example, Black Americans may need to forgive the Africans who participated in the slave trade. They may also need to forgive Blacks who denigrate other Blacks because of the color of their skin or the texture of their hair and those Black parents, who because they were emotionally unavailable or physically abusive, had a profoundly negative effect on their child's development (see, e.g., Barras, 2000). Furthermore, some Blacks may have to forgive themselves for passively accepting or actively colluding with a system that denied them and their associates their humanity. Accepting that all communities are, to some degree, responsible for the nature of race relations in the United States makes forgiveness more likely (Exline et al., 2003).

The Process of Forgiving

Being the victim of prejudice and discrimination has serious economic and psychological consequences (e.g., Branscombe, Schmitt, & Harvey, 1999; Gibbons, Gerrard, Cleveland, Wills, & Brody, 2004). The cost of not dealing with these transgressions effectively can be substantial. Yet how do we determine who and what to forgive? Perhaps Black Americans need to begin the healing process by acknowledging all of the ways they have been transgressed against economically, politically, socially, and psychologically (Robinson, 2000), the effects of those transgressions (see, e.g., Danieli, 1998), and, as a community, systematically forgive the transgressors.

Black Americans must then focus their anger and energy, as they did in the 1960s, on changing the system that supports and maintains behavior that dehumanizes anyone. Forgiveness, if it is to be used to create social harmony between Black and White Americans, must be part of a comprehensive social movement whose ultimate aim is to create a community that embraces everyone.

A Framework for Forgiving

Fincham and Kashdan (2004) have developed an expanded framework for facilitating forgiveness that is especially useful if we are to see racial forgiveness as a social movement. Their framework acknowledges that existing clinically based forgiveness interventions are not adequate for reaching every Black American suffering from a racially motivated transgression and that a social climate that supports forgiveness must be created.

The model includes five levels of intervention: (a) a mass media-based forgiveness information campaign to promote the importance of forgiveness, (b) psychoeducation to make the public aware of the generic factors that facilitate forgiveness, (c) psychoeducation with forgiveness implementation to assist those who are ready to forgive a specific transgression, (d) psychoeducation with relationship skills training to teach interested parties forgiveness as a general skill, and (e) forgiveness-focused therapeutic intervention to assist those who have been severely damaged by a transgression.

Attempts at forgiveness will be more effective if there are community norms that support forgiveness and if the individual who wishes to forgive has been taught how to forgive. Worthington (2001) has developed, what appears to be, a psychologically reasonable five-step procedure to guide the individual forgiveness process. It is summarized by the acronym REACH: R for recalling the transgression as objectively as possible, E for empathizing with the perpetrator, A for giving the altruistic gift of forgiveness, C for committing yourself to forgive publicly, and H for holding on to forgiveness.

A core feature of the forgiveness process is the victims telling their stories. Story telling allows for personal healing by reducing the painful emotionality contained in the narrative (Niederhoffer & Pennebaker, 2002) and by helping the teller find a life enhancing meaning in the offense (Goleman, 1995). Story telling also reveals the victim's humanity to the transgressor. That revelation can trigger a transformation in the transgressor and invite the transgressor to share his story. Sharing stories fosters empathy and empathy expands one's social identity. Racial discord continues to exist because racial groups have exclusive social identities.

Empathizing and offering the altruistic gift of forgiving are difficult requirements, but would be facilitated if Blacks are able to (1) share their story in a safe and respectful climate, (2) hear their transgressor's story, (3) and attribute the transgressor's behavior to something other than unrepentant racism. The gift of altruism would also be easier if the transgressor apologized (Darby & Schlenker, 1982). While an apology would be helpful, it is not, however, a necessary condition for forgiveness. And even though a number of states have officially apologized for participating in slavery, the wish for an apology can become an obstacle to creating harmonious race relations. In an ABC News.com poll conducted in 2000, a minority of the Whites polled (38%) felt that the federal government should apologize to Black Americans for the slavery that once existed in this country. The desire for an apology was not unanimous in the Black community. Only 68% of the Blacks polled felt the federal government should apologize. As we consider whether forgiveness is a viable race relations strategy, we must also consider whether Whites feel they must be forgiven.

A Complication with Conferring Forgiveness

Publicly forgiving the White community may, in fact, engender resentment (Exline et al., 2003). In an ABC news poll, 53% of the Whites polled said that the federal government should not apologize to Black Americans for the slavery that once existed in this country (ABC News.com Poll, 2000). These Whites may feel that (1) because they are relatively recent immigrants they had nothing to do with slavery or discrimination, (2) they should not be held responsible for the transgressions of their ancestors, and (3) they have never discriminated against Blacks and have not benefited from Blacks being systematically disenfranchised. To them, Black forgiveness may appear to be rather presumptuous. Except where the transgression is undeniable and the perpetrator can be unmistakably identified, asking White Americans to assume responsibility for the circumstance of present-day Black Americans could lead to greater racial antagonisms.

Forgiveness Is Not Enough

As I explored interracial forgiveness, the importance of assertively responding to transgressions became keenly apparent. Without the possibility of retribution, with its attendant notion of accountability, there is little to stop the transgression from reoccurring. Social psychological research has shown that a tit-for-tat strategy is more likely to lead to cooperative solutions (Au & Komorita, 2002; Pruitt, 1998) than a strategy where a player remains unconditionally forgiving (Komorita, Chan, & Parks, 1993). South Africa's Truth and Reconciliation Commission, which advocated absolution, was brought about, at least in part, because of the efforts of the African National Congress (ANC), the harsh court of world opinion, and the fact that those offenders who did not publicly acknowledge their politically motivated transgression would be subject to criminal court (Crocker, 2000) in a Black-led South Africa.

The Rwandan Genocide also serves as a painful example. In 1994, between 500,000 and 1,000,000 Tutsis and moderate Hutus were murdered by two extremist Hutus militia groups. The killing did not end until a Tutsi-dominated rebel movement overthrew the Hutu government. Likewise, one could argue that in the United States Martin Luther King Jr.'s peaceful activism was made more effective because of the perceived threat posed by the Black Panthers and Malcolm X.

A tit-for-tat strategy, however, creates the possibility of escalating violence. The Cold War arms race between the United States and the Soviet Union serves as a historical example. And the Rwandan conflict seems to have spilled over into neighboring countries. Without a credible external agent – the United States, the United Nations, or a world court, for example – that is willing to maintain order through force of law and military/police power, the powerless who forgive will continue to be subject to social, economic, and political exploitation. Forgiveness as a race relations strategy can only work if norms of civility are created and enforced (see Osgood, 1962). For forgiveness to be effective, the relationship that exists between antagonistic groups must be transformed.

In addition, the personal benefits possibly conferred by forgiving will not last if the social and economic conditions that reflect the contemporary and historical injustices persist. Perhaps reparations, reconciliation, or developing an especially strong norm of cooperation between all Americans could help to create and maintain the social harmony that forgiveness would produce.

Moving Beyond Forgiveness

The Question of Reparations. Germany has given reparations to Jews and the United States has given reparations to the descendents of the Japanese Americans who had been interned during World War II. But would reparations to Black Americans be a legitimate policy initiative or an expedient way to deal with a complex issue?

It is clear that uncompensated Black slave labor contributed significantly to the economic well-being of the United States. And it is clear that Black America lags behind American communities that have not had to contend with the legacy of slavery on a number of social indicators, life expectancy and infant mortality are two prime examples. So perhaps reparations to Black Americans are the fair thing to do and those reparations can be used to address a number of social ills facing the Black community. There are, however, strong arguments against reparations.

Some may argue that (1) Blacks have received compensation for past practices of discrimination: the voting rights act, historically Black colleges, and 30+ years of affirmative action; (2) it is unreasonable to think that slavery, which ended over 200 years ago, accounts for the state of Black America today; and (3) money that was distributed for reparations has benefited a select few (see Cose, 2004, for a thorough discussion of these concerns). In addition, if reparations were to be considered, two important questions would have to be answered: (1) how much is reasonable compensation and (2) who will be compensated?

These questions and concerns should be debated. They have, however, served to legitimize the reluctance to politically address the issue of reparations (Robinson, 2000). I, however, do not believe the political determination to completely address the pros and cons of reparations will emerge until the norms that guide race relations in the United States have been effectively transformed.

The Question of Reconciliation. Desmond Tutu (1999) has suggested that the United States could benefit from a South African-type of Truth and Reconciliation Commission. This recommendation is open to question. In 1979 Klansmen and Nazis were videotaped shooting at a multiracial crowd that was marching to unionize workers in the textile mills. Five of the marchers were killed and a number of others were wounded. Even though the event was videotaped no one was convicted of the murders. In response to a failed initiative to openly address the "Greensboro massacre," Cose (2004, p. 124) argued that "It's extremely difficult to convince groups of people who see no need for collective healing to get deeply involved in a process that supposedly will heal them or heal their community. It's even more difficult when that process requires them to acknowledge so-called truths that their very self-image requires that they reject or deny." Who is really willing or ready to acknowledge that their relatives were racist and that the privileges that they enjoy were gotten because others were exploited?

South Africa was able to have a Truth and Reconciliation Commission because there was a restructuring of political power. In addition, (1) the new political leadership, symbolized by Nelson Mandela, was actively committed to the peaceful transformation of South Africa, (2) there was a clear sense as to who committed the transgressions, and (3) there was the possibility of amnesty for even the most egregious politically motivated offenders.

Reconciliation also appears to have worked in East Timor. East Timor is a poverty stricken country which, after its liberation from Indonesia, successfully brought together former enemies. Several factors made this possible:

1. The citizens of East Timor could hold Indonesia responsible for the conflict.
2. They have a common enemy: poverty.
3. They have a common history and culture.
4. There are limited racial distinctions.
5. There are few economic distinctions.
6. The leadership has established a norm of cooperation.

According to Cook (1984) these are exactly the elements needed to establish favorable relationships between members of different racial groups. Unfortunately, a number of these elements do not exist in the United States. Even though White Americans tend to feel that Black Americans have been treated unfairly in the past (Katz et al., 1986), present-day Black and White Americans have distinctly different views as to the degree to which racism still exists (Dovidio & Gaertner, 1996). More importantly, in addition to Black and White Americans differing in terms of their perceptions of modern day racism they also do not have a shared vision of the future.

Martin Luther King, Jr. attempted to provide a vision with his "I Have a Dream" speech, but the vision was not the result of an inclusive national dialogue and, therefore, not shared by critical constituencies. And President Clinton's 1998 national dialogue on race, while being a bold and important initiative, reviewed what individuals in many circles believed was already known. In one case the vision was not shared by all Americans, in the other case no new ground was covered and, therefore, neither catalyzed Americans to embrace comprehensive social reform.

Appreciative Inquiry

I believe that if we are interested in fostering greater racial harmony and a more equitable and racially just society then discussions of reparations, reconciliation, and forgiveness need to take place in a social climate that is informed by a shared vision of the future. A vision that is grounded in the conditions that were present when members of diverse racial and cultural groups were able to work together harmoniously and productively.

Cooperrider and his associates (Cooperrider, D. L., Sorensen, Jr. P. F., Whitney, D., Yaeger, T. F., 2000) developed a social technology that has been especially effective in achieving this vision on a large scale, Appreciative Inquiry.

> Appreciative Inquiry is a collaborative and highly participative, system-wide approach to seeking, identifying, and enhancing the "life-giving forces" that are present when a system

is performing optimally in human, economic, and organizational terms. It is a journey during which profound knowledge of a human system at its moments of wonder is uncovered
and used to co-construct the best and highest future of that system. (Watkins & Mohr, 2001)

Appreciative Inquiry (AI) has five generic processes: (a) choosing the positive as
a focus of inquiry; (b) inquiring into stories of life-affirming forces; (c) locating
themes that appear in the stories and selecting topics for further inquiry; (d) creating
shared images for a preferred future; and (e) finding innovative ways to create that
future (Watkins & Mohr, 2001). These processes have been used to successfully
address a number of challenging social issues and to develop a positive interracial
climate.

An international corporation used AI to create greater gender equity (Schiller,
2001), *Imagine Chicago* (Browne, 1998) used it to stimulate dialogue across racial,
cultural, economic, and generational boundaries; develop frameworks to understand, imagine, and create projects that build community; and to link individuals
and organizations committed to developing a positive future for Chicago's children.
Imagine South Carolina (Stewart & Royal, 1998) used AI to create a state-wide
initiative focused on developing effective communities and addressing issues of
race. Imagine South Carolina was recognized in two publications, *Racial Divide* and
Interracial Dialogue Groups across America as one of the nation's most successful
programs on improving racial dialogue.

AI works because a positive collective vision of the future that is grounded is
what is best about our shared experience and is given precedence over assigning
blame. This positive vision, and the process that creates it, promotes optimism, trust,
a norm of openness, and a positive view of the other. This is exactly the social
context that is needed for forgiveness to take place and for people to discuss how to
create a society that honors all of its members.

Racial healing in the United States will not begin with White Americans
acknowledging their complicity in the oppression of Blacks or with Black Americans forgiving Whites or with the federal government establishing a trust fund for
Blacks who have suffered from the legacy of slavery. All of these initiatives are
noteworthy but will, in the best case, offer temporary relief and, in the worst case,
increase the racial divide. To be optimally effective an appropriate social context
must be created. Appreciative Inquiry provides the tools and the processes to create
that context.

Racial healing will begin when the different communities which make up the
United States come together to discuss when race relations were at their best and
to use those instances to "help ignite the collective imagination of what might be"
(Hammond & Royal, 1998).

References

ABC News.com Poll. (2000, July). Retrieved August 18, 2007, from http://www.pollingreport.
    com/race.htm
Affinito, M. G. (1999). *When to forgive*. Oakland, CA: New Harbinger.

Aquino, K., & Reed, A. (2002, December). The self-importance of moral identity. *Journal of Personality and Social Psychology, 83*(6), 1423–1440.

Au, W., & Komorita, S. (2002, October). Effects of initial choices in the prisoner's dilemma. *Journal of Behavioral Decision Making, 15*(4), 343–359.

Barras, J. R. (2000). *Whatever happened to daddy's little girl? The impact of fatherlessness on black women.* New York, NY: The Ballantine Publishing Group.

Bobo, L. D. (2001). Racial attitudes and relations at the close of the twentieth century. In N. J. Smelser, W. J. Wilson, & F. Michael (Eds.), *American becoming.* Washington, DC: National Academy Press.

Branscombe, N., Schmitt, M., & Harvey, R. (1999, July). Perceiving pervasive discrimination among African Americans: Implications for group identification and well-being. *Journal of Personality and Social Psychology, 77*(1), 135–149.

Browne, B. (1998). Imagine Chicago: A study in intergenerational appreciative inquiry. In Hammond, S. A. & Royal, C. (Eds.), *Lessons from the filed: Applying appreciative inquiry.* Plano, TX: Practical Press, Inc.

Clark, K. B. and Clark, M. P. (1957). Racial identification and preference in Negro children. In T. M. Newcomb and E. L. Hartley (Eds.), *Readings in social psychology,* New York: Holt, Rinehart and Winston.

Cook, S. W. (1984). Cooperative interaction in multi-ethnic contexts. In N. Miller & M. B. Brewer (Eds.), *Groups in contact: The psychology of desegregation.* New York: Academic Press.

Cooperrider, D. L., Sorensen, P. F., Jr., Whitney, D., & Yaeger, T. F. (Eds.). (2000). *Appreciative inquiry: Rethinking human organization toward a positive theory of change.* Champaign, IL: Stipes Publishing, LLC.

Cose, E. (2004, February 15). *Bone to pick: Of forgiveness, reconciliation, reparations, and revenge.* New York: Atria Books.

Crocker, D. A. (2000). *Retribution and reconciliation.* Retrieved August 18, 2007, from http://www.puaf.umd.edu/IPPP/Winter-Spring00retribution_and_reconciliation.htm

Cross, W. E. (1991). *Shades of black: Diversity in African American identity.* Philadelphia, PA: Temple University Press.

Cross, W. E., Jr., & Vandiver, B. J. (2001). Nigrescence theory and measurement: Introducing the Cross Racial Identity Scale (CRIS). In J. G. Ponterotto, J. M. Casas, L. A. Suzuki, & C. M. Alexander (Eds.), *Handbook of multicultural counseling* (2nd ed., pp. 371–393). Thousand Oaks, CA: Sage.

Danieli, Y. (1998). *International handbook of multigenerational legacies of trauma.* New York: Plenum Press.

Darby, B. W., & Schlenker, B. R. (1982). Children's reactions to apologies. *Journal of Personality and Social Psychology, 43*, 742–753.

DeGruy-Leary, J. (2005). *Post traumatic slave syndrome: America's legacy of enduring injury and healing.* Milwaukie, OR: Uptone Press.

Dovidio, J., & Gaertner, S. (1996, Winter). Affirmative action, unintentional racial biases, and intergroup relations. *Journal of Social Issues, 52*(4), 51–75.

Dovidio, J. Gaertner, S. L., Validzic, A. Matota, K., Jonson, B., & Frazier, S. (1997). Extending the benefits of recategorization: Evaluations, self-disclosure and helping. *Journal of Experimental Social Psychology, 33*, 401–420.

Enright, R. D., & Fitzgibbons, R. P. (2000). *Helping clients forgive: An empirical guide for resolving anger and restoring hope.* Washington, DC: American Psychological Association.

Enright, R., Santos, M., & Al-Mabuk, R. (1989, March). The adolescent as forgiver. *Journal of Adolescence, 12*(1), 95–110.

Exline, J., Baumeister, R., Bushman, B., Campbell, W., & Finkel, E. (2004, December). Too proud to let go: Narcissistic entitlement as a barrier to forgiveness. *Journal of Personality and Social Psychology, 87*(6), 894–912.

Exline, J. J., Worthington, E., Hill, P., & McCullough, M. E. (2003). Forgiveness and justice: A research agenda for social and personality psychology. *Personality and Social Psychology Review, 7*(4), 337–348.

Fincham, F., & Kashdan, T. (2004). *Facilitating forgiveness: Developing group and community interventions.* Hoboken, NJ: John Wiley & Sons Inc.

Fiske, T. E. (2004). *Social beings: A core motives approach to social psychology.* New York: John Wiley &Sons, Inc.

Franzoi, S. (2000). *Social psychology* (2nd ed.). New York: McGraw-Hill.

Gibbons, F., Gerrard, M., Cleveland, M., Wills, T., & Brody, G. (2004, April). Perceived discrimination and substance use in African American parents and their children: A panel study. *Journal of Personality and Social Psychology, 86*(4), 517–529.

Goleman, D. (1995). *Emotional intelligence.* New York: Bantam.

Grier, W., & Cobbs, P. (1968). *Black rage.* New York: Basic Books.

Hammond, S. A., & Royal, C. (Eds.). (1998). *Lessons from the filed: Applying appreciative inquiry.* Plano, TX: Practical Press, Inc.

Helms, J. E., & Parham, T. A. (1992). The relationship between black identity attitudes and cognitive styles. In J. E. Helms (Ed.), *Black and White racial identity: Theory, research, and practice.* Westport, CT: Greenwood Press.

Holmgren, M. R. (1993). Forgiveness and the intrinsic value of persons. *American Philosophical Quarterly, 30*, 341–352.

Ilibagiza, I. (2006). *Left to tell: Discovering God amidst the Rwandan holocaust.* Carlsbad, CA: Hay House.

Kaplan, B. (1992, February). Social health and the forgiving heart: The type B story. *Journal of Behavioral Medicine, 15*(1), 3–14.

Kardiner, A., & Ovesey, L. (1951). *The mark of oppression: Explorations in the personality of the American Negro.* New York: Norton

Katz, I., & Hass, R. (1988, December). Racial ambivalence and American value conflict: Correlational and priming studies of dual cognitive structures. *Journal of Personality and Social Psychology, 55*(6), 893–905.

Katz, I., Wackenhut, J., & Hass, R. (1986). *Racial ambivalence, value duality, and behavior.* San Diego, CA: Academic Press.

King, M. L., Jr. (1957). *Loving your enemies.* Retrieved August 18, 2007, from http://www.creighton.edu/ mlk/speeches/enemies.html

Kohlberg, L. (1963). The development of children's orientations toward a moral order: Sequence in the development of moral thought. *Vita Humana, 6*(1), 11–33.

Komorita, S., Chan, D., & Parks, C. (1993, May). The effects of reward structure and reciprocity in social dilemmas. *Journal of Experimental Social Psychology, 29*(3), 252–267.

Liem, R. (2007). Silencing historical trauma: The politics and psychology of memory and voice. *Peace and Conflict: Journal of Peace Psychology, 13*(2), 153–174.

McCullough, M., & Witvliet, C. V. (2002). *The psychology of forgiveness.* New York: Oxford University Press.

McCullough, M., Worthington, E., & Rachal, K. (1997, August). Interpersonal forgiving in close relationships. *Journal of Personality and Social Psychology, 73*(2), 321–336.

Miller, T., Smith, T., Turner, C., Guijarro, M., & Hallet, A. (1996, March). Meta-analytic review of research on hostility and physical health. *Psychological Bulletin, 119*(2), 322–348.

Niederhoffer, K., & Pennebaker, J. (2002). *Sharing one's story: On the benefits of writing or talking about emotional experience.* New York: Oxford University Press.

Osgood, C. (1962). *An alternative to war or surrender.* Urbana, IL: University of Illinois Press.

Pruitt, D. (1998). *Social conflict.* New York: McGraw-Hill.

Robinson, R. (2000). *The debt: What America owes to Blacks.* New York: Penguin Putnam, Inc.

Reed, A., & Aquino, K. (2003, June). Moral identity and the expanding circle of moral regard toward out-groups. *Journal of Personality and Social Psychology, 84*(6), 1270–1286.

Ripley, J., & Worthington, E. (2002, September). Hope-focused and forgiveness-based group interventions to promote marital enrichment. *Journal of Counseling & Development, 80*(4), 452–463.

Scarville, J., Button, S. B., Edwards, J. E., Lancaster, A. R., & Elig, T. W. (1999). *Armed Forces Equal Opportunity Survey*. (Rep.) Arlington, Virginia: Defense Manpower Data Center Survey & Program Evaluation Division.

Seligman, M. (2002). *Authentic happiness: Using the new positive psychology to realize your potential for lasting fulfillment*. New York: Free Press.

Sellers, R., Rowley, S., Chavous, T., Shelton, J., & Smith, M. (1997, October). Multidimensional inventory of Black identity: A preliminary investigation of reliability and construct validity. *Journal of Personality and Social Psychology, 73*(4), 805–815.

Sellers, R., Smith, M., Shelton, J., Rowley, S., & Chavous, T. (1998). Multidimensional model of racial identity: A reconceptualization of African American racial identity. *Personality and Social Psychology Review, 2*(1), 18–39.

Shelton, J., & Richeson, J. (2005, January). Intergroup contact and pluralistic ignorance. *Journal of Personality and Social Psychology, 88*(1), 91–107.

Schimmel, S. (2002). *Wounds not healed by time: The power of repentance and forgiveness*. New York: Oxford University Press.

Schiller, M. (2001) Case study: Avon Mexico. In J. M. Watkins & B. J. Mohr (Eds.). *Appreciative inquiry: Change at the speed of imagination*. San Francisco, CA: Jossey-Bass/Pfeiffer.

Snyder, C., & Higgins, R. (1988, July). Excuses: Their effective role in the negotiation of reality. *Psychological Bulletin, 104*(1), 23–35.

Steele, C. (1997). *Race and the schooling of Black Americans*. Englewood Cliffs, NJ: Prentice-Hall, Inc.

Stewart, A. K., & Royal, C. (1998). Imagine South Carolina: A citizen's summit and public dialogue. In S. A. Hammond & C. Royal (Eds.), *Lessons from the filed: Applying appreciative inquiry*. Plano, TX: Practical Press, Inc.

Taylor, D., Wright, S., & Porter, L. (1994). *Dimensions of perceived discrimination: The personal/group discrimination discrepancy*. Hillsdale, NJ, England: Lawrence Erlbaum Associates, Inc.

Tutu, D. (1999). *No future without forgiveness*. New York: Random House

Underwood, B., & Moore, B. (1982, January). Perspective-taking and altruism. *Psychological Bulletin, 91*(1), 143–173.

U.S. Merit Systems Protection Board. (1997). *Fair & equitable treatment: A progress report on minority employment in the federal government*. (Rep.) Washington, DC: U.S. Merit Systems Protection Board Office of Policy and Evaluation.

Vandiver, B., Cross, W., Worrell, F., & Fhagen-Smith, P. (2002, January). Validating the Cross racial identity scale. *Journal of Counseling Psychology, 49*(1), 71–85.

Wade, N., & Worthington, E. (2005, June). In search of a common core: A content analysis of interventions to promote forgiveness. *Psychotherapy: Theory, Research, Practice, Training, 42*(2), 160–177.

Watkins, J. M., & Mohr, B. J. (2001). *Appreciative inquiry: Change at the speed of imagination*. San Francisco, CA: Jossey-Bass/Pfeiffer.

Williams, R., & Williams, V. (1993). *Anger kills*. New York: Random House.

Witvliet, c. V., Ludwig, T. E., Van der Laan, K. L. (2001). Granting forgiveness or harboring grudges: Implications for emotion, physiology, and health. *Psychological Science, 121*, 117–123.

Wohl, M., & Branscombe, N. (2005, February). Forgiveness and collective guilt assignment to historical perpetrator groups depend on level of social category inclusiveness. *Journal of Personality and Social Psychology, 88*(2), 288–303.

Worthington, E. (2001). *Five steps to forgiveness*. New York: Crown.

Worthington, E., Sandage, S., & Berry, J. (2000). *Group interventions to promote forgiveness: What researchers and clinicians ought to know*. New York: Guilford Press.

Chapter 11
Rwanda: Repentance and Forgiveness – Pillars of Genuine Reconciliation

Antoine Rutayisire

In less than a hundred days from April 7th to July 4th, 1994, more than 1 million Tutsis and moderate Hutus of Rwanda were massacred in one of the worst genocides of the century. Up to date, people are still trying to process the causes of this madness. How could such a thing happen? How to explain such madness?

The Hard Questions

From time immemorial, Rwanda has been populated by Hutus, Tutsis, and Twas, three groups that have been and are still frequently mistaken for ethnic groups or tribes. The three groups speak the same language without even a distinguishing dialect, and they share the same culture and live in the same villages next to each other, thus defying any scientific delineation into tribes and ethnic distinctions. Even physical traits are not a reliable reference for the distinction. We have the same skin color and the height and facial traits that are at times presented as undeniable distinctives, but are also presented as misleading stereotypes.

Then come the hard questions – "if it be so, then how do you explain that the Hutu hated the Tutsi so much that they tried to wipe them out in one of the worst human tragedies of the century, namely the genocide of 1994?" "If it is impossible to distinguish between a Hutu and a Tutsi, how did people know who to kill and who to spare?" As the major focus of this chapter is to give an analytical answer to the first question, I will first clear the second one in one sentence: Ethnically marked identity cards made it easy to know who was Hutu and who was Tutsi. As for the why, many factors have been identified such as ethnic hatred, bad politics and power struggle, colonial and neo-imperialist manipulations, as well as socio-economical frustrations. Most of the root causes of collective violence like structure-based inequalities, difficult life conditions, destructive intergroup ideologies (Staub, 1989) were all there and the climate was ripe for a genocide. But this was the culmination of four decades of "episodic violence" against the Tutsis – including killings in the period 1959–1963 and in 1973, deprivation of rights through institutionalized injustice called "ethnic equilibrium," and an "incriminating ideology" making of them the former oppressors. The genocide against Tutsis in 1994 came as another historical evidence that "memory, one taproot of civic peoplehood, can also be a time bomb ready to explode into political conflict" (Shriver, 1995, p. 4).

Ani Kalayjian, Raymond F. Paloutzian, *Forgiveness and Reconciliation*, Peace Psychology Book Series, DOI 10.1007/978-1-4419-0181-1_11,
© Springer Science+Business Media, LLC 2009

In the first part of this chapter, I will look at wounded collective memory as the taproot of the long lasting ethnic animosity, my major contention being that collective hurts of the past, if not healed, will fester into future social sores. Unhealed social wounds in the Rwandan history born out of bad group relationships between the two major social groups – the Hutus and the Tutsis – motivated the politics of hatred and exclusion that eventually culminated into the genocide. This explains the importance of forgiveness, reconciliation, and long lasting measures aimed at peace building in areas that have known group tensions and conflicts.

In the second part of the chapter, I will focus on the challenges of peace building through structural transformation, the role of restorative justice through the Gacaca Community Courts, and the importance of repentance and confession, healing and forgiveness as prerequisites for genuine reconciliation. Drawing from different experiences in my personal life and from the daily practice in the National Unity and Reconciliation Commission, on which I served as a commissioner since 1999, my conclusion is that peace building must be a multidimensional exercise at the group level. Drawing from the experiences with the Gacaca Community Courts (whose motto is "Justice for Reconciliation"), my second contention is that reconciliation at the interpersonal level is only possible when, on the one hand, the perpetrator has come to terms with his evil deed, has repented from it, and confessed and asked for forgiveness; and on the other hand, the victim has healed from the wounds and is ready to forgive. Forgiveness alone will not lead to reconciliation though it may help the offended to get release and healing from the pain of past wounds. Forgiveness alone will heal the individual, with lots of difficulties if the offender refuses to recognize and acknowledge the evil, but it will not restore group harmony and cooperation. Even by its very etymology, reconciliation is a reciprocal process. It is the restoration of a broken relationship. And for that to happen, you need a change of heart and behavior on the part of the offended (through healing and forgiveness) and of the offender (through repentance and confession). Forgiveness is only one part of a two-way give and take process.

The chapter is presented under the form of narrative for three major reasons. First, it is just a cultural bias, ours being an oral culture that favors narrative over analysis. Second, narrative is factual and lends itself to possibilities of multiple reinterpretations. But the main reason is that I am simply more of an amateur practitioner of forgiveness and reconciliation than a trained psychologist and analyst of trauma. My conclusions will thus be directly drawn more from daily examples and practice than from academic interpretation.

Understanding the Madness

From Father to Son: Intergenerational Transmission of Trauma

Peace psychologists have tried to identify systemic and cultural origins of violent episodes. "Violent events are viewed as manifestations of interactions among a host of destructive inputs that are embedded in social, cultural and historical factors" (Christie, 2006). These factors include social injustices, bystander passivity, militarism, globalization, and "a range of cultural narratives that support violence including, for example, ideologies that normalize social exclusion and violence" (Christie, 2006, p. 6). What were the factors and cultural narratives that led to the 1994 Rwanda genocide?

In 1993 when Rwanda was tense with all types of conflicts I asked one young militiaman "Interahamwe" (the youth wing of the MRNDD party in power that was later on turned into a killing machine) why he was doing what he was doing, hating and persecuting Tutsis indiscriminately. "How old are you?" I asked him. "Nineteen", he answered. "Now, you were not even born when the Tutsis lost their power. What have they done to you?" I asked again. "Data yarabambwiye (My father told me)." Very revealing words. This is a clear case of generational transmission of trauma. "My father, my grandfather, they... have told me." Manipulated history, past wounds kept on the heart and not dealt with, become like a hidden landmine on which future generations will step to be blown up. Unlike physical wounds, inner wounds are transmitted from father to son, from generation to generation, becoming worse and more irrational the further down the line away from the original offense.

Most of our Rwanda present social misfortunes are the sour harvest of our national past, an unfortunate legacy of psychological scars, social injustices, economical and political/ideological ills. Our fathers sowed the wind and we reap the tempest! As one old prophet put it "our fathers committed sins and they are no more, and we bear their iniquities" (Lamentations 5:7). Manipulated history taught to children has become "leftover debris of our national past that continue to clog the relationships of diverse groups" (Shriver, 1995, p. 4). And Shriver concludes, "the debris will never get cleaned up and animosity will never drain away until forgiveness enters these relationships in some political form" (p. 4). The cultural narratives that our generation inherited from the parents and from opportunistic politicians have been stories of intergroup mistrust, hatred, and exclusion – continuously poisoning the stream of our group relationships.

Sowing the Wind: Rwandan History as I Learned it in School

Social and cultural narratives are transmitted from generation to generation through stories and anecdotes parents tell the children, through the media, and through school lessons. Research done in 2006 by a Commission of the Rwanda Senate, the IRDP, one of the institutions working on peace building in Rwanda, showed that racial prejudices were learned from parents (12.8%), teachers and school curriculums (75%), peers and political party rallies (42.3%), and through the media and other means (27.4%). This obviously was for the recent times because there was a time when the media was the greatest channel of hate propaganda (1990–1994). This part of the chapter looks at how intergenerational animosities were transmitted through history teaching, as an example of transgenerational transmission of past group trauma.

Rwanda history as taught to us in school had it that Rwanda is populated by three ethnic groups: The Batwa (1%), the Batutsi (14%), and the Bahutu (85%), commonly referred to as Twas, Tutsis, and Hutus, respectively, in English and French. The Twas, we were taught, were the first to occupy the land but they were only nomadic hunters who belonged to the short pygmoid group. They initially had their dwellings in forests and trees, feeding on animals they killed, fruit they picked from the trees, and roots they dug from the ground. Even then, they are said to have been very small in number and have remained so. No one ever told us where the Twas came from. They have always been despised, not allowed to share from the same pot of drinks as our social customs have it, and they do not intermarry with the two other groups. No wonder even today they are almost invisible in our social spheres.

When I was appointed as a commissioner on the National Unity and Reconciliation Commission in 1999, I took time to analyze the roots of our problems and I was amazed to find out how blind I had been to the plight of that small group. I had simply accepted and taken for granted that they do not belong because they do not like to belong! But the memory of one incident in my early school years in primary school flashed back in a revelatory way. One day, our teacher was telling us about the origins of the three Rwandan groups. The first thing he did was to ask those who belonged to each group to stand up. "The Hutus, stand up." They proudly stood up. "The Tutsis, stand up," we hesitantly stood up, a smaller number. "The Twas, stand up." No one! Then the teacher called out "Mukabuduwe, why are you not standing up, you are a Twa, aren't you?" The girl called by that name stood up, shyly, as if ashamed of being who she was. We all turned in her direction, looked at her, and laughed. The teacher reprimanded us for the behavior and did something I will never forget. He turned to us and asked, "Why do you behave like that? Do you despise the Twas?" Then he asked, "Who of all of you cannot share from the same drink with a Twa?" All of us, Hutus and Tutsis alike, stood up like one man! The girl had remained sitting, alone. Then all of a sudden she broke into tears, stood up, and dashed out of the classroom, weeping. For a whole week she did not come back to school. The teacher shrugged it off, scolded us a little, and just went on with his teaching on our origins. That was another way of forming a destructive social narrative. The more I work with issues of healing and reconciliation, I have come to understand why the girl left school that day and stayed away for a whole week. I have come to understand why the Twas are not with us in the church, in the army, or in politics. We have rejected them. Wounded as they are, they keep away from our contempt, afraid to be rejected again. Who would like to sit next to a person who despises him? When a social group has been despised for a period long enough to get to a point of believing the lie, their spirit becomes like a broken spring that will not bounce when pushed down. We all tend to shy away from places where we are made to feel rejected.

The Hutus, we were told, came second from somewhere around the Lake Tchad and settled in different places under different names according to different countries and they make up what is called the "Bantu" group. They were mainly cultivators and were consequently sedentary by nature.

The Tutsis came last after many centuries and found the Hutus well established. They came in small numbers and were very well received by the Hutus. They came from Abyssinia somewhere around Ethiopia and Somalia and belong to the "Nilotic-Hamitic" group. They came with cows. Later on they started conquering the land of their hosts and enslaved them.

Dissension Step-by-Step

This is a summary of the narrative of the origins of the three groups in our land. A close look reveals how the seeds of dissensions were sown.

First, the way the Twas are presented explains why we have never given them any recognition: after all, their ancestry was less than human, they were just "next to the monkeys." Despising the Twas was just normal from that perspective. In the 1980s the government tried to amend their lot but it was done in such a condescending way that it did not bear any tangible fruit. Small brick houses were built for them in some places and in other places they were given iron sheets for roofing their houses, but this was just a way of appeasing the feeling of guilt on the national conscience. But there was no confession, there was no effort to change the prejudices, and even the above efforts seemed to reinforce them. During our first term on the National Unity and Reconciliation Commission (1999–2002), one of the commissioners was a Twa. The first day of our meeting I went to him and told him I wanted to apologize for the way we had treated his group. He was amazed and he did accept the apology and since then we have been friends and mutual admirers!

Second, the way the relationships between the Hutus and the Tutsis are presented reveals an undercurrent of intentional manipulation. The narrative runs as if the country belonged to the Hutus who were sedentary agriculturalists, who were the first comers and toiled to cut the forest to turn the forest into a habitable country. The Hutus are presented as naive and good-hearted hosts who welcomed the Tutsis into their land. Then the Tutsis are presented as the bad guests – "ucumbikira mu mfuruka bakaguca mu mbere" (you give them a sleeping place in the guest room and the following day they have chased you out of your bedroom), as goes the popular saying that reflects that stereotype.

So all the historical conquests by Tutsi kings are not considered in their real value but rather as usurpation of "Hutu Power." The traditional Rwanda kingdom started as a small chiefdom in the Northeastern part of the present Rwanda territory under the leadership of Tutsi leader and slowly expanded by the conquest of other chiefdoms. The conquests were not discriminatory: regions under pastoralist (later on called Tutsis) and agriculturalist (referred to as Hutus) chiefs were all subjected to attacks and conquests in the non-stopping expansion of the kingdom that went on until the arrival of the white colonialists in the region at the end of the 19th century (1896). In the presentation of our history, however, the conquests have always been interpreted as a kind of usurpation of "Hutu power," passing in silence over the fact that chiefdoms under pastoral leaders (Tutsi) were also conquered. No wonder "Hutu Power" became the leitmotiv theme of the songs and slogans used before and during the genocide. One of the songs says, "nanga abahutu batibuka, ngo bibuke Nyagakecuru mu Bisi bya Huye, ngo bibuke 'Nice Mpandahande, mvire Ruhande rimwe,' ngo bibuke Nzira ya Muramira. Icyo bazize se ntimukizi?" (I hate Hutus who do not remember, Hutus who do not remember the conquest of Ibisi near Huye the kingdom of Nyagakecuru, Hutus who do not remember the invasion of the land of Mpandahande who lived in Ruhande; who do not remember Nzira son of Muramira. Will you ignore the cause of their fall?) The story of the renowned conqueror Tutsi King Ruganzu as presented in that song reflects how the Tutsis were presented in the eyes of the younger generation in our schools: tactful usurpers. This idea of Tutsi being foreigners from Abyssinia who came to usurp the Hutu Power was exploited by demagogues and propagandists of the genocide. Many people were killed and thrown into the Akagera River, one of the rivers feeding the Nile River as "a shortcut back to their homeland of Ethiopia." Why was the hate propaganda so successful? Simply because the unhealed wounds of the past served as a detonator for the ethnic bomb that unleashed the genocide of 1994. But where did the bitterness come from?

Rwanda Before the Arrival of the Europeans

Nostalgics will always look at the past as a lost paradise. Today, a certain reading of history has glamorized our past before the arrival of the whites and all the misfortunes are simplistically blamed on the white colonialists. Listening to some people, you would think our ancestors lived in a paradise without social blemishes. This is another dangerous narrative – scapegoating only the white colonial powers for all the ills of our nation.

The first whites arrived in Rwanda around 1896 and found the Hutus, Tutsis, and Twas all living together under the leadership of an uncontested monarchy. All were servants to the same king, who was said to be above "the mêlée" although he belonged to the Tutsi group. In his enthronement ceremony he was always reminded that "umwami ntaba umuhutu, ntaba umututsi, ntaba umutwa" (the king is never a hutu, a tutsi, or a twa). He was the unifying element of the people and was supposed to be impartial to all. But this is only partly true as promotion in the system often came from family relationships and the scheming traffic of influence. In actual fact, the power was in the hands of one clan – the Abanyiginya – which gave the king with few satellite clans who gave the queen mothers and thus waged great power and influence. Nevertheless, it was possible for anybody from the three groups to access higher positions through personal achievements and performance (military, economic, artistic, and even personal service to the royalty).

Although it is true that no single clash or war on an ethnic basis is recorded in our history, it is clear that a bitter root was already there poisoning the relationships between our three groups. The Twas, as already seen, were despised by the two other major groups. The relationships between the Hutus and the Tutsis were twisted by many factors. The aristocratic system was built on stereotypical myths that made everything beautiful and good to be Tutsi and everything bad and ugly to be Hutu. A close analysis of our social stereotypes as reflected in our proverbs, popular jokes, and sayings shows that our standards of beauty and handsomeness favored the tall height and the fine facial traits that in many cases came to be identified with the Tutsis. During the genocide, the paranoia on this physical appearance was so high that even statues of the Virgin Mary in Catholic churches were cut into pieces simply because "they looked Tutsi!" The Tutsis were thought to be refined in behavior while it was expected and acceptable for Hutus to be raw, rude, and gluttonous. The word "imfura" used by Tutsis to talk of themselves refers not only to physical beauty but also to nobility of character and behavior. The rough, the uncouth, the glutton, and the uncultured were referred to as "Hutu."

The wounds created by this kind of rejection, negation, and belittlement of the other in his humanness, breed bitterness that will eventually explode into destructive behaviors. A good reading of history will show that all violent atrocities committed against aristocratic nobilities in social upheavals and revolutions (like the French Revolution) have always been fuelled by this undercurrent of emotional woundedness. Stories collected during the genocide and before show that resentments based on ethnic rejection was one of the deep roots of the genocide. Some of the killers mutilated Tutsi women saying "Umva ko muri beza, tuzareba ko uzongera kuba mwiza" (you are said to be beautiful, let us see if you will be beautiful again after this). Others raped Tutsi women saying "reka twumve uko umututsikazi amera" (let's taste how it feels to have sex with a tutsi woman).

1900–1959: The Colonial Period

Rwanda was first a German colony; then it became a Belgian protectorate when Germany lost World War I. The Germans had not had enough time to leave their fingerprints on the slate of Rwandan history as the Belgians did. With their firm hand on the administration of the country, the Belgians changed many factors in the social equation. First, the king lost his unifying role when promotion was taken over by the Belgians who promoted exclusively the sons of Tutsi chiefs who were considered as born leaders at the expense of the two other groups. They created what the African American activist Malcolm X once called the "House Negroes" and the "Field Negroes":

> There were two kinds of negroes. There was that old house Negro and the field Negro. And the house Negro always looked out for his master. When the field Negroes got too much out of line, he held them back in check. He put them back on the plantation.

> The house Negro could afford to do that because he lived better than the field Negro. He ate better, he dressed better, and he lived in a better house. He lived right up next to his master- in the attic or the basement. He ate the same food his master ate and wore his same clothes. And he could talk just like his master- good diction. And he loved his master more than his master loved himself. That's why he did not want his master hurt. If the master got sick he'd say "what's the matter, boss, we sick? When the master's house caught a fire, he'd try and put the fire out. He didn't want his master's house burned. He never wanted his master's property threatened. And he was more defensive of it than the master was. That was the house Negro.

And then you had some field Negroes, who lived in huts, had nothing to lose. They wore the worst kind of clothes. They ate the worst food. And they caught hell. They felt the sting of the lash. They hated their master. Oh, yes, they did. If the master got sick, they'd pray that the master died. If the master's house caught fire, they'd pray for a strong wind to come along. This was the difference between the two.

And today you still have the house Negroes and the field Negroes. I'm a field Negro. If I can't live in the house as a human being, I'm praying for a wind to come along. If the master won't treat me right and he is sick, I'll tell the doctor to go in the other direction. But if all of us are going to live as human beings, as brothers, then I'm for a society of human being that can practice brotherhood." (quoted in DeYoung, 1997, 22–23)

The Tutsi chiefs, "born leaders," were used like the "House Negroes": adulated, sent to the colonial school, taught to speak like the master, and even given some advantages over the others. And they were used for the tasks of keeping the others in line. And this created obvious jealousies. With their new system of administration, the Belgians introduced tough measures of forced labor, fines, imprisonments, lashing, and other systems of punishment and exploitation that had never existed before. These were resented by the population and all was blamed on the Tutsi chiefs who were the policy implementers! This myth of the "Tutsi born leader" was to be exploited against the Tutsis during the period of "Hutu Regimes" after independence. Nobody loves to sit next to a "born leader" who makes you feel little and threatens to take your place! And the fact of having been collaborators with the colonial system was to be later exploited to identify their leadership with colonialism. During the "Hutu Regimes," they always spoke of "ingoma ya gihake na gikolonize," "the leadership of feudalism and colonialism," one referring to the Tutsi (feudalism) and the other referring to the whites (colonialism). This formed another social narrative based on the wounds of colonial leadership.

1959–1994: The Ethnic (Hutu) Regimes – Politics of Revenge

Miroslav Volf (1996) writes that when victims do not heal from their wounds, with time they tend to "mimic the behaviour of the oppressors, (they) let themselves be shaped in the mirror of the enemy" and they "will become perpetrators tomorrow who in their self-deceit, will seek to exculpate their misdeeds on account of their own victimization" (p. 117). This should serve as a warning, as history over and over again shows that the oppressed of yesterday will become a worse oppressor when opportunity comes for him to seize power. "The factual-moral claim is: absent forgiveness and its twin repentance, political humans remember the crimes of ancestors only to entertain the idea of repeating them" (Shriver, 1995, p. 6). Wars of revenge, politics of revenge are all "debris of the past" that are still visible in many events all over the world. Who would have believed that the battle of Kosovo in 1398 would still be remembered in the minds of ordinary Serbian soldiers in 1993? But "constantly watered with intergenerational resentment, the memory of past horrors prepares the ground for their repetition in the future" (Shriver, 1995, p. 67). And that is what happened in Rwanda.

From 1957, Hutu activists started claiming for equal treatment while the Tutsi leadership was asking for independence for the country. The Belgians simply exploited the situation and turned the two groups against each other. From 1959 to 1962 the country went through a period of social turmoil that has come to be known as the "Social Revolution" that overthrew the monarchy and established a "Hutu Republic." It was unfortunate that all Tutsis, even those who had never ruled, were corporately tagged and bundled with former rulers and exploiters and were all subject to the same fate. Some were killed, others were beaten, all lost property. Many decided to leave the country and settled in refugee camps in the neighboring countries. Many went to Uganda, Burundi, Tanzania, Congo, and even beyond. The killings, the looting, the cruelties were all justified on the basis of former grievances.

As if the killings and other atrocities had not been enough, the Hutu politician put in place "politics of revenge" camouflaged under the acceptable colors of "affirmative action." All the policies on education and power sharing were based on the false assumption that all the Tutsis had had their share of the national power cake and now was time for the Hutus to take their turn. Ethnic belonging had become a criterion for access to political power during colonial rule and unfortunately the Rwandan takeover did not change the trend but rather exacerbated it by perpetuating it as a system. From this misconception and all the former stereotypes came the following policies.

Subordination. The Tutsis were not allowed in the army leadership except in a "tokenish" representation: only one senior officer in the army. More than once when discussing with friends, they would say "what do you want, you are well represented in the army. It's simply that you are never satisfied when you don't have everything." The system was even pushed further and it was later on explicitly forbidden for Hutus in high army and political positions to marry Tutsi women.

Restricted Social Positions. The Tutsi were not allowed in high positions of leadership in the government and other institutions (even the church!). But some token representation was always there again to muzzle every claim for justice. This tokenish representation in power position is another formula for the House Negro and Field Negro syndrome. It is enough to recruit someone who is harmless and inoffensive by his submissive character, someone you will use to endorse your line and even defend it to outsiders and even to people of his own group. The psychology of this approach is to treat that person well but the loss of his job being always a possibility when he is no longer loyal or when he becomes openly vehement on injustices he may see being done to his group. The token representative remains in position as long as he does not see and talk about the problems in the system. The Tutsi who lived in the system know what it means when you have to keep silent and back up the party line because you cannot afford to lose your security (being put in jail), your job, or even your life. I often remember grumbling and cursing under my breath when asked to sing the slogans of the MRND (one) party calling President Habyarimana "umubyeyi w'igihugu" (the father of our nation) even when he was oppressing us with his ethnic equilibrium policies.

Limited Access to Education. The Tutsis had limited access to education and this was established into a system since 1973. The policy of "équilibre ethnique" (ethnic quotas) could not be explained and when challenged, the proponents of the system were always fast to remind you that "Tutsis have had their time, this is time for the Hutus." In normal situations, ethnic quotas systems are used to protect a minority that may be overlooked because of its small size. They may as well be applied as a measure of affirmative action in contexts where a minority has held the power monopolizing all the political, economic, and educational privileges (like during the apartheid system in South Africa). In the Rwandan situation, however, Tutsis, Hutus, and Twas live in the same neighborhoods, go to the same schools, markets, and churches, and share the same miseries. It cannot be proved that by 1959 Tutsis had achieved a level of life standard beyond Hutus in the same social category. A few Tutsis belonging to the aristocracy had enjoyed the privileges of power but not everybody was the son of a chief!

Ethnic Division. The narrative of ethnic division was not only translated into national policies but was equally enshrined in our symbols like the national anthem, logo, and flag, all exalting the victory of one group (Hutus) against the other (Tutsis). There was for instance one stanza of our national anthem I always jumped because it exalted what the Hutus called the "exploits" of the liberators while for some of us it was the killings of our fathers and relatives. This is the dilemma of a polarized nation: the heroes of one group are villains for the other and their exploits are villainies.

Guilt. The refugees who were outside in foreign countries since 1959 kept claiming for their right to come to their homeland but they were constantly reminded that they had been the former exploiters, and the population inside was told that if they came back "you will be back to forced labour." This guilt creation in the oppressed helped the oppressors to feel at ease in their injustices even during the perpetration of the genocide. Another example of "perpetrators exculpating their misdeeds on their misdeeds on account of their past victimisation" (Volf, 1996). When the second generation of exiles organized themselves into a political front (Rwanda Patriotic Front) cum army (Rwanda Patriotic Army) and attacked the country in 1990, those accusations became the main slogan lines to incite the population not only against them but also against every Tutsi wherever he may be in the world, this eventually culminating in the genocide. Literature coming from some of the groups of perpetrators and their foreign supporters are still trying to explain away that horrible act by the same accusations that it was the RPF that attacked first and supposedly shot down the plane of the Hutu President Juvenal Habyarimana, thus sparking off "Hutu anger."

Episodic Violence. The genocide was in actual fact the culmination of "a widening gyre" of episodic violence against Tutsis since 1959. Killings were carried out every time the refugees in neighboring countries attacked the country as a reminder of their presence in refugee settlements. In 1963, 1967, 1973, and 1990–1994 there were killings and property destruction accompanied by propaganda exploiting the same old fears and accusations. The victims were always presented as the cause of their own demise!

Peace psychology identifies two types of violence: "episodic violence" where direct violence occurs from time to time and kills or harms people directly through bodily insult and "structural violence" with social inequalities resulting in slow death by depriving people of basic human need satisfaction (Christie, 2006). This brief overview shows an insidious combination and interplay of both types of violence, eventually culminating into a remorseless genocide.

Rebuilding on the Ruins of the Past

The genocide of 1994 and the war that followed to stop it left us with a nation shaken from every fiber of its foundation. The Hutu regime crumbled under the weight of its criminality, and when the RPF took power in July 1994 only the shell of the nation had survived. Everything in the country was like a ghost – people, cities, the whole country. Most of the physical infrastructures, roads, schools, hospitals, private houses, and properties had been looted and/or destroyed. The genocide had claimed more than 1,000,000 human lives in less than 3 months, while causing other grave consequences in the social fabric. For more than 2 years, more than 3,000,000 Rwandese, mainly Hutus, were trapped into the refugee camps in the neighboring countries of Burundi, Congo, and Tanzania. Many of them died of outbreaks of diseases like cholera, others died of fatigue and malnutrition on their long trekking, others got separated from their families, etc. By the end of 1994, more than 500,000 children inside the country were counted as unaccompanied, i.e., orphans or separated from their parents.

But more than anything else, the most destructive lasting effect of that man-made human tragedy is the way it affected the relationships and the emotions of people. The genocide left deep wounds on the minds and hearts of all people, the victims suffering from trauma, bitterness, anger, and hopelessness, while the perpetrators were overburdened with the guilt of having done something that was initially presented to them by their leaders as acceptable but eventually ended up condemned by the whole world.

The new government put in place in July 1994 had to come up with solutions to all those problems in the context of a very confused international opinion. Some came with compassion and understanding, others came with criticisms and judgments; but all in all, everybody saw the future with justified apprehension. The victims of yesterday had become the victors of today. Will they adopt the Churchill principle of "magnanimity in victory" or will they go for "eye for eye, tooth for tooth?" Will the Tutsis get over the hurts and wounds of the past and live peacefully with the Hutus? Will they be magnanimous enough to forgive such evil? Will the Hutus get over the burden of guilt and shame to live peacefully next to their yesterday victims? Some people were already suggesting to cut the small land into a Hutuland and a Tutsiland, so deep was the divide that many feared it could not be bridged. Some Hutus and even Tutsis were exploring and adopting the option of leaving the country to live somewhere else, echoing the musing of Jurgen Moltmann about living in Germany after World War II: "How could one belong to a nation on which such a burden of guilt lay? Should not one renounce it and make a fresh start somewhere else?" (quoted by Shriver, 1995, p. 85). Questions were fusing from everywhere, all wondering how to get over the evils of the past and transform the society for the better.

Systems Approach

Peace psychologists recommend that in the aftermath of man-made social tragedies the rebuilding of society should be made through the interplay of multiple constructive inputs such as peacekeeping, conflict resolution, reconciliation, peace education, nonviolent social justice movements, trauma reduction, and societal reconstruction. This requires a "systems approach that promotes changes in human relationships across levels of societal complexity from interpersonal to intergroup" (Christie, 2006).

In the case of Rwanda, the first signs of hope for change came with the appointment of the transition government in July 1994. The Rwanda Patriotic Front had opted for a "Broadbased Government of National Unity": Hutus and Tutsis were well represented. Not only was the new government bent on shaping more equitable structures, it was also determined to change the social narratives and the national symbols. The government started calling back and resettling the refugees and consented great efforts and financial expenses to visit refugee camps, encouraging all to repatriate. The ethnically marked identity cards were soon banned and the ethnic quota system was replaced by a more just system based on performance. Today access to secondary education, university scholarships, and jobs is solely based on performance. This does not mean that ethnicity is dead and buried in our communities but the seeds of change have been sown. Laws that had served as the foundation of ethnic divisions have been revised, our symbols (national logo, flag, and anthem) that exalted one ethnic group against the other have been changed, all in a general attempt to create a Rwanda where all the Rwandans will feel equal, united, and reconciled. A Commission for National Unity and Reconciliation, a Commission for the Human Rights, and the Office of the Ombudsman have been put in place to see to it that we do not go back into the old paths. Reconciliation has been enshrined as a non-negotiable value for the survival of the nation. At this moment, our National Unity and Reconciliation Commission is working at producing a National Policy on Reconciliation that will help keep the country focused until the nation is healed. Programs of civic education for the general population and the youth in and out of the schools have been put into place to inculcate the ideals of unity and peace. Different stakeholders are coordinated to bring about total healing for all. While all these processes were going on, one thorny question remained: What policy to adopt for justice?

The survivors of the genocide were claiming for justice and compensation while the international community was calling for clemency and amnesty because of the great numbers of perpetrators. Some survivors had started even committing acts of revenge while at the same time some hardhearted perpetrators were still bent on "finishing the job" of eliminating the Tutsi survivors in their neighborhoods and even beyond. The challenge was how to punish and at the same time restore and forgive a group that has either committed atrocities or just stood by and watched. The general consensus was well summarized by these words by the then Vice President Paul Kagame: "the problem of justice is not just a problem of texts and tribunals. We need to find a way in-between the classical justice, the rebuilding of the social tissue, and the prevention of another tragedy, of another genocide."

Reconciliatory Justice: Gacaca Courts

The prison statistics show that the number of imprisoned suspects of the genocide has been fluctuating between 128,000 and 115,000 between 1998 and 2001. This happened at a time when all the government and judicial infrastructures had been shattered and grounded to a halt. The killing of many judges and other justice administrative employees, the exile of many others, and the imprisonment of another number because of their participation in the genocide had contributed to a total paralysis of the judicial system. It was necessary to recreate the system while at the same time a large number of people were being put in jail in an attempt to eradicate the culture of impunity and to defuse a certain hunger for revenge from the survivors of the genocide. During most of 1994 and 1995, everybody thought justice would be our healing solution. By 1996, we already knew it would not work! That is when "reconciliation" became the word of the day. That is when came the idea of resurrecting our traditional system of reconciliatory justice called Gacaca.

The name Gacaca comes from a short grass commonly found around the compounds of traditional Rwanda. When the name is applied to courts, it represents the space with gacaca grass where people sat to listen to different problems of the community in order to find solutions together. In the traditional context, Gacaca was not a court in the modern sense of the term because it did not have written laws and it did not have prisons. The Gacaca assembly was usually made up of "people of integrity" (Inyangamugayo) and recognized as such by the community because of their honesty, age and experience, wisdom, and even political or economic influence. All the members of the community around were allowed to take part and to give their views although the final decision was made by the Inyangamugayo by consensus and in public.

The major role of the "people of integrity" was to listen to the case, to hear both antagonistic parties, and to pronounce a sentence establishing clearly the culpability of the offender on the one hand and the reparation to be paid on the other. The offender was always asked to ask for forgiveness and the case was always terminated by a celebration of the recovered unity by sharing a pot of local beer that was given by the family of the offender. The penalty was always a matter of all the family although the fault may have been individual. When the offense was judged too big to settle in the Gacaca, it was referred to the higher authority, usually the chief of the area and rarely the king. The objective of Gacaca has always been to rebuild the social tissue and to restore right relationships.

The new system kept the same spirit but it was readjusted with borrowings from other systems, mainly the Nuremberg Courts and the South African Truth and

Reconciliation Commission. From Nuremberg, they borrowed the idea of "the most guilty and the less guilty" (Shriver, 1995, p. 81), making the distinction between the leaders and the mere participants (implementers) of the genocide. From the South African Truth and Reconciliation Commission came the idea of forgiving and reducing the penalty of those who accepted to speak the truth, confess, and ask for forgiveness. Other elements like written laws and punishments were borrowed from formal justice.

The new legislation as applied today categorized the genocide perpetrators into three categories. Category 1 is made up of those who masterminded the genocide by planning, organizing, and supervising the genocide as well as those who became famous for their cruelty and those who raped women and/or engaged in crimes of sexual torture or mutilation. Category 2 is made up of those who killed or wounded the victims with the intention of killing. Category 3 is made up of those who committed infractions to property (looting or destroying). This new legislation already offers the reduction of penalties in exchange of truthful confession and asking for forgiveness from the victims and the community.

Gacaca courts are today on the final phases; the collection of information is finished, and the judgments have already started in some areas. Without going into detail about the procedures and their evolution, let me highlight some lessons the process has taught us in the area of reconciliation and forgiveness.

Bring Parties Together. For real reconciliation to happen, both parties need to be together. Gacaca courts bring together the families of the survivors of the genocide and the families of the perpetrators who live in the same neighborhood. It serves as a social platform for talking again and sharing as a community. We have noticed that people leave the place in the right mood when there is consensus, when both sides agree on the truth of what happened without any cheating. When that happens, we become community again. We are together. This confirms the idea that "as repair of broken social relations, forgiveness has to be learned in a community." ... "You can do it but you are not to try to do it alone" (Shriver, 1995, pp. 34–35).

Confessions. It is not enough to recount the truth to bring real healing and reconciliation. We have noticed that the survivors of the genocide start feeling released when somebody not only confesses his evil deed but does so with a contrite heart and readiness to ask for forgiveness. Truth is not enough to heal. People want to feel and see that the offender is really sorry for what he did. Without contrition and remorse, the confession is often resented as mockery and cynicism and instead of healing it "rubs salt in the wound" and irritates.

Psychological Freedom. Confession is difficult but those who have done it have acquired great release and psychological freedom. I remember one day when I was preaching in one prison and one man became fidgety on his bench. By the time I finished he stood up and asked "is it really true that God can forgive all sins?" I was puzzled by the question but I answered "yes." Then he said, "do you really mean it is all sins?" Then I answered, "that is what the Bible says, God forgives us of all sins when we repent." The man started confessing all types of crimes he had committed: people he had killed, women he had raped, property he had destroyed. At the end of the confession, he looked peaceful when he concluded "now, it is all over. I have said it. I feel released, I feel at peace. Let them do with me what they want, but I have peace." I have heard many similar confessions and seen similar releases in many similar occasions. And it is happening in many Gacaca courts situations. It is true that "a person who thus admits his guilt and complicity renders himself defenseless, assailable and vulnerable. He stands there, muddied and weighed down. Everyone can point at him and despise him. But he becomes free from alienation and determination of his actions by others; he comes to himself, and steps into the light of a truth which makes him free and brings him into a new comradeship with the victims-readiness for reconciliation" (Jurgen Moltmann quoted in Shriver, 1995, p. 85).

Trauma Reduction. Forgiveness comes easy when the offended has gone through a process of healing from the inner wounds. Trauma reduction and healing play a great role in the process of forgiveness and reconciliation. Today we have witnessed many wonderful stories of forgiveness and most, if not all, come from people who have accepted to come to terms with their inner wounds. Wounds that have been inflicted on us, particularly through mass tragedies like a genocide, tend to be "sacralized" and people like to hold on to them, not daring to desecrate them. This refusal to let go of the wounds of the past is a sure road to an eternal state of victimhood. In that case, the offender is still controlling your life. Lewis Smedes (1996) put this so well when he wrote "it would give us some comfort if we could only forget a past that we cannot change. But the ability to remember becomes an inability to forget when our memory is clogged with pain inflicted by people who did us wrong. If we could only choose to forget the cruelest moments, we could, as time goes on, free ourselves from their pain. But the wrong sticks like a nettle in our memory. The only way to remove the nettle is with a surgical procedure called forgiveness. It is not as though forgiving were the remedy of choice among other options, less effective but still useful. It is the only remedy" (p. xi).

I will illustrate this with a personal testimony. I grew up hating the Hutus because they killed my father and many other members of my family during the 1959–1963 social upheaval. Then they kicked us out of school in 1973. In 1983 I lost my job with the university because of the "ethnic equilibrium" policy. Then when I was 35, I was thrown into the furnace of the genocide. Every 10 years of my life (at my ages of 5, 15, 25, and 35) I had to go through a traumatic event from the hands of the Hutus. All throughout those years, every sad event triggered sad remembrances and I blamed everything on the Hutus that had killed my father. Many times I found myself thinking about them, judging them, wishing them misfortunes. I was a victim. Many nights I went without sleep. Many days I went without food. Every time I remembered what they had done to us, it sparked off a negative response. When you remember your hurts just for the sake of ruminating them without any intention of letting them go, you are crucifying yourself on the cross of your past suffering. And you suffer more. That does not bring any healing at all. When I was 26, I accepted Jesus as my savior. It was his prayer for his tormentors when he was on the cross – "Father forgive them, for they do not know what they are doing" – that turned my life back into the right position. My faith not only enabled me to forgive and love my enemies, it did sustain me through the fire of the genocide and I came out still forgiving. Forgiveness is not just another gift from God, it is not a character predisposition although a well-balanced character is an enabling factor. Forgiveness is a reasoned decision! For more details about my personal pilgrimage in woundedness and forgiveness, see my book *Out of the Fire: Stories of Healing, Forgiveness, Repentance and Reconciliation,* to be published in the near future. It is only when you choose to let go of your right to hate that it becomes easy to forgive your enemies and to live with them at peace.

Repentance. Forgiveness alone is not enough to bring reconciliation: you need the offended to heal and forgive but you also need the offender to be contrite, to repent and confess, and ask for forgiveness. Reconciliation happens when the repentant offender meets the healed offended and they restore their community of mutual friendship and trust. We are witnessing so many cases of that and I have collected such stories in the book mentioned in the preceding paragraph. Gacaca courts are bringing people together to find the truth about what happened, we are presently studying how to involve the faith communities in the next step of bringing the offenders and the offended together to achieve real reconciliation. The journey may be long, but at least we know where we are going and how to get there. Reconciliation is possible – when the offender has confessed and the offended has forgiven.

Conclusion

From the experience of Rwandan history, it is easy to see the importance of forgiveness not only in individual lives but also in the building of our nations. When wounds of the past have not been well processed and healed, they will come back like ghosts to haunt the future. Wounds of the heart do not heal with time, they simply sink deeper into the individual or collective psyche and come back in disguised forms, influencing perceptions of people and reality and shaping in a twisted way individual and collective convictions, character, and conduct. And as Lewis Smedes (1996) puts it, "forgiving is not the remedy of choice among other options, less effective but still useful. It is the only remedy" (p. xii). It is only through the release that comes with healing and forgiveness on the part of the offended and the repentance and contrite confession of evil on the part of the offender that individuals and even nations can start living real freedom from the shackles of a wounded past. In nations that have suffered from inequalities and mass crimes, it may be wise to first dismantle the reinforcing systems often found under the form of laws and national symbols and also to put in place systems of education that help groups and individuals to heal from their past wounds. This process of trauma reduction and healing is often left out in the process of peace building and reconciliation.

The big challenge remains of extending forgiveness and confession beyond the interpersonal level to the group level. In our traditional Gacaca system, the guilt and shame was carried out by the family of the offender and they corporately confessed through the mouth of a family elder (spokesman). But in the political context, it is not easy to find a spokesman for a given group to speak with collective consent on their behalf. Confession means vulnerability and it is not a popular stand, mainly in politics. The same applies to forgiveness. Can somebody express forgiveness on behalf of a whole group? Forgiveness is often associated with religion. Can it become a political agenda? As Shriver (1995) puts it so rightly, forgiveness needs to "escape its religious captivity and enter the ranks of ordinary political virtues" (p. 7), or is it that scientific researchers need to rediscover religion as "an extremely potent source of values for individuals as well as cultures?" (Park, 2005)

Recommended Reading on Rwanda

Bourdanne, D. (Ed.). (2002). *Le tribalisme en Afrique.* Abidjan: PBA
Dallaire, R. (2003). *Shake hands with the devil: The failure of humanity in Rwanda.* Toronto: Random House Canada.
De Lacger, L. (1961). *Rwanda.* Rwanda: Kabgayi.
Gourevitch, P. (1998). *We wish to inform you that tomorrow we will be killed with our families.* New York: Picador.
Guillebaud, M. (2002). *Rwanda: the land god forgot? Revival, genocide and hope.* Oxford: Monarch Books.
Guillebaud, M. (2005). *After the locusts: how costly forgiveness is restoring Rwanda's stolen years.* Oxford: Monarch Books.
National University of Rwanda: Center for Conflict Management. (2001). *Les juridictions gacaca et les processus de reconciliation nationale.* Kigali: Palloti Press.
Prunier, G. (1995). *The Rwanda Crisis 1959–1994: History of a genocide.* Kampala: Fountain Publishers.
Rutayisire, A. (1996). *Faith under fire: stories of Christian bravery.* London: African Enterprise.

References

Christie, D. J. (2006). What is peace psychology the psychology of? *Journal of Social Issues, 62,* 1–17.
DeYoung, C. P. (1997). *Reconciliation: our greatest challenge...our only hope.* Valley Forge, PA: Judson Press.
Park, C. L. (2005). Religion as a meaning-making framework in coping with life stress. *Journal of Social Issue, 61,* 707–729.
Shriver, D. W., Jr. (1995). *An ethic for enemies: forgiveness in politics.* Oxford: Oxford University Press.
Smedes, L. B. (1996). *The art of forgiving: when you need to forgive and don't know how.* Nashville: Moorings.
Staub, E. (1989). *The roots of evil: The origins of genocide and other group violence.* Cambridge: Cambridge University Press.
Volf, M. (1996). *Exclusion and embrace: a theological exploration of identity, otherness, and reconciliation.* Nashville: Abington Press.

Chapter 12
Darfur: Efforts to Forgive and Reconcile in an Unresolved Conflict

Suliman A. Giddo

Disasters, whether natural or man-made, have a tremendous psychological impact on individuals, communities, societies, and nations. In the case of natural disasters, the affected people blame their life circumstances (e.g., they live in an earthquake-prone area) even as considerable bitterness remains in their soul and they suffer from lingering trauma. However, in the case of man-made disasters, grievance and bitterness expand beyond the posttraumatic disorder (PTSD) seen in natural disaster victims to become posttraumatic disorder that stems from the violent behavior a victim suffers at the hand of an actual person (Digeser, 2001). In order to discuss this in more depth, let us use the Darfur Genocide as a case study. This chapter will emphasize the psychological impact resulting from the conflict and will focus especially on ways to reach the forgiveness necessary for the healing of a society.

Darfur

The Region and the Crimes

The Darfur region in western Sudan (North Africa) is a complex society with two basic ethnic groups, the Arabs and the non-Arabs (Indigenous Black African Tribes). The roots of the diverse tribal populations extend to neighboring countries. It is a society of deeply embedded tribal tradition; in particular, the land is the identity and the heritage of the tribe. Women and animal wealth, on the other hand, are the dignity of the tribe. All tribal males are responsible for protecting and defending every woman and tribal properties as well as its traditions.

For centuries, the tribes in Darfur (Arabs and non-Arabs) have had occasional conflicts of varying degrees of seriousness, but all disputes were solved by an indigenous administration system called Ajaweed. Ajaweed dealt with disputes of all types, including serious family problems; it prevented the win–lose orientation to conflict resolution that can deteriorate into cycles of suspicion, anger, and destruction. Security instability became common in Darfuri culture after the Sudanese government dissolved this time-honored arrangement in the early 1980 s.

The current government replaced this historical and valuable social structure with an Emirates administration and judicial system to reflect Arabic and Islamic

Ani Kalayjian, Raymond F. Paloutzian, *Forgiveness and Reconciliation*, Peace Psychology Book Series, DOI 10.1007/978-1-4419-0181-1_12, © Springer Science+Business Media, LLC 2009

concepts that were familiar but not practiced in Darfur. These imported concepts did not allow for the dignity of some ethnic groups in Darfur. In turn, self- or government-identified Arab groups were favored in disputes of all kinds. This accentuated ethnic and racial sensitivities and resulted in insecurity and instability in the Darfur region.

The problem of resolving tensions between the two ethnic groups escalated, with both groups suffering continual marginalization by the central government. In 2003 tribal tensions reached a boiling point and erupted in violence. That tension has been used by the government of Sudan to favor Arabs over the native Africans. It was at this point that Darfur began its horrific experience of systematic genocide – the organized destruction of lives and properties of the non-Arabs – with the perpetrators being the Government of Sudan and its proxy militia alliance, the Janjaweed.

Additionally, with the onset of mass killing and gang rapes, traditional community leaders lost any control they had as protectors of their people. Understandably, the people became frightened when they realized that their own leaders could no longer really help them. As a consequence, Ajaweed for tribal reconciliation and forgiveness became inapplicable in Darfur.

The intention of the Government of Sudan and its illegal government-supported militia to target the non-Arabs became clear in 2003. The crimes were deliberately committed and were among the most appalling known to humankind (United Nations, 2005a). These included the wholesale destruction of villages; humiliation of the people; the mass rape of women and young girls; the murder of men by the government forces and militia (Janjaweed), either in raids or by execution. Some disappeared, some were abducted, and Arabs took the land. The infrastructure was destroyed; Darfur became a state in terror.

Stages and Levels of Forgiveness Needed

This chapter will use the case of Darfur to explore ways to promote forgiveness. We should consider the process of forgiveness in three stages: individual, community and tribe (ethnic group), and society (Worthington, 2005; Volkan, 2001).

One must first consider the atrocities suffered by the marginalized non-Arab people. Women were raped in front of their husbands, sons and daughters, other relatives, or all at the same time. In some cases, they were permanently branded on their faces and hands as signs of disgrace to carry for the rest of their lives. In several incidents, children were burned to death in torched huts while their parents were forced to watch. The case of Khadija A. Abdalla, a 9-year-old girl, is one of thousands who met with a similar fate: she was gang raped and then murdered. To add extra humiliation and to stymie attempts at identification, her face was skinned off. There were thousands of victims in all; the exact number will never be known.

Women and men were traumatized by the rapes. Pregnancies resulted, and the births of the rape offspring caused further agony to the victims. There have been many reports of mothers refusing to nurse their infants born of rape. Many husbands abandoned their wives as they refused to accept this humiliation and disrespect to their life. In Darfuri culture, it is a terrible disgrace to be raped; there have been many suicides because of the shame. Consequently, many rape survivors have not made official reports.

Thousands of villages were looted and burned. Millions were displaced to the wilderness or to enormous displaced persons' camps. Darfur became a completely chaotic place to the individuals, communities, and tribes of non-Arab ethnic groups.

To restore peace and foster forgiveness, certain procedures have been shown to be effective and society must be involved in the process at all levels (Wade & Worthington, 2005). At the individual level, the perpetrators should be tracked down (they could be easily identified by victims); the victim's properties, including land, should be returned; and there should be a guarantee that organized war by the government, or any other internal force, will never target them again.

On the community and tribal levels, restoration of the *status quo ante* is required. Concrete settlement of the conflict is expected in order to create a bridge of confidence between the ethnic groups. The international community has repeatedly affirmed the duty of other States to end the impunity with which these crimes are committed and to prosecute and bring to justice those who are responsible. This, in addition to respecting the rights of the victims, will lead to forgiveness in this complex society (Digeser, 2001). If the perpetrators are not held accountable for their crimes, then the traumatized group will not easily cooperate with any proposed conflict resolutions and will not be able to move forward in the process of forgiveness and reconciliation. A consequence might instead be acts of revenge, which would create a second traumatized group in the area.

The widely escalated war in Darfur has had a tremendous psychological impact on individuals, communities, and ethnic groups. Unless the victim's cycle of revenge is broken by forgiveness and solid reconciliation, the memories of fear, anger, guilt, and humiliation will never end; the poisonous aftereffects will trickle down to the young for generations. The memories of those dark days of atrocities will fester, becoming an obstacle to a genuine peaceful resolution.

Resolving Aggression in the Darfur Context

Let me briefly summarize theories of aggression and offer comprehensive details about forgiveness from the Darfur context. There will be a focus on tribal conflict analysis in Darfur, a discussion of the psychological impacts of this conflict, and a proposal of the methods that could heal this ongoing conflict as seen through concepts of traditional and spiritual practices of forgiveness (Exline & Baumeister, 2000; Worthington, 2005).

Aggression has been described as a social problem, but why does aggression exist and how is it generated? Several theories regarding the nature of aggression can help us understand human behavior. They provide a basis for explaining, predicting, and modifying aggression (Bandura, 1973). To protect ourselves from destruction and to resolve conflicts, it is imperative that we analyze aggression and learn to reduce its role in social violence.

Aggression is a behavior of dominance through physical and verbal force that individuals use to obtain valued resources; change rules to fit their own wishes; gain control over and extract subservience from others; eliminate conditions that affect their well-being; and, remove barriers that block or delay attainment of desired goals. Even so, aggression can appear in people when no such reaction seems reasonable or warranted. Minor annoyances can erupt into aggressive action with the potential for the infliction of emotional and/or physical injury. This behavior may be attributable to the repression of anger and miscommunication about the true reason for the aggressive action.

There is disagreement about whether aggression is learned social behavior or a reaction to frustrations in the aggressor's environment (Yoder & Zehr, 2005). As stated by Freud, it is primarily a pleasure-seeking or pain-avoidance behavior. Different theories, including psychoanalytic theory, propose that people are driven to behave destructively to prevent self-destruction. On the other hand, ethological theories emphasize that aggression is an instinctual system that generates its own source of aggression, depending on external stimuli (Bandura, 1973).

Aggression is not an inevitable or unchangeable aspect of humankind, but a product of the intricate conditions operating within a society. Humans have the power to reduce levels of aggression. However, whether this occurs depends on how this capacity is used – wisely or destructively (Yoder & Zehr, 2005). In Darfur, this capacity has unfortunately been used to perform every conceivable form of appalling violence, including mass killing, gang rape, and abduction.

What Is Forgiveness and Why Do People Forgive?

Hating people is like burning down your own house to get rid of a rat.
  – Harry Emerson Fosdick

Forgiveness and Reconciliation

I would like to start with this question: Why do people forgive? What are the benefits of forgiveness? Research shows that those who forgive are happier, and perhaps even healthier, than those who will not or cannot forgive (Berry & Worthington, 2001; Karremans, Van Lange, & Ouwerkerk, 2003; Lawler et al., 2003; Maltby, Macaskill, & Day, 2001; McCullough, Pargament, & Thoresen, 2000). Fitzgibbons, Enright, and O'Brien (2004) have cited several benefits to the one who forgives. These include decreased levels of anger and hostility, improved ability to control anger, enhanced capacity to trust, no repetition of negative behavior, improved physical health, and an improvement in those with psychiatric disorders (*Working to Forgive*). Forgiveness is also an aspect of love; it serves as a bridge from hatred and alienation to liberation from a kind of hell, bitterness, and victimhood on one side and, guilt, shame, and self-recrimination on the other (Karen, 2003).

Reconciliation is the restoration of confidence in a relationship in which the trust has been damaged, often quite severely (Worthington, 2001). Keeping that in mind, in Darfur – where the war has destroyed a complete social structure – reconciliation has become very important to rebuilding respect for interpersonal coexistence.

The theme of forgiveness integrated with reconciliation has a static and dynamic coordination – who, what, where, how to? The question "Who forgives?" usually applies in a case in which one person or party is expected to forgive; but in reconciliation the question of "Who?" can extend to include two or more people or parties. Healing and peace are gifts granted in forgiveness, but earned in reconciliation. How to forgive can be an emotional response; but reconciliation is a behavioral response. Where to forgive has to be within one's actual being, but reconciliation has to be done within the relationship with the other party. A procedure for how to forgive can be seen like a pyramid, as a sequence of steps from one instance of forgiveness to another, so that eventually each wrongdoing has been forgiven. Then from each instance of forgiveness there can follow the bridge of reconciliation that connects the two parties (Worthington, 2006).

Steps Toward Forgiveness and Healing

The most simple, straightforward notions about the possibility of forgiveness in Darfur hold that those who engineered, mastered, recruited, financed, and implemented this genocide must be brought to trial and prosecuted. The perpetrators of mass killings and gang rape should be held accountable for their crimes.

To be unforgiving is harmful (Worthington, 2006). Forgiveness can also be defined as a key that unshackles us from a past that will not rest peacefully in a grave. As long as our minds are captive to the memory of having been wronged, they are not free to wish for reconciliation (Smedes, 1984).

However, forgiveness is not a quick fix (Enright, 2001), but is instead a matter of a willed change of heart, the successful result of an active endeavor. In the uncovering of one's anger, the decision to forgive, the working toward forgiveness, and in finally doing so, there is release from an emotional prison.

Alongside the above-stated position, there is another theory of forgiveness that summarizes three types of forgiveness. *Detached forgiveness* is a reduction in negative affect toward the offender, but with no restoration of the relationship. *Limited forgiveness* consists of a reduction in negative affect toward the offender and a partial restoration of, and decreased emotional investment in, the relationship. Finally, there is *full forgiveness* that is similar to traditional concepts of forgiveness; it includes total cessation of negative affect toward the offender and a full restoration and growth of the relationship (Nelson, 1992).

Keeping the above theories in mind (which are compatible), a model of forgiveness was developed that has four stages in the decision-making process: awareness, change, interaction, and reconciliation. The movement through these stages needs four consecutive decisions from each side, offender and victim; those are judgment, vulnerability, intimacy, and trust building. The stage of awareness requires an admission of the violent occurrence. It becomes the responsibility of the person aware of the violation, and its effect on the relationship, to take steps to change or not change the situation. Each situation is unique. It might very well be that the victim comes forward initially because the offender may be unaware that they have committed an offense. The decision to be intimate is the basis of the interaction stage. When all three decisions have been made constructively for forgiveness, the fourth decision to build trust can be made and the reconciliation stage can begin (Johnson, 1986).

The Darfur Complexities

The name Darfur comes from two words: *Dar* means "land" and *Fur* is the name of the largest tribe in the region, but it does not necessarily mean that the Fur is the only tribe. There are over 36 different ethnic groups in the region. These are divided mainly into two ethnic groups. African farmers make up about 62% of the population and Arab nomads who mainly depend on animal wealth make up about 38% of the population.

Darfur was an independent sultanate (kingdom) from the fifteenth century; it had its own international, political, and economic relationships that were specifically focused on Egypt and Turkey as well as other kingdoms in central and western Africa. In 1916, Darfur was annexed to Sudan by the British colonial power. The king was once the sole authorized individual to distribute land, and indeed, he had allocated land to large tribes in Darfur, known as Dar Zaghawa, Dar Masalit, Dar Rizigat, Dar Bani Halba, Dar Gimir, etc.

After the collapse of the kingdom, the colonial government (in 1922) formalized the existing land distribution with the consent of the major tribes in Darfur. This agreement became the status quo and all tribe leaders were expected to maintain the integrity of the arrangement. Darfur was also subdivided into six administrative districts, with each district further organized into several administrative units under the native administration of indigenous tribes. This administrative system was accepted and respected by all concerned parties.

The greater Darfur area is the size of France, with a population of 6.5 million inhabitants. It enjoyed a common understanding and respect among the different ethnic groups until it was divided into three states by the current government in 1989. Even so, Darfur has been the scene of more than 24 ethnic conflicts during the last two decades. Some of the reasons attributed to these conflicts include the central government's large role in the region's marginalization; political parties; land disputes; drought; water scarcity; natural migration; and ethnic sensitivity. In addition, there is the major issue of neighboring countries' conflicts.

There are two aspects of the conflicts in Darfur: *External* and *Internal*.

External Factors

Chad Rebels vs. Chadian Government. Darfur is bordered by three countries: Libya, Chad, and the Republic of Central Africa. For decades, Chadian rebels used Darfur as a backyard for their military operations. Darfur has always been the launch point for their opposition movements. Founog, North Darfur, where I was born and raised, was the headquarters for several Chadian rebel groups, including those led by Hussain Habri and Idris Déby. As a result, they were able to defeat and change the governments in Chad, while disregarding their destructive behavior's effect in Darfur. This detrimental behavior came from the continuous threat of violence to Darfurians; there was an influx of weaponry which is always frightening to a civilian populace; a feeling of unease, even imminent violence, can exist in an atmosphere even if there is not direct daily violence. It is very destructive and leads to a change in people's perception of what is safe and what is not. It can make children, especially, feel very insecure.

In Darfur, children began to mimic in play what they saw in militia behavior. The children adopted nicknames and personas of well-known militia members and began to use play "weapons"; they became steeped in war culture simply by being near it and observing it. This sort of thing is natural enough, of course, in childhood. In America, the reader will be familiar with children playing "cops and robbers," for instance. But when the play becomes constant and this serious, it can psychologically warp young minds.

This situation created by the perpetual ominous presence of fighters remains a key component of Darfur's instability. Even at the time of this writing, the two current Chadian rebel groups still operate from Darfur.

Libya–Chad War. Ouzo has been a disputed zone between Chad and Libya for decades. In the mid-1980s Libya used Darfur as the proxy battlefield for fighting Chad. Eventually some Darfurians were recruited, trained, armed, and financed by Libya and sent back to Darfur in 1986. The dispute was settled by referring the case to the international community, but there is still tension regarding the rich natural-resources area that falls between the two countries' borders. This poses a serious risk for a future dispute that will again add to the instability in Darfur.

Internal Factors

The Central Governments in Khartoum. When Sudan annexed Darfur in 1916, the region lost the ability to control and manage its affairs. After Sudan's independence in 1956, the central government marginalized Darfur and intentionally left it undeveloped. Since then, Darfurians have been a cheap labor source for agricultural schemes in central Sudan, as well as low-ranking military soldiers. The people of Darfur are generally considered to be second-class citizens in Sudan. Since religion could not be used as leverage, as it was in the south (the overwhelming majority of Darfurians are Muslim), the government manipulated ethnic sensitivities to bring about the desired instability in the region.

The Arab Alliance. In 1987, certain Arab ethnic tribes established the Arab Block (Alliance) mainly as a competitive social, cultural, and political caucus. Lately, that group has deviated from their original mission and developed claims that their ethnic group has been marginalized within Darfur. Out of this new self-perception as outsiders came much misunderstanding resulting in a widening gap between the two broad ethnic groups in the Darfuri community. This greatly increased regional tensions and was the seed out of which the current conflict grew.

Water Sources. Drought and desertification have caused the unplanned migration of certain ethnic groups from affected areas in North Darfur to the south and west seeking food and pasture. Thoroughly studying the distribution of water sources, such as wells and dams, will reduce unplanned migration. This will result in the reduction of ethnic disputes.

Generally, a dispute evolves out of the migrated group's attempt to keep its traditions and leaders in power as they were in their homeland. However, the hosting group often tries to show its supremacy and control. Disputes emerge when the migrated group must choose between abandoning its traditions or resist being controlled. Sharing the scarce resources is a major element within the dispute; by providing accessible water sources, these conflicts may be avoided.

Land Ownership. In 1922 Darfur was divided by the colonizing British into *Hawakier* (i.e., each ethnic group was allocated a specific area as a homeland). All Darfurians, such as Dar Masalit, Dar Zaghawa, Dar Rizigat, Dar Ziyadia, and Dar Fur, accepted this arrangement. Considerable pasture paths were given to nomad Arabs on which they could move freely after the farmers cultivated their crops. As seasons have changed over time, the nomad Arabs began to use these pastures even before the farmers cultivated their land. Creation of a new Arab Emirates in the land of the farmers, along with the establishment of a new "native" administration, was not accepted by Darfur's indigenous groups. This situation only served to exacerbate the already-existing tensions.

If the sensitive issue of land ownership is handled properly there is great potential to alleviate the tension between nomads and farmers and make way for peaceful coexistence. With such a large land area, there is adequate space for the entire population to sustain itself by sharing the land again in an appropriate and fair manner. Darfur is one of the richest regions in Sudan. With a better understanding of natural resource utilization, Darfur can be shared without the eruption of disputes. However, this kind of agreement must be mutual and emerge from within the Darfuri community, in the spirit of compromise and peace and in the best interests of all parties. Forced land redistribution by the central government would be a recipe for disaster.

Disaster Contingency, Preparedness, and Management. There is no early warning system for projected droughts upon which farmers can rely. Farmers start plowing their fields by April/May and continue planting until December when they might encounter a scarcity in rain resulting in failed crops. They have nothing to show for 6 months of work and nothing to feed their families. This economic threat leads to migration, which as noted previously, leads to disputes.

Ethnic Sensitivity. A tribe is the heritage, power, and dignity of all Darfurians. It is the center around which most life activities revolve. Today Darfur is deeply divided by the current government's manipulation of one side against the other. This conservative community has separated into two ambiguous ethnic groups: Arabs and Africans. The division was an ominous development and many feared that it would become a very serious problem for Darfur's future. Surely, there is no doubt about the seriousness of this now.

Political Parties. Political parties in Sudan have a long history of considering Darfur a fruitful "backyard." While the people of Darfur were the backbone of support for key Sudanese policy makers, they were not actually directly engaged.

Usually, political candidates made local appearances only during the election periods in Darfur.

All political parties – in one way or another – have played a major role in creating the tension that has led to the current conflict. The Uma Party was behind the Arab Alliance, while the Unity Democratic Party supported the ethnic African groups. The National Islamic Front (NIF) recruited its members from the smaller African tribes. The Communist Party recruited members within Darfur using its social ideas and communist theory as an alternative to the other parties.

When tensions reached a peak, due to the political parties' intentional failure to bring stability to the region, people retreated to their own ethnic groups rather than continue their efforts to achieve solidarity as Darfurians. At this point, the people of Darfur reached a level of zero tolerance for the government of Sudan.

Situation Before and During the Conflict

The war in 2003 erupted out of the frustrations of Africans regarding the bias of the Government of Sudan against the Afro-Arab ethnic groups. The Sudan Liberation Army (SLA/Rebel Group), which is dominated by the African groups, began with no political agenda. The main reason for the formation of the SLA was to offer protection to their ethnic groups; on the other hand, the Justice and Equality Movement (JEM) organized under a somewhat political agenda; nevertheless, the war began. To exploit the religious differences in the North–South War, the central government in Khartoum used the people of Darfur (for years) to fight in the name of Islam against the Christians in south Sudan. The current government Islamized the war by introducing Jihad (holy war) within one nation.

Because Darfur was intentionally left undeveloped, Darfurians were left with little choice but to work as cheap labor elsewhere in Sudan and to serve in the lower ranks of the military. Darfurian soldiers were carefully and deliberately selected by officers from North Sudan and deployed to fight in south Sudan. The reason I mention this is to emphasize that many Darfuri men have served in the military and were well trained early in their lives to commit violence. When the current war began in 2003, the reaction of the central government was to recruit and finance a large number of Arab men, organizing them under the name of Janjaweed. It is through the mobilization of this armed proxy militia that the massive and murderous destruction has occurred.

Trauma and Forgiveness in Darfur

Traumatizing the Native Darfurian

In Darfur, families share the hardships of life. The mother is the master of economic strength in the rural areas. Her responsibility is to make the home a better place, but in many cases, females are doing the hardest part of keeping these families together. Women and girls collect and carry firewood, transport water from wells, look after the animal wealth, and prepare the food. The male's job is to earn money; the main source of income is to work as low-paid labor in the central part of Sudan for 1 to 2 years, and sometimes longer.

Rape as a Weapon in the Darfur Genocide. The number of rape cases is uncountable because it has occurred on such a massive scale; at the same time, women rarely report what has happened to them. It will become a permanent shame on them and the women will be isolated and degraded by the community. In any case, rapes have occurred and it is still used as a tool to threaten the people of Darfur. In Tawilla, North Darfur, immediately after an air attack upon a school, government forces and the Janjaweed raped over 42 school students, as well as their female teachers. Despite numerous, consistent, and credible reports documenting the patterns of rape and sexual violence that amount to war crimes against humanity, the Sudanese government repeatedly and adamantly refuses to acknowledge the scale and the gravity of the crimes (United Nations, 2005a-c).

Despite the denials of the government that rape as a weapon of war has occurred, the rape victims and their parents believe that injustice has occurred and that their rights to punish the perpetrators have been denied. In one incident of so many, in December 2004, a victim and her lawyer were informed that a court hearing that same morning would be public, even though the lawyer had requested a closed session; the request was refused by the Chief Judge. The refusal to hold a closed hearing can lead to serious consequences for the victim. Some in the community assume this is an admission by the victim that she has committed *Zinah* (prostitution). In Sharia, a woman can be held accountable if she cannot prove that rape has taken place. Proof requires two men or one man and two women to testify that they have seen the rape. Darfur has been traumatized by atrocities, including mass rapes, which fulfill the legal definition of crimes against humanity (United Nations, 2005a-c). A few incidents reflect thousands in Darfur. To write this chapter, I interviewed hundreds of genocide survivors and all share stress and severe trauma at varying levels according to their individual stories. I interviewed a 43-year-old tribe leader and local trader who was forced by government soldiers and Janjaweed militia to undress his wife. She was raped in front of their two young sons. After the gang rape, she was murdered. This left him and his two sons to suffer humiliation and sorrow on behalf of their mother. The man is psychologically destroyed; his first reaction was to take revenge.

In another case, an eyewitness described the horrifying situation of a woman who refused to allow her body to be raped. The perpetrators, two horsemen, dipped their knives into her private parts. To humiliate her further before she died, the men tied her legs to different horses and made each horse run in a different direction; she was split in half.

The sexual humiliation of Darfuri women and girls must be addressed. This traditional society has a long way to go to accept the atrocities of the war. A lot of work and consolation is needed to recover and it will take the entire community, represented in the tribes, to accomplish it.

Mass Killing in Darfur. Uncovered by a restless wind, skulls and bones poke above the thin dirt in a corner of Darfur, lying surrounded by half-buried, rotting clothes (*Mass Grave Memories Feed Fear in Darfur*, 2007). Darfur has become a place where there is no control and survival of the fittest is the brutal reality. This war is the result of an accumulation of resentment over several recent tribal and ethnic conflicts. This increased the chances that severe violence would eventually occur – as it certainly has. Mukjar, in west Darfur, is the scene of one of the notorious murder cases in the whole region. The Associated Press interviewed an eyewitness, Ibrahim, in April 2007. He testified about an incident that involves Janjaweed leader Ali Mohamed Abdel-Rahman, also known as Ali Kushayb, and the junior minister of humanitarian assistance, Ahmed Haroun. The International Crime Court (ICC) at The Hague has indicted both men on 51 counts, including crimes against humanity (*International Criminal Court*).

Kushayb ordered his men to "get rid of every Fur" and then turn their property and land into "Dar Arab" instead of Dar Fur. Kushayb then opened a barred door of a cell, pulled out a prisoner, and split his head open with an ax (*Mass Grave Memories Feed Fear in Darfur*, 2007). Then he axed two more prisoners to death while his men shook their right fist and shouted "Janjaweed, Janjaweed." Haroun, Kushyab's boss, sat in the shade and he cheered. This unambiguous message to the Africans will never be forgotten; the horrific memories will be with the survivors forever. A comprehensive trauma-healing program should start immediately for their recovery.

In Darfur's case there is a complicated twofold problem with respect to the resulting bitterness of the conflict. There is tension between and among individuals and also between the Darfur community and the central government. With all of the atrocities and catastrophes that the indigenous Africans have endured in Darfur, the level of distress differs from individual to individual. Trauma differs from stress in intensity and duration. Nevertheless, the bottom line is that both stress and trauma have occurred and they have deeply affected individuals and the community-at-large on many levels: physically, emotionally, cognitively, behaviorally, and spiritually.

As many survivors of the genocide in Darfur still suffer from trauma, the social interaction of the community in general is where constructive healing might be more difficult than at a personal level. When a traumatic event or series of events affects a large number in a community, it becomes a societal or collective trauma. A group experience of trauma can set off widespread fear, horror, helplessness, or anger that might affect the situation at a regional level, resulting in societal trauma (Volkan, 2001). These collective traumas, if left untreated, have a long shelf life and are often transmitted to the following generation. Untreated wounds and stress become a chosen trauma, a shared mental representation of a massive tragedy that the group's ancestors suffered at the hand of the enemy (Karen, 2003).

A Common Response to Trauma

The feeling of being a victim, and the shame that often comes with it, and the self-righteous fury that explodes out of it and seeks to erase it bring to mind what the sociologist Jack Katz has referred to as the "seductions of the crime" (Karen, 2003). *I will never tell the stories that I went through to my children*. With that statement, a man promised himself to bear his suffering in silence and not transfer it to the coming generation. *I will never forget those days until I revenge* – that statement was made by another man of similar age. These two statements indicate the level of trauma that they experienced, even if they have suffered through the same incident. There is trauma, stress, and violence, in both cases, though they may be manifested differently due to individual psychologies. The survivor cycle listed below (Karen, 2003; Yoder & Zehr, 2005) depicts common trauma responses when violence shatters our sense of security.

Survivor Victim Cycle

1- Traumatic acts of aggression
2- Psychological changes
3- Shock, injury, denial, fear
4- Realization of loss and panic
5- Suppression of grief and fears, numbness, isolation
6- Anger, rage, spiritual questions, and loss of meaning
7- Survivor guilt, shame, humiliation
8- Helplessness
9- Reexperiencing the acts and the events, thoughts of avoiding reminders, hypervigilance

Losing Hope and Escalating the War

The atrocities committed in Darfur would not have been so horrendous and miserable if the international community, especially the United States that acknowledged these crimes as genocide, had dealt properly with international laws. These laws give the responsibility to protect defenseless civilians to the United Nations (UN) if their own state is incapable or unwilling to secure the safety of its citizens.

For the last 5 years, the indigenous Africans in Darfur have been intimidated by the silence of the international community; the continuous violence by their own government; and the systematically decreasing level of humanitarian aid. The whole region has become an anarchic state of terror and fear; nobody feels safe and secure. Even the play behavior of young children has taken the shape of war. Instead of hide and seek, Umshalilk, and other games, pretend shootings and attacks have become the only play of interest among the children. This is a serious indication of trauma in child behavior and is an ominous warning for the future. I called a friend of mine in Nyala; he has a 4-year-old son. As his father was standing and talking on the phone, I heard his son shouting, "Baba, Baba, lie down." I asked my friend, "Why does your son want you to lie down?" He answered, "Because he heard a plane."

It is the same at the adult level; many people never express their sorrow and sadness when they have lost a loved one. This is because so many people have died; the community has never seen such terrible behavior before. It is going to be an ever-present trauma and the response to such horror will require new behavior standards in the society.

A humanitarian crisis exists because more than 3,000 indigenous African vil-lages have been destroyed and because the Government of Sudan and its militia destroyed almost all of the hospitals, schools, farms, millers, and small clinics. In addition, several hundred villages in the non-African areas were affected. Upward of three million people have fled their homes because of this. They are living in Internal Displaced Camps (IDP) within Darfur and refugee camps in Chad. Before the persons currently living in the concentrated camps return to their former homes, the villages and public service facilities should be reconstructed.

Methods of Forgiveness in Darfur

The people in Darfur are mostly Muslims, and killing an individual is a great sin as well as a crime. The murderer is not only punished by law but also rejected by the community. In most cases, even if the judiciary does not charge a murderer, there is no way to return as a member of the community. It is common for murderers to leave the area of their residence forever. They travel to an area where people do not know of their crimes because he/she will be denied even the privilege of marriage. This cultural reaction to crime is a mixture of local tradition and Islamic rules. In Islam, there are two aspects of forgiveness: Allah's forgiveness and Human forgiveness. We need both, because we do wrong in our relations to Allah as well as in our relations to each other (Ali, n.d.). However, a part of being human is that we make mistakes and some mistakes are not deliberate and without intent. Sometimes, though, crimes are planned. Atrocities such as the massive killing in Darfur are a true example of intentional crime.

Bowers (2005) theorized that revenge was universal among early societies largely because there was no state and violence, even killing for revenge, was not considered a crime but a kind of wild justice (Nelson, 1992). This is not the case in Darfur, as there is compensation for crime; the methodology used is Ajaweed (community leaders who mediate disputes).

Within Islamic concepts, in order for forgiveness to be accepted, some conditions should be met including that the crime is committed out of ignorance, not intent. The perpetrator is quick to acknowledge shame and repents after committing a crime (out of ignorance). After asking for forgiveness, the guilty party must make a promise to mend their ways and not commit the crime again. The following texts are examples of the bases of these practices: "If any of you did evil in ignorance, and thereafter repented, and amended Lo! Allah is Oft-forgiving, most Merciful" *Holy Qur'an: Al-Shura 6:54*; "Those who avoid major sins and acts of indecencies and when they are angry, even then forgive" *Holy Qur'an: Al-Shura 42:37*; "... The reward of the evil is the evil thereof, but whoever forgives and makes amends, his reward is upon Allah" *Holy Qur'an: Al-Shura 42–40*; "If any shows patience and forgive, that truly would be an exercise of courageous will and resolution in the conduct of affairs" *Holy Qur'an: Al-Shura 42:43*. Thus, with the above quotations, we can see that forgiveness has been a conventional behavior in Darfur; it was necessary to base human relations on forgiveness as it is required by the Muslim faith practiced in the region.

> The way of forgiveness is hard. Forgiveness is not for wimps and wusses. In many ways, the destructive power of unforgiveness is much easier than the tough, steely pull of forgiveness. (Worthington, 2001)

Along with over three million displaced people, there is also the terrible toll of 450,000 dead. Their own government, along with the Janjaweed, has already killed a large percentage of certain ethnic groups. What makes forgiveness more difficult in Darfur's case is that the victims – the native Africans – hosted the Janjaweed, who are mainly from Arab tribes. After hundreds of years, they now want to take the land from their traditional and long-time owners.

A human rights organization interviewed a war victim and his testimony about the Janjaweed is as follows: "They hung me with hooks piercing my chest. They also burned me. I was arrested with thirty other men. They tied us together and interrogated us about animals. We said we did not know so they called us liars, shot and slaughtered some of the men in front of my eyes. I was tortured" (Human Rights Watch, Report, 2005).

This victim has seen the killing and he knew the people who committed this crime; how will he be able to live with the killers? How will he live with these bad memories? The trauma has a reached such a high level that the people will take no more. If fair trials do not take place, then revenge will be the alternative.

Building Individual and Community Trust in Darfur After the War

To overcome the conflict and return peace to this destroyed region, as well as develop a much-needed, robust infrastructure, the following measures will guide us to an effective solution: the United Nations/African Union hybrid mission in Darfur (UNAMID) must be fully deployed and fully supported materially. The Janjaweed and rebels must disarm; impartial trials must be held for perpetrators of atrocities. Fair compensation, rehabilitation, and repatriation (with former native administrations in place) must be provided to victims of the conflict. These will lead to forgiveness and peaceful coexistence in Darfur. It will also help to facilitate a political settlement for all states in Sudan.

In Darfur, rehabilitation and repatriation have become *the* critical issue that must be thought through clearly *before* discussions begin regarding the return of the war-affected population. It is also imperative to consider security as a main constraint in this context.

Protection. The protection of the displaced innocent civilians, who have become increasingly vulnerable in this conflict, displaced from their homelands, and fleeing to Chad, must be given the highest priority. Many are still inaccessible to international organizations. The African Union, with its very weak mandate, lack of logistics, commanders, and political support, has been a complete failure for the last

3 years. UN peacekeeping forces have the potential to bring security and hope to Darfur. However, it will take major political will on the part of the actor countries in the UN to achieve any stability in Darfur. Refugees have understandably lost hope and faith after too many promises not kept.

Dispute Resolution. Since the war that began in February 2003, all negotiations for political settlements have proved to be failure. This is due to various political reasons and the lack of consideration given to the innocent victims of Darfur. The conflict will be among the rebels who are deeply divided into ethnic groups. We must continue to focus on negotiations with all rebel groups and reemphasize that the attempt to facilitate political settlement is the correct path to progress and peace in Darfur.

Disarmament. Within the political settlement, *disarming Janjaweed* should be the focus. It should follow immediately after an agreement is reached. The UN Security Council adopted this request in Resolution 1556 on 30 July 2004; but, as usual, there was no will in the international community to enforce it, largely due to the political interests of key players on the Security Council.

The Janjaweed has created a state of terror among the native Africans in Darfur. To bring feelings of safety to the people, the international community should disarm these Sudanese militia groups. Though several thousand men have been incorporated into government forces and the National Popular Defense, militia groups remain the primary cause of insecurity in Darfur.

The government will make a media show of disarming the Janjaweed militia. However, it is almost certain that the Janjaweed will remain active under the media's radar, collaborating with the central government. Both government leaders and Janjaweed face the possibility of punishment by the International Criminal Court; therefore, they will make every attempt to remain unified so that complete details of their crimes can remain undisclosed. Many more tragedies will occur if the UN peacekeeping forces are not immediately deployed to enforce disarmament of the Janjaweed and all rebel groups in Darfur.

Rebel groups should be controlled and disarmed in accordance with the terms of any signed agreement. The government of Sudan has lost the trust of its own citizens and the international community. History has proven that this government is not to be trusted to comply with any agreement's decrees and obligations. Therefore, nobody believes that the government will disarm the Janjaweed without more political pressure from the international community and UNAMID in place to monitor the disarmament.

Disarming the rebels will solve two major expected problems:

- First, it will reduce the possibility of war among the dozens of rebel groups who have mutual interests but different approaches to implementing their common goals.
- Second, it will build trust among estranged ethnic groups in Darfur.

Prosecution. As previously stated, those who engineered, recruited, financed, and implemented this genocide must be brought to trial and prosecuted. Those perpetrators who committed these massive killings and practiced gang rape should be held accountable for their crimes. In addition, the people of Darfur deserve an apology from the Government of Sudan. This will go a long way to help inspire trust and confidence in Darfurians.

The International Commission for Darfur. For Darfur's stability, the international community must establish a commission to monitor the compensation process. The task of this commission is to fund, establish, and work for the resettlement of the large affected population of Darfur. It is evident that the government of Sudan will do nothing to be responsible for the administration of such a commission.

Compensation, Rehabilitation, and Repatriation. The financial compensation terms in the Darfur Peace Agreement (DPA) signed in 2006 were not reasonable and fair. The amount of money stated in this partial agreement (the equivalent of about $30 million) will at best amount to a mere $10 per person. No one can replace his/her entire belongings, let alone land or a family compound, for that amount of money. Because the number of people affected by this war is so great and their losses have been so total in terms of loved ones, dignity, heritage, property, and resources, if there is not fair compensation the world is going to end up with more than three million poor Africans in the isolated land of Darfur who will face uncertainty their entire lives. This is not simply a moral issue but a long-term security matter as well. Alternatively, just compensation would become a solid foundation for future sustainable development in the area and would aid victims in the creation of a new beginning for a new life in a new era.

Conclusion and Hope

Darfur is a complex and conservative society, with tribes that have differences in historical backgrounds, geographic roots, economic, political, and social customs. The region has become vulnerable to several disputes within and among these individuals and tribes. Unless the root causes of this conflict are addressed properly and comprehensively, Darfurians will never feel secure and will endure a life of grinding poverty. Darfur will never be stabilized unless the Government of Sudan considers the people to be true citizens of Sudan, with full rights and duties, a fair share of power and wealth, reasonable compensation for crimes, and justice delivered to the perpetrators of atrocities committed during the conflict. Only then will the possibility of revenge among ethnic groups be reduced and forgiveness can be realized. Then we will dream of social coexistence.

References

Ali, M. A. (n.d.). *The Importance of forgiveness in Islam.* Institute of Islamic Information & Education. http://www.iiie.net/node/52. P.O. Box 410129, Chicago, Illinois 60641-0129, U.S.
Bandura, A. (1973). *Aggression: A social learning analysis.* Englewood Cliffs, NJ: Prentice-Hall.

Berry, J. W., & Worthington, E. L., Jr. (2001). Forgivingness, relationship quality, stress while imagining relationship events, and physical and mental health. *Journal of Counseling Psychology, 48*, 447–455.

Bowers, R. (2005). *Fullness of forgiveness*. Oregon City, OR: Living Free Publications.

Digeser, P. E. (2001). *Political forgiveness*. Ithaca, NY: Cornell University Press.

Enright, R. (2001). *Forgiveness is a choice*. Washington, DC: American Psychological Association.

Exline, J. J., & Baumeister, R. F. (2000). Expressing forgiveness and repentance: Benefits and barriers. In M. E. McCullough, K. Pargament, & C. Thoresen (Eds.), *Forgiveness: Theory, research, and practice*. New York: Guilford Press.

Fitzgibbons, R., Enright, R., & O'Brien, T. F. (2004). Learning to forgive. *American School Board Journal, 191*(7), 24–26.

Human Rights Watch; Entrenching Impunity: Government responsibility for International crimes. (2005) hrw.org/reports/2005/darfur1205/darfur1205text.pdf

International Criminal Court (ICC). All legal documents in the cases of ICC-02/05-01/07 Case. The Prosecutor v. Ahmad Muhammad Harun ("Ahmad Harun") and Ali Muhammad Ali Abd-Al-Rahman ("Ali Kushayb"). http://www.icc-cpi.int/cases/Darfur.html

Johnson, K. A. (1986). *A model of forgiveness: Theory formulation and implications*. La Mirada, CA: Biola University.

Karen, R. (2003). *The forgiving self: The road from resentment to connection*. New York: Random House/Anchor Books.

Karremans, J. C., Van Lange, P. A. M., & Ouwerkerk, J. W. (2003). When forgiving enhances psychological well-being: The role of interpersonal commitment. *Journal of Personality and Social Psychology, 84*, 1011–1026.

Lawler, K. A., Younger, J. W., Piferi, R. L., Billington, E., Jobe, R., Edmondson, K., et al. (2003). A change of heart: Cardiovascular correlates of forgiveness in response to interpersonal conflict. *Journal of Behavioral Medicine, 26*, 373–393.

Maltby, J., Macaskill, A., & Day, L. (2001). Failure to forgive self and others: A replication and extension of the relationship between forgiveness, personality, social desirability and general health. *Personality and Individual Differences, 30*, 881–885.

Mass Grave Memories Feed Fear In Darfur. (2007, May, 27 Sunday). (AP). Reprint http://www.sudantribune.com/spip.php?article22064

McCullough, M. E., Pargament, K. I., & Thoresen, C. E. (2000). The psychology of forgiveness: History, conceptual issues, and overview. In M. E. McCullough, K. I. Pargament, & C. E. Thoresen (Eds.), *Forgiveness: Theory, research, and practice* (pp. 1–14). New York: Guilford.

Nelson, M. (1992). *A new theory of forgiveness*. Bloomington, IN: Purdue University.

Smedes, L. B. (1984). *The relationship between forgiveness and reconciliation*. Oxford: Oxford University Press.

United Nations (2005a, January). *International commission of inquiry on Darfur*. Report, Executive Summary, pp. 3–4; Section I: p. 26 ff. http://www.un.org/news/dh/sudan/com_inq_darfur.pdf

United Nations. (2005b, January). *International commission of inquiry on Darfur*. Executive Summary (p. 5). http://www.un.org/news/dh/sudan/com_inq_darfur.pdf

United Nations. (2005c, January). *International commission of inquiry on Darfur*. Report, Section III, 1–5 (pp. 135–140). [Sections on perpetrating, aiding, abetting, planning, and ordering international crimes against humanity.] http://www.un.org/news/dh/sudan/com_inq_darfur.pdf

Volkan, V. D. (2001). *Mind and human interaction*. Charlottesville, VA: University of Virginia.

Working to Forgive. Everett L Worthington: A campaign for Forgiveness Research, http://www.forgive.org/

Wade, N. G., & Worthington, E. L., Jr. (2005). In Search of a common core: A content analysis of interventions to promote forgiveness. *Psychotherapy: Theory, research, practice and training, 42*(2), 160–177.

Worthington, E. L. (2001). *Five steps to forgiveness: The art and science of forgiving*. New York: Random House/Crown.

Worthington, E. L. (Ed.). (2005). *Handbook of forgiveness*. New York: Routledge.

Worthington, E. L. (2006). *Forgiveness and reconciliation: Theory and application*. East Sussex, UK: Taylor & Francis/Brunner-Routledge.

Yoder, C., & Zehr, H. (Eds.). (2005). *The little book of trauma healing: When violence strikes and community is threatened*. Intercourse, PA: Good Books.

Chapter 13
India and Pakistan on the Brink: Considerations for Truth, Reconciliation, and Forgiveness

André L. Brown, Rhea Almeida, Anita Dharapuram, Asma Warsi Choudry, Lisa Dressner, and Pilar Hernández

This chapter offers a perspective that promotes peace and forgiveness through a framework of accountability and reparations. Understanding the contemporary political and peace-building efforts in the India and Pakistan conflict requires an analysis of India's history of colonization. We review the historical context of the current conflict and offer an overview on the pre-partition, partition, and post-partition periods.

Transmission of Trauma Over Time

Pre-partition: Dividing a People – The 1947 Partition

> No citizen of India can avoid being Hindu/Muslim, Bengali/Kannadiga, shopkeeper/laborer, man/woman, father/mother, lower caste/upper caste at the same time. (Pandey, 1999, p. 629)

Many rulers, from Alexander the Great to the Mughal Empire to the British Raj, presided over the South Asian subcontinent which was comprised of a collection of kingdoms and territories rather than a nation under a unified government. Prior to British colonization, there were 88 "true kingdoms," each with its own rulers, distinct culture, language, and religions (Udayakumar, 1997). Through the centuries, South Asian identity has focused primarily on regional culture as opposed to religion alone. In contemporary India and the entire Indian diaspora, Indians identify with a particular region – Bengali, Kannadiga, Maharashtrian – before identifying as Hindu or Muslim (Anderson, 1991). However, it is important to note that during and after the Mughal period, many Hindus converted to Islam, viewing it as a more compassionate and life-affirming religion. It offered them an opportunity to challenge the oppression of the caste system. Numerous battles were fought with the Rajput generals (Hindus) leading the Mughal (Muslim) armies to victory. This close military collaboration also came with a 200-year pattern of intermarriage between the Mughal princes and the Rajput princesses. Unlike other rulers, the British colonization (1757–1947) instigated the growth of religious communalism which they used strategically to "divide and rule." The resurgence of religion and culture coupled

Ani Kalayjian, Raymond F. Paloutzian, *Forgiveness and Reconciliation*, Peace Psychology Book Series, DOI 10.1007/978-1-4419-0181-1_13,
© Springer Science+Business Media, LLC 2009

with a strident British national identity reshaped contemporary South Asian identity in a manner that highlighted and promoted divisiveness and competition amongst ethnic and religious groups (Chatterjee, 2004; Kumar, 1997; Pandey, 1999).

In 1600, the Honorable East India Company received its charter from the British monarchy and eventually trading rights from Jahangir, the reigning emperor of the Mughal Empire. Its primary intent was to tap into the lucrative spice trade in Asia, with India as an important hub in the trade network. There was no overt policy toward empire building. In the 18th century, with the British East India Company prevailing over its French counterpart, La Compagnie francaise des Indes orientales, and the Mughal Empire's decline, the company began its penetration into the Indian government. The First War of Independence in 1857 (known as "The Great Mutiny" by the British) was fought by both Muslims and Hindus in response to the steady encroachment of the British beyond their original commercial interests. In 1857, the Mughal Empire ended its rule and in 1858 the British East India Company was dissolved. The British seized this opportunity and took direct control over India, ushering in the period known as the British Raj. Despite never visiting the territory, Queen Victoria coroneted herself empress, naming India the Crown Jewel in her expansive empire (Kuah, 2003; Robb, 2002; Wolpert, 2006).

In 1920, Mohandas Karamchand Gandhi entered politics and began his Satyagraha campaigns of non-cooperation with the British Raj (Wolpert, 2006). Muhammad Ali Jinnah, a Muslim politician, leader of the All India Muslim League and eventual founder of Pakistan, did not agree with Gandhi's tactics. Gandhi, on the other hand, considered Jinnah's methods old-fashioned and a waste of energy. The tension between these two leaders continued over time and influenced how India and Pakistan initially positioned themselves before and after the partition. This ongoing conflict gave the British an opening to renege on promises of "dominion status" for India and legitimized their reintroduction of martial law.

With India's growing restlessness for independence the British contemplated relinquishing rule of the region. The Government of India Act of 1935 was hastily written by the British in an effort to leave a government intact in India. Muhammad Ali Jinnah, Jawaharlal Nehru, and Mohandas Gandhi,[1] as leaders of their political parties, participated in the creation of a new India. Although these political parties were working toward the same goal of establishing a new government, relations between them were marred with fear and disharmony and was fueled by the British, who were anxious to leave India by 1948. Partition lines were drawn through thickly populated and long-settled areas in Punjab and Bengal (Philips & Wainwright, 1969; Wolpert, 2006). This ill-conceived plan is captured in W.H. Auden's (1976) poem, "Partition-1947," which tells of Sir Cyril Radcliffe's task of setting the borders of the new counties:

> Unbiased at least he was when he arrived on his mission,
> Having never set eyes on the land he was called to partition
> Between two peoples fanatically at odds,

---

[1] Jawaharlal Nehru and Mohandas Gandhi were both leaders in the Indian National Congress.

With their different diets and incompatible gods.
"Time," they had briefed him in London, "is short. It's too late
For mutual reconciliation or rational debate:
The only solution now lies in separation."

Aftermath of Partition

The fall of the British Empire and the aftermath of the partition have been described as "beastlier than anything beasts could have done to each other" (Singh, 1956). On 14 and 15 August 1947 the United Kingdom granted independence to British India, creating two sovereign states: the Dominion of Pakistan, later known as the Islamic Republic of Pakistan, and the Union of India, later known as the Republic of India. The British pulled out prematurely without an orderly exit strategy that would ensure basic law and safety for people who lived in their communities for centuries. An estimated 10 million Hindus and Sikhs living in West Punjab, North-West Frontier Province, Baluchistan, East Bengal, and Sindh fled to India in fear of domination and suppression in Muslim Pakistan. Communal violence killed an estimated 1 million Hindus. The violence was interrupted in early September due to the cooperative efforts of both Indian and Pakistani leaders, especially because of the initiatives of Gandhi. The assassination of Gandhi on 30 January 1948 was a major setback to the young nation. Gandhi was murdered by a Hindu fanatic who held Gandhi responsible for the partition and charged that he was appeasing Muslims.

In 1949 India recorded close to 1 million Hindu refugees flooded into West Bengal and other states from East Pakistan, owing to communal violence, intimidation, and repression from Muslim authorities. The plight of the refugees outraged Hindus and Indian nationalists, and the refugee population drained the resources of Indian states, which were unable to absorb them. Prime Minister Nehru signed a politically progressive pact with Liaquat Ali Khan, the first prime minister of Pakistan, that pledged both nations to the protection of minorities and creation of minority commissions. Steadily, hundreds of thousands of Hindus returned to East Pakistan, but the thaw in relations did not last long, with the decision of control over Kashmir still in disagreement (Ganguly, 2006; Ganguly & Hagerty, 2005; Philips & Wainwright, 1969; Singh, 1956; Wolpert, 2006).

Contemporary India and Pakistan Relations

Since the partition there have been three wars (1965, 1971, and 1999) between India and Pakistan. There was a brutal crackdown by the Pakistani army in 1971 that required India's intervention around the rise of Bengali subnationalism. This military onslaught led to the flight of 9.8 million people into northeastern India and West Bengal. A civil war ensued in which Indian troops supported the Bengalis leading to the creation of Bangladesh. The conflicts along the Kashmir border were minimal (Ganguly, 2006; Ganguly & Hagerty, 2005).

Efforts toward truth and reconciliation in the South Asian context are characterized by "competitions for victimhood" (Montville, 2001). Both India and Pakistan have competing historical narratives that are built upon individual stories of atrocities committed during the partition era until the present. The painful memories and scars of the partition have left both parties with the experience that each side is fundamentally untrustworthy and vicious (Ganguly, 2006). As a result, the subcontinent is driven by deep chasms between people based on religion, geography, language, caste, and class. This was a time marked by the congealing of new identities, relations, and histories and the questioning of all that previously existed (Pandey, 1999). A major historical factor that contributed to these deep conflicts, the role of British colonization, remains unspoken.

As we write this article, Pakistan is burning. Benazir Bhutto was assassinated on 27 December 2007 while rallying for the presidential bid (Jan & Khan, 2007). This created further turmoil in Pakistan, which in recent months has seen a spate of conflicts stemming from the house arrest of members of the judiciary and from the political wrangling of the major Pakistani parties. The world watches with bated breath as Pakistan struggles through these issues while keeping its finger on the nuclear button.

General Pervez Musharraf seized power in Pakistan in a bloodless military coup in October 1999 from the government of Nawaz Sharif. Pakistan is a pervasively militaristic society in which democratic institutions lack civic authority. In the years since the 1947 Partition of India and Pakistan, no democratically elected government has completed its term. All of these governments were terminated by the incursion of the army into politics. The army is a constant and omnipresent force in both daily life and Pakistan's political institutions. The landlord class and family dynasties that were destroyed in India were left relatively intact in Pakistan. Currently, that landlord class is the principal base from which Pakistani political leaders arise. Further, the global rise of Islamist forces in Muslim countries has disarmed Pakistani civil society (Hoodbhoy, 2004).

Initially, Musharraf was heralded as a democratic moderate reformer who could lead Pakistan forward. In the post 9/11 era, Pakistan began to play a critical role in the global war on terror and in particular in the United States' war on Afghanistan. As a leader of a client state of the United States, Musharraf positioned himself as the bulwark against the rising tide of Islamism that would sweep into the United States. He justified his autocratic decisions by stating that the United States was better off dealing with him rather than allowing jihadist elements to take over as they had done in Iran and Afghanistan. Not unlike his predecessors General Zia-ul-Haq and Benazir Bhutto, Musharraf has continued giving these radical Islamists tacit support to counter Indian troops stationed at the Kashmiri border (Shah, 2004).

The United States continues to navigate its complex relationship with Pakistan in light of a political regime that struggles to create a democratic state. In fact Pakistan has changed its constitution three times since the partition. India on the other hand has maintained democracy since partition and is clearly a more stable nation. In spite of this however, the religious wounds created at partition continue to fester. The

2002 Gujarat riots were responsible for the killing of 2000 Muslims; 13 individuals were eventually convicted for this crime (Ali, 2002; Majumder, 2008).

The unique historical experience of British colonization has indelibly imprinted itself upon the national identities of both countries. Not unlike Britain, the United States' policy of imperialism continues to demand a presence in the region. This presence is not welcome by most of the people, especially the religious fundamentals. The Government of Pakistan is not likely to turn away from enormous packages of economic aid and the outward alliance with the United States. To add to this complexity is the failed United States' foreign policy on terrorism. Pakistan under Musharraf offered promises to both hunt down the terrorists and permit US military activity within and across Pakistani's borders. Pakistan and India are constantly engaged in political and military jousting. American foreign policy appears to gloss over the historical roots of the conflict between these two countries and the ascendant conflict between Muslims and Hindus. American military aid and economic support to Pakistan has existed since the partition. Having an American presence in the region first due to the Cold War and now due to terrorism has defined this alliance. In light of these past and current political events, reconciliation and forgiveness between India and Pakistan is a major human rights endeavor.

The political and religious identities foisted upon the people of Pakistan and India by the partition is in direct opposition to the cultural identities that existed before. For example, in Punjab, a state that was partitioned in 1947 with one half going to Pakistan and the other half to India, cultural identity is very strong. This pattern of cultural identity is reflected throughout India as a strongly rooted experience of intersectionality. To reiterate earlier periods in Indian history offered a more fluid definition of identity. The colonial policy by the British to bifurcate people's identities along religious lines in order to control communities was the launching point for this partition conflict. Perhaps this bond between people in Punjab, separated by an international border, could be a starting point for peace. Reclaiming cultural identity after British colonization would not be easy, however.

Noteworthy is the role of Kashmir, the site where much of the military aggression smolders. The decision about Kashmir's independence was generated by the British and was largely influenced by Cold War concerns and an anticommunist focus prevalent at that time, as well as an interest in maintaining Anglo-American presence in Pakistan (Ganguly, 2006). With a Hindu monarch and mainly Muslim population, Indians and Pakistanis vied for control over this territory. Pakistanis believed Kashmir was necessary to create the complete state of Pakistan. For India the inclusion of Kashmir would exemplify that Muslims could live under Hindu rule. Although there were a number of resolutions designated through the United Nations, requiring Pakistan to stop all assaults, India to pull back its forces, and Kashmiris to have a voice in their destiny, none of these resolutions were implemented.

Pakistan's continued desire for sovereignty and India's successful democracy and entrance into the global economy, post-independence is the landscape for forgiveness and peace-building efforts. Neither of these can occur without beginning a dialogue focused on truth and meaningful efforts toward accountability and reparations involving the British, the Pakistanis, and the Indians.

Beginning the Healing Process: Critical Consciousness, Empowerment, and Accountability

> There is no person without family, no learning without culture, no madness without social order; and therefore neither can there be an I without a We, a knowing without a symbolic knowing, a disorder that does not have reference to moral and social norms. (Martín-Baró, 1994, p. 41)

In *Pedagogy of the Oppressed*, Freire (1971) critiques the traditional model of education as an instrument of oppression that serves to reinforce social inequities. He goes on to describe how knowledge is used as a tool for oppression rather than an experience to share. Education for critical consciousness invokes a *dialogical* approach to change, requires critical *reflection*, and promotes preparedness toward *action* (Freire, 1971). Empowerment then involves the development of a critical consciousness, the level of consciousness in which the person becomes aware of being creator and owner of his/her own destiny. In understanding how persons/individuals are embedded within social, economic, and political systems, knowledge is demystified. Through this analysis of social critique comes awareness that experiences of oppression require public, institutional as well as individual, family, and community solutions. Like Freire, Martín-Baró (1982, 1989, 1990) clarifies that his view does not make a distinction between trauma and hope. He relies on the process of *concientización* to shift the focus of healing from individual alienation to group de-alienation through a critical understanding of the reality of war that shapes people's lives. Through dialogical teaching, reflection, and action, people can understand and articulate their experiences and then appropriate a personal remodeling in their lives and communities. As critical consciousness develops, we no longer see current realities as "the unquestioned and unchangeable nature of things." Instead, we see options for change (Freire, 1971). Most peace efforts are directed toward a conflict resolution of some sort with no foundation of critical inquiry or discussion of accountability and reparations (Lira, 1988; Lira, Weinstein, & Salmovich, 1986; Weinstein, 1987). Superficial solutions toward peace initiates, not unlike conflict resolution in schools addressing violence that fail to address the social critique surrounding the conflict and violence, collude with the history of perpetration. Such solutions are laid upon a smoldering landscape that will eventually explode or remain perpetually volatile, as is the case of India and Pakistan. A peace initiative through raising critical consciousness offers a social critique and solutions designed to reclaim the integrity and soul of these communities.

Within a postcolonial context, the process of raising consciousness is central to healing and societal change. Martín-Baró (1994) further elaborated this concept by identifying three aspects in the consciousness raising process. They are as follows:

1. The human being is transformed through changing his or her reality.
2. Through the gradual decoding of their world, people grasp the mechanisms of oppression and dehumanization. Critical consciousness of others and of the surrounding reality brings with it the possibility of a new praxis, which at the same time makes possible new forms of consciousness.

3. People's new knowledge of their surrounding reality carries them to a new under-standing of themselves and, most important, of their social identity. They begin to discover themselves in their mastery of nature, in their actions that transform things, in their active role in relation to others. (p. 40)

The process of raising critical consciousness is about developing empowerment in the following ways: first, by framing individual suffering in context, stories are opened up to be understood as forming part of the social and political ways in which suffering is maintained. Second, by emphasizing the community aspects of healing, webs of relationships are reconstructed through affiliation and trust, and therefore hope becomes an avenue for change involving groups of people and not solely individuals.

Critical to this discussion is the relationship between violence and trauma. Sluzki (2003) explains that violence destroys any sense of order as well as the personal stories constructed in that world. It creates confusion, disintegration, and loss of identity. In trying to understand violence and its effects, people look for descriptions and explanations to make sense of cruelty. Concerning India and Pakistan, these explanations are ensconced within dominant religious, political, and cultural narratives. The bystanders and perpetrators' roles in this process of narration contribute to obscuring the fact that violence took place. Sluzki (2003) argues that when the victimizers' voices prevail, the possibility for building com-munity and developing relational reliance and moral reparation is robbed. The victims cannot confront the victimizers, and the learning and healing processes are obstructed.

With this integration in mind, trauma and healing takes into account the devel-opment of new social identities and therefore contributes to the building of social movements that question existing social orders. In a broad manner, healing inter-ventions at a community level contribute to the restoration of social networks and the restructuring and re-storying of people's lives (Hernandez, Almeida, & Del-Vecchio, 2005; Sluzki, 2003). Bringing neighborhoods together to remember and retell their experiences prior to and after partition is a beginning point to this healing process. Families and communities that were once defined through the experience of partition can now redefine their lives through expanded narratives. Indian activists have attempted to use a peace memorandum to create healing and forgiveness. It represents an invitation to commemorate the bloody violence that many families and communities fell prey to during and after the partition (Singh, 1956).

While such an invitation should be upheld as an important contribution toward peace building, it stops short of accountability and empowerment for families and communities going forward. It does not, for example, demand a dialogue, inquiry, and action between key players. It does not embrace the notions of cultural identity, a key factor in the history of Indian civilization, pre-colonization. Redefining experi-ences of cultural identity, within networks of social, economic, and political power, can begin to identify sources of power and victimization. This process creates new boundaries for families and communities wanting to bring justice, equity, and peace to their experience.

Fostering a culture of peace demands more than just focusing on conflict-resolution and antiwar work. Establishing peace in a postcolonial era requires healing from sufferings endured and accountability for traumas perpetrated. Postcolonial approaches respond to questions regarding values, assumptions, and practices in a way in which empowerment and accountability are central tenets in the healing process (Hernandez et al., 2005; Seuffert, 2005). These approaches intend to promote balance between self-determination and distributive justice while locating individuals within the concrete realities of communities. Ideals regarding a good life and a good society are grounded in the notions of mutuality, social obligations, and the overcoming of oppression. For example, in her critique of the modernization/globalization policy of India, Vandana Shiva, a world-renowned environmentalist/scientist, describes how the neoliberal forces of global, economic, and social exclusion policy unite to perpetrate violence on vulnerable groups around the world (Shiva, 2005). In rallying international attention to her call for peace she reminds the world of the British policies that privatized land displacing and povertizing millions of people together with exhorting natural resources. This is a brutal reminder of the continued ravaging of resources and destruction of lives, mostly of the poor, by postcolonial policies and complicit governments. She goes on to challenge the industrial world's notion of development as simply the genetic engineering of food, the theft of culture. and privatization of natural resources. In *Earth Democracy,* Shiva (2005) lays out the bedrock principles for building living economies, living cultures, and living democracies, toward a just and sustainable future.

A central task in elucidating the meaning of empowerment and accountability from this perspective is an understanding of the process whereby communities and governmental and societal entities develop critical consciousness. This is required on the individual, familial, national, and cultural levels by all parties; including Great Britain, India, Pakistan, and Hindu and Muslim citizens. The processes of forgiveness, healing, and reconciliation are grounded in the principles of critical consciousness, accountability, and empowerment. Specific examples of these outcomes might be a memorial that the British would create along the path of violence from India to Pakistan during the partition. Another example, in alliance with Shiva (2005), might be an effort by the colonial powers to give back the environmental rights to seed and water along the path of the partition. These rights are now corrupted by genetic engineering and the position of local governments to passively accept these "innovations." Another example of healing might involve a regular city/village meeting where perpetrators of violence (legitimized by the partition) confess and discuss options for rebuilding peace and trust.

The evolution of public hope in India and Pakistan after the partition was galvanized by winning of socialist leaders on platforms of bread, food, and work. This platform is essential to any nation where poverty is the result of large-scale inequity and unrest. With the failure of Russian alliances in this part of the world and the invitation to a world platform for economic participation, hope was reignited through religious ideology in the form of fundamentalism, both Muslim and Hindu (Chomsky & Archer, 2006). Clearly the religious ideology did not bring with it the promise of bread, food, and work but it did offer hope and spirituality. Most importantly the fundamentalist movements in Pakistan are galvanized against the West which obscures the role of their own government in perpetuating poverty. India, on the other hand, has entered the global market despite its fundamentalist populations. Nonetheless the divide between the middle class and the poor has grown substantially in India. Poverty and desperation always have the potential of aligning with fundamentalist movements.

With the rise of fundamentalism in all nations dogma takes precedence over rational or logical process and life circumstances. Such dogma perpetuates a life of its own without a filter of critical thinking. The building of critical consciousness is a necessary foundational step to creating systems of critical action and accountability. In this case creating a standpoint of knowledge that would place colonization/imperialism at the head of this disaster seems credible and fair. It would demystify the violence between two countries that did not exist for centuries. Accountability and reparations for the holocaust can serve as a blueprint for other nations, even though the intersections of violence and oppression between other nations may be different. There is a common thread running through many nations in current conflicts exacerbated by dictators.

Accountability begins with acceptance of responsibility for one's actions and the impact of those actions upon others. However, accountability moves beyond blame and guilt. It results in reparative action that demonstrates a willingness to ensure safe and democratic life for all involved parties (Almeida, Dolan Del Vecchio, & Parker, 2007).

Restorative and Reparatory Justice

"The restorative justice movement is a global social movement with huge internal diversity" (Johnstone & Ness, 2007, p. 5). Although there are common philosophical foundations and comparable practices, each region and country of the world develops its own way of implementing restorative justice (Johnstone & Ness, 2007). Reviews of the growing restorative justice literature (Doolin, 2007; Walker, 2006) indicate that there are core values that remain consistent. Restorative justice:

- Aims above all to repair the harm caused by wrong, crime, and violence.
- Requires acknowledgment that a wrong has been committed.
- Makes central the experiences and needs (material, emotional, and moral) of victims.
- Insists on genuine accountability and responsibility taking from those who are responsible for harm. Ideally, this process should be made directly to those who have suffered harm and to larger affected or interested communities.
- Aims at offering those responsible for wrong and harm the opportunity through accountability and repair to earn self-respect and to be reintegrated into their communities.

- Builds and strengthens individuals' and communities' capacities to do justice actively and not to surrender the role of doing justice to experts, professionals, or "the state." These agents should play facilitating roles.
- While process values (participation, dialogue, encounter, collective resolution) are emphasized, restorative justice should be appraised in terms of achievable outcomes.

Restorative justice is referred to by many names including informal, reparative, transformative, holistic, relational, corrective, and problem solving (Daly & Immarigeon, 1998; Walker, 2006). Johnstone and Ness (2007) posit that while the differences are more than just a disputes over models, they are not so profound as to conclude that any of the perspectives is outside the restorative justice movement. The distinctions are over alternative conceptions of restorative justice and influence where emphasis is placed and the process through which results are achieved. Within this internally complex concept, the focus can be placed on *encounter, repair,* or *transformation.* The restorative emphasis of the *encounter conception* is that the parties to a crime should be offered an opportunity to meet and decide the most satisfactory response to that crime and is guided by principles that help describe the desired results. The emphasis of the *reparative conception* is that the response to crime or offense must seek to repair the harms resulting from crime and is guided by processes and outcomes designed to bring healing. The *transformative conception* places emphasis on the restorative insight that fundamentally we are relational beings connected through intricate networks to others, to all humanity, and to our environment. The restorative nature of those relationships is guided by a vision of transformation of people structures and our very selves. Reparations in the Indian and Pakistani context should be provided within a framework that incorporates and emphasizes principles of all of the aforementioned foci: encounter, reparations, and transformation.

Defining reparation is easy; it is the "doing" that makes discussions enraging and processes complicated. Simply put, reparations are the act of making amends for a wrong, the act of repairing something. This may include efforts to compensate for a loss, injury, or suffering (Costello, 1993; Pearsall, 1999). Reparations are legislative and court action designed to address historical injustices. They are also used by communities to bring corrective justice (correcting past harm) and in so doing creating distributive justice (Brophy, 2006). Reparations can include compensations such as return to sovereignty or political authority, group entitlements, truth commissions, apologies, community development programs, and money or property transfers, or some combination of these. The form that reparations take depends on the particular demands of the victimized group and the nature of the wrong committed (Brophy, 2006; Westley, 1998)

Transitional societies moving in a liberal-democratic normative direction should employ a model of reparatory justice (Verdajo, 2006). Nations emerging from recent histories of mass atrocity or violent authoritarian rule face many ethical and practical challenges. India and Pakistan must reconcile how to achieve some degree of social and political stability, maintain democratic governments, and create policies for a stable economy. They must also confront a sizable number of victims and perpetrators and decide to what extent accountability can be sought without undermining peace (Brophy, 2006; Verdajo, 2006).

Reparatory justice focuses on distributive justice issues for both the individual and the collective. It seeks to provide resources to individuals and groups with the aim of creating the material basis and security necessary for them to become full participants in social, political, and economic life. It is imperative to note that for many victims, reparations are not simply about financial compensation but also about the moral force of state acknowledgment. Therefore, collapsing reparations into development is normatively problematic because this is often a way for governments to obfuscate their responsibilities. For example, what the state may call reparations for victims can be viewed as part of the state's duties to all citizens, allowing the government to build moral and political capital while actually satisfying basic obligations. This is often couched under the auspices of welfare programs and by building roads and schools. Soyinka (1999) notes that reparation movements fail when grantors in the process of forgiveness and reconciliation do not include specific reparations.

For example, the Asian Women's Fund, established in 1995 by Japan to compensate the aging victims of its wartime sexual slavery (i.e., "comfort women"), was widely criticized. Japan claims that postwar treaties absolved them of any guilt following World War II. Therefore, instead of providing state-held reparations for this fund, the government used money obtained through private collections. This dubious strategy was employed by the government in an effort to discourage additional claims by victims of Japanese crimes and militarism. Of the $4.8 million raised from private contributions, 285 women in South Korea, Taiwan, and the Philippines received almost $17,000 each, accompanied by a letter of apology from the Japanese prime minister. The government has also provided, out of the Asian Women's Fund, $6.3 million in "welfare services" to the 285 women, as well as to 70 women in the Netherlands. Only a small fraction of the comfort women accepted the money by the time the fund closed (Brophy, 2006; Onishi 1999; Soh, 2001). In order for reparations to be truly meaningful, it must be provided from the resources of the grantor and must be distinctively targeted to the victims (Brophy, 2006; Cha-Jua, 2001; Johnstone & Ness, 2007).

Considering these factors, restorative justice for India and Pakistan should include reparations from the British government to Pakistan and India, reparations from the Indian and Pakistani governments to their own respective citizens, and reparations from the Indian government to the Pakistani government and vice versa. Such reparations could include the following:

1. A Reconciliation and Reparation Committee should be created to oversee the process, inviting an international peace-keeping committee to oversee the process and ensure accountability.
2. A citizens' committee should be created to determine the atrocities that each of their governments has engaged in due to the partition.

3. The British government should offer a public acknowledgment and apology for the colonization, underdevelopment, and exploitation of India and Pakistan under British rule.
4. The British government should also provide a public acknowledgment and apology for the partition of India and Pakistan into two nations.
5. A reparations program financed by the state and international actors should be created to include compensation for serious injuries and losses, psychological-rehabilitation initiatives, and the restitution of or compensation of stolen property.
6. A series of monuments, parks, and national festivals should be created and funded by the Indian, Pakistani, and British governments, designed to acknowledge and memorialize the loss of civilian lives that occurred during the partition.

Conclusion

While the theory of restorative justice has been developed mainly to address criminal justice for individual victims and perpetrators, its core values provide a framework for community, national, and international peace building. When addressing multigenerational injustice it is critical that the historical accounting have a clear and relevant starting point. That is, many might think about apology and reparations with India and Pakistan from the point of the partition onward, seemingly because that is when the conflicts began between these two countries. This leaves one feeling hopeless and confused about possibilities for peace. How can either side be helped to shift their positions when they are locked in competing stances? However, when the point of reference for understanding the conflict is pre-partition, we can bring people together for critical dialogue and inquiry around the common themes of imperialism and the struggle for redefining one's people and postcolonial national identity. For example, the Englishman Cecil Rhodes in 1877 stated, "I contend that we Britons are the first race in the world, and the more of the world we inhabit, the better it is for the human race. I believe it is my duty to God, my Queen, and my country..."(Haggard & Monsman, 2002, p. 278). In addition to the economic and trade benefits that Britain experienced, colonization was an effort to further white supremacy and Christianity (Ani, 1994; Brown, 2004; Kambon, 1998). Given the deleterious impact of colonization at multiple levels this chapter elucidates openings for the process of accountability, reparations, and peace.

With accountability grounded in the critical consciousness of pre- and post-partition, reparations can then focus on reparative and restorative justice. Bringing ambassadors from Britain, Pakistan, India, and members of the UN together, first within their respective countries and then with each other, offers possibilities for some of the reparations we have outlined and other potential reparative efforts, both symbolic and concrete. While similar in some respect to other dialogue and problem-solving models, this model for restorative justice holds Freire's and Martín-Baró's concepts central to the process of understanding and defining accountability and developing reparations that aim toward social justice and structural change beyond individual and relational repair.

Following the recent assassination of Benazir Bhutto, the Women's Action Forum (2007) expressed in their Requiem for her a complex analysis of their loss:

> Benazir Bhutto lived a tragic and tumultuous life,
> Fraught with pain and loss,
> A celebrated life,
> Of success and exhilaration,
> One that reached out and responded to the anguish and hope of people,
> And articulated and converted these hopes, giving sustenance to so many.
>
> Women's Action Forum while sometimes critical of her policies
> Took pride in the fact that she was a woman.
> A woman who controlled her own destiny,
> A woman who instinctively and wholeheartedly
> Embraced equal rights and opportunities,
> For women and religious minorities,
> A brave woman, a woman of courage.

In spite of this ray of hope that Bhutto offered, her own legacy is peppered with violence and corruption. Her party was responsible for the murder of her brother who represented the opposition during one of her campaign cycles. Her stunning will to name the heir of her party much like a dynasty rather than a democracy continues to leave a chilling legacy for Pakistan.

India on the other hand, while plagued by its masses, poverty, and pockets of fundamentalism, still heralds a democratic vision of government and citizenry. With its historic role of non-alignment with the West, it maintains a specific narrative of political independence and economic entrepreneurship for its people. Heeding the call to action put forth by Vandana Shiva, this economic force within a democracy could only benefit the process of peace building with Pakistan.

References

Ali, K. A. (2002, May 9). The band played on. Continued Military Rule in Pakistan. *Middle East Report Online*. Retrieved on January 22, 2008 from http://www.merip.org/mero/mero050902.html

Almeida, R. V., Dolan Del Vecchio, K., & Parker, L. (2007). *Transformative family therapy: just families in a just society*. Thousand Oaks, CA: Sage.

Anderson, B. (1991). *Imagined communities: Reflections on the origin and spread of nationalism*. London: Verso.

Ani, M. (1994). *Yurugu: An African-centered critique of European cultural thought and behavior*. Trenton, NJ: African World Press.

Auden, W. H. (1976). *W.H. Auden Collected Poems*. Westminster, MD: Random House.

Brophy, A. L. (2006). *Reparations pro & con*. New York: Oxford University Press.

Brown, A. L. (2004). *Exploring Blackness as a site of resilience for street life oriented young Black men living in the inner-city*. Dissertation. Seton Hall University.

Cha-Jua, S. K. (2001, Summer). Slavery, racist violence, American Apartheid: The case for reparations. *New Politics, 8*, 3, Retrieved January, 13, 2008, from http://www.wpunj.edu/newpol/issue31/chajua31.html#r28

Chatterjee, I. (2004). *Unfamiliar relations: Family and history in South Asia.* Piscataway, NJ: Rutgers University Press.

Chomsky, N., & Archer, G. (2006). *Perilous power: The middle east & U.S. foreign policy: Dialogues on terror, democracy, war and justice.* Boulder, CO: Paradigm Publishers.

Costello, R. B. (1993). *The American heritage college dictionary* (3rd ed.). New York: Houghton Mifflan Company.

Daly, K., & Immarigeon, R. (1998). The past, present, and future of restorative justice: Some critical reflections. *The Contemporary Justice Review, 1*(1), 21–45.

Doolin, K. (2007). But what does it mean? Seeking definitional clarity in restorative justice. *Journal of Criminal Law, 71*(5), 427–440.

Freire, P. (1971). *The pedagogy of the oppressed.* New York: Herder and Herder.

Ganguly, S. (2006). *India Pakistan relations.* Foreign Research Policy Institute. Retrieved December 28, 2007 from http://www.fpri.org/enotes/ 200604. asia.ganguly. indiapakistanrelations.html

Ganguly, S., & Hagerty, D. (2005). *Fearful symmetry: India-Pakistan crisis in the shadow of nuclear weapons.* New Delhi: Oxford University Press.

Haggard, H. R., & Monsman, G. (Ed.). (2002). *King Solomon's Mine.* Ontario: Broadview Press.

Hernandez, P., Almeida, R., & Dolan-Del Vecchio, K. (2005). Critical consciousness, accountability, and empowerment: Key processes for helping families heal. *Family Process, 44*(1), 105–119.

Hoodbhoy, P. (2004, November/December). Can Pakistan work? A country in search of itself. *Foreign Affairs, 83*(6). Retrieved on February 28, 2008 from http://www.foreignaffairs. org/20041101fareviewessay83611/pervez-hoodbhoy/can-pakistan-work-a-country-in-search-of-itself.html

Jan, S., & Khan, J. (2007, December 28). *Pakistani opposition leader Bhutto killed in suicide attack on campaign rally.* Associated Press. Retrieved February 23, 2008, from http://abcnews. go.com/International/wireStory?id=4055924

Johnstone, G., & Van Ness, D. W. (Eds.). (2007). *Handbook of restorative justice.* Portland Oregon: William Publishing.

Kambon, K. K. (1998). *African/Black psychology in the American context: An Africancentered approach.* Tallahassee, FL: Nubian Nation Publication.

Kuah, D. (2003). *The epic of race: The Indian mutiny, 1857.* The Victorian Web. Retrieved February 23, 2008 from http://www.victorianweb.org/history/empire/ mutiny.html

Kumar, R. (1997). The troubled history of partition. *Foreign Affairs, 76*(1), 22–34.

Lira, E. (1988). Efectos psicosociales de la represión en Chile [Psychological effects of repression in Chile]. *Revista de Psicología de El Salvador, 28*, 143–152.

Lira, E., Weinstein, E., & Salmovich, S. (1986). El miedo: Un enfoque psicosocial [Fear: A psychosocial model]. *Revista Chilena de Psicología, 8*, 51–56.

Majumder, S. (2008, January 18). Thirteen convicted for India riot. *BBC News.* Retrieved February 1, 2008 from http://news.bbc.co.uk/go/pr/fr/2/hi/ south_asia/7196017.stm

Martín-Baró, I. (1982). A social psychologist faces the civil war in El Salvador. *Revista Latinoamericana de Psicología, 2*, 9–111.

Martín-Baró, I. (1989). Political violence and war as causes of psychosocial trauma in El Salvador. *International Journal of Mental Health, 18*, 3–20.

Martín-Baró, I. (1990). *Psicología social de la guerra: trauma y terapia* [The social psychology of war: trauma and therapy]. San Salvador: UCA Editores.

Martín-Baró, I. (1994). *Writings for a liberation psychology.* Cambridge: Harvard.

Montville, J. (2001). Justice and the burdens of history. In M. Abu-Nimr (Ed.). *Reconciliation, coexistence, and justice: Theory and practice* (pp. 129–145). Maryland: Lexington Books.

Onishi, N. (1999, April 25). Japan's 'atonement' to former sex slaves stirs anger. *New York Times.* Retrieved December 23, 2007, from http://www.nytimes.com/2007/04/25/ world/ asia/25japan.html

Pandey, G. (1999). Can a Muslim be an Indian? *Comparative Studies in Society & History, 41*(4), 608–629.

Pearsall, J. (1999). *The concise Oxford dictionary* (10th ed.). New York: Oxford University Press.

Philips, C. H., & Wainwright, M. D. (Eds.). (1969). *The partition of India: Policies and perspectives*. Cambridge: The MIT Press.

Robb, P. (2002). *A history of India*. New York: Palgrave.

Seuffert, N. (2005). Nation as partnership: Law, "race", and gender in Aotearoa New Zealand's treaty settlements. *Law & Society Review, 39*(3), 485–526.

Shah, A. (2004). The transition to 'guided' democracy in Pakistan. In J. Rolfe (Ed.), *The Asia-Pacific: A region in transition* (pp. 207–218). Honolulu, HI: Asia –Pacific Center for Security Studies. [Electronic version]. Retrieved March 10, 2008 from http://www.apcss.org/Publications/Edited%20Volumes/RegionalFinal%20chapters/RegionalFinal.html

Shiva, V. (2005). *Earth democracy – Justice, sustainability, and peace*. Boston, MA: South End Press.

Sluzki, C. E. (2003). The process toward reconciliation. In A. Chayes & M. Minow (Eds.), Imagine coexistence: Restoring humanity after violent ethnic conflict (pp. 21–31). San Francisco, CA: Jossey-Bass.

Singh, K. (1956). *Train to Pakistan*. London: Chatto & Windus.

Soh, S. (2001, May). Japan's responsibility toward comfort women survivors. Working Paper No. 77. *Japan Policy Research Institute*. Retrieved January 13, 2007 from http://www.jpri.org/publications/workingpapers/wp77.html

Soyinka, W. (1999). *The burden of memory, the muse of forgiveness*. New York: Oxford University Press.

Udayakumar, S. P. (1997). South Asia: Before and after. *Futures, 29*(10), 919–935.

Verdajo, E. (2006). A normative theory of reparations in transitional democracies. *Metaphilosophy, 37*(3–4), 449–468.

Walker, M. U. (2006). Restorative justice and reparations. *Journal or Social Philosophy, 37*(3), 377–395.

Weinstein, E. (1987). Problemática psicológica del retornado del exilio en Chile: Algunas orientaciones psicoterapéuticas. [The psychological problem of the return from exile in Chile: Some psychotherapeutic orientations] *Boletin de Psicologia (El Salvador), 6*(23), 21–38.

Westley, R. (1998). Many billions gone: Is it time to reconsider the case for Black reparations. *Boston College Law Review, 40*, 429–476.

Wolpert, W. (2006). *Shameful flight: The last years of the British Empire in India*. New York: Oxford University Press.

Women's Action Forum. (2007, December 28). *Requiem for Benazir Bhutto*. Retrieved February 28, 2008, from http://www.madre.org/about/wafbhutto.html

Chapter 14
Forgiveness in the Context of the Armenian Experience

Viken Yacoubian

Can Armenians forgive the Turks for the 1915 genocide? While Armenians have endured many forms of oppression and calamities throughout their history, as victims of the first genocide of the 20th century they have been in the unfortunate position of forming a collective identity with this national tragedy as a backdrop. The wounds have yet to heal as the perpetrators continue to deny that they engaged in genocide. In this context, the question revolves around the usefulness and feasibility of forgiveness in light of the fact that such an act implies relinquishment of negative feelings toward the transgressor (Boon & Sulsky, 1997; Exline & Baumeister, 2000; Sandage, Worthington, Everett, & Hight, 2000). While researchers have documented that forgiveness allows for the conflicting sides to successfully move beyond the negative emotions that are perpetuated when forgiveness is lacking (Minow, 1998; Zechmeister & Romero, 2002) and that forgiveness promotes positive emotional reactions (McCullough, Bellah, Kilpatrick, & Johnson, 2001; McCullough & Hoyt, 2002), it is not clear whether the act of forgiveness can occur within a milieu absent of historical and social justice. Recent research on peace psychology has suggested that there is an inseparable link between peace-building and social justice movements (Montiel, 2001; Mayton, 2001), implying that acts of forgiveness and reconciliation must emanate from "equitable and cooperative interpersonal and social arrangements" (Christie, 2006, p. 14).

Forgiveness Versus Reconciliation

Before proceeding further, I must first clarify certain terminologies used in this chapter. Although both forgiveness and reconciliation are being used interchangeably, the two terms do not mean precisely the same thing. Research has explored distinctions between *interpersonal* forgiveness and other conceptually related terms such as excusing, forgetting, condoning, and pardoning (Enright & Coyle, 1998). While reconciliation has also been conceptually distinguished from forgiveness

---

Dedicated to the memory of Dr. Frederick J. Hacker, a mentor and friend.

Ani Kalayjian, Raymond F. Paloutzian, *Forgiveness and Reconciliation*, Peace Psychology Book Series, DOI 10.1007/978-1-4419-0181-1_14, © Springer Science+Business Media, LLC 2009

(Hargrave & Sells, 1997; Worthington, 1988), this distinction is not as clear as those previously mentioned.

One distinction that has been proposed posits that reconciliation implies restoration of a broken relationship, thereby requiring goodwill from both parties (Fincham, 2000). According to Orcutt (2006) "for reconciliation to occur, forgiveness must be present" (p. 350). Therefore, in some ways, reconciliation follows forgiveness and is a consequence of it. Forgiveness, on the other hand, can occur unconditionally, without reconciliation necessarily following it.

In this chapter, the focus is on intergroup conflict and mass trauma rather than interpersonal transgressions. Thus, the meaning of forgiveness must be construed from an intergroup perspective. In this chapter, the usefulness of viewing forgiveness as a prerequisite for reconciling relationships is explored. The thesis advanced is that forgiveness of mass trauma, such as genocide and the consequent experience of dislocation and uprooting, is a necessary requirement and antecedent of reconciliation. This is especially true in the case of Armenians where the traumas are deep and extensive. Further, it is suggested that in the case of Turks and Armenians, in order for forgiveness to occur, Turks would have to acknowledge the genocide had taken place. In this way, the victim's status, power, and sense of fundamental fairness are honored. Therefore, for the purposes of this discussion, reconciliation is conceptualized as a natural and desirable consequence of forgiveness.

The 1915 Armenian Genocide

In the years extending from 1915 to 1918, the Ottoman Empire, which was ruled by Muslim Turks, conceived, planned, and executed a policy aimed at eliminating its Christian Armenian population (Adalian, 1997). Beginning in 1894, widespread massacres had already begun against Armenians, the worst of which occurred in 1895 with the killing of some estimated 100,000–300,000 innocent civilians (Bliss, 1896/1982). As a result of these massacres, the 1915 Armenian genocide, and other post-1915 massacres, by 1922 Armenians were exterminated from their historic homeland (Adalian, 1997; Bryce, 1916).

As with other genocides, the 1915 Armenian genocide was also meticulously planned in a manner that affected all strata of the population. Intellectuals and able-bodied men were the initial targets of elimination. Thousands were drafted into the Ottoman army and subsequently slaughtered. The remaining adult population was summarily arrested, transported into remote areas, and systematically killed (Adalian, 1997). Subsequently, under the pretext of safety concerns, a vast number of women, children, and the elderly were deported, the majority of whom perished in transit (Adalian, 1997). Many suffered unfathomable cruelties, primarily in the form of sexual abuse. Many girls and young women were forcefully taken away from their families as slave-brides (Sanasarian, 1989). By 1918, almost 1.5 million Armenians were butchered and the few who had survived had been dispersed throughout the world (Adalian, 1997).

It is important to highlight that the genocide of Armenians, like many others, was not the result of a spontaneous act of unchecked aggression. It was very carefully planned over a long period of time and executed like a wartime military operation. There was a master plan to eliminate Christian Armenians from an area where Young Turks intended to implement their vision of "Turkification" and where Armenians were perceived as an obstacle in the way (Adalian, 1997). Accordingly, the plan called for not only the physical annihilation of the entire Christian Armenian population of the country, but also the obliteration of all traces that hinted to a past, so that the memory and history would also be wiped out along with the physical disappearance of the populace. This fact is supported by an even cursory look at the efficiency by which the Young Turks implemented the blueprint of their genocide, systematically assigning fitting roles to all members of the extended official apparatus, from government agencies, to party functionaries, to the local gendarmerie, and even "butcher battalions" made up of convicts released from prisons for the specific purpose of operating as killer units (Trumpener, 1968). Thus, all goods and assets, from homes, farms, buildings and lands to bank accounts and personal wealth and possessions, were systematically and almost casually transferred from Armenian to Turkish hands.

Psychological Implications of Dislocation and Uprooting

Before one can successfully address the question of forgiveness, it would be instructive to explore the nature of the loss that is prompting the need for forgiveness. The question to be asked here is, "Is forgiveness feasible given the depth and horridness of the act perpetrated, in this case the act of genocide?"

Aside from the obvious physical destruction caused to an entire group, the trauma of genocide also deeply and often irreversibly affects subsequent generations of survivors. The fissure in the psyche of the genocide victim or survivor is one that involves a separation "from one's original personal, social, and historical groundings (connections)" (Apfelbaum, 2000, p. 1009). In the case of Armenians, 1915 signified a year where an entire people was suddenly stripped of a heritage that dated back 3000 years. Their churches were defiled, towns and villages destroyed, cultural symbols desecrated. All manifestations of Armenian culture were destroyed, relegating such symbols to a collective memory that would now be wrought with the calamitous consequences of genocide. Furthermore, in this case, the aforementioned "genocidal fissure" was further amplified by the continuous denial of the perpetrators and the silence or complicity of others. Halbwachs (1924/1952) has eloquently discussed the need for personal narratives and experiences to be contextualized and memorialized collectively, by way of public accounts. He has suggested that the public chronicling of personal narratives plays an anchoring role through which personal stories gain legitimacy and resonance. Without this interplay between personal and collective, individual narratives are marginalized to the extent of being lost, silenced, and forgotten. In this respect, denial of genocide ultimately signifies the victim's alienation from his or her own experience and therefore represents a psychological uprooting that is fundamentally irreversible. Yet, to this day the Turkish government vehemently refuses to acknowledge that the Young Turks committed genocide against the Armenians in 1915, even though right after World War I the extensive documentation of the genocide played a prominent role in postwar negotiation debates by the Allied Powers (Adalian, 1997; Harbord, 1920). Unfortunately, in 1922, when Nationalist Turks in Ankara took over the country, earlier criminal sentences against those who had organized and executed the genocide were annulled along with any hope that the perpetrators would acknowledge the Armenian genocide (Dadrian, 1989). This set the stage for the social and psychological milieu in which virtually every Armenian's identity was formed after the 1915 genocide.

As Apfelbaum (2000) has noted, psychologists have failed to seriously explore and address the implications of dislocation and uprooting, issues such as the psychological reconstruction of a life that has been virtually obliterated by the grief, loss, and wholesale destruction, caused by massacres and genocide. One can argue that denial of the transgression by the perpetrator promotes a silence that in essence perpetuates the trauma for the children and grandchildren of the survivors of genocide (Altounian, 1990; Apfelbaum, 2000; Hoffman, 1989). Some have suggested that in fact the denial preserves the experience of the trauma such that it is transferred to those who were not directly targeted by the assault, i.e., children and grandchildren of survivors (Guroian, 1988; Smith, 1989).

In addition, although some researchers have suggested an idiosyncratic pattern in individual reactions to the Armenian genocide, all have agreed that there is a common thread in the collective experience of trauma which plays a defining role in the formation of the Armenian identity (Boyajian & Grigorian, 1986; Der-Karabetian, Berberian, & Der-Boghossian, 2007; Miller & Miller, 1986). Furthermore, as framed by Tololyan (2001), stories of sustained victimization (at times peppered with acts of heroism) are transferred across generations through cultural narratives, thus encapsulating the original experience for the new generations (Kalayjian, 1999; Kalayjian & Weisberg, 2002). Consistent with this, one study found that even in the face of a natural calamity (i.e., the Soviet Armenian earthquake of 1988), a group of Armenian youths in Los Angeles interpreted the event within the larger context of the injustices against and the persecution and oppression of the Armenian people (Yacoubian & Hacker, 1989).

Is Forgiveness a Feasible Option? The Context of the Armenians

A host of studies have suggested that forgiveness results in the replacement of negative emotions with positive ones and in the promotion of a renewed constructive relationship between conflicting parties. The analysis here relates to the necessity of certain antecedents to impel the process of forgiveness in cases of mass trauma where the grief, dislocation, and experience of uprooting caused by the original act continue to impact subsequent generations. Recently, Christie (2006), examining the nature of peace psychology, suggested a distinction between episodic and structural violence whereby the first, among other factors, is dramatic, characterized by direct violence and by an acute insult to people's well-being, while the latter is indirect, normalized, causing a chronic insult to well-being. In this context, episodic peacebuilding, characterized by a successful conflict management regime where opposing sides ultimately achieve a more constructive relationship, seems to result in the reduction of episodic violence. In contrast, structural peacebuilding effectively addresses issues of social injustice that underlie the societal fabric itself, ultimately resulting in structural shifts that promote equitability and justice. Obviously, the act of genocide itself is characterized by episodic violence. However, collective violence that culminates in genocide is most likely the result of structural inequalities that have systematically subjugated a segment of the population (Staub, 1999). Along these lines, one might argue that structural violence continues after genocides, especially in cases, such as the Armenians', where there is an adamant denial of the act on the perpetrator's part. Hence, the sense of inequality, injustice, and oppression, at least symbolically, is perpetuated through the silence that denial imposes.

Conceptually, a desirable consequence of forgiving, aside from its mitigating effect on the victim's emotional burden, would be the achievement of a permanently reconstructed positive relationship between the groups in conflict. In this respect, it is important that the structural conditions are reconfigured to reflect a milieu that promotes "the equitable and sustainable satisfaction of human needs" (Christie, 2006). Such structural changes can play a crucial role in assuaging the grief and pain of the victim, thereby creating a viable context for forgiving. As noted by Bretherton and Mellor (2006), reconciliatory processes can greatly benefit from the rectification of historical injustices.

Context for Forgiving: The Empowerment of the Victim

In a recent study, Shnabel and Nadler (2008) have proposed a needs-based model of reconciliation, focusing on the necessity of addressing the differential needs of victims and perpetrators so that forgiveness and, ultimately, reconciliation can occur. Accordingly, the researchers have posited that for the victim the threat lies in the loss of one's status and power, while for the perpetrator the threat is in the loss of one's moral position and social acceptability. This discussion is important in the context of intergroup conflict, especially as it pertains to the experience of Armenians, because it explores psychological and emotional dimensions that can potentially play a critical role in fostering a climate conducive to forgiveness and reconciliation.

While conflict resolution focuses on practical outcomes for the opposing factions, in essence promoting an attitude of cost–benefit analysis in the parties at odds, reconciliatory approaches advocate the necessity of an emotional or psychological reorientation for positive changes to occur (Staub, Pearlman, Gubin, & Hagengimana, 2005). From this perspective, the resolution of the underlying emotional issues is regarded as a prerequisite for positive changes in the relationship (Nadler,

2002; Nadler & Liviatan, 2004). In fact, Nadler (2002), in his conceptualization of the *socioemotional route to reconciliation*, effectively argues that the potential of failure of reconciliatory efforts is increased when the emotional needs of the adversaries are ignored. Furthermore, researchers in the area of negotiation have reported that the practice of dismissing the emotional issues in the process in favor of a focus on the so-called tangible matters, such as money, often results in a state of deadlock (Zubek, Pruitt, Peirce, McGillicuddy, & Syna, 1992).

The profound socioemotional and psychological consequences of genocidal victimization have been eloquently discussed by many researchers (e.g., Apfelbaum, 2000; Laub & Auerhahn, 1989; Sternberg, 2003). In this respect, individual and collective losses are monumental and the destruction traverses from the intrapersonal all the way to the communal. In the context of the above-discussed pathway to forgiving and reconciliation, the socioemotional need of the victim transcends the mere acquisition of a sense of power by way of the perpetrator's acknowledgment of the act of genocide; it requires a process that can potentially address the genealogic loss, what some have called the cultural orphanage of surviving generations of victims of genocide (Altounian, 1990; Apfelbaum, 2000). It is therefore surprising that the socioemotional dimension of reconciliation and forgiveness has received much less attention in the research than issues such as level of social category inclusiveness (Wohl & Branscombe, 2005) or the instrumentality of the relationship (Rusbult & Van Lange, 1996; Rusbult, Verette, Whitney, Slovik, & Lipkus, 1991). Shnabel and Nadler (2008) have proposed that it is necessary for conflicting parties to engage in a process of social exchange to "facilitate the recovery of the parties' impaired psychological resources" (p. 117). Through such a process, a psychological shift in the attitudes of the conflicting parties can take place making forgiveness and reconciliation a much more tenable option.

In the case of Armenians, then, let us entertain the following question. What are the socioemotional needs that must be addressed in order to increase the viability of forgiveness and ultimate reconciliation? Researchers have noted that in the victimization experience, different aspects of the psychological resources of victims and perpetrators are impaired. The experience of the perpetrator is one of moral inferiority (Exline & Baumeister, 2000; Zechmeister & Romero, 2002), a fear of being rejected from the moral community (Tavuchis, 1991). The victim on the other hand feels a sense of disempowerment (Foster & Rusbult, 1999), a loss of self-esteem (Scobie & Scobie, 1998), as well as a loss of perceived control (Baumeister, Stillwell, & Heatherton, 1994). According to Shnabel and Nadler (2008), the victim's loss of these psychological resources creates in the individual a sense of deprivation that needs to be satisfied. That is, the victim's sense of power must be restored. As a result, an increase is observed in the victim's power-seeking behavior (Foster & Rusbult, 1999). Hence, one can view the refusal of forgiveness in the context of this type of power-seeking behavior. In light of this dynamic, the perpetrator's acknowledgment of responsibility for the injustice caused to the victim would effectively create a milieu where the victim's sense of power is reestablished by way of his or her prerogative to forgive the perpetrator, thereby restoring this latter's ability to be accepted in the moral community (Akhtar, 2002; Minow, 1998; Schonbach, 1990).

As highlighted by the Turkish government's denial of the Armenian genocide, perpetrators often avoid feelings of guilt through a denial of culpability or responsibility for their action (Mikula, 2002). Perpetrators of genocide may even perceive their actions as having some merit or justification (Baumeister, 1996; Sternberg, 2003). The victims, on the other hand, emphasize the injustice inflicted upon them and the imperative of the perpetrators' acknowledgment of responsibility, a phenomenon that Exline and Baumeister (2000) have coined as the *magnitude gap*. Thus, as noted by Shnabel and Nadler (2008), "restoring victims' sense of power will enhance their willingness to reconcile with perpetrators" (p. 118). On the other hand, the victim's forgiveness will increase the perpetrator's willingness to reconcile in light of the fact that such an action would restore the perpetrator's public moral image.

Ethnoracial Identity Development and Willingness to Forgive

One of the most significant consequences of the 1915 Armenian genocide has been the creation of a diaspora due to the worldwide scattering of genocide survivors. Wherever they have found themselves at the end of their forced migration, Armenians have built organized and sophisticated cultural infrastructures through which their cultural narrative has endured and evolved. While there are many intracultural differences among this geographically and demographically diverse group of people (Bakalian, 1993), value orientations, as reflected in language structures and sociopolitical institutions, together with the shared experience of uprooting and trauma, unify Armenians in ways that transcend physical boundaries. Armenian American writer William Saroyan (1936) has captured this experience of "Armenianness" with lyrical vivacity as he describes his accidental encounter with an Armenian waiter from Fresno, California, in a beer parlor during his visit to Rostov, Russia:

> And the Armenian gestures, meaning so much. The slapping of the knee and roaring with laughter. The cursing. The subtle mockery of the world and its big ideas. The word in Armenian, the glance, the gesture, the smile, and through these things the swift rebirth of the race, timeless and again strong, though years have passed, though cities have been destroyed, fathers and brothers and sons killed, places forgotten, dreams violated, living hearts blackened with hate. (p. 181)

In Saroyan's image, one can readily sense how the resilience of Armenians is attributed to their will to survive attempts of annihilation and destruction. Implied in this attribution is also a position of defiance, one akin to the "never again" used in reference to the Jewish Holocaust. To an important extent, the ethnoracial identity of Armenians is formed in this context of determined survival and pursuit of recognition of the Armenian genocide (Bedoyan, 1979; Boyajian & Grigorian, 1986; Der-Karabetian, 1980). Miller and Miller's (1986) observation that second- and third-generation Armenian Americans were found to be even more revengeful toward the perpetrators of the genocide than the actual survivors further underscores this fact. One researcher has suggested that highly organized community-based sociopolitical structures such as the ones found in all diasporan Armenian communities may in fact play a role in preventing, in its most socioculturally active individuals, the development of a racial identity that is characterized by a mature ability to resolve identity conflicts (Yacoubian, 2003). In light of this interesting and somewhat unique dynamic, it would be informative to briefly explore the potential impact of forgiveness on the ethnoracial identity development of the diasporan Armenian. Parenthetically, it should be noted here that the term ethnoracial is being used in consideration of the yet unresolved discussion in the current literature regarding terminologies used in ethnic and racial identity development research (Quintana, 2007).

Many researchers have contended that ethnoracial identity is formed through a discernible developmental pattern (Cross, 1971; Helms, 1985). Accordingly, it is argued that this pattern is sequentially developed and that stages toward the end of identity formation signify a well-adjusted and healthy ethnoracial identity. All these models assert that a resolved ethnoracial identity has at its core a sense of cultural empowerment that nevertheless embraces an attitude of openness, tolerance, and inclusiveness toward the larger society. In the case of Armenians, one might reasonably argue that an obstacle in the way to achieving such a synergistically resolved identity is the individual's inability to work through the trauma of genocide in the presence of a perpetrator who refuses to take responsibility for the committed act. This difficulty is further exacerbated by highly organized and sophisticated community infrastructures whose very existence is propelled by the perpetrator's continuous denial of the genocidal act. Thus, the milieu of the diasporan Armenian's ethnoracial identity development (especially for those who are active participants in community-based networks) is predicated upon an invested and committed attitude to undo the injustice inflicted upon its people. Such an attitude, more often than not, requires an immersion, as described by Helms (1990), in one's culture. In turn, there is a clear dissonance between such an attitude of immersion and one that is characterized by a settled equilibrium as is the case in higher stages of ethnoracial identity development. In sum, another potential implication of denial could be the arrest of ethnoracial identity development, especially among those who are actively involved in community-based activities.

In the context of the above, it is also interesting to highlight Wohl and Branscombe's (2005) recent work on social category inclusiveness. The researchers hypothesize that forgiveness would be facilitated for the victimized group (in this case survivors of the Jewish Holocaust, as well as subsequent generations) if this latter is able to reframe its categorization of the perpetrator (in this case Germans from the Nazi period) by perceiving the perpetrator and itself not as distinct social groups but as members of a single inclusive superordinate group (i.e., humans). In this way, according to the authors, collective guilt assignment would not be transferred to the new representatives of the historical perpetrators, the subsequent generations. Thus, by perceiving the perpetrators as human beings rather than a specific social group (i.e., Germans, Turks, etc.), the likelihood of forgiveness and psychological rehabilitation is increased.

While an interesting moral and ethical discussion can be generated from Wohl and Branscombe's proposition as delineated above, our focus here does not allow for such a digression. However, in the framework of our discussion of the Armenian's ethnoracial identity development pattern, one can question as to how a perception of social category inclusiveness can develop when, as a result of the continuous denial of the crime itself, the infrastructures of the Armenian Diaspora promote unequivocal immersion in one's real and symbolically represented cultural narrative – a narrative that, directly and indirectly, highlights the genocidal carnage and the perpetrator's failure to take responsibility for the wholesale slaughter. Reframing of any kind, be it cognitive or emotional, is very difficult when the assault itself has not been officially acknowledged (Altounian, 1990; Apfelbaum, 2000; Laub & Auerhahn, 1989) and when sentiments of hate continue to percolate in a highly polarized situation (Sternberg, 2003).

Conclusion

In a general sense, psychologists agree that many positive factors are connected to the act of forgiveness (McCullough et al., 2001; McCullough & Hoyt, 2002; Minow, 1998; Zechmeister & Romero, 2002). Thus, as it relates to transgressions and painful inflictions, psychological and emotional benefits are derived from the act of forgiving the perpetrator. In this chapter, we examined the conceptual validity of this notion as it relates to mass trauma, the act of genocide. As noted throughout the chapter, genocide is a form of violence that occurs on a mass level and whose consequences are far reaching, including trauma experienced by subsequent generations of the affected group who were not direct victims of the act. Furthermore, focusing on the experience of the Armenians, a thesis was developed here in which the implications of the perpetrator's failure to take responsibility for the act of genocide were considered in the context of forgiveness and reconciliation. Accordingly, it was asserted that denial not only exacerbates the pain of the original trauma in subsequent generations, but also plays a significant role in preventing the launch of a healing process which could potentially lead to forgiveness on the part of the victim and subsequent reconciliation. It was suggested that acknowledgment of responsibility by the perpetrator or its representative (in this case, the Turkish government) for the genocidal act was a necessary precursor to creating the milieu where forgiveness and reconciliation become viable alternatives. In the absence of such an acknowledgment, the emotional burden of the victims, especially in the context of undoing the injustice perpetrated against its group and of an ethnoracial identity formed around cultural narratives of dislocation, trauma, and uprooting, prevents them from achieving an inner sense of equilibrium that would allow for ultimate forgiveness and reconciliation. Thus, it is imperative that victims of mass trauma experience external sources of validation through the acknowledgment of the impact of their monumental loss, a loss that has obliterated the most basic expectations and needs of human existence – a need for safety, security, and a sense of connectedness to one's roots, family, and home. In sum, a loss of identity and raison-d'etre (Apfelbaum, 2000; Apfelbaum & Vasquez, 1984). Such a validation, surely not only on the part of the perpetrator but also on the part of the larger society, is an imperative step toward the victim's ultimate internalization of the necessary emotional resources that could feed the potentiality of healing and repair. It is only after such an internal transformation that the act of forgiveness can find meaningful expression in the victim.

Apfelbaum (2000) has eloquently highlighted the importance of a genealogical continuity in the anchoring of one's life and identity. She has also noted that for victims of mass trauma, as is the case of genocide victims, a collective public discourse can become a crucial forum through which some form of meaning could be derived for "one's uprooted and disrupted personal history" (Apfelbaum, 2000, p. 1011). The presence of at least a functionally reconstructed identity is necessary for the mourning of one's fundamental personal and collective loss and for triggering a healing process that could potentially result in forgiveness and reconciliation.

References

Adalian, R. P. (1997). The Armenian genocide. In S. Totten, W. S. Parsons, & I. W. Charny (Eds.), *Century of genocide: Eyewitness accounts and critical views* (pp. 41–77). New York: Garland.

Akhtar, S. (2002). Forgiveness: Origins, dynamics, psychopathology, and technical relevance. *Psychoanalytic Quarterly, 71*, 175–212.

Altounian, J. (1990). *Ouvrez-moi seulement les chemins d'Armenie: Un genocida aux deserts de l'inconscient* [If you only could open the road to Armenia: A genocide at the limits of the unconscious]. Paris: Les Belles Lettres.

Apfelbaum, E. R. (2000). And now what, after such tribulations? Memory and dislocation in the era of uprooting. *American Psychologist, 55*(9), 1008–1013.

Apfelbaum, E. R., & Vasquez, A. (1984). Les realites changeantes de l'identite [identity in the light of changing realities]. *Peuple Mediterraneens, 24*, 83–100.

Bakalian, A. (1993). *Armenian Americans: From being to feeling Armenian*. New Brunswick, NJ: Transaction Publishers.

Baumeister, R. F. (1996). *Evil: Inside human violence and cruelty*. New York: Henry Holt.

Baumeister, R. F., Stillwell, A. M., & Heatherton, T. F. (1994). Guilt: An interpersonal approach. *Psychological Bulletin, 115*, 243–267.

Bedoyan, H. (1979). The social political and religious structure of the Armenian community in Lebanon. *Armenian Review, 32*(2), 119–130.

Bliss, E. M. (1982). *Turkey and the Armenian atrocities*. Fresno, CA: Meshag. (Original Work published 1896).

Boon, S. D., & Sulsky, L. M. (1997). Attributions of blame and forgiveness in romantic Relationships: A policy-capturing study. *Journal of Social Behavior and Personality, 12*, 19–44.

Boyajian, L., & Grigorian, H. (1986). Psychological sequelae of the Armenian Genocide. In R. G. Hovannisian (Ed.), *The Armenian genocide in perspective* (pp. 177–185). New Brunswick, NJ: Transaction Publishers.

Bretherton, D. J., & Mellor, D. (2006). Reconciliation between Aboriginal and other Australians: The "stolen generations." *Journal of Social Issues, 62*(1), 81–98.

Bryce, V. (1916). *The treatment of the Armenians in the Ottoman Empire 1915–1916*. New York: G. P. Putnam's Sons.

Christie, D. J. (2006). What is peace psychology the psychology of? *Journal of Social Issues, 62*(1), 1–17.

Cross, W. E., Jr. (1971). The Negro-to-Black conversion experience: Toward a psychology of Black liberation. *Black World, 20*(9), 13–27.

Dadrian. V. N. (1989). Genocide as a problem of national and international law: The World War I Armenian case and its contemporary legal ramifications. *Yale Journal of International Law, 14*(2), 221–334.

Der-Karabetian, A. (1980). Relation to two cultural identities of Armenian-Americans. *Psychological Reports, 47*(1), 123–128.

Der-Karabetian, A., Berberian, S., & Der-Boghossian, A. (2007). Armenian ethnic orientation questionnaire-revised. *Psychological Reports, 101*, 485–496.

Enright, R. D., & Coyle, C. T. (1998). Researching the process model of forgiveness within psychological interventions. In E. L. Worthington, Jr. (Ed.), *Dimensions of forgiveness: Psychological research and theological perspectives* (pp. 139–161). Philadelphia: Templeton Foundation Press.

Exline, J. J., & Baumeister, R. F. (2000). Expressing forgiveness and repentance: Benefits and barriers. In M. E. McCullough, K. I. Pargament, & C. E. Thoresen (Eds.), *Forgiveness: Theory, research, and practice* (pp. 133–155). New York: Guilford Press.

Fincham, F. D. (2000). The kiss of the porcupines: From attributing responsibility to Forgiving. *Personal Relationships, 7*, 1–23.

Foster, C. A., & Rusbult, C. E. (1999). Injustice and power seeking. *Personality and Social Psychology Bulletin, 25*, 834–849.

Guroian, V. (1988). Post-Holocaust political morality: The litmus of Bitburg and the Armenian genocide resolution. *Holocaust and Genocide Studies, 3*(3), 305–322.

Halbwachs, M. (1952). *Les cadres sociaus de la memoire* [The framework for memory]. Paris: Presses Universitaires de France. (Original work Publisher 1924).

Harbord, J. G. (1920). *Report on the American military mission in Armenia.* Washington, DC: Government Printing Office.

Hargrave, T. D., & Sells, J. N. (1997). The development of a forgiveness scale. *Journal of Marital and Family Therapy, 23*, 41–62.

Helms, J. E. (1985). Toward a theoretical explanation of the effects of race on Counseling: A Black and White model. *The Counseling Psychologist, 12*, 153–165.

Helms, J. E. (1990). *Black and White racial identity: Theory, research, and practice.* Westport, CT: Greenwood Press.

Hoffman, E. (1989). *Lost in translation.* New York: Penguin.

Kalayjian, A. S. (1999). Forgiveness and transcendence. *Clio's Psyche, 6*(3), 116–119.

Kalayjian, A. S., & Weisberg, M. (2002). Generational impact of mass trauma: The Ottoman Turkish genocide of the Armenians. In J. S. Piven, C. Boyd, & H. W. Lawton (Eds.), *Jihad and sacred vengeance* (pp. 254–279). New York: Writers Club Press.

Laub, D., & Auerhahn, N. C. (1989). Failed empathy: A central theme in the survivor's Holocaust experience. *Psychoanalytic Psychology, 6*(4), 377–400.

Mayton, D. M. (2001). Gandhi as peacebuilder: The social psychology of satyagraha. In D. J. Christie, R. V. Wagner, & D. D. Winter (Eds.), *Peace, conflict, and violence: Peace psychology for the 21st century* (pp. 307–313). Upper Saddle River, NJ: Prentice-Hall.

McCullough, M. E., Bellah, C. G., Kilpatrick, S. D., & Johnson, J. L. (2001). Vengefulness: Relationships with forgiveness, rumination, well-being and the Big Five. *Personality and Social Psychology Bulletin, 27*, 601–610.

McCullough, M. E., & Hoyt, W. T. (2002). Transgression-related motivational Dispositions: Personality substrates of forgiveness and their links to the Big Five. *Personality and Social Psychology Bulletin, 28*, 1556–1573.

Mikula, G. (2002). Perspective-related differences in interpretations of injustice in close relationships. In C. F. Graumann & W. Kallmeyer (Eds.), *Perspective and perspectivation indiscourse.* Amsterdam: John Benjamins.

Miller, D. E., & Miller, L. T. (1986). An oral history perspective on responses to the Armenian Genocide. In R. F. Hovannisian (Ed.), *The Armenian Genocide in perspective* (pp. 187–203). New Brunswick, NJ: Transaction Publishers.

Minow, M. (1998). *Between vengeance and forgiveness*. Boston: Beacon Press.

Montiel, C. J. (2001). Toward a psychology of structural peacebuilding. In D. J. Christie, R. V. Wagner, & D. D. Winter (Eds.), *Peace, conflict, and violence: Peace psychology for the 21st century* (pp. 282–294). Upper Saddle River, NJ: Prentice-Hall.

Nadler, A. (2002). Post-resolution processes: Instrumental and socio-emotional routes to reconciliation. In G. Salomon & B. Nevo (Eds.), *Peace education: The concept, principles, and practices around the world*. Mahwah, NJ: Erlbaum.

Nadler, A., & Liviatan, I. (2004). Intergroup reconciliation process in Israel: Theoretical analysis and empirical findings. In N. R. Branscombe & B. Doosje (Eds.), *Collective guilt: International perspectives* (pp. 216–235). New York: Cambridge University Press.

Orcutt, H. K. (2006). The prospective relationship of interpersonal forgiveness and psychological distress symptoms among college women. *Journal of Counseling Psychology, 53*(3), 350–361.

Quintana, S. M. (2007). Racial and ethnic identity: Developmental perspectives and research. *Journal of Counseling Psychology, 54*, 259–270.

Rusbult, C. E., & Van Lange, P. A. M. (1996). Interdependence processes. In E. T. Higgins & A. W. Kruglanski (Eds.), *Social psychology: Handbook of basic principles* (pp. 564–596). New York: Guilford Press.

Rusbult, C. E., Verette, J., Whitney, G. A., Slovik, L. F., & Lipkus, I. (1991). Accommodation processes in close relationships: Theory and preliminary empirical evidence. *Journal of Personality and Social Psychology, 60*, 53–78.

Sanasarian, E. (1989). Gender distinction in the genocidal process: A preliminary study of the Armenian case. *Holocaust and Genocide Studies, 4*(4), 449–461.

Sandage, S. J., Worthington, E. L., Everett, L., & Hight, T. L. (2000). Seeking Forgiveness: Theoretical context and an initial empirical study. *Journal of Psychology and Theology, 28*, 21–35.

Saroyan, W. (1936). *Inhale and exhale*. New York: Arno Press.

Schonbach, P. (1990). *Account episodes: The management or escalation of conflict*. New York: Cambridge University Press.

Scobie, E. D., & Scobie, G. E. W. (1998). Damaging events: The perceived need for forgiveness. *Journal for the Theory of Social Behaviour, 28*, 373–401, 41–52.

Shnabel, N., & Nadler, A. (2008). A needs-based model of reconciliation: Satisfying the differential emotional needs of victim and perpetrator as a key to promoting reconciliation. *Journal of Personality and Social Psychology, 94*(1), 116–132.

Smith, R. W. (1989). Genocide and denial: The Armenian case and its implications. *Armenian Review, 42*(1), 1–38.

Staub, E. (1999). The origins and prevention of genocide, mass killing, and other collective violence. *Peace and Conflict: Journal of Peace Psychology, 5*, 303–336.

Staub, E., Pearlman, L. A., Gubin, A., & Hagengimana, A. (2005). Healing, reconciliation, forgiving and the prevention of violence after genocide or mass killing: An intervention and its experimental evaluation in Rwanda. *Journal of Social and Clinical Psychology, 24*, 297–334.

Sternberg, R. J. (2003). A duplex theory of hate: Development and application to Terrorism, massacres, and genocide. *Review of General Psychology, 7*(3), 299–328.

Tavuchis, N. (1991). *Mea Culpa: A sociology of apology and reconciliation*. Palo Alto, CA: Stanford University Press.

Tololyan, K. T. (2001). Cultural narrative and the motivation of the terrorist. In D. C. Rapoport (Ed.), *Inside terrorist organizations* (pp. 217–236). Southgate, London: Frankcass Publishers.

Trumpener, U. (1968). *Germany and the Ottoman empire 1914–1918*. New Jersey: Princeton University Press.

Wohl, M. J. A., & Branscombe, N. R. (2005). Forgiveness and collective guilt Assignment to historical perpetrator groups depend on level of social Category inclusiveness. *Journal of Personality and Social Psychology, 88*(2), 288–303.

Worthington, E. L. (1988). Understanding the values of religious clients: A model and its application to counseling. *Journal of Counseling Psychology, 35*, 166–174.

Yacoubian, V., & Hacker, F. J. (1989). Reactions to disaster at a distance: The first week after the earthquake in Soviet Armenia. *Bulletin of the Menninger Clinic, 53*(4), 331–339.

Yacoubian, V. (2003). *Assessment of racial identity and self-esteem in an Armenian American population.* Unpublished doctoral dissertation, University of Southern California, Los Angeles.

Zechmeister, J. S., & Romero, C. (2002). Victim and offender accounts of interpersonal conflict: Autobiographical narratives of forgiveness and unforgiveness. *Journal of Personality and Social Psychology, 82*, 675–686.

Zubek, J. M., Pruitt, D. G., Peirce, R. C., McGillicuddy, N. B., & Syna, H. (1992). Disputant and mediator behaviors affecting short-term success in mediation. *The Journal of Conflict Resolution, 36*, 546–572.

Chapter 15
Forgiveness in Spite of Denial, Revisionism, and Injustice

Ani Kalayjian

> *History, despite its wrenching pain, cannot be unlived, but, if faced with courage, it need not be lived again.*
>
> Maya Angelou

This chapter focuses on how to forgive in the presence of denial, revisionism, and injustice. In particular, it addresses coping with the denial of the Ottoman-Turkish Genocide of the Armenians. Additionally, two cases are presented to illustrate the challenge of forgiveness and how, when governmental denial exists, the practice of forgiveness is not only a challenge, but an unending process. A seven-step Biopsychosocial and Eco Spiritual Model is presented as the approach used for transforming anger, hatred, and resentment into forgiveness, in both individual and group settings (Kalayjian, 2002). Since 1989, this model has been applied world-wide in more than 20 post-disaster humanitarian outreach projects, as part of the Mental Health Outreach Programs (MHOP) organized by this author. It is distilled here into its most essential form. However, it can be adapted for application in a wide range of situations.

The Non-forgiveness Cycle

Forgiveness is a concept that tends to be misunderstood and seldom practiced. In situations that range from individual resentment caused by frustration and disappointment to mass trauma that is perhaps acknowledged or denied, traumatized individuals do not frequently choose forgiveness as their response. One way to define forgiveness is as a peaceful inner state, irrespective of one's experienced individual or mass trauma, which best follows the catharsis, expression, and processing of negative feelings. In difficult and trying situations individuals can have many and varied negative emotions such as anger and resentment. As with every other emotion, the more one experiences it, the more one will be familiar with and attached to it. Thus, the more a person practices the negative emotional components of victimization trauma and the negative feelings that follow, the more he or she can become a slave to or driven by that emotion – as if trapped in or addicted to it. As a

Ani Kalayjian, Raymond F. Paloutzian, *Forgiveness and Reconciliation*, Peace Psychology Book Series, DOI 10.1007/978-1-4419-0181-1_15,
© Springer Science+Business Media, LLC 2009

consequence, the negative feelings can create a loss of perspective so that the person is less aware of other possible responses and/or options. The following clinical case illustrates this notion of being driven by an emotion that is repeatedly practiced and therefore nurtured or reinforced.

Mr. M., a 22-year-old college junior, expressed that since his girlfriend left him so abruptly and hurt his feelings, he intends to slash her vehicle's tires in retaliation. After empathizing with his anger, this author asked what he hoped to accomplish by doing that. Mr. M. quickly responded: "Then she will suffer, and understand a little more how much she has hurt my feelings." The author continued asking, "What, then, would follow?" Mr. M. stated, again very quickly, that his girlfriend would then not hurt him again. The author tried to provide another scenario by saying, "What if your girlfriend came and slashed your tires in retaliation – what makes you think that she will not react and retaliate like you did?" Mr. M. pondered this for a moment and then replied, "Well, I never thought of that."

Often, people who are in the midst of pain, hurt, and sadness feel that by causing pain to others, and thereby trying to overcome their feelings of trauma by way of retaliation, they will be able to resolve their emotional pain. In fact, they enter a vicious cycle of retaliation and pain, from which one can seldom exit. This method of coping and recovery becomes a compulsive habit; due to the rush of neurotransmitters associated with each negative emotion, the body experiences the chemical equivalent of riding a roller coaster.

Traumatized individuals often succumb to the immediacy of the influence of the trauma and therefore react semi-automatically, instead of first defining all possible and healthy responses, selecting the best option, and moving ahead to learn a deeper lesson about themselves. In addition, quotes such as, "Forgetting what is behind and straining toward what is ahead, I press on toward the goal to win the prize for which God has called me heavenward in Christ Jesus" (Philippians 3:13–14), which mentions forgetting the past, are widely misunderstood and wrongly associated with forgiveness. For example, when considering the notion of forgiveness, individuals in the author's Armenian community as well as in her private practice state that they are afraid to forget, they feel guilty when they forget, and they feel the bones of their loved ones turning in their graves. Thus, instead of striving for a future that is focused singularly on positive and fulfilling goals, they seem stuck, imprisoned, in a long-passed traumatic event.

Peace Psychology and Forgiveness

According to Christie (2006), for many scholars the "peace" in peace psychology continues to be associated with a narrow and post–Cold War focus on the prevention of nuclear war. This is a limited view, as the violence and need for peace around the world extends well beyond this focus. Christie offers a 2 × 2 matrix as a model of the peace-building process, incorporating a systems perspective. This systems perspective traces the preconditions of violent episodes to structure-based disparities in human well-being. As such, for large-scale violence and genocide to occur, there needs to be structure-based inequalities that produce difficult living conditions for part of a society, which in turn cause a rise in negative psychological and social processes including destructive intergroup ideologies (Staub, 1999). Christie (2006) presents a thorough review of the recent literature and research on peace-building, peace-keeping, and peace-making in psychology, and focuses on the promotion of intergroup contact and nonviolent management of conflict, citing Gandhi as an exemplar; this author adds Martin Luther King, Jr.'s example as well.

Christie (2006) emphasizes the role of both episodic and structural peace-building. According to him, when taken together, episodic and structural peace-building can form a larger peace-building system that addresses both peaceful means and peaceful ends. Christie hopes that incorporating nonviolent management of conflict while maintaining social justice will be the wave of the future. However, without the practice of forgiveness, the residue left from past conflicts will erupt at a later time and place. This is what is currently happening in South Africa even after all the efforts of the Truth and Reconciliation Commission, in Rwanda, and in former Soviet Republics. This author has received several e-mail testimonials from Cape Town and Rwanda that retaliation is taking place, since there were no long-term systematic efforts to help people practice forgiveness.

Forgiveness is also missing from many scientific research projects because it is related to religion and spiritual beliefs. Almost all religions indicate the spiritual value of forgiveness, and state unanimously how God/Allah/Buddha/Universe is all-forgiving.

Other literature not immediately related to peace psychology indicates positive outcomes of meaning-making post-trauma (Park & Folkman, 1997) and forgiveness, specifically using conflicts in Northern Ireland as an example (Luskin, 2002). According to Luskin, forgiveness does not require reconciliation or forgetting; rather, it insures that unkindness stops with you. Those who do not discover positive meaning from their traumatic situation may find themselves in incongruence with their positive global beliefs and become depressed or experience full-blown post-traumatic stress disorder (Park & Folkman, 1997). Worthington (2005), who has a campaign for forgiveness research, documented the effectiveness of practicing and teaching forgiveness. Although there is no one definition of forgiveness, the evidence seems clear on what happens when one is unforgiving: One experiences anger, bitterness, hostility, even hatred, and is stuck in a negative cycle of repeating the trauma.

Additionally, there are many novels, biographies, and personal case studies that indicate how valuable and essential the practice of forgiveness is for peace-building, peace-keeping, and peace-making. Such a first-hand account is exemplified in the case of Immaculée Ilibagiza, a victim of the Rwandan genocide. She escaped death by hiding from the Hutu killing squads in her pastor's bathroom with seven other women for over 91 days. She later came to the United States and wrote *Left to Tell* (2006), a book that tells her personal story. When the Rwandan genocide was finally over, Ilibagiza met in person with one of her family's murderers, and he could barely face her. However, ultimately Ilibagiza decided to grant him forgiveness.

According to Enright (2001), there are universal phases experienced by people in the process of forgiving. He identifies 20 steps with four major phases: (1) the uncovering phase, in which one feels and explores the pain, which can eventually be recognized as limited and lead to (2) the decision phase, in which the option to forgive is considered. Once forgiveness is chosen, then there is (3) the work phase, in which one reframes the entire context of the hurtful situation, which often leads to empathy and compassion and involves acceptance and the processing of pain. The final phase (4) occurs when the individual experiences healing and realizes forgiveness. Enright and other researchers have tested the 20-step model with various populations and consistently found encouraging results whereby individuals and groups found recovery and release possible.

Kalayjian's (2002) model for recovery from genocide consists of eight stages: These stages are (1) acknowledgment by others, the perpetrator, and the self; (2) validation of the perpetrator, others, and the self; (3) reparation; (4) facing fear, anger, shame, and humiliation; (5) facing denial and revisionism; (6) accepting that which cannot be changed, taking responsibility for one's own responses; (7) practicing forgiveness; (8) meaning-making, identifying lessons learned and closure. These stages have been observed in numerous Armenian Diasporan communities and found to be therapeutic and effective. Follow-up assessment revealed release of negative thoughts and feelings, building positive outlooks, and learning the positive lessons through discovering a new meaning. For example, one of the respondents stated: "I cannot control others; I can only control my own responses. I can choose to respond authentically instead of reacting."

Frankl (1962) insists that when one does not forgive, that person is connecting him or herself to the perpetrator in an angry and destructive way. When this author asked Frankl how she should help her own Armenian communities resolve the anger stemming from the Turkish government-sponsored denial of the genocide of the Armenians, he stated without hesitation: "You have to help them forgive" (Kalayjian, 1999). It has been a profoundly transformative journey for this author. Casarjian (1992), Frankl (1962), and Kalayjian (1999) wrote of the healing powers of forgiveness on the part of the victim/survivor, even in the absence of remorse on the part of perpetrators, and of the positive meaning that can be discovered even in the worst of experiences.

The Biopsychosocial and Eco Spiritual Model

Traumatology, or the study of trauma, its effects, and how to treat them, has greatly improved over the last 50 years. Although formally acknowledged in the 1970s and despite the fact that academic writing in this field increased during the last decade, there is still controversy about which treatment modality is approved, effective, and optimal. However, almost none of the modalities address the idea of forgiveness. Instead, they look at general symptomatology, address the need to process feelings, and tend to glorify a "victim identity."

Looking further back, although emotional reactions to highly stressful events have been documented in every century for which records of human behavior exist, these records leave us no single definition or one method to best approach rehabilitation. Instead, theories, explanations, analyses, clinical interventions, and complementary approaches have varied; and symptoms of flashbacks, dissociation, and startle responses have been interpreted variously as the works of God, evil, the devil, spirits, and agents from outer space (Ellenberger, 1970).

The Biopsychosocial and Eco Spiritual Model is based on the idea that any trauma can cause physical, emotional, and spiritual symptoms of illnesses. Such illnesses include post-traumatic stress disorder (PTSD), major depression, generalized anxiety disorder, phobic disorders, somatic disorders, addictions, aggression turned inward and outward; as well as physical illnesses such as back pain, gastrointestinal diseases, and cardiovascular diseases. On the spiritual level, traumas cause spiritual vacuums and loss or disillusionment of faith. The list of psychological symptoms includes nightmares, night terrors, flashbacks, regression, loss of or increase in appetite, loss of hope, loss of status, and helplessness. Also, a trauma may affect not only the survivors themselves, but often also families over several generations (Kupelian, Kalayjian, & Kassabian, 1998).

The Seven Steps

The model incorporates the following seven steps through which various aspects of traumatic exposure are assessed, identified, explored, processed, and integrated.

1. *Assess Levels of Distress:* Participants are brought together at a meeting place and given a written questionnaire, the Reaction Index Scale, revised and used by Kalayjian in approximately 20 previous mass disasters to determine the level of post-traumatic stress symptomatology, coping, and meaning-making. Additionally, they are given a forgiveness scale.

2. *Encourage Expression of Feelings:* One at a time, each member of the group is encouraged to express his or her feelings in the "here and now," in relation to the trauma. The author's research findings indicate the universal predominance of feelings of fear, uncertainty of the future, flashbacks, avoidance behaviors, anger at the perpetrator(s), sleep disturbances and nightmares, somatic symptoms, substance abuse, and domestic abuse.

3. *Provide Empathy and Validation:* The members of the group validate each survivor's feelings by using statements such as "I can understand. . ." or "It makes sense to me. . .." and sharing information about how other survivors from around the world have coped. Intentional therapeutic touch, such as holding a survivor's hand, is also used. In this step it is emphasized that the survivor's feelings of grief, fear, and anger, as well as the joy of surviving, are all natural responses to the disaster and need to be expressed. When trauma ruptures an individual's connection with a group, an intolerable sense of isolation and helplessness may ensue. Providing validation and empathy in a group setting addresses these effects by reestablishing the mutual exchange between the individual and the group, and the individual and

the universe. Forgiveness is introduced as a mechanism for creating inner peace in spite of unjust acts committed against the individual and in spite of ongoing denial of injustices. It is reinforced that when someone angers us, they control us. When we feel controlled we feel helpless. Therefore, participants are encouraged to find ways to transform their anger and sublimate it, or use it in a therapeutic way.

4. *Promote Discovery and Expression of Meaning:* Survivors are asked, "What lessons, meaning, or positive associations did you discover as a result of this traumatic experience?" This question is based on Frankl's logotherapeutic principles, which stipulate that a positive meaning can be discovered in the worst catastrophe, and on the Buddhist assertion that it takes darkness to appreciate and reconnect with light. Again, each member of the group is invited to focus on the strengths and meanings that naturally arise from any disaster situation. Some of the positive lessons learned and expressed by survivors from around the world are that interpersonal relationships are more important than material goods; it is important to release the resentments; working through anger and practicing forgiveness is healthy; it is possible to take charge of one's own life; and it is important for nations to come together for the purpose of peace. Once forgiveness is practiced regularly, one feels freer to move into this phase of searching for a meaning and is more likely to recognize the positive growth that can occur after a hardship.

5. *Supply Didactic Information:* Practical tools and information are given on how to gradually return to one's daily routine by using the systematic desensitization process. The importance of preparation in advance of disasters is taught and elaboration is provided on specific ways to prepare. Handouts are given to teachers and prospective group leaders on how to conduct disaster evacuation drills and create safe and accessible exits from buildings, homes, factories, and other potential disaster sites. Booklets are distributed to parents and teachers on how to understand and respond to their children's nightmares, fears, and disruptive behaviors after wars. In addition, assessment tools are given to mental-health professionals. Handouts are provided on grief as well as on how to take care of oneself as a caregiver and prevent secondary traumatization.

6. *Eco Centered Processing:* Practical tools are shared to connect with Gaia, Mother Earth. Discussions and exercises conducted around environmental connections. Ways to care for one's environment are shared. Startin with one's environment and expanding to the larger globe, being mindful of system's perspective and how we can impact our environment, and how the environment in turn impacts us. A list of mindful acts is shared to help co-create an emerald green world.

7. *Demonstrate Breathing and Movement Exercises:* Breath is used as a natural medicine and a healing tool. Since no one can have full control over nature, others, or what happens outside of one's self, survivors are assisted in learning how to control the way that they respond to traumas. A demonstration is provided of exercises that bring a sense of harmony to the mind, body, and spirit by focused and guided attention, imagery, and suggestion; this may be uniquely adapted to the beliefs or customs of the people being helped. This is the experiential section of the model. Survivors are given instructions on how to dissipate fear, uncertainty, and resentments from mind-body-and-spirit. In addition, survivors are instructed on how to use breathing exercises and how to move toward self-empowerment as well as to

engender gratitude, compassion, faith, strength, and forgiveness in response to disasters, mass trauma, and denial of the trauma. Forgiveness meditation exercises are conducted. Forgiving oneself as a first step is introduced. Compassion and love is reinforced as Martin Luther King Jr. states: "The ultimate weakness of violence is that it is a descending spiral, begetting the very thing it seeks to destroy. Instead of diminishing evil, it multiplies it. Through violence you may murder the liar, but you cannot murder the lie, nor establish the truth.Through violence you murder the hater, but you do not murder hate. In fact, violence merely increases hate...Returning violence for violence multiples violence, adding deeper darkness to a night already devoid of stars. Darkness cannot drive out darkness; only light can do that. Hate cannot drive out hate: Only love can do that" (Rev Dr. Martin Luther King Jr., *Where Do We Go From Here? Chaos or Community*, 1967).

Major Symptoms, Syndromes, and Problems Treated

Vicious Cycle. After a person has suffered years of trauma, victimization, anger, and retaliation, healthy approaches to dealing with life's challenges diminish. As a consequence, one may turn the anger inward (resulting in poor self-esteem and unconsciously hurting oneself through addictions and ways of life) or outward (by wanting to hurt others or wishing ill upon them) through envy, retaliation, jealousy, or malicious thoughts and intentions. Similar to cases of drug addiction, if one does not hit rock bottom, one may not be motivated to reach out to get the necessary help and may instead repeat the cycle of pain and violence over and over. If one is not aware of this cycle, the person is preconditioned, to continue to point the finger outward and blame others. As a Middle-Eastern friend once said, "Feelings are like donkeys; they are a useful and important part of our life (in a village called Kessab, Syria) but you need to know how to lead and direct them, and not let them lead you."

This vicious cycle, with its deep emotional roots and extreme swings of high and low feelings, is hard to stop. When one feels the pain of victimization on a daily basis, the individual becomes more familiar with it and its expression as an outburst of anger and as a wish to retaliate and have others "pay for" their emotional pain and suffering. This occurred in the small-scale example given at the beginning of this chapter, the case of Mr. M who wanted to slash the tires of his girlfriend's car. On a larger scale, this pattern may be part of the reason for wars that have been taking place for centuries. Perhaps, even the American government's invasion of Iraq is partly due to this pattern. After the terrorist attack on the World Trade Center as well as other U.S. government buildings on September 11, 2001, the invasion of Iraq could be construed as a large-scale display of displaced anger, humiliation, and emotional pain.

According to Frankl, we can all transcend our current level of being and go to a higher level by wanting to be free from that vicious cycle. Human beings are capable of moving forward to make better choices, to serve better causes, and to love the other (Frankl, 1962). However, one cannot exercise this self-transcendence if one does not see peace-building through forgiveness as an option, as a better choice. One must accept and experience it as one's own dream and make it come true. Just as negative conditioning and negative habits are routed in the past, the old, and the unconscious, choosing forgiveness can be what happens now, the new way of being and behaving, routed in the conscious choice to enact peace within oneself and in interpersonal and intergroup relations. Then each one, piece by piece, will contribute to the collective transformation of the world into a more positive, caring, and mutually forgiving and respectful community.

Horizontal Violence. Horizontal violence is a phenomenon that appears in oppressed groups of people such as women, minorities, and indigenous groups. Stereotypical statements such as "Armenians know how to hurt one another," "women eat their young," "nurses eat their young," "Black on black violence," "Greeks don't like one another," and the latest one I heard, "Sierra Leoneans can't trust one another, they hate each other," all depict this phenomenon. When oppression is exercised for a long time, with no periods of justice or human-rights practices, those who are oppressed can easily express their built up anger and hatred horizontally, manifesting it toward one's own brothers and sisters and/or those closest to them. This phenomenon is found in almost all oppressed groups. Generations of oppression of a larger group can lead to generations of smaller subgroups that dislike one another, distrust one another, and are unable to celebrate, love, and empathize with one another.

Generational Transmission of Trauma. Although some, but not all children of Holocaust survivors suffer pathological consequences including guilt (e.g., Davidson, 1980; Steinberg, 1989), according to Albeck (1994) a variety of inter-generational consequences do occur. However, the feeling of guilt does not have a parallel among the Armenian survivors of Turkish attacks (Kalayjian, Shahinian, Gergerian, & Saraydarian, 1996). Kalayjian et al. (1996) found two variables unique to the Armenians survivor community – the meaning construed by the individual of the profoundly invalidating experience of the denial of the genocide by the perpetrators, and the degree of the family's involvement in the Armenian community. According to Kalayjian (1995), the nightmares of second-generation genocide survivors who had experienced the devastating 1988 earthquake in Armenia were not of the earthquake, but of the Turkish gendarmes beating them on the death march, although they were not eyewitnesses to the atrocities that had taken place some 73 years before the quake. Therefore, these nightmares were the result of the generational transmission of the trauma of the genocide passed to them by their parents and grandparents.

Case Illustrations

The Impact of Trauma on the Individual

This case study is based on my personal trauma in Turkey in 1999. As a child of survivors of the Ottoman-Turkish Genocide, I was traumatized by learning the tragic stories of the genocide of the Armenians. I learned that during World War I, the Young Turks declared Armenians to be enemies of the state. Adult males, particularly those identified as potential leaders, were taken from their families, escorted to a desolate area, and shot. Others were forcibly gathered in churches and burned alive. This process was designed to deprive Armenians of leadership and representation, so that deportations might proceed without resistance. Ultimately, forced deportations, famine, thirst, torture, epidemics, pillage, and plunder resulted in the death of two-thirds of the Armenian population in Asia Minor. Both my father's and mother's families had survived the long, forced deportation march and related the hardships endured while crossing the desolate terrain to the neighboring country of Syria, where they were allowed to reside in fear. My parents met and married in Aleppo, Syria, and my family and I immigrated to the United States in the early 1970s.

The pain and suffering collectively contained in my community and the continued official denial of the genocide by the Turkish government for over 90 years have caused me tremendous psychic pain and feelings of helplessness. The best way I found to deal with those negative feelings is to sublimate them via taking positive and proactive measures. I developed a United Nations Non-Governmental Organization (NGO) dedicated to the scientific study of the stresses of genocide and other mass traumas, fostered the understanding and resolution of generational transmission of trauma, and worked with conflict-resolution and transformation groups.

I was fortunate to have met Viktor Frankl and found his logotherapeutic school of thought to be very helpful. While researching the long-term impact of the genocide on survivors, I witnessed a lot of anger and suffering. While studying with Frankl, I asked him how I could assist the surviving members of the Armenian community cope with the trauma of the genocide. With great understanding and empathy he responded, "You have to help them forgive. Your people have waited for justice long enough. They cannot wait any longer. Help them to practice forgiveness" (Kalayjian, 1999). I then began to lecture about forgiveness and its healthy impact on the survivors. The Armenian community did not understand this message and did not know how and why to forgive – and indeed, whom to forgive.

I continued my journey toward forgiveness and integration of genocidal trauma. I submitted a paper to an International European Traumatic Society's Congress on Psychotraumatology and Human Rights that took place in Istanbul, Turkey. Being fully cognizant of the Turkish government's denial propaganda, I revised my research abstract and entitled it "Mass Human-Rights Violations: Resilience vs. Resignation." Upon my arrival at the conference, I noticed that the keynote speakers talked freely regarding the host country's more recent human-rights violations against the Kurds. I felt encouraged by these candid discussions and decided to distribute my original abstract on the genocide against Armenians. At this point, the threats began. First, my life was threatened by two men claiming to represent the Turkish National Intelligence Organization (MIT), to whom I responded with skepticism, stating that I did not believe that anyone would dare kill me in front of the 600+ scholars from 48 countries who were present at the conference. The following day, I was threatened to be tortured if I talked about the genocide. On the third day, the abstracts of my presentation were snatched from my hands. On the last

day of the conference, when my lecture was scheduled, I was called by the organizers from Istanbul and the (British) then-president of the European Association
for Traumatic Stress Studies for a private meeting in the basement of the Marmara
Hotel. At this meeting, I was presented with an ultimatum: Either I must sign the
letter that was presented to me or forcibly leave the conference escorted by the Turkish police (who were waiting at the door) without addressing the conference. The
typed letter stated that I would agree to refrain from talking about the genocide that
the Armenian community had suffered. The letter was served to me only 20 minutes
prior to my scheduled lecture, which was to take place during the last hour of the
conference. Although I reminded the police and president that they were attending
a human-rights conference and that they were in fact violating my human rights as
a presenter, it was to no avail. They reiterated that because of the political situation,
they were obliged to "protect the conference organizers from the government."

After a difficult deliberation, I chose to sign the letter so that I would not lose
the opportunity to address the conference. Colleagues helped me revise my trans-
parencies by covering the controversial words with a special marker provided by
the audiovisual department. When I began delivering my lecture and the first transparency was projected, I apologized for the black lines without looking at the screen,
and then noticed that many of my colleagues had smirks on their faces. The Turkish
audience was enraged. When I turned around to look at the screen, I saw that the
censored words were showing through the black marks. I then spontaneously said:
"Whoops, the light is so bright it is coming through. I guess we cannot hide it any
longer." Tension grew in the audience. The Turkish attendees were extremely anxious; others were laughing, seeing the irony in my statement, and the Chair of the
panel was banging his gavel. At that point, I told the audiovisual department to turn
off the projector, and reinforced that I was there to focus on transcending hatred and
embracing forgiveness through dialogues. I focused on the importance of empowerment and moving on to the next phase of dialogue, education, and collaboration. I
asserted that the admission of genocide is a very difficult task to take on, especially
when survivors of the perpetrators have been misinformed for almost a century.
I then asked the scientific community to assist the Turkish community to accept
responsibility and apologize for the wrongs of their ancestors. They too need to forgive their ancestors in order to overcome denial and accept responsibility. After the
lecture, numerous international colleagues came forward and hugged and congratu-
lated me for my courage and for the depth of my message. I cried in their arms out
of relief, happiness for being alive, and for having delivered that important message.

I returned safely to the United States, planning to write about my experience. I
was spiritually enriched but emotionally and physically drained. I kept on postpon-
ing my writing out of fear of reprisal. Then a devastating earthquake hit Turkey.
Since I had been working with post-disaster recovery for over a decade, I began to
wonder if I should go to Turkey to help. I decided to go and assist, in spite of my colleagues' assertions that I must be crazy to take such a risk. For me, a humanitarian
outreach eschews geographic and political boundaries. Having fully incorporated
Frankl's message of forgiveness, I viewed this as yet another challenge and another
step forward in my journey of forgiveness, empowerment, and transcendence. I

developed the Mental Health Outreach Project for Turkey, and spearheaded a team that worked for several weeks under tents with more than 500 survivors via group therapy, debriefing, and application of the Biopsychosocial and Eco Spiritual Model.

The Impact of Mass and Unresolved Trauma

The collective impact of mass trauma is evident in the vicious cycles of violence and retaliation in countries such as Lebanon, South Africa, Sudan, Bosnia, and Armenia. During the Mental Health Outreach Projects (MHOP) that I have organized and directed in Lebanon, Syria, Bosnia, and Armenia, it was clear to all of the MHOP teams that these countries were suffering from a vicious cycle of violence, rage, retaliation, and generational transmission of anger without being mindful of the possibility of choices of forgiveness, transcendence, love, and the knowledge that they can create a new reality.

In May of 2007, while on a postwar humanitarian recovery and outreach effort in Lebanon, the MHOP team discovered the generational transmission of the hatred, anger, retaliation, and war of over 30 years. While training the psychologists and the mental-health practitioners, the MHOP team observed how difficult empathy was when the practitioners themselves had been suffering for so long and how there was virtually no post-trauma period, rather, only continuous trauma. By that time, there was not only generational transmission of trauma, but also horizontal violence. The traumatized groups were now inflicting pain on one another (Kalayjian, 2007). This is a common phenomenon in traumatized and oppressed groups (Kalayjian, 2002). A few professors were highly critical of the aid received from America, and were angry that more is not done to prevent these traumas, wars, civil wars, and political infighting.

In July of 2007 in Sarajevo, at the biennial conference of the International Association of Genocide Scholars (IAGS), I witnessed the anger and rage of the Bosniak conference chair directed at one of the Serbian student conference participants. In response to a question raised by the Serbian student, the chair reacted violently, accusing the student of being responsible for the genocide inflicted on the Bosniaks. The student was shocked at this reaction, as were I and other colleagues. The student, a 22-year-old male, burst into tears, and as he attempted to leave the auditorium, he collapsed right in front of the podium and went into an emotional seizure so uncontrollable that the emergency service had to be called in. The next day, I began generational healing workshops and groups among the youth of Bosnian, Serbian, and Croatian descendents. The group used the Biopsychosocial and Eco Spiritual Model and students were able to witness one another's expression of feelings, their traumatic experiences of the war, and their commitment to forgive and respect one another. The most amazing part is that they were able to be empathic with one another, but they stated that their parents and teachers were having the hardest time letting go of the past and embracing one another.

In October 2007, while delivering training for mental-health professionals in the Republic of Armenia, tension was observed and deeply felt. The MHOP team lectured in universities, mental-health centers, orphanages, and children's centers, and was interviewed for television and radio regarding the development of peace with the neighboring Republic of Azerbaijan. When the concept of forgiveness was introduced, people were extremely puzzled, and stated that they could not envision themselves forgiving their neighbors for all the atrocities committed against them during the Sumgait pogrom, and the small-scale massacres committed from 1989 to 1992. A few, in extreme distress, shared tears and disappointment that some Armenians had in fact retaliated and committed some atrocities against the Azeris during the 15-year civil war. This retaliation had made the observers extremely distressed and unable to live normal lives. There is a fine line between a victim and a perpetrator, and this case clearly demonstrates this phenomenon.

Summary

States, governments, religions, NGOs, even the United Nations, all working on peace-keeping, peace-building, and conflict transformation have not been able to maintain peace globally. Over 20 large-scale conflicts have erupted even after WWII – larger in number, and based on old unresolved conflicts, old hurts, and territorial and other claims. In addition, new injustices are also erupting around the world, fueled by generational transmission of trauma, horizontal violence, and other reasons based on greed, hate, selfishness, and loyalty to one clan or another.

What has clearly worked thus far is the nonviolence promoted by Martin Luther King, Jr., Gandhi, Henry David Thoreau, and Mother Teresa. These forms of nonviolent techniques cannot be practiced if one is not able to practice compassion and forgiveness. Practicing forgiveness is creating peace within. There are no shortcuts, no easy ways out, and no clear formulas. *Everyone* has to do the work of processing one's generationally transmitted feelings of human-rights violations, aggressions, and injustices, so that one can feel empathy and compassion and express it to others, including their oppressors. To be able to extend empathy and compassion to one's opponents, one first needs to forgive whatever injustices they have caused.

The research is consistent on the positive impact of practicing forgiveness. Further research on this issue is merited. International research is also needed to compare how forgiveness is practiced around the world and its impact on the health of the mind, body, and spirit.

References

Albeck, J. H. (1994). Intergenerational consequences of Trauma: Refraining traps in treatment theory: A second-generation perspective. In M. B. Williams & J. F. Sommer (Eds.), *Handbook of post-traumatic therapy* (pp. 106–125). Westport, CT: Greenwood Press.

Casarjian, R. (1992). *Forgiveness: A bold choice for a peaceful heart*. New York: Bantam.

Christie, D. J. (2006). What is peace psychology the psychology of? *Journal of Social Issues, 62* (1), 1–17.

Davidson, S. (1980). Transgenerational transmission in the families of holocaust survivors. *International Journal of Family Psychiatry, 1*(1), 95–112.

Ellenberger, H. F. (1970). *The discovery of the unconscious: The history and evolution of dynamic psychiatry*. New York: Basic Books.

Enright, R. D. (2001). *Forgiveness is a choice: A step-by-step process for resolving anger and restoring hope*. Washington, DC: American Psychological Association.

Frankl, V. E. (1962). *Man's search for meaning: An introduction to logotherapy*. Boston: Beacon. Press. (Original work published in 1946).

Ilibagiza, I. (2006). *Left to tell: Discovering god amidst the Rwandan holocaust*. Carlsbad, California: Hay House.

Kalayjian, A. S. (1995). *Disaster and mass Trauma: Global perspectives on post disaster mental health management*. Long Branch, NJ: Vista Publishing.

Kalayjian, A. (1999). Forgiveness and transcendence. *Clio's Psyche*, 6(3).116–119.

Kalayjian, A. (2002). Biopsychosocial and spiritual treatment of Trauma. In R. Massey & S. Massey (Eds.), *Comprehensive handbook of psychotherapy: interpersonal/ humanistic/existential* (Vol. 3). New York: John Wiley & Sons.

Kalayjian, A. (2007). *Eight stages of healing from genocide*. Presented at the United Nations panel on Human Rights Violations: Challenges to the Mind-body-spirit Continuum.

Kalayjian, A. S., Shahinian, S. P., Gergerian, E., & Saraydarian, L. (1996). Coping with Ottoman-Turkish genocide: An exploration of the experience of Armenian survivors. *Journal of Traumatic Stress*, 9(1), 87–97.

Kupelian, D., Kalayjian, A. S., & Kassabian, A. (1998). The Turkish genocide of the Armenians: Continuing effects on survivors and their families eight decades after massive Trauma. In Y. Danieli (Ed.), *International handbook of multigenerational legacies of Trauma* (pp. 191–210). New York: Plenum Press.

Luskin, F. (2002). *Forgive for good: A proven prescription for health and happiness*. New York: Harper Collins.

Park, C., & Folkman, S. (1997). Meaning in the context of stress and coping. *Review of General Psychology*, 1(2), 115–144.

Staub, E. (1999). The origins and prevention of genocide, mass killing, and other collective violence. *Peace and Conflict: Journal of Peace Psychology*, 5, 303–336.

Steinberg, A. (1989). Holocaust survivors and their children: A review of the clinical literature. In P. Marcus & A. Rosenberg (Eds.), *Healing their wounds: Psychotherapy with holocaust survivors and their families* (pp. 23–48). New York: Praeger Publishing.

Worthington, E. L., Jr. (Ed.). (2005). *Handbook of forgiveness*. New York: Routledge.

Chapter 16
Reconciliation and Forgiveness in Divided Societies: A Path of Courage, Compassion, and Commitment

Paula Green

> *It is hard to imagine a world without forgiveness.*
> *Without forgiveness, life would be unbearable.*
> *Without forgiveness, our lives are chained,*
> *Forced to carry the sufferings of the past and repeat them*
> *with no release.*

(Kornfield, 2002, p. 21)

From the Ottoman Turkish Genocide of Armenians in the early years of the 20th century to the genocides in Bosnia and Rwanda in its final decade, this century that was to see the end of war has been stained by unremitting violence. From our century of suffering, a new movement has emerged to establish legal, ethical, psychological, and spiritual reconciliation processes to nurture communal healing and enable former enemies to build a future as neighbors and fellow citizens. These reconciliation practices have developed in response to patterns of contemporary violence, where frequently revenge is fueled by powerful collective narratives and advanced by opportunistic leadership. Our collective survival will require our adherence to this growing international reconciliation agenda; we must protect victims, hold perpetrators accountable, and develop methods of facing truth, establishing justice, and expressing compassion.

South Africa's Truth and Reconciliation Commission (TRC) stands as the most remarkable and visible experiment in post-conflict reconciliation, offering guidance and inspiration to others who choose to embark upon this path. Elsewhere, from Rwanda to North Ireland, generous overtures of reconciliation and forgiveness arising from societies shattered by mass violence bestow the possibility of renewed life to those who have suffered incalculable loss and invite healing for fractured communities. These processes, new in the human community and still in the investigational stage, offer the best hope we have for social healing in the 21st century (Minow, 1998).

This chapter will discuss global applications of reconciliation, forgiveness, and restorative justice processes, with examples from the Conflict Transformation Across Cultures (CONTACT) Program and from Bosnia, Rwanda, the Middle East, South Africa, and other regions. The central question to be explored is how we can

Ani Kalayjian, Raymond F. Paloutzian, *Forgiveness and Reconciliation*, Peace Psychology Book Series, DOI 10.1007/978-1-4419-0181-1_16, © Springer Science+Business Media, LLC 2009

best support the arduous process of social healing for all of those involved in mass violence, whether as victims, perpetrators, or bystanders.

Those of us who have not directly experienced the utter anguish and devastation of genocidal violence can hardly understand its profound and lasting consequences. While there has been an increase in the theoretical literature on the practices of post-conflict social reconstruction, we must remember that monstrous atrocities do not lend themselves to formulaic responses. Healing, if such a concept can be applied, is often irregular and episodic. In a sense, "no response can ever be adequate" (Minow, 1998, p. 5). Nonetheless, we must learn from those brave souls who have survived the outer edge of human experience and courageously returned to teach us how to rebuild lives on the remnants of all that has been lost.

Defining Reconciliation in Divided Societies

The meanings and demands of reconciliation vary according to each individual's experience during mass violence. Victim recovery frequently commences through tangible acknowledgments of their distress. Violators may feel an inner calling to atone and repent. Political leaders and their minions may be intent on revenge, denial, or blame, and the international community may choose to stabilize, politicize, criticize, or ignore, thereby helping or hindering the whole complex process. A national reconciliation process may become a creative vehicle for substantive exploration, healing, and change, or be manipulated to promote self-serving narratives and power struggles. Ethical leadership within and beyond the communities in conflict can guide the reconciliation procedures toward wisdom and compassion, using moral persuasion to encourage safety and justice and to restrain vengeance and retribution. We have seen striking moral leadership emerge in post-apartheid South Africa and lamented its absence in the years following the Dayton Accord that ended the wars in the former Yugoslavia (Tutu, 1999).

Reconciliation in divided societies, like conflict itself, is fundamentally about relationships, perhaps especially an encounter between the shattered past and the envisioned future. Reconciliation, from the Latin root *conciliatus*, which means drawing together a council, is a sustained process that, at its best, rekindles community and restores harmony where violent conflict has set people against each other. Reconciliation also requires intentionality and perhaps even generosity. Of all the steps in peacemaking, intercommunal reconciliation may be the most demanding. It requires those who participate to surrender hatreds passed on for generations, release chosen narratives, relinquish fantasies of vengeance, and reestablish relations shattered by betrayal and brutality.

Approaches to Reconciliation

Communities must approach reconciliation through an interconnected social, psychological, spiritual, legal, and political web that supports truthfulness, acknowledgment, justice, protection, compassion, repentance, and restoration. In societies divided by mass violence, reconciliation is too multifaceted for a one-dimensional response. Each aspect of the process reflects and affects the other dimensions. Reconciliation without compassion, for example, could be legal and dry, whereas reconciliation without justice would offer no hope of official protection to victims or prevention of future harms. Similarly, acknowledgment of wrongdoing by perpetrators without genuine repentance may seem formulaic, and justice without reparations would seem dismissive and disrespectful. Inner and outer healing is interdependent, as are psychosocial and structural approaches to reconciliation.

Legal processes alone do not create social transformation, yet they are essential for successful reconciliation, in that they provide a framework of legislation to protect victims and authorize the range of acceptable behaviors. If legal institutions fail to strongly condemn the appalling acts of violence, the perpetrators may believe they have the upper hand, leaving victims to feel vulnerable to further attack. In post-conflict circumstances, it is critical that political and legal mechanisms offer safety, communicate very clearly that there will be zero tolerance for further perpetration, and usher in a new era of sanctuary under the law (Minow, 1998).

For national or intercommunal political reconciliation, Amnesty International spells out four main tasks that must be accomplished: establish the truth; strengthen the rule of law; build on a foundation of maximum participation and transparency; and include the moral right to compensation and reparation (Bronkhorst, 1995, p. 150).

These four requirements have become cornerstones in national reconciliation processes in countries such as South Africa, which embraced all aspects of the healing process, including legal, psychological, and spiritual dimensions. Legal amnesty was offered to perpetrators in exchange for complete truth, which was needed both for the historical record and for families of victims. Although reparations remain a contentious issue, they were promised in the TRC structure. No national reconciliation process to date has matched the scope, size, drama, visibility, and integrity of the TRC, partially due to the moral leadership provided by TRC Chairperson Archbishop Desmond Tutu and the then South African President Nelson Mandela (Tutu, 1999).

Victims must draw upon extraordinary reservoirs of psychological resilience following communal atrocities, far beyond what is needed in recovery from common experiences of grief and loss. In mass violence, trusted neighbors or religious leaders, and sometimes even family members, have betrayed the very foundations of psychological security. All of these betrayals occurred in Bosnia and Rwanda, leaving emotionally shattered adults and children whose difficulties challenge us to question the limits of healing possible in fragile post-conflict environments (Neuffer, 2001). The cycles of violence that repeat themselves generation after generation between victims and violators are caused in part by unhealed distress transmitted to their descendants. The result is cyclical revenge rather than reconciliation. Without deep transformation of the attitudes, behaviors, and social institutions of those involved in mass violence, the dangers of renewed violence lie in waiting, with the descendants of both perpetrators and victims caught in the wounds of their ancestors (Minow, 1998).

Illustrative of the psychological struggle to restore humanity and surrender hatreds is a dialogue group called *One by One* (www.one-by-one.org), composed of second-generation survivors of the Holocaust and second-generation descendants of the Third Reich. These mostly Boston and New York area American Jews and Berlin area Germans have been meeting together in dialogue for more than 10 years, facing their ghosts, staring down their ancestors, and dueling with the wrenching history and internal messages that keep them apart. Although these are dialogues among the adult children of survivors and violators, they carry the rage, pain, and shame of their parents' generation, so that fear of encounter, mistrust, and misapprehensions remain strong. Using tools of structured dialogue, they and similar groups from other historic conflicts have made tremendous breakthroughs in the process of re-humanization, understanding and befriending each other against all odds. For those who persist, discourse and relationship are within reach, and reconciliation is visible on the horizon.

The range of human behaviors and psychological responses to trauma is so vast that there are no formulas for recovery or healing. I have seen remarkable transformations of those whose lives have been shattered and witnessed others enduring similar tragedies with much less resilience and capacity to cope. Individuals bear loss and sorrow differently, even within comparable circumstances. Some victims are able to use their suffering in service to others, becoming what mental health professionals call *wounded healers*, a term first coined by philosopher Henri Nouwen (1972) to describe those in ministry to others who identify the suffering in their own hearts as the starting point of their healing assistance. I know victims whose history leads them to struggle for peace and justice, and I have seen others lost in bitterness, recrimination, self-destruction, and fantasies of revenge. A comprehensive reconciliation process offers many avenues for victims to reshape their lives, mend their broken hearts, and serve their communities.

Spiritual Perspectives in Reconciliation and Forgiveness

For victims, there can be an element of sacredness in the journey toward reconciliation and forgiveness, with its internal triumph over emotional impulses toward unending hatred or bitterness. It takes a spiritual mastery to forgive the unforgivable. "Forgiveness does not overlook the deed," TRC commission and psychologist Gobodo-Madikizela (2003) writes, "It rises above it. 'This is what it means to be human' it says. 'I cannot and will not return the evil you inflicted on me' " (p. 117). The capacity to let go of fantasies of revenge and to remove the toxins of hatred from the heart signifies a level of ethical and spiritual development that serves as a moral compass, illuminating a path for others to follow.

For some victims of mass violence, the desire to forgive arises through the powerful practices of community worship or inner contemplation. Forgiveness is frequently an inward spiritual decision made by a victim to let go of the burden of pain and hate, not in order to forget, but to release heart-constricting grief and loss. Forgiveness and reconciliation require courage, commitment, and compassion. Each step in the passage entails deliberation and reflection and cannot be rushed or demanded by others. Forgiveness, which promises no exemption from punishment for the perpetrator, can remove a crippling burden of hatred carried by the victim and offer release as well to the violators and community.

In my practice as a peacebuilder, I meet ordinary yet extraordinary individuals who have been aided in their reconciliation journey by spiritual practices. Eddie, a Rwandan workshop participant, recounted his intention to kill 23 Hutus, because Hutus had murdered 23 members of his Tutsi family. However, he found a healing church and became an active peacebuilder instead of a victim in search of revenge. Vahidin from Bosnia, a young Muslim imam, thought he would never speak to a Serb again, and yet several years later, through his religious exploration as well as through our structured dialogue experiences, he was partnering with Serb colleagues in shared programs of healing their fractured communities. Jaya, a Sri Lankan Tamil involved in a violent struggle for rights, described a spiritual awakening about the harm he was inflicting through violence. He now works as a leading peacebuilder in his region, encouraging active nonviolence. In these young lives, forgiveness has been in the end a solitary and brave decision, in each case going against popular opinion in the community, yet resulting in a renewed and rewarding life of service, purpose, and vision. Under certain circumstance, spiritual teachers or community leaders model and teach forgiveness, as illustrated in the following stories.

South Africa

Archbishop Tutu (1999) developed his conviction about forgiveness from the South African concept of *ubuntu*, which translates roughly as "a person is a person only through others" (p. 31). This orientation implies that we are not solitary, but interdependent; our humanity is caught up in each other's existence. Dehumanization of others inexorably dehumanizes the self, and the act of forgiveness ultimately serves the self and others, extends out to the community, and sets an example for all of humanity.

Archbishop Tutu (1999) reflected that the Truth and Reconciliation Commission testimony made him realize "... that there is an awful depth of depravity to which we can all sink, that we do possess an extraordinary capacity for evil" (p. 110). Yet somehow, sitting through overwhelming testimony on the extent of these brutal crimes, a number of victims and their families sought forgiveness. The archbishop believes that without forgiveness we are chained to the past, victims to our victimization. He closes his *No Future without Forgiveness* (1999), with these words: "Our (South African) experiment is going to succeed because God wants us to succeed, not for our glory or aggrandizement but for the sake of God's world. God wants to show us that there is life after conflict and repression – that because of forgiveness, there is a future" (p. 230).

Tibet

In Tibet, many of the monks imprisoned by the Chinese emerged from long years of privation and torture without hatred for their Chinese captors. Remarkably, the monks felt compassion for the circumstances that led the Chinese to behave so brutally, believing that their vicious behavior would haunt their destiny in this life and the next. The Dalai Lama often commends the monk Lopon, who was imprisoned and tortured for 18 years and yet remained gentle and loving. Lopon informed the Dalai Lama that his only fear while imprisoned was losing his compassion for the Chinese (Dalai & Chan, 2004). Like Archbishop Tutu and the other peacemakers mentioned above, the monk Lopon refused to surrender his moral compass or to sink in the miasma of hatred and revenge. Lopon's extraordinary capacity for compassion and forgiveness enabled him to preserve his moral integrity and protect his spiritual fidelity under drastic circumstances.

Rwanda

Joseph Sebarenzi, the former Speaker of the Parliament of Rwanda, a former student, and currently a colleague, uses his own experiences to teach about the potency of forgiveness (Sebarenzi, 2006, personal communication). His losses in the genocide were tragic beyond imagining, including the murder of his parents and almost all his siblings and their families. He now lives in the United States, where he speaks publicly about the long process that took him from anguish, rage, futile denial, and feeling betrayed by God, to practices of prayer and compassion, and finally to reconciliation and forgiveness.

Reflecting on his journey toward forgiveness, Sebarenzi believes that he gained a shift of perspective some years after the genocide by visiting prisons and observing the dismal conditions where accused perpetrators were held. Through this exposure to the suffering of others, he felt the stirrings of compassion, which opened what he calls *the endless grief* in his heart. As his emotions surfaced, Sebarenzi become aware that culturally conditioned prohibitions on displays of emotions for Rwandan men constricted his rage and sorrow. He saw that his inability to express his rage and grief became increasingly detrimental to his physical and mental health and also harmed his children. He called on his deep Christian beliefs for guidance in releasing emotions and letting go of hatred, which led to an interior process of forgiveness that brought peace to himself and his family. Sebarenzi believes that reconciliation and forgiveness are not signs of weakness but of strength; they are his gifts to himself, his children, and future of his country.

Meaning-Making in Reconciliation and Forgiveness

The human story is comprised of narratives mined from observation, experiences, beliefs, and legends, transmitted and embellished through the generations. We are meaning-making creatures and order our lives through these collected wisdom teachings, which provide us with coherence and behavioral guidelines. Tutu and his church, for example, emphasize the practice of forgiveness as a path to healing for grieving victims. The Dalai Lama encourages compassion toward those responsible for violence and destruction. Approaches to reconciliation and forgiveness emerge through these collectively held teachings, and in turn the experiments with reconciling and forgiving reshape the living narratives. Experiences of war and chaos frequently involve changing one's beliefs about the world and the self, resulting in new meanings about life (Park, 2005). Meaning-making thus remains interactive and highly contextual, sometimes adding more layers of nuance and complexity leading to reconciliation and at other times reducing and simplifying events to rationalize hatred and revenge.

Sebarenzi discovered that culturally acquired prohibitions about male behavior in the grieving process intensified his pain. Observing the suffering of the perpetrators in prison shifted his thinking about revenge, moving him to a more nuanced and complex story about forgiveness. In this way his narrative was enlarged and his fundamental understanding of meaning opened up, allowing for a new range of attitudes and ultimately of behaviors. His reinterpretation of the traumatic events is now his legacy to those around him, even those who harmed him. Because Sebarenzi is currently a teacher and public speaker, his capacity to forge new meaning from the ashes of genocide impacts many others, and his new story ripples out into his community.

Massive crimes against humanity such as experienced in the Holocaust, South Africa, Rwanda, Bosnia, and Tibet can destroy normal structures of meaning. Religion provides a powerful source of meaning, especially in drastic circumstances that interrupt the coherence of one's prior experiences and beliefs about safety in the world and trust in others. In crisis situations, even victims not familiar with spiritual teaching may turn inward in their search for understanding (Silberman, 2005). Religious narratives, while enduring, are not necessarily permanent, but rather adapt to changing times and circumstances. Spiritual teachings and practices of reconciliation and forgiveness serve as a feedback loop, offering meaning, changing meaning, and being changed by experience and observation. Tutu's inspirational leadership and his plea for forgiveness for the sake of the future has no doubt influenced and changed religious teaching and the reconciliation and forgiveness paradigm. The Dalai Lama likewise engages the spiritual dimensions of meaning-making in reconciliation, teaching people how to tame hatred and to practice compassion and forgiveness. These practices of forgiveness and compassion benefit both self and others, enriching meaning in one's own life and restoring humanity to others, even the so-called enemies.

Perhaps the most famous commentator on meaning is the well-known author, Holocaust survivor and psychiatrist Viktor Frankl (1984), who wrote in *Man's Search for Meaning*: "We who lived in the concentration camps can remember those who walked through the huts comforting others, giving away their last piece of bread. They may have been few in number but they offer sufficient proof that everything can be taken from us but the last of human freedoms. . .the freedom to choose our spirit in any circumstance" (p. 86). Frankl alleges that meaning can be maintained in the most seemingly meaningless existence and, in fact, may serve as a lifeline to sanity in a world gone insane. Starving concentration camp prisoners who offered their bread to others must have preserved an internal dignity, an active compassion for the suffering of others, and an unfathomable humanity, all of which may have offered meaning to fellow victims as well as some measure of internal coherence.

Restorative justice, as we shall see below, also requires expanding the narrative of meaning, from the common practice of punishing wrong doers to achieve revenge and restore honor, to the practice of rehabilitating and then reintegrating wrong doers back into the human community through a new, reconciling social vision.

Restorative Justice as a Reconciling Process

Restorative justice aims to reinstate the humanity of offenders, to repair rather than punish, to rehabilitate rather than incarcerate, and to mend social connections so that broken communities can renew relationships. Reparative approaches help to build bridges between victims and those who harmed them. Restorative justice may require symbolic or economic reparations as well as acknowledgment and contrition. Fueling the restorative justice movement is the insight that the injustices and abuses embedded in our social structures contribute to antisocial and criminal behavior. At the deepest level, restorative justice calls for social reform to eliminate the sources of violent crime.

Illustrative of restorative justice in its relationship to reconciliation and forgiveness is the story of Amy Biehl, who was a US university student volunteering in the black townships of South Africa during the apartheid years (in Tutu, 1999, pp. 118–121). She was murdered by a small group of young men from that township. Rather than spend their years in bitterness, her parents found the courage and compassion to turn this tragedy into a remarkable story of restorative justice. They established the Amy Biehl Foundation, met the men who murdered their daughter, sought clemency in their sentencing, and helped rehabilitate and develop employment for these men and others in their community. The Biehls believed that acts of restorative justice best honored the legacy of their daughter and offered a model of hope and reconciliation for all those caught in the legacy of apartheid in South Africa.

Similarly, over 300 families whose children have been killed in the Israeli–Palestinian conflict met together as the Bereaved Families' Forum (www.mideastweb.org/bereaved_families_forum.htm). Members recognize the pull of revenge, but relinquish vengeance in favor of sharing their grief with families from all sides of the conflict who have lost children. This organization has had an impact in Israel and Palestine, where there are currently very few circumstances for shared mourning and endless opportunities for blame and recrimination. Likewise, Families of Peaceful Tomorrows (www peacefultomorrows.org), a group of Americans who lost loved ones on September 11, 2001, extends support to Afghan and Iraqi citizens. Their members have turned loss and bitterness into acts of reconciliation, receiving in turn greater meaning and new purpose through their losses. They take their name from Dr. Martin Luther King Jr.'s reflection: *Wars are poor chisels for carving out peaceful tomorrows* (Families for Peaceful Tomorrows).

The restorative justice demonstrated by the Amy Biehl family, the Bereaved Families Forum, and the Families of Peaceful Tomorrows rejects punishment and revenge as a response to violence. Members of these groups convert their suffering into the service of peace, promoting awareness of our common humanity and the futility of retribution.

Expanding the Circle of Compassion

In the Amy Biehl story, the parents of their murdered daughter grew in compassion toward her murderers and their families, recognizing that these young men and their community were victims of the apartheid regime. Sebarenzi's story of visiting Hutu prisoners accused of genocide likewise awakened his compassion, opening him to a renewed life of forgiveness and reconciliation. Lopon, the imprisoned Tibetan monk, maintained compassion for his Chinese jailers and tormenters. Compassion, the capacity to feel the suffering of others, may serve as the gateway to reconciliation and forgiveness, opening the heart to new dimensions. Although the ability to feel compassion for one's torturers is a rarified phenomenon, requiring an almost transcendent state of mind, compassion itself can be consciously cultivated and nourished.

In the CONTACT (Conflict Transformation Across Cultures) Summer Peace-building Institute that I direct at the School for International Training in Vermont, each year in June we gather 60–75 participants from around the world for a month of exploring the causes and consequences of peace, war, and reconciliation (Green, 2002). Many of our participants have witnessed or personally survived communal violence, frequently directed at their particular religious, ethnic, racial, or national groups. Some have been victims of mass violence, enduring great loss. Others belong to groups who committed atrocities; some were bystanders or, less frequently, rescuers. Many arrive filled with hatred for the identified *other* and hold stereotypes and prejudices against Americans, Muslims, Christians, Africans, and many others who they have never met and toward whom compassion would seem impossible.

However, within a few weeks these participants are approaching what Dr. Martin Luther King Jr. frequently called *the beloved community*, full of empathy, understanding, and joy in each other's presence. CONTACT shapes new insights into the reality of multiple and overlapping identities and the value of tolerance and diversity. Students absorb powerful lessons about cycles of revenge and the disasters that result from generations of endless prejudices and injustice. Differences in historical context shrink in the face of overwhelming evidence of a shared human bond. Profound personal changes and shifts in worldview ripple through the learning community. Group members expand their loyalties from their own identity group to the global commons, including even those who have caused them harm in the circle of life. An environment that affirms both the distinctions of identities and the universality of shared humanity helps nurture compassion and reconciliation.

Granted, these participants are not in direct competition for scarce resources or positions of power, nor do they command armies or votes. None are current warriors, although some have seen combat. Nonetheless, their experience stands as testimony to the power of personal witness and exchange in the reconciliation process, where the capacity of one to forgive motivates another who is not yet ready, leading to increased change through mutual encouragement, example, and inspiration. Group members who have risked and encountered each other at deep levels, celebrated and grieved together, and experienced a reconciling community have savored an undreamed-of reality. A vision of another world has been touched, one that will guide their future choices and actions as peace leaders in their communities (Green, 2002).

Stages in the Journey of Reconciliation and Forgiveness

In regions suffering from recent violent conflict, an atmosphere of silence frequently prevents any public conversations about mass violence and its traumatic legacy. Because speaking of the past feels dangerous and may indeed be life threatening, particular skill and sensitivity is essential for those who are invited to help a community move toward recovery and future reconciliation. In the next section we will explore a social healing program in Bosnia, undertaken at the invitation of Bosnian Muslims just a few years after the 1995 Dayton Accord that officially ended the war in Bosnia.

Working as a peacebuilder in war-torn societies, I have been humbled by the daunting tasks confronting both the wounded and the aggressors in binding their own pain as well as finding repair, justice, and healing for their communities. From 1997 to 2002, I taught conflict transformation and facilitated dialogues for educators from two cities in northern Bosnia: Sanski Most and Prijedor (Green, 2000a). This region of Bosnia, formerly of mixed ethnicity, became an epicenter of agonizing ethnic conflict between 1992 and 1995. Betrayal by neighbors and colleagues shattered basic human trust, caused profound trauma, and left the victim community of Bosnian Muslims devastated.

Karuna Center was invited by some courageous Bosnian Muslim residents to guide the first steps in the social healing process, first with women and later with educators. There were few building blocks upon which to establish relationships and restore any semblance of community, and introducing the vocabulary of reconciliation and forgiveness would have felt like an inappropriate affront to their reality in those first postwar years. With our Bosnian colleagues, we created a program of intercommunal dialogue for educators called *Projekt Dijakom*, the Project for Dialogue and Community Building in Bosnia. As outsiders, we provided a safe connection between Muslim and Serb communities for coexistence measures and trust to emerge slowly and in keeping with participants' readiness and comfort. After

6 years of facilitated dialogue and training, the Bosnian participants established their own peace-building organizations.

Acknowledgment

The first and most critical step in reconciliation, as I observed in the Bosnian process, is acknowledgment from the perpetrator group to the victims that wrong has been done. Acknowledgment is the cornerstone upon which apology, remorse, reparations, and reconciliation can be built. While extremely difficult for members of perpetrating communities, acknowledgment is essential for victims, allowing them to feel that violators and bystanders at least recognize their losses and grief. The Bosnian educators' group was composed of both Muslim victims of the 1990's genocide and Bosnian Serbs, whose community carried out the genocide. Although none of the Serbs in our group had been directly involved as perpetrators, the Muslim survivors needed the Serb participants to acknowledge the genocide committed in their name. To the extent that Serb participants did not directly and fully acknowledge the 1990's genocide or rationalized it as a response to past wrongs, progress in the dialogue remained thwarted.

Complicating the circumstances in Bosnia, there is a long history of mutual oppression and mistreatment, with the result that perpetrator groups confounded the past and the present, in a sense taking refuge in historical grievances. Others have documented this tendency to merge the past and present and thereby cast blame rather than accept responsibility. "What seems apparent in the former Yugoslavia is that the past continues to torment because it is not the past. . ... Reporters in the Balkan Wars often observed that when they were told atrocity stories they were occasionally uncertain whether these stories had occurred yesterday or in 1941, 1841 or 1441" (Ignatieff in Minow, 1998, p. 14). In the struggle against painful acknowledgment of wrongdoing, recalling one's historic victimhood displaces more recent realities and serves as psychological protection against the atrocities committed in one's name.

For the Serb educators, acknowledgment evoked shame and guilt about their own bystander status and the war crimes committed by their ethnic group. Serb group members thus frequently attempted to equalize responsibility for the genocide among all ethnic groups. Gobodo-Madikizela (2003) writes about the same pattern in post-apartheid South Africa, and I have observed this phenomenon in the Caucasus and other Balkan countries. I believe this behavior springs from a desire to distance from those parts of one's identity that have been shamed by the debauched behavior of members of one's ethnic, religious, or national reference group.

Perhaps one specific case can illustrate the enormous hurdle that acknowledgment can present. During 3 days in 1992, 58,000 Muslim residents had been forcibly expelled from their homes in their previously well-integrated city. Many were killed and some raped; many were taken to camps, others put on busses at gunpoint for points unknown, their homes exploded or torched behind them. Eight years and many structured dialogues later, when we were training an advanced group to become peace-building facilitators themselves, one of our more skilled Serb participants spoke of the expulsion of the Muslim community as the time the Muslims *left*, or *migrated*. Her choice of words, misrepresenting and denying the Muslim experience of expulsion, had serious consequences within the group. The failure to acknowledge the misfortunes of the Muslim community created a wall of separation between participants, each group retreating behind its particular wounds. Although they worked long and hard to overcome the damage of that moment, the breach could not fully be repaired.

We can see this same need for acknowledgment on the part of many women who have been battered at home or raped on the streets, through Holocaust survivors in the One by One dialogue groups, and with family members who have been hurt by each other emotionally. In the United States, there has never been a presidential acknowledgment or sufficient national dialogue on the evils of slavery or the genocide of the Native Americans (Minow, 1998). In its absence, the histories and suffering of descendants of victims remain unrecognized. A classic example is the Ottoman Turkish Genocide of Armenians, mentioned elsewhere in this volume. Despite consistent Armenian organizing and protest, the Turkish government has not yet acknowledged the reality of this early 20th century genocide, a denial that harms descendants as well as the international community in its quest to establish truthful accounts of the past.

As the leader of South Africa's TRC, Archbishop Tutu has learned more than most human beings about the journey toward national and communal healing. He writes powerfully about the role of acknowledgment in the reconciliation process and of the forgiveness and compensation that may flow in its own time if acknowledgment is present:

> If we are going to move on and build a new kind of world community there must be a way to deal with our sordid past. The most effective way I know is for the perpetrators or their descendants to acknowledge the horror of what happened and the descendants of the victims to respond by granting the forgiveness they ask for, providing something can be done, even symbolically, to compensate for the anguish experienced, whose consequences are still being lived through today. (Tutu, 1999, p. 226)

As members of perpetrating groups acknowledge the atrocities committed in their name or by their fellow community members, relationships between perpetrators and victims become more authentic. When the acknowledgment comes from religious or political leaders, the impact increases. "To give the vocabulary (of reconciliation) greater permanence and lend it a multiplier effect throughout the larger society, it needs to be reinforced at the level of political leadership" (Gobodo-Madikizela, 2003, p. 132). Unfortunately, political leaders accountable for the decisions leading to communal violence seldom accept responsibility for the consequent mass atrocities. Additionally, the admission and possible apology offered may be more expedient than heartfelt and may carry no obligations. Genuine acknowledgment of wrongdoing by political and religious leaders should be encouraged, as it sets a behavioral example, assigns responsibility, and may promote a moral tone for the reconciliation process.

The Role of Apology

In the best of circumstances, apology would follow acknowledgment. Sincere apology expresses regrets or remorse for the injury done and responsibility for one's own role either as violator or as bystander. Truth is such a relief, both for victim and for violator, setting the stage for apology and enabling the individual or the community to look back together at past suffering and its causes. In our interpersonal relationships, genuine apology allows love to flow again; it releases both parties from the gloom of withholding love while nursing our private hurt. It seems to me that apology is a two-way gift; we benefit both when we offer and when we receive apology.

In Rwanda's *gacaca* (ga-cha-cha, or grassroots) process of community justice, some prisoners offer what seem to be lightweight apologies in hopes of gaining release from prison, but these pseudo-apologies are roundly rejected by the community of victims, who sense the presence or absence of genuine spiritual remorse, sorrow, and repentance (Neuffer, 2001). In our Bosnia dialogues, Milka, a Serb educator, broke ranks with her ethnic group, challenged the silence, and offered sincere and repeated apologies to the Muslim group members, who in turn expressed their profound gratitude and extended their hands in friendship. The Bosnian Muslims could reach out to Milka because they trusted the earnestness of her apology. Ties between Milka and the Muslim participants have remained strong because of this critical experience; relations between the other Serbs and the Muslim participants never reached such a high level of trust, as there had been no full, remorseful, and direct apology.

Apology, in a way, is a mysterious process. All of us have given and received apologies for various wrongs. Apologies play a role even in small hurts, touching the heart and melting the distance created by the offense. After mass violence, any apology is inevitably inadequate and can in no way match the scale of the suffering and humiliation experienced by victims. And yet, even in extreme circumstances, the spirit of apology matters and may help the healing journey. "Apology speaks to something larger than any particular offense and works its magic by a kind of speech that cannot be contained or understood merely in terms of expediency or the desire to achieve reconciliation" (Tavuchis in Minow, 1998, p. 91).

Apology is relational, requiring an offering and a response. The victims must acquire and retain the power to accept, reject, or otherwise respond to the apology (Minow, 1998). There is much debate in the professional field of reconciliation about the viability of apologies from the second generation of violators to the second generation of survivors. Some argue that the apology–forgiveness process can only occur between victims and their aggressors while others recognize the efficacy of even belated, next-generation apologies, as they attempt to right the historical record and speak for the larger community. In the One-by-One dialogue group discussed earlier, second-generation apology seems to have had a significant impact. "Members of the victim side often hear the profound apologies they have waited a lifetime to hear, and members of the perpetrator side often meet descendants of victims for the first time and hear from them that they are not to blame for atrocities committed by their parents, grandparents, and countrymen" (www.one-by-one.org).

My own observations from years of intercommunal teaching in postwar communities is that silence in the face of atrocities is both offensive to the victims, in that they continue to feel unseen and insignificant, and dangerous for the society, as there is no moral standard for righting wrongs. Belated, sincere apologies, it seems to me, are better than never speaking of a shameful past.

Commitment and Action

After apology, then what? Is that the end of the story? In mass violence, apology is essential but does not signify the end of the process. What will prevent the perpetrators from repeating the crime? How do we know this community remorse is genuine? What would help to restore trust in the other side? After apology must come attention to the rule of law and commitment from the aggressor side not to repeat the transgression. In Bosnia, for example, war criminals remain on the loose, and Bosnian Muslims fear that when the UN peacekeepers and human rights monitors leave, which will happen someday, they will once again be unsafe (Neuffer, 2001). This fear is more than the voice of trauma speaking; it is the voice that has known international neglect and local deficiency in both political will and economic resources. The lack of acknowledgment, the absence of remorse, the failed commitment to a new future, and the inattention to the rule of law leave Bosnia divided, fragile, and dangerous. None of the four recommendations cited earlier in this chapter by Amnesty International has been accomplished: the truth has not been established; the law is weak; processes are not transparent; and there is no right to compensation.

During the Israeli–Palestinian dialogues in the Oslo years of the 1990s before the second *Intifada*, I observed another challenge of intercommunal restoration (Green, 2000b). For the Palestinians, dialogue was an instrumental activity to help their community attain freedom and human rights. As such, they expected their Israeli dialogue partners to join them in their political struggle for justice. For the Israelis in the group, on the other hand, dialogue was an interpersonal process that helped them build relationships with Palestinians and partially assuage their guilt as part of a society that oppressed Palestinians. The Israelis resisted public demonstration of political solidarity with Palestinians, which greatly frustrated their Palestinian counterparts and reduced their faith in the Israeli group as partners in the struggle. Acknowledgment and apology by the aggressor group, without action and visible commitment to redress injustices, can seem insufficient and relatively empty to communities who feel oppressed.

Victims expect the aggressor community to probe the causes of the genocide or mass violence and deal with its war criminals. They must feel partnered in the restoration of justice and observe that spiritual and political leaders on the aggressor side are engaged in a full process of introspection and repentance. In the former

Yugoslavia, this has not yet happened, leaving the victim communities unsettled, anxious, and certainly mistrustful (Neuffer, 2001).

A major study directed by Croatian peace psychologist Dr. Dinka Corkalo (in Stover and Weinstein, Eds, 2004) investigates three formerly well-integrated cities in the former Yugoslavia: Vukovar in Croatia and Mostar and Prijedor in Bosnia. (As the reader will recall, Prijedor is one of the cities where the Bosnian dialogues described earlier took place.) The Corkalo study found that 10 years after the mass atrocities in these cities, there is almost no reintegration of populations and great resistance to the restoration of intercommunal relations. Corkalo observed sharp divisions along ethnic lines among former friends and neighbors, with superficial relations replacing multicultural friendships. Deep distrust appears to have created insurmountable barriers to social recuperation. The process of acknowledgment and repair has barely begun and victims do not feel protected by any legal mechanisms. Corkalo observes,

> The three most apparent forms of group self-deception among our participants were denial of what happened during the war, biased memories of the events or embellishment of particular historical episodes, and the downplaying of war crimes committed by members of their own national group. These manifestations of group self-deception offer fertile ground for building national myths instead of national history. (Stover & Weinstein, Eds, 2004, p. 149)

For any change to occur in this frozen post-conflict condition, Corkalo recommends that four levels of social reconstruction be planned and monitored to occur simultaneously from the top down and bottom up. These should include individual recuperation from trauma; renewal of communal networks; new civic and economic initiatives; and the establishment of the rule of law with guaranteed security (2004, p. 159). In the absence of these measures, there is little hope for healing in the Balkans.

Reparations in the Reconciliation Process

Economic or symbolic reparations serve as a vital chain in the process of social rebuilding after mass violence. Victims have rights of compensation, which in no way should close the books on the issue or block further examination of the moral and legal implications of the violence. Avoidance or engagement to reparations reflects on the commitment of individuals and their governments to express remorse and redress past wrongs. Some leaders may resist offering a national apology for fear that it would lead to demands for reparations, which many people believe to be the case in the United States' lack of apology to descendants of slaves and to Native Americans (Minow, 1998).

In Rwanda, reparations take the form of communal services performed by released prisoners who have confessed their sins at community *gacaca* trials. Prisoners are returned to the very place where they participated in the genocide: they build homes for families devastated by genocide, construct schools and health clinics, or work the land (Neuffer, 2001). In Germany, reparations have been paid to individual Holocaust survivors or their descendants, as well as to the Israeli government. Not every government or institution agrees to offer reparations. Swiss banks, for example, have contested reparations to Holocaust victims. Many European countries, including some who fought with Germany, have not compensated victims or their families. Bosnia has no structural process for addressing this issue, nor do the other former Yugoslav states. It took Japanese-Americans 30 years of legislative battle to receive compensation from the US government for the loss of their homes seized in WWII when they were interred, and the compensation was considered quite inadequate by survivors (Minow, 1998).

Compensation is complicated. No compensation ever repairs the loss and betrayal, the suffering and endless nightmares, the lifetime spent without loved ones or trust in humanity. Mental and physical health often cannot be restored. And yet, reparations offer a token of care and connection, of economic or psychological help, especially in the context of remorse and contrition, and with assurance that the violence will never be repeated. Compensation allows victims and their descendants to feel visible and *to walk between vengeance and forgiveness* (Minow, 1998, p. 106).

Compensation demanded of descendants of perpetrators can fuel resentment and embitter future generations. Why should second- or third-generation post-Holocaust Germans pay for the sins of previous generations? Why should today's white Americans compensate African-Americans for slavery? We can look at the negative responses to affirmative action, a form of group compensation in the United States for denied opportunity, to see both the need and the challenges of delayed reparations. In South Africa, monetary compensation has not been forthcoming to victims as pledged, causing anger among young generations of victim families. In most cases, victims have asked for modest financial redress, such as for medical or educational expenses, yet these requests are often denied. The refusal to grant even such a token gesture has soured some survivor families to the reconciliation process.

Symbolic reparations also aid the restorative process. Museums, monuments, memorials, public literary and artworks, days of commemoration, new historical narratives, and revised history books can all play a role in re-humanization and national healing (Minow, 1998). I find it revealing that the most visited monument in Washington DC is the haunting Vietnam Memorial Wall, symbol of America's brokenness and unhealed national wounds. I shudder to think about Iraq in the context of the Vietnam Wall, yet someday the painful lessons of the Iraq War will also need to be acknowledged and memorialized.

Forging a Joint Future After Mass Violence

So far we have reflected on acknowledgment, apology, atonement and remorse, restorative justice, tangible commitment to not repeating the offense, and reparations in responding to mass violence, all steps in the long journey toward reconciliation and forgiveness. There is one final stage: forging a joint future after mass violence. Both victim and aggressor groups must cooperate to establish a just and mutually satisfying relationship. The victims, or their descendants, for this often takes many generations, are ready to reengage with the perpetrator group or their descendants. For the victims, this signifies that the apologies and atonement, the reparations and commitments have been sufficiently genuine and trustworthy. The victim group must firmly reject attempts to avenge the deaths of their ancestors. For the aggressor group, reengagement requires their pledge to be trustworthy to those they have harmed.

Most groups must live side by side after mass conflict, as there are no empty spaces on this planet. We see the suffering that ensued in Palestine from believing that there was empty land to be dispensed to people who had no safe homeland. To live together as neighboring countries, such as in the former Yugoslavia, or as one country such as in South Africa, Rwanda, or Northern Ireland, enemy groups must become collaborators in sharing land, water, borders, government, and citizenship. Fairly administered programs of justice, equality, and reconciliation effect stability and promote peace. Where there is no full restorative process, no re-humanization or rapprochement, the lack of healing may lead over time down the dark path of counter-revenge, where victims and perpetrators, in the same or reverse roles, reengage in communal violence.

Reconciliation is fragile, and post-conflict mistrust lives on in the narrative of victims and their descendants. Similarly, fear of revenge remains in the minds of aggressors and their descendants. Trust must be given and earned by every generation. Mutual regard must be repeatedly expressed and demonstrated. Human relations must be cultivated actively lest we slide into greed-driven or fear-driven separation fueled by the ambitions of ruthless leaders tugging on the sentimental walls of nationalism and ethnic identity. Each of us is vulnerable to the seductions of demagogues and to the illusion of separateness. Our task as a human family is to monitor our own fallibility, to recognize that each of us is both victim and violator, and to acknowledge that the journey of reconciliation and forgiveness always awaits us. "Our survival depends on a significant portion of the human race accomplishing a change in worldview, from patriotic and tribal loyalties to loyalty to life itself" (Green, 2002, p. 105).

References

Bereaved Families' Forum. Available at http://www.mideastweb.org/bereaved_families_forum.htm

Bronkhorst, D. (1995). *Truth and reconciliation: Obstacles and opportunities for human rights.* Amsterdam, Netherlands: Amnesty International Dutch Section.

Dalai, L., & Chan, V. (2004). *The wisdom of forgiveness: Intimate journeys and conversations.* New York: Riverhead Books.

Families for Peaceful Tomorrows. Available at www.peacefultomorrows.org

Frankl, V. (1984). *Man's search for meaning.* New York: Touchstone Books.

Gobodo-Madikizela, P. (2003). *A human being died that night: A South African story of forgiveness.* Boston: Houghton Mifflin.

Green, P. (2000a). For a future to be possible: Bosnian dialogue in the aftermath of war. *Journal of Medicine, Conflict, and Survival, 16*(4) 441–450.

Green, P. (2000b). Shadows and light: Encounters in the holy land. *Journal of Medicine, Conflict, and Survival, 16*(4), 434–440.

Green, P. (2002). CONTACT: Training a new generation of peacebuilders. *Peace and Change, 27*(1).

Kornfield, J. (2002). *The art of forgiveness, loving-kindness and peace.* New York: Bantam Books.

Minow, M. (1998). *Between vengeance and forgiveness.* Boston: Beacon Press.

Neuffer, E. (2001). *The key to my neighbor's house: Seeking justice in Bosnia and Rwanda.* New York: Picador Books.

Nouwen, H. (1972). *The wounded healer.* New York: Doubleday Books.

One by One. *Dialogue among descendants of survivors, perpetrators, bystanders and resisters.* Available at <www.one-by-one.org>

Park, C. (2005). Religion as a meaning-making framework in coping with life stresses. *Journal of Social Issues, 61*(4).

Sebarenzi, J. (2006). Interview by the author. Brattleboro, Vermont.

Silberman, I. (2005). Religion as a meaning system: Implications for the new millennium. *Journal of Social Issues, 61*(4).

Stover, E., & Weinstein, H. (Eds.). (2004). *My neighbor, my enemy: Justice and community in the aftermath of mass atrocity.* Cambridge, UK: Cambridge University Press.

Tutu, D. (1999). *No future without forgiveness.* New York: Doubleday, A Division of Random House Inc.

Chapter 17
Dialogue, Forgiveness, and Reconciliation

Barbara S. Tint

The individuals in the room sat silently facing one another for a long time. The former relationships within the group seemed to dissolve, as for the moment, the group members became only Arabs and Jews, polarized in their experiences, beliefs and desires. Among the feelings in the room, the predominant ones were surprise and betrayal; how could this well-meaning group of peace-oriented descendants of the Middle East find themselves so mired in the polarization they had come together to analyze and heal? How could the good intentions have gone bad? How could they have gone from perceived partners to felt enemies? And where could they/should they go from here?

So goes the difficult work of dialogue, the process by which members of differing groups come together with the hope of increasing understanding and transforming deep-rooted issues of conflict. It is rarely a smooth road; there is no formulaic path to understanding, forgiveness, or reconciliation. In most cases, dialogue requires people to encounter painful feelings that have polarized them for so long and to face themselves and others in ways that lead to new perceptions and relationships. In many historically conflicted communities, dialogue processes are often used to provide safe and structured dimensions to reconciliation among fractured parties. This chapter will explore both the theoretical and practical dimensions of dialogue as a tool in forgiveness and reconciliation and a particular case study where dialogue has served as a platform for moving conflicted parties forward at the intergroup level.

Principles of Dialogue

Derived from the Greek term *dialogos* –*dia* meaning "through" and *logos* meaning "the word" – dialogue speaks to the flow of connection and exchange through words. At its most fundamental, dialogue refers to parties coming together with the goal of increased mutual understanding. Though dialogue can occur between individuals or groups of random parties, in peace-building work, it is most commonly used as an intergroup process between members of conflicted societies. One definition suggests

Ani Kalayjian, Raymond F. Paloutzian, *Forgiveness and Reconciliation*, Peace Psychology Book Series, DOI 10.1007/978-1-4419-0181-1_17,
© Springer Science+Business Media, LLC 2009

that intergroup dialogue is "a form of democratic practice, engagement, problem solving, and education involving face-to-face, focused, facilitated and confidential discussions occurring over time between two or more groups of people defined by their different social identities" (Schoem, Hurtado, Sevig, Chesler, & Sumida, 2001, p. 6). Harold Saunders, one of the most influential scholars on this topic, suggests that dialogue is "a process of genuine *inter* action through which human beings listen to each other deeply enough to be changed by what they learn" (1999, p. 82). Dialogue processes derive from contact theory (Allport, 1954), which proposes that one of the most successful ways to reduce intergroup conflict, prejudice, and enmity is positive intergroup contact. The goal is that through contact experiences, parties are able to shift the relationship of enmity and reduce the dynamic of competing social identities.

While many groups, particularly within indigenous communities, have long used dialogue as a means by which to deal with group conflict, recent decades have shown an increase in the use of structured dialogue as a peace-building tool. Today, in fractious communities worldwide, dialogue is implemented at different stages of societal fissures to create possibilities for movement and transformation. It can be used while conflict and structural divisions are still very much alive, as is the case in Cyprus (Volkan & Itzkowitz, 1994) and Israel/Palestine (Abu-Nimer, 1999; Kelman, 2001; Reich & Halabi, 2004). It is often used in a post-conflict phase where rebuilding and reconciliation are the main tasks of a fractured society as is the case in South Africa or Rwanda (Villa-Vicencio & Savage, 2001) and the Balkans (Botcharova, 2001). Or dialogue processes can be utilized long after a conflict is over but where enduring emotional scars survive into future generations, as is the case with dialogue between descendants of Holocaust survivors and Nazi perpetrators (Bar-On, 1999, 2006; Busse, Emme, Gerut, & Lapidus, 1999). In some cases, dialogue occurs between groups that live in coexistence such as the Tamils and Sinhalese in Sri Lanka (Stokes & Green, 2002), differing factions in Northern Ireland (Fitzduff, 2001; White, 2003), and interracial communities in the United States (Day, Bernard, & Smith, 1999; Hubbard, 2001) or with groups that have minimal contact beyond the dialogue process itself, as with participants in Korean/Japanese reconciliation efforts (Hundt & Bleiker, 2007).

In addition to being a tool used in different phases of a conflict cycle, dialogue can also be effective at multiple levels of intervention. It has been used successfully within official governmental contexts, unofficial Track II arenas, and grassroots community groups. While useful at any phase, dialogue has been used primarily at the Track II and the grassroots levels; while governments negotiate peace treaties, citizens are left to do the healing work that rebuilds communities. While there are often cases of "representative forgiveness" where a leader extends the olive branch in an attempt to move a society forward, this top-down approach can backfire and does not allow for citizen healing if there is no investment and participation on the part of the community. These processes are difficult to execute at the community level even when political agreements have been reached. In societies where there has been history of trauma and conflict, the concepts of reconciliation and forgiveness can be overwhelming; the ability for whole groups to forgive and reconcile is challenging and often elusive. Dialogue work conducted at the grassroots level can allow for reconciliation processes to impact large numbers of people over long periods of time so that official decisions are more successfully integrated and accepted among communities in conflict. It is a tool that is essential in bringing different levels of peace processes together to heal a fractured society.

Within both the content and the process of dialogue, relationship is the focal point for transformation among conflicted parties (Lederach, 1997; Saunders, 1999; Schoem et al., 2001). An intentional process that seeks to create deep understanding and transformative experiences for group members, dialogue provides a structure in which parties explore how their thoughts, emotions, consciousness, beliefs, and narratives diverge and how they come together. According to Saunders (1999), relationship combines a variety of elements: *identity, interdependent coexistence of needs and interests, nature and working of effective power, and limits on behavior and evolving perceptions.* Each of these elements is significantly impacted during long-term conflict and must be addressed in its healing. Dialogue focuses on the transformative possibilities within these elements and addresses each of them in the process of intergroup engagement. Additionally, Ellinor and Gerard (1998) identify four essential and interrelated qualities of dialogue work: suspension of judgment, suspension of assumptions, listening, and inquiry and reflection. Through these processes, there is an emphasis on vulnerability rather than strategy, transparency rather than protection, and curiosity rather than conclusion.

Because dialogue is a reflective and reflexive process, participants are invited to reconsider their experiences in ways that allow for new constructs to emerge. Bohm (1996) suggests that dialogue involves the evolution of a new culture among participants, where meaning becomes more important than truth and members of a dialogue process develop shared meaning around emerging issues. The concept of meaning systems (Park, 2005; Park & Folkman, 1997) suggests that at the very core of human existence is the need to find meaning and value in life. Global meaning systems – beliefs, values, goals, feelings – are typically constructed unwittingly on the part of group members so that a group culture develops in deep and often unconscious ways. In societies where there has been collective trauma, the process of meaningless often occurs when trust, beliefs, or values are violated. Meaning-making becomes the process by which individuals and groups set about trying to restore meaning after a trauma and it is through dialogue that meaning-making can occur in safe and transformative ways.

Types of Dialogue

While the use of dialogue in different contexts has certain shared principles, as outlined above, there are variations to its practice as well. These include differences in group goals, participant numbers, process duration, meeting frequency, facilitator roles, content or process focus, and post-dialogue follow-up options. Zuniga and Nagda (2001) divide dialogue processes into four general types: *collective inquiry,* a process by which groups attempt to find shared meaning and synergistic relationships through collective thinking and discourse; *critical-dialogical education*, a focus on consciousness raising and looking at group differences from a social justice perspective toward the goal of individual and systemic change; *community building and social action*, a process that attempts to bring large numbers of people together around community issues needing attention and mobilization; and *conflict resolution and peace-building* processes where group members in conflicted societies come together to look at new ways to approach the conflict and deal with the substantive and the psychological issues embedded in the situation. These models often overlap and will all typically pass through certain general process stages including setting an environment, developing a common base, exploring questions and issues, and moving from dialogue to action.

As we consider dialogue between groups mired in historical grievances, it is primarily in the realm of conflict resolution and peace building that we focus our attention. This form of dialogue differs from other kinds of dialogue in a number of ways. First, these processes are often laden with more traumatic and emotional content than those rooted in other issues. While it is not to be confused with therapy, dialogue of this nature does have a therapeutic and healing component that is not as fundamental to other intergroup processes. Second, in most dialogue work associated with reconciliation, the fracture between groups is rooted squarely in the past. While any dialogue process will focus on certain dimensions of the past, dialogue around painful and conflicted histories demands that parties address past injuries as a primary focus of what has brought them together. Third, in peace-building work, groups are brought together as a way of dealing with larger societal issues that impact almost all members of the groups. Members are attempting to simultaneously process both personal and structural dimensions of a pervasive phenomenon that they are often unable to influence; the focus then is on the individual experience of these large-scale issues. Last, while some dialogue processes tend to develop spontaneously through what arises between parties when they come together with dialogic intent, dialogue work in deeply fractured societies typically requires a more focused or structured process to serve as a safe container for the deeply challenging issues that arise in the encounter.

One form of structured dialogue is called interactive problem solving (IPS) pioneered by Kelman (1997, 1999) and Fisher (2001) and has been implemented in multiple contexts including Northern Ireland, Cyprus, Israel/Palestine, Afghanistan, Cambodia, and the Horn of Africa. IPS is an intergroup process whereby unofficial representatives of conflicted groups come together for several days of dialogue and problem solving around a protracted national conflict. The facilitators of these workshops – typically academics or other social scientists – structure the process toward greater mutual understanding between parties, strengthened relationships, increased trust, new perspectives on old problems, and de-escalation of entrenched and polarizing positions. Because the participants in these workshops are not officials, the goal is not to reach a formal agreement; however, because they are often influential citizens, they can return to their domains and offer new perspectives toward shifts in their communities. Furthermore, participants in IPS workshops often later move into official positions where they can have a greater impact on national decisions by offering analyses, recommendations, and strategies derived from the dialogue.

While reconciliation and forgiveness are not necessarily stated goals of these dialogue processes, there are several dimensions to this work that create space for them to arise. First, there is a shared walk through history (Montville, 1993, 2001) with an emphasis on acknowledging grievances, accepting responsibility, and expressing contrition. Acknowledging differing narratives of group histories is an essential element of finding other, more mutually acceptable narratives to replace the ones mired in enmity. Another core element is the telling of personal stories of loss; whereas political or national stories tend to reinforce polarization, personal stories allow participants to hear and understand each other's pain and fear in very different ways (Tint, in press). Additionally, these encounters provide a forum for participants to spend informal and personal time together, thus making it more difficult for parties to maintain enemy images of each other. Through these dimensions of the process, new ways of considering old problems emerge.

Saunders (1999) has developed a model of dialogue based on his many years of experience in interethnic conflict situations. What he dubs a "public peace process" is very much rooted in the utilization of citizen peace building as a way to address long-term fractures in divided societies. Particularly, his work centers around citizen dialogue groups held during and following parallel processes occurring at the official level. Saunders' model centers around five stages: (1) *deciding to engage* includes overcoming resistance to interacting with the other, offering a commitment to the process, and defining guidelines for the dialogue; (2) *mapping and naming problems and relationships* includes each side sharing its experiences of loss, their historical narratives, and identifying the issues as they see them; (3) *probing problems and relationships to choose a direction* is a deeper exploration of the issues that emerge and a sense of where parties want to go with them; (4) *scenario building – experiencing a changing relationship* is a stage where parties begin to actually experience a shift in their relationship and move from opposing groups to joint problem solvers; and (5) *acting together to make change happen* is where participants develop the ideas generated in stage four toward action. While these stages provide a framework for dialogue, they do not suggest a linear process; Saunders acknowledges that these stages are fluid and circular and develop in ways that are dependent on the context and population.

Within all of these types of dialogue, there are key dimensions that inform the process. Of greatest importance is establishing willingness of the participants. While there will naturally be some level of resistance, participants must be motivated and feel assured in the safety of the experience. Once safety is established, as participants share their histories and experiences there is also the sharing of pain, loss, and fear. As parties revisit these difficult emotions, increased polarization and impasses can occur. It is in these moments that transformative opportunities arise; as parties have their pain witnessed *and* acknowledged by the other, the possibility of moving through the impasse emerges. Parties can then consider their circumstances through new eyes and explore alternatives for the future that may have previously been beyond their capacity to see. As participants look toward the future, follow-up can take the form of education, social action, therapeutic support, or continued contact experiences. The rocky road toward reconciliation has begun.

Forgiveness and Reconciliation Through Dialogue

The relationship between forgiveness and reconciliation is well documented (Auerbach, 2004; Gopin, 2001; Helmick & Peterson, 2001) and while the complexities of this relationship are not the focus of this chapter, certain salient issues within this dynamic are key to our understanding these processes as they relate to dialogue. While forgiveness is typically regarded as an internal process for those who have suffered injury or trauma, reconciliation is seen as a process where parties come together to repair injured relationships and fractious histories. Therefore, forgiveness work may not necessitate dialogue, but reconciliation will almost always require some space in which parties come together to heal the past and imagine a different future.

Dialogue is well aligned with forgiveness and reconciliation in a number of ways. Reconciliation is a process, like dialogue, which focuses on relationship as the transformative dimension in peace building (Bloomfield, Barnes, & Huyse, 2003; Kriesberg, 1998; Lederach, 1997). Lederach suggests that reconciliation is a place of encounter and acknowledgment, where past and future meet; dialogue is a practical manifestation of this concept of encounter and provides the link in the present between past and future. Forgiveness and reconciliation are also seen as both processes and outcomes (Bar-Tal & Bennink, 2004; Lederach, 1997) rooted in a depth of exploration that transcends typical peace-making processes. Dialogue supports this exploration through its intensive nature and transformational possibilities.

Through the experience of long-term traumas, groups develop societal beliefs about the other that perpetuate fractures in societies. These beliefs are typically accompanied by emotions, values, and perceptions of the other that are often as intractable as the conflict that informed them. Therefore, any effort toward reconciliation and forgiveness must attempt to shift these beliefs so that not only forgiveness of past events, but the possibility for a new future as well is possible. This shifting of relationship must happen on the emotional as well as the intellectual levels; the reconstruction of meaning and identity occurs when there is deep movement around the issues that have brought parties together.

Within dialogue, it is the humanization of the other that allows the fractured past to emerge into a different vision of the future. Reconciliation work is deeply rooted around issues of identity and the emergence of new identities developed through the process (Halabi, 2004; Hicks, 2001; Kelman, 2004). As a large majority of communal conflicts worldwide are assessed to be identity-based (Rasmussen, 1997; Rothman, 1997), exploring issues of identity through dialogue is key to finding paths toward forgiveness and reconciliation. In identity-based conflicts, one of the core elements that contributes to the entrenchment and polarization impeding reconciliation is the manifestation of a zero-sum perception of identity on the part of social groups (Hicks, 2001; Kelman, 2001, 2004). Parties often feel that the very survival of their own group or identity is inextricably tied up with the negation of the other – that the two literally cannot coexist. Threats to identity on both sides contribute to a sense of self-protection, attachment to one's own group narrative or beliefs, and a high resistance to receptivity to the other. In dialogue, the opportunity to challenge this experience of identity as zero-sum is presented and parties avail themselves to a shift that precludes the negation of the other for their own survival. When parties are able to do this it allows for the possibility of a new transcendent identity that can emerge freed from the entrenched beliefs that have polarized for so long.

Kelman (2004) suggests five components necessary for reconciliation: *mutual acknowledgment of the other's nationhood and humanity, development of a common moral basis for peace, confrontation with history, acknowledgment of responsibility, and establishment of patterns and institutional mechanisms of cooperation.* The principles and practices of dialogue clearly parallel these components and provide the ideal mechanism by which to achieve them. While many conflict resolution and peace-building practices achieve some dimensions of this view of reconciliation, dialogue is more comprehensive in that it focuses deeply on content *and* process, on substance *and* relationship, and on the psychological *and* concrete dimensions to conflict.

Though forgiveness can be the result of transformative dialogues and reconciliation processes, it is rarely the stated goal or agenda. In some cases, dialogue is a process that people enter because they are motivated to address the uncomfortable feelings of unforgiveness – "a cold, emotional complex consisting of resentment, bitterness, hatred, hostility, residual anger and fear" (Worthington, 2001, p. 162). Dialogue often begins with reducing unforgiveness, which can then open the door for forgiveness to emerge. Seen as the spiritual-moral dimension to the psychological aspect of reconciliation work (Auerbach, 2004), forgiveness is a process that evolves organically. While it cannot be prescribed or mandated, it does typically pass through certain phases. Botcharova (2001) offers seven steps toward forgiveness that are highly consistent with the dialogue processes outlined above: *mourning and expressing grief, accepting loss and confronting fears, rehumanizing the enemy, choosing to forgive and committing to taking risks, establishing justice, reviewing history, and negotiating solutions and joint planning.* As the processes of forgiveness and reconciliation are so personal to the parties involved, any attempt to push or force them is ill-advised. Dialogue can provide a container for this work, but it cannot assure the path that will unfold. And while it is possible for fractured parties to achieve a full sense of forgiveness and reconciliation, it is more often the case that these processes evolve over long periods of time and are achieved in shades of grey. Forgiveness and reconciliation are seen as developmental processes whereby parties might shift partially through dialogue and continue with their own internal process long after group meetings are over. Because dialogue can take place between parties that live in coexistence or between parties that do not, complete reconciliation or forgiveness may ultimately occur only within people's hearts.

Challenges to Dialogue Work

Though dialogue is a process that facilitates many dimensions of intergroup heal-ing, it is not a panacea for all situations nor is it always the prudent choice for intergroup conflicts. Dialogue presents the opportunity for parties to sit with each other with the intent to respect, listen, and transform historically fractured relation-ships, but it must be used cautiously and deliberatively so that it maximizes its positive potential and minimizes its potential for further harm or injury. Zartman's (2001) notion of ripeness – the conditions of readiness that allow for individuals and groups in conflict to avail themselves to conflict resolution or transformational processes – applies to dialogue work as well. Groups brought together prematurely run the risk of being too raw or protective to benefit from the process; conversely, groups brought together belatedly run the risk of being either so entrenched in their histories that they may not benefit as well or so removed from them that they have passed the transformational window of opportunity.

A significant challenge of dialogue work is in addressing power imbalances that typically exist between parties in conflict. While contact theory suggests that ideal intergroup experiences should promote equal status among participants (Allport, 1954; Pettigrew, 1998), equal status rarely exists in conflicted societies and both real and felt inequality do not cease when parties enter into dialogue. For parties of lesser power, it can be injurious to conduct dialogues from the perspective of "we are all in this together" because it can minimize the impact of power differentials in the development of the conflict as well as minimize the realities of real structural injus-tices occurring in the present. In many scenarios, groups are brought together while there are still very significant power differentials between dominant and subordinate groups (i.e., among different racial groups in the United States, between Israelis and Palestinians, between blacks and whites in South Africa). Therefore, groups having less power come to dialogue with a very different agenda than those in a higher power role. Majority participants tend to be more interested in communication and understanding whereas minority participants are more interested in action and jus-tice that will challenge the status quo (Abu-Nimer, 1999; Hubbard, 2001). While majority participants often want to get to know more about the other, minority par-ticipants have less of a need or desire for this as their position in society has already required that they know more of the other than the other knows of them – knowledge and ignorance of the other's experience is hardly symmetrical in conflicts between groups of unequal power (Baker Miller, 1995; Rouhana & Korper, 1996).

Because dialogue work is a process by which peace building occurs slowly through relational change rather than structural change, it can be challenging for small groups of individual to address larger structural issues that they are unlikely to impact in significant or immediate ways. This can become frustrating for partici-pants who are invested in societal shifts. This reality becomes even more challenging when the view of the other as "enemy" is reinforced by ongoing structural issues of oppression; minority participants tend to be weary of processes that create a "feel good" experience only to be followed up by continued injuries and injustices within their everyday worlds. For true, sustainable peace building to occur, dialogue needs to be linked to action and change that address injustices that have perpetuated the conflict. Forgiveness and reconciliation are difficult, if not impossible, if there are ongoing injuries in current circumstances that restimulate injuries from the past.

Not only do those who come from different power positions have different agendas in dialogue and reconciliation work, but they have different responsibilities as well. If the goal of dialogue is a transformed identity, then both parties have to seriously reconsider and shift parts of their own identities as a way of creating more room for the other (Hicks, 2001). Those from high-power groups need to reconcile that their behavior, or that of their group, has been responsible for the suffering, pain, and humiliation of the other. This can lead to a sense of exposure, humiliation, or self-loathing. Those from the low-power group are challenged to let go of their "victim" identity, which has allowed them some of their own source of power – the moral high ground – during the conflict. While these shifts are challenging for both groups, it is particularly difficult to ask this of victimized parties. In dialogue, a skilled facilitator needs to support perpetrators in taking responsibility while helping them maintain their dignity and to support the low-power group to find alternatives to their victim identity without denying them the justification of their pain.

Attempting to address power inequities becomes particularly challenging in cases where the roles of victims and perpetrators are not clear-cut or where power inequities manifest in different ways for different parties. In some conflicts, there is more of a delineation of victim and perpetrator (Nazi perpetrators and Holocaust survivors), while in others, both sides have been victimized and both sides have perpetrated atrocities (Serbs and Croats during the Balkan conflict). In certain scenarios, structural and institutional asymmetries present significant challenges, but individual or group acts of violence by members of the subordinated group toward the dominant group and historical cycles of violence add a different layer of victimization (acts of violence toward Jewish Israelis from Palestinians). There are many conflicts where there are "competitions of victimhoods" (Montville, 2001) which suggest that dialogue, reconciliation, and forgiveness work require that both sides share the roles of assuming responsibility and relinquishing the sole victim position if there is to be significant movement or change.

Another challenge to dialogue work is the potential lack of follow-up in many cases of intergroup encounters (Abu-Nimer, 1999). Well-intentioned organizations, community leaders, and third-party interveners often bring parties together for intense encounters without appropriate follow-up which can create a number of significant problems. First, parties (particularly youths) can be vulnerable upon reentry to their home communities; if they have just undergone a shift in meaning, perspective, or identity, it can be difficult for them to retain this in the face of familiar conditions that reinforce their previous selves. Second, parties from all groups run the risk of estrangement or hostility from their own communities if they are perceived as betraying their group by joining with "the other"; this phenomenon can create a new set of fissures at the intragroup level. Third, parties who experience a positive, transformational experience in dialogue can often experience a feeling of betrayal following the encounter when they reengage in their worlds with some of the same intergroup difficulties or social injustices that precipitated the conflict.

This sense of betrayal can produce a hardening that is sometimes more impenetrable than their original barriers to the other, as now it is layered with "see, I trusted them, and look what happened." While dialogue work is certainly not an infallible process, it is still one of the most useful and successful methods of dealing with groups in conflict. Having considered some of the key theoretical elements of dialogue work, we now turn our attention to a particular case study of dialogue at work.

Dialogue in Action

Authored by Wilma J. Busse, Martina Emme, and Rosalie Gerut.

In 1993, a group composed of descendants of Holocaust survivors and descendants of perpetrators of the Third Reich met in Germany to serve as research subjects in a study examining the interaction of the two groups during a structured group experience. Following their time together in Germany, the 13 people who took part in the research study decided to form their own organization called One By One. The goal of One By One was to develop venues in which other descendants of the Holocaust and the Nazi era could address their shared, yet distinct, histories and gain a deeper understanding of themselves and each other. In 1996, One By One held its first Dialogue Group (DG) in Berlin, Germany.

The facilitators simultaneously structured the DG process, shared their own individual and group experiences, and served as witnesses to the experiences of the group members. The facilitators held the powerful impact of bearing witness to the consequences of family histories in the presence of the other. For 5 days, everyone present both witnessed and experienced the heightened emotional tension and the acute feelings of fear, anger, guilt, and shame in the room. The intensity of Holocaust-related feelings, coupled with the opportunity to tell one's personal story and be truly heard, promoted transformation in many members. Participants came to know one another as individuals, thus challenging stereotypes and preconceived notions of the other. Following their participation in the DG, many members have continued contact with one another, spoken publicly about their experiences and the merits of dialogue, become actively involved with issues of social justice, and engaged in creative expression of their experiences through artistic endeavors.

Since 1996, One by One has conducted numerous Dialogue Groups in Berlin. The groups are composed of descendants from both sides and, in smaller numbers, survivors and perpetrators themselves. Participants have come from England, Peru, Germany, Italy, Poland, the former Yugoslavia, and the United States. Throughout this chapter, "descendants of perpetrators" is used to represent those members descended either from actual perpetrators – to varying degrees – of Nazi crimes, bystanders who did not resist Nazi goals, or witnesses to atrocities. "Descendants of survivors" refers to participants whose family members were persecuted, imprisoned, enslaved, killed, forced to hide or flee from their homes and/or countries.

The DG process has three main goals. The first is to facilitate the individual's reexamination of his/her relatives' experiences and their impact on his/her own life. The second is to provide members with an opportunity to gain a better understanding of the "other." The third is to help members give greater personal meaning to their post-War II legacies and identities. Although forgiveness and reconciliation are not explicit goals of the One By One model, dialogue is viewed as a necessary precursor to reconciliation and, in some cases, forgiveness. In One By One we generally do not use the term "forgiveness," since it carries different meanings and connotations for people of different faiths and spiritual beliefs. However, several Christian DG members have stated that "Although it is not in our power to forgive on behalf of our parents, forgiveness may be a necessary part of healing and a means to achieving peace in our own lives." In this context, forgiveness does not mean excusing or forgetting, but rather understanding the 'other' and moving beyond revenge and closed-mindedness.

Reconciliation or "shalom" (peace and wholeness) requires, in the Jewish tradition, the perpetrator to have a deep turning within the soul (t'shuvah). This includes acknowledging the wrong committed directly to the victim, realizing what the impact has been on the victim, offering assistance to the victim, and promising to live his/her life with integrity, thereby returning integrity and peace to both sides. This act of atonement leads to "at – one – ment" (Bina Gibson, DG member). The victim can refuse the overture, but through the DG process, the overtures lead to a release of previously held fear, pain, grief, and shame, which can be nothing short of miracle (Busse, Emme, & Gerut, 2007). It is the hope of One By One that together we can bring the highest moral principles of all our faiths to transform our legacies of darkness and brutality into acts of kindness, compassion, justice, and social action. In this manner we seek to repair the world, one by one, just as we seek to repair ourselves.

One tenet of trauma theory that was influential in the design of the DG is the importance of recalling and talking about trauma in order for those affected by it to heal. The transformation of these stories from inert and senseless to emotional and meaningful is central to the healing process. "We may find meaning in life even when confronted by a. . . fate that cannot be changed. For what matters then is to bear witness to the uniquely human potential at its best, which is to transform personal tragedy into a triumph. . . . Suffering ceases to be suffering at the moment it finds a meaning" (Frankl, 1984, p. 133). The model adheres to the belief that group work provides special opportunities for healing that do not exist in individual processes (Herman & Shatzow, 1984) and draws upon Carl Rogers' person-centered approach (1942, 1986), which fosters openness to and respect for the validity of the other's thoughts, feelings, and opinions.

Another principle of the DG model is the importance of the physical presence of the "other." Their presence not only heightens tension and vulnerability, but also makes manifest the historic chasm that separates them – the Holocaust/Shoah. For the descendants of survivors the chasm is filled with the memories of murdered or persecuted relatives. They may hear the intergenerational statements: "Do not forget." "You are the guardian of our memories." "Don't trust the German." "Don''t have anything to do with them." The descendants of the perpetrators, torn between the desire to accuse or defend their family members, to discover or deny their histories, hear "Do not be disloyal." "Stay with us in the silence." Levi (1992) advocated reaching across the gulf: "Time has come to explore the space which separates the victims from the persecutors. . . . [That] space. . . is studded with figures with whom it is indispensable to know if we want to know the human species" (p. 40). He maintains that it is possible to extend an offer for dialogue to the former enemy and still maintain a desire for justice. For Levi (1993), the purpose of dialogue is to seek the truth about the past and the present, but not necessarily to forgive or to achieve harmony. He offered the notion of a "gray zone," a way of underscoring the mixture of good and bad in people, victims and perpetrators alike. In the perpetrators, he found acts of bravery and generosity, without excusing the bad. In the victims, he described cruel acts of aggression and competition together with acts of extraordinary kindness and courage. The DG attempts to create a bridge to the "gray zone," serving as a way to reach across the chasm that separates the participants from one another and themselves.

The Dialogue Group Model

Preparation. Individuals interested in participating in a DG are interviewed by the facilitators in either Germany or the United States. Each potential member is asked about his/her motivation for joining the group, what he/she hopes to achieve, family background, support systems (especially for the period immediately following the group), health concerns, and fears/anxieties. The facilitator explains the overall agenda and provides a description of the 5-day group experience and the 2 days of post-group activities. In choosing participants, facilitators try to ensure that the group contains a relatively equal number of members of the perpetrator and survivor groups. In Germany, pre-DG meetings are offered for those who are interested in attending. In the USA, pre-DG groups are less likely to occur due to the great physical distances between members so pre-group discussions are often conducted by telephone. All potential members are provided with each facilitator's contact information and are encouraged to call and discuss any questions or issues that arise prior to the actual group experience.

The Dialogue Group Format. The DG is facilitated by 2–4 people who are either cofounders of One By One and/or trained therapists or group facilitators. All facilitators are descendants of perpetrators or survivors and all have been participants in a DG. All members and facilitators are required to reside at the conference center and translators are present at all times. The opportunity to live and share space together is considered essential for group bonding. Typically, people arrive a day early and have a chance to get settled and acquainted with one another before work begins. The DG usually meets Monday through Friday and is followed by 2 days of optional organized activities. The 5 days are structured as follows:

Day 1: The group, composed of 10–16 members, convenes in the morning and begins with each person providing a short self-introduction. The facilitators then model self-disclosure by telling their stories to the group; this serves as a trust-building and bonding exercise. Members are then asked to sign up for a time when they would be willing to share their story. There is a long lunch break to allow for the group to eat together, talk with one another, or rest prior to the afternoon session. During the afternoon, two group members share their stories. Participants are asked to begin their stories by addressing the question: "How did the Shoah/the Holocaust or the Nazi period affect my life"? Participants are given 30 minutes to tell their stories, followed by another 15 minutes in which the speaker may either continue his/her story or take questions from the group. Group members then discuss what has arisen for them during story-telling, including similarities or parallel experiences and/or what they found moving or difficult.

Days 2, 3, and 4: These 3 days are divided into morning and afternoon sessions as well, with each session devoted to individuals telling their stories. The same format used on the afternoon of Day 1 is employed in the morning and afternoon sessions. On Day 4, sessions are held in the morning and evening. The afternoon is spent visiting the House of the Wannsee Conference, where the "Final Solution" was planned.

Day 5: The last day of the DG is devoted to discussing themes and issues that surfaced throughout the previous 4 days. Those identified are put on the agenda and discussed, explored, and analyzed using the themes as a basis for interaction. Various formats are used including full group discussion, dyadic pairings, and small group clusters. Numerous themes arise from the story-telling including trust, unresolved emotions between individuals, and group process dynamics.

Post-dialogue Group Activities. Following the fifth day, all members leave the conference center. Participants from abroad stay in Berlin with people they have met during the group or with Berliners from former dialogues. Former DG members come to the conference center and escort the new members to their respective homes. This interaction between former DG members and the new DG members is considered an important cultural experience in which individuals get to experience everyday life in Berlin. This is often a very poignant experience for non-German-born Jews who stay in a non-Jewish German home as it is for non-Jewish Germans who accompany Jews to a synagogue.

Friday night is typically devoted to attending a Shabbat service together; Saturday is reserved for sightseeing in Berlin with One by One members serving as guides through Jewish Berlin. Destinations include the Jewish Museum and memorial sites related to the Nazi era. Saturday night, a social gathering is organized to welcome the new participants who are given the opportunity to describe what they have experienced. Almost all of them make use of this opportunity and, in doing so, begin to share their experience in the presence of new people, also engaging in intense individual discussions of their experience with former DG members. On Sunday, the last day of organized activities, DG members are given the opportunity to visit a former concentration camp (Ravensbrück or Sachsenhausen).

A Chance Encounter

Sitting within the circle of DG members at a Berlin meeting there was a German woman who had recently learned that her father, an SS officer, had participated in the murder of thousands of Jews in White Russia. We listened intently as she spoke of her discoveries about her father and of the abuse she had suffered as a child at his hands. The pain of these memories, together with the knowledge of what her father had done, had led her to attempt to take her own life. Also sitting in this circle was a young man from the United States, who was completely taken aback at the realization that he was in the presence of the daughter of the SS officer who had directly participated in the murder of his father's family. These two people, separated by the chasm of the Holocaust, found themselves in an emotional and moral dilemma as they struggled to decide what to do with the threads of history that connected them. What was he to do with his rage? How was he going to respond to this woman? What could she possibly say to him? The entire group spent many hours struggling to find meaning in this chance meeting. In the end, the young man announced to the group what we all had come to realize: the German woman too was a victim – both of her father and of history – as well as a survivor. She had both suffered and survived her perpetrator. In spite of his turbulent emotions, the young man recognized her sincerity in wanting to confront the truth, and he respected her determination to break with her family's and her country's silence. She had taken the necessary steps to confront and bear witness to her father's crimes. He embraced her and together they crossed the bridge over the chasm that separated them and entered the "gray zone." As they did so, the group was moved to tears. From that point on, they were – and continue to be – connected. She continues to work to help others unveil family secrets from the Nazi era, and he continues to publicly tell the story of his confrontation with truth. Their friendship has endured and has inspired many others.

Conclusion

As is seen in this moving example of dialogue in action, transformation through the bearing of witness can happen in the most extreme circumstances. Deep forgiveness and true reconciliation can emerge through the powerful process of dialogue. If those who have been so wounded by the past are willing to come together in the spirit of encounter, then conflicted groups can begin to heal the traumas of history and imagine a different future. When this level of healing can occur side by side with official processes and decisions, then lasting structural change and peace building can occur. It is then that true peace can trickle down and up through all levels of society.

References

Abu-Nimer, M. (1999). *Dialogue, conflict resolution, and change.* Albany: State University of New York Press.

Allport, G. W. (1954). *The nature of prejudice.* Cambridge, MA: Addison-Wesley.

Auerbach, Y. (2004). The role of forgiveness in reconciliation. In Y. Bar-Siman-Tov (Ed.), *From conflict resolution to reconciliation* (pp. 149–176). New York: Oxford University Press.

Baker Miller, J. (1995). Domination and subordination. In P. Rothenberg (Ed.), *Race, class & gender in the United States: An integrated study* (pp. 57–64). New York: St. Martin's Press.

Bar-On, D. (1999). Children of victims and perpetrators of the holocaust in dialogue & post-genocide reconciliation between perpetrators and victims as seen by a holocaust researcher. In I. W. Charny (Ed.), *Encyclopedia of genocide* (Vol. I., pp. 142–147). Oxford: ABC-CLIO.

Bar-On, D. (2006). *Tell your life story: Creating dialogue among Jews and Germans, Israelis and Palestinians*. Budapest, Hungary: Central European University Press.

Bar-Tal, D., & Bennink, G. (2004). The nature of reconciliation as an outcome and as a process. In Y. Bar-Siman-Tov (Ed.), *From conflict resolution to reconciliation* (pp. 11–38). New York: Oxford University Press.

Bloomfield, D., Barnes, T., & Huyse, L. (Eds.). (2003). *Reconciliation after violent conflict*. Stockholm: International Institute for Democracy and Electoral Assistance.

Bohm, D. (1996). *On dialogue*. New York: Routledge.

Botcharova, O. (2001). Implementation of track two diplomacy: Developing a model of forgiveness. In R. Helmick & R. Peterson (Eds.), *Forgiveness and reconciliation* (pp. 269–294). Radnor, Pennsylvania: Templeton Foundation Press.

Busse, W., Emme, M., & Gerut, R. (2007). *Journeys of transformation*. Sudbury, MA: One By One Publishers.

Busse, W., Emme, M., Gerut, R., & Lapidus, J. (1999). Descendants of the Holocaust meet descendants of the Third Reich: The one by one dialogue concept. *Journal of Humanistic Psychology, 39*(2), 106–133.

Day, W. J., Bernard, J., & Smith, F. J. (1999). Baton Rouge: Dialogue on race relations. In H. Saunders (Ed.), *A public peace process*. New York: Palgrave.

Ellinor, L., & Gerard, G. (1998). *Dialogue: Rediscovering the transforming power of conversation*. New York: John Wiley and Sons, Inc.

Fisher, R. (2001). Social-psychological processes in interactive conflict analysis and reconciliation. In M. Abu-Nimer (Ed.), *Reconciliation, justice, and coexistence* (pp. 25–46). Lanham, Maryland: Lexington Books.

Fitzduff, M. (2001). The challenge to history: Justice, coexistence and reconciliation work in Northern Ireland. In M. Abu-Nimer (Ed.), *Reconciliation, justice, and coexistence* (pp. 255–273). Lanham, Maryland: Lexington Books.

Frankl, V. (1984). *Man's search for meaning*. New York: Pocket Books.

Gopin, M. (2001). Forgiveness as an element of conflict resolution in religious cultures: Walking the tightrope of reconciliation and justice. In M. Abu-Nimer (Ed.), *Reconciliation, justice, and coexistence* (pp. 87–99). Lanham, Maryland: Lexington Books.

Halabi, R. (2004). Reconstructing identity through the encounter with the other: The facilitator training course. In D. Reich & R. Halabi (Eds.), *Israeli and Palestinian identities in dialogue: The school for peace approach* (pp. 79–96). New Jersey: Rutgers University Press.

Helmick, R., & Peterson, R. (Eds.). (2001). *Forgiveness and reconciliation: Religion, public policy and conflict transformation*. Radnor, Pennsylvania: Templeton Foundation Press.

Herman, J. L., & Shatzow, E. (1984). Time limited group psychotherapy for women with a history of incest. *International Journal of Group Psychotherapy, 34*, 605–610.

Hicks, D. (2001). The role of identity reconstruction in promoting reconciliation. In R. Helmick & R. Peterson (Eds.), *Forgiveness and reconciliation* (pp. 129–149). Radnor, Pennsylvania: Templeton Foundation Press.

Hubbard, A. (2001). Understanding majority and minority participation in interracial and interethnic dialogue. In M. Abu-Nimer (Ed.), *Reconciliation, justice, and coexistence* (pp. 275–290). Lanham, Maryland: Lexington Books.

Hundt, D., & Bleiker, R. (2007). Reconciling colonial memories in Korea and Japan. *Asian Perspective, 31*(1), 61–91.

Kelman, H. (1997). Group processes in the resolution of international conflicts: Experiences from the Israeli-Palestinian case. *American Psychologist, 52*(3), 212–220.

Kelman, H. C. (1999). Interactive problem solving as a metaphor for international conflict resolution: Lessons for the policy process. *Peace and Conflict: Journal of Peace Psychology, 5*, 201–218.

Kelman, H. C. (2001). The role of national identity in conflict resolution: Experiences from Israeli-Palestinian problem-solving workshops. In R. D. Ashmore, L. Jussim, & D. Wilder (Eds.), *Social identity, intergroup conflict, and conflict reduction* (pp. 187–212). Oxford: Oxford University Press.

Kelman, H. C. (2004). Reconciliation as identity change. In Y. Bar-Siman-Tov (Ed.), *From conflict resolution to reconciliation* (pp. 111–124). New York: Oxford University Press.

Kriesberg, L. (1998). Coexistence and the reconciliation of communal conflicts. In E. Weiner (Ed.), *The handbook of interethnic coexistence* (pp. 182–198). New York: Continuum.

Lederach, J. P. (1997). *Building peace: Sustainable reconciliation in divided societies.* Washington DC: United States Institute of Peace.

Levi, P. (1992). *Ist das ein mensch* [If this is a man]. Muenchen, Wien: Deutscher Taschenbuch Verlag. (Original work published 1961).

Levi, P. (1993). *Survival in Auschwitz.* New York: Simon & Schuster.

Montville, J. (1993). The healing function in political conflict resolution. In D. J. D. Sandole & H. Van der Merve (Eds.), *Conflict resolution theory and practice: Integration and application* (pp. 112–127). Manchester: Manchester University Press.

Montville, J. (2001). Justice and the burdens of history. In M. Abu-Nimer (Ed.), *Reconciliation, justice, and coexistence* (pp. 275–290). Maryland: Lexington Books.

Park, C. (2005). Religion as a meaning-making framework in coping with life stress. *Journal of Social Issues, 61*(4), 707–729.

Park, C., & Folkman, S. (1997). Meaning in the context of stress and coping. *Review of General Psychology, 1*(2), 115–144.

Pettigrew, T. F. (1998). Intergroup contact theory. *Annual Review of Psychology, 49,* 65–85.

Rasmussen, J. (1997). Peacemaking in the twenty-first century: New rules, new roles, new actors. In W. Zartman & J. Rasmussen (Eds.), *Peacemaking in international conflict: Methods and techniques* (pp. 23–50). Washington, DC: United Sates Institute of Peace Press.

Reich, D., & Halabi, R. (Eds.). (2004). *Israeli and Palestinian identities in dialogue: The school for peace approach.* New Jersey: Rutgers University Press.

Rogers, C. (1942). *Counseling and psychotherapy.* Boston: Houghton Mifflin.

Rogers, C. (1986). The rust workshop: A personal overview. *Journal of Humanistic Psychology, 26*(3), 23–45.

Rothman, J. (1997). *Resolving identity-based conflict in nations, organizations and communities.* San Francisco, California: Jossey-Bass Publishers.

Rouhana, N., & Korper, S. (1996). Dealing with power asymmetry: Dilemmas of intervention in asymmetrical intergroup conflict. *Negotiation Journal, 12,* 315–328.

Saunders, H. (1999). *A public peace process: Sustained dialogue to transform Racial and ethnic conflicts.* New York: Palgrave.

Schoem, D., Hurtado, S., Sevig, T., Chesler, M., & Sumida, S., (2001). Intergroup dialogue: Democracy at work in theory and practice. In D. Schoem & S. Hurtado (Eds.), *Intergroup dialogue: Deliberative democracy in school, college, community, and workplace* (pp. 1–21). Ann Arbor: The University of Michigan Press.

Stokes, D. O., & Green, P. (2002). Preparing for peace: Interethnic dialogue and communal healing in Sri Lanka. *The Journal of Intergroup Relations, 4,* 89–96.

Tint, B. (in press). History, memory and conflict resolution, part II: An empirical study. *Conflict Resolution Quarterly.*

Villa-Vicencio, C., & Savage, T. (2001). *Rwanda and South Africa in Dialogue: Addressing the legacies of genocide and a crime against humanity.* Rondebosch, South Africa: Institute for Justice and Reconciliation.

Volkan, V., & Itzkowitz, N. (1994). *Turks and Greeks: Neighbors in Conflict.* Cambridgeshire, England: Eothen.

White, I. (2003). Victim-Combatant Dialogue in Northern Ireland. In D. Bloomfield, T. Barnes, & L. Huyse (Eds.), *Reconciliation after violent conflict* (pp. 89–96). Stockholm: International Institute for Democracy and Electoral Assistance.

Worthington, E. (2001). Unforgiveness, forgiveness, and reconciliation and their implications for social interventions. In R. Helmick & R. Peterson (Eds.), *Forgiveness and reconciliation* (pp. 161–182). Radnor, Pennsylvania: Templeton Foundation Press.

Zartman, W. (2001). The timing of peace initiatives: Hurting stalemates and ripe moments. *The Global Review of Ethnopolitics, 1*, 8–18.

Zuniga, X., & Nagda, B. (2001). Design considerations in intergroup dialogue. In D. Schoem & S. Hurtado (Eds.), *Intergroup dialogue: Deliberative democracy in school, college, community, and workplace* (pp. 306–327). Ann Arbor: University of Michigan Press.

Name Index

Subject Index